REEL
TERROR

Also by David Konow

Bang Your Head
Schlock-o-Rama

THOMAS DUNNE BOOKS.
An imprint of St. Martin's Press.

www.thomasdunnebooks.com
www.stmartins.com

ISBN 978-0-312-66883-9 (paperback)
ISBN 978-1-250-01359-0 (e-book)

First Edition: October 2012

10   9   8   7   6   5   4   3   2   1

REEL
TERROR

THE SCARY, BLOODY, GORY, HUNDRED-YEAR HISTORY OF CLASSIC HORROR FILMS

DAVID KONOW

THOMAS DUNNE BOOKS
ST. MARTIN'S GRIFFIN ≋ NEW YORK

This book is dedicated to the fans of horror, whose passion and love
for the genre have kept it alive and well for many years,
and will hopefully continue to do so
for many years to come.

CONTENTS

REEL
TERROR

INTRODUCTION

WHY WE LOVE BEING SCARED

At the 2009 Academy Awards ceremony, there was a tribute to horror films, and watching it made it clear why the horror genre is still not taken seriously in many corners. Kristen Stewart and Taylor Lautner of *Twilight* introduced the segment, and there was too much CGI, and not much of a clue of what really constitutes true horror films (Johnny Depp in *Edward Scissorhands*?). As Jay Fernandez wrote in *The Hollywood Reporter,* "If the idea was to bring back some respect to the genre, consider that mission run through a wood chipper."

There have been horror films since the dawn of cinema, and the genre still has a strong following today, not that it's gotten much respect from mainstream Hollywood. As Wes Craven once said, "It's one of the hardest things about doing horror films, that the people involved with them don't want to admit that they do them and don't want to admit the possibility of any real value in them, and the commercial things they're interested in are boring. It really is painful."

And in 1987, right as Clive Barker was breaking through in the States, he said, "Most genres are judged by the best in their fields. Horror, unfortunately, is often judged by the worst. . . . It's a very subversive, but relevant genre."

As Brian De Palma once put it, the major studios treated the horror genre "like retarded stepchildren," even though he also said "the horror genre is a very filmic form. Certainly it's the closest thing we have today to pure cinema. And the fact that most horror films are so badly made doesn't mean there isn't a tremendous amount of artistry in the genre. I sometimes feel compelled to work in it just to show what can be done."

And indeed, whatever the mainstream and the critics will think of them, the level of skill and artistry it takes to pull off a successful horror film is considerable. No less a master of fear than Val Lewton has said, "No type of picture reacts so favorably to better staging, better casts, more time and money spent on quality than the horror film. Horror films must be filmed carefully. They must be just right."

A number of horror films have certainly been cynical exercises in commerce, and they can make a lot of money back on small budgets. Horror has been a subject of controversy, with those who don't understand it finding it something a civilized society shouldn't put up with, but for many, horror films are a necessary catharsis.

Jonathan Demme has only made one horror film in his career, *The Silence of the Lambs*, but he has long been a fan of the genre, and has often said that every director wants to make a movie that scares its audience.

"It's a subtle and recorded truth that people love to be terrified in the safety of a work of fiction," said Demme. "I believe in the positive aspects of experiencing certain kinds of catharses. When I saw *Rosemary's Baby* or *Texas Chain Saw Massacre,* I left the theater feeling purged and cleansed."

In his review of *Phantasm,* Charles Champlin wrote in the *L.A. Times,* "The shriek of laughter sounds like a contradiction but it has kept the horror movie profitable for almost as long as there have been movies. Audiences dance to the macabre with great pleasure, glad to be scared only half to death and evidently glad for both the tingling excitement and for the safe release that makes calm reality not half bad to see again."

"It allows us in groups to confess that we're frightened," says Stanley Mann, the screenwriter of *Damien: Omen II*. "And we need outlets for being frightened, as we need outlets for being excited, feeling in love, which is why we go to the movies."

"We're subjected to fear on a daily basis," says Joseph Stefano, the late screenwriter of *Psycho*. "And here it's like saying, 'If you will pay money for the ticket, we're really gonna scare you, but it won't be real. When you leave the theater, none of this will be there.' Fear is something we must feel. When you're watching *Psycho*, you don't think about the real things that are frightening you. You're allowing yourself to be frightened by fantasy, and that's more bearable."

Of course, the value of the horror genre, or the fun of being scared, doesn't need to be explained to the fans, who are very loyal to their favorite directors, and who keep these movies alive year after year. "People that love horror are kind of like a family," said Reggie Bannister, costar of *Phantasm*. "When I go to conventions and appearances, it's like . . . talking to family."

Horror was a great place for a lot of filmmakers to start because you didn't need a ton of money to pull one off, and they were easy to market. Where some directors used it as a launching pad, many like George Romero, Wes Craven, and Dario Argento would call it home. Many would try to branch out and do different things, and some eventually realized scaring audiences was what they did best.

Although many Hollywood chronicles don't mention it, in addition to making a lot of money, many horror films have broken new ground in cinema, kept major studios in business, and have been highly influential to filmmakers of all genres. And long before the days of Miramax, some of the most successful independent cinema success stories that were made completely outside the studio system were horror movies.

This book is not just a love letter to a great and underappreciated genre, but it also tries to show what makes a great horror film effective, even decades after it's been made. There are rules to crafting scares and suspense, and just as often the great horror films break those rules, or didn't know there were rules in the first place, creating new innovations in terror. Some of the best horror films in history were also made by filmmakers who didn't like the genre, or only dabbled in it once. Again, by not knowing the rules or the genre conventions, they were able to transcend them beautifully.

There are many reasons why the best horror films in the genre have lasted, and why many are still scary today. These are the common denominator films no self-respecting fan wouldn't have on their DVD shelves: the Universal classics starring Chaney, Karloff, and Lugosi. *Psycho*. The British Hammer Films. The undead films of George A. Romero. *The Exorcist. The Texas Chain Saw Massacre. Jaws. The Omen*. The work of the Italian troika consisting of Dario Argento, Mario Bava, and Lucio Fulci. John Carpenter's *Halloween* and *The Thing. Alien* and *An American Werewolf in London*. The work of David Cronenberg. The work of Wes Craven. And many, many others to be found inside.

The history of the horror genre is a rich and varied one, as well as a fascinating and fun one to track throughout its milestones. All at once, horror can be great art, an escape from fear, and a way of confronting it head-on by giving it a shape, say of a great white shark, then blowing it to hell. Horror can also be so much more, and the masters of the genre have crafted great cinematic fear in and out of its boundaries.

Ultimately it's what a strong filmmaker brings to a scary story, and the fear we bring to the theaters that makes us lose our minds the way we do when watching a great horror film. A book that gives the genre its due is long overdue, and as long as there is fear, there will probably, thankfully, always be horror films to help us deal with it.

ONE

THE FOUNDATIONS OF FEAR

How horror's been with us from the dawn of cinema, how Universal built their empire with monsters, how *The Twilight Zone* created clever, thoughtful terror with a twist, and how *Famous Monsters of Filmland* and *Tales from the Crypt* became required reading for the monster kid generation

When Sam Raimi was making movies for Universal, he loved to spend his free time roaming the backlot, where the great movie monsters of the thirties once dwelled. "There's a certain feeling you get walking down the hallowed streets of Universal Studios," Raimi said. "Big stages towering to your left and right, thinking, 'They made the classics here.'"

For horror fans, it was like visiting ancient Rome, and walking where great warriors once stood, a time where Chaney, Karloff, and Lugosi made the movies that made them eternally famous, and cemented the studio's foundation. Fans visiting Universal would constantly take themselves back in the time machines of their imaginations, trying to recapture what it must have been like to make the classics back then, and wondering if the ghosts of Chaney, Karloff, and Lugosi still wander the lot.

Back in the thirties, there was new ground broken practically everywhere you stood. This was where the modern horror film began, not long after film itself began. Universal watched what was going on in Europe with *The Cabinet of Dr. Caligari*, *Nosferatu*, as well as the 1927 sci-fi masterpiece *Metropolis*, and they drew from all of these classics. But Universal also had its own sensibilities, and combined with the European filmmaking styles, built its own horror foundation in the States.

Looking back on the Universal days is a valuable lesson for horror fans, because you can see where history repeats itself many times throughout the genre, and in many ways, the appeal of the horror film often leads back to the Universal classics. At Universal, horror films broke new ground with special effects, and stars like Lugosi, Karloff, and Chaney became synonymous with horror, and quickly became stereotyped. Other studios jumped on the horror bandwagon when they saw how much money it was making, eventually lowballing the genre, just wanting to just churn 'em out fast and cheap.

Horror also would eventually become more reflective of the outside world in times of trouble. *The Creature from the Black Lagoon* was a reaction against the fear of nuclear power and pollution, and horror films like *Night of the Living Dead* and *The Last House on the Left* reflected the turmoil at the end of the sixties, even if it often creeped in unconsciously. The public has often turned to horror to help deal with the worst of times.

The Universal films still stand strong as classics today because of the great stars like Karloff, Lugosi, and Chaney who embodied the monsters and brought them to life. The incredible, iconic monster designs by the founding fathers of special effects makeup also became stars in their own right. The limitations of film technology then, like the beautiful black-and-white cinematography that captured the looming shadows and textures, proved to be an asset that helped make the films timeless. (Another obvious limitation that became an asset, which a lot of people making horror today would have a hard time doing without, is that horror films couldn't have gore back then.)

Between *Dracula* and *Frankenstein*, the Universal films progressed not just with special effects and the growing language of cinema, but also with the complexity of the creatures. As Universal's movies proved, they were much more than just monsters. Dracula was clearly a creature of the night who embraced the dark, where Frankenstein and the Wolfman were much more complicated and tragic. The Frankenstein Monster was childlike in that he didn't understand the damage he caused, and the Wolfman had an element of Greek tragedy because he couldn't escape his destiny, and his story also had elements of a deeper psychological drama with the father-son conflict.

In the early thirties, the original *Dracula* and *Frankenstein* films didn't just make stars out of Bela Lugosi and Boris Karloff, they were major moneymakers that kept Universal's doors open during the Great Depression. When the studio tried to move away from horror, the public still couldn't get enough, and monsters would save Universal from going out of business more than once.

The classic Universal monsters would eventually be brought together in the "monster rally" movies of the forties like *Frankenstein Meets the Wolf Man,* and *House of Frankenstein.* They would also be reinvented with comedy, and given their send-off in 1948 with *Abbott and Costello Meet Frankenstein.* Moving with the times, next came *The Creature from the Black Lagoon*, and Universal monsters were now directly reflecting the modern fears of the cold war. Later, with the advent of television, a new generation of young fans would rediscover the Universal classics on *Shock Theater,* launching the "monster kid" generation that would make their own fantastic scarefests when they grew up.

In the seventies when Universal was trying to decide whether to go forward with *Jaws 2* or not, some executives worried it would bring about another era of monster movies at the company. Some at Universal were embarrassed by the company's monster past, but the classic monsters were the stars the company was built on, and it was a strong foundation that held up well for decades.

Carl Laemmle, an immigrant from Germany, was originally in exhibition and distribution, and he built Universal Studios in North Hollywood, Lankershim Township. Laemmle bought the land for $165,000, and the studio opened their doors for business on March 15, 1915.

Norman Zierold, author of *Moguls: Hollywood's Merchants of Myth,* wrote that Laemmle was "the prototype of the more than slightly mad movie mogul, impulsive, quixotic, intrepid, unorthodox and unpredictable." But it was Laemmle's son who moved the company into much different directions.

Universal was a company heavy in nepotism, and when Carl Laemmle, Jr., became general manager of the studio when he was twenty-one, many considered his hiring the most obvious example of it. Carl Sr., was worried his son wouldn't do well without his help, but once Junior was in power, he expanded Universal's repertoire by setting up a wider variety of movies than the usual Westerns and serials the studio was churning out, including the 1930 Technicolor musical *King of Jazz,* and the war drama *All Quiet on the Western Front,* which would win Best Picture for 1930 (it would be the last time a Universal film would win Best Picture until *The Sting*).

Before Universal got in the horror business, horror pictures were already causing quite a stir with *The Cabinet of Dr. Caligari* and *Nosferatu*, released in 1920 and 1922, and both films were remarkable steps forward in the art of cinema when it was a brand-new medium. It's a testament to the staying power of both films that they're still well regarded in an era where many young film fans still haven't seen a black-and-white movie.

The expressionism of *Dr. Caligari*, with its use of composition, shadow, architecture, and dark psychological themes, would show itself repeatedly in horror and film noir. Many have remarked that the off-kilter design of *Dr. Caligari* draws you into the film, and closes in on you at the same time. (Considering how far horror has come in terms of extremity, it's also remarkable to note that one modern fan raving about the film on the Internet Movie Database recommended not showing *Dr. Caligari* to children.)

The image of *Nosferatu* with its hideous, rodentlike features is still disturbing after all these decades, and the scene of the vampire rising straight up out of his coffin is still a terrifying vision today. Where *Dr. Caligari* utilized hand-painted, surreal settings, *Nosferatu* was shot in real locations that are still standing in Germany today, shooting on location and using nonactors for realism, again while cinema was a brand-new medium.

In creating their own horror films, Universal was looking to combine the European influences of *Dr. Caligari* and *Nosferatu* with its own sensibilities. Universal wanted make the big-screen adaptation of *Dracula* as early as 1915. It was what Hollywood would call "a hot property," but it was considered too extreme for the time. It took Lon Chaney, the legendary "Man of a Thousand Faces," to break the ice for horror at the studio with *The Hunchback of Notre Dame* in 1923 and *The Phantom of the Opera* in 1925.

Irving Thalberg, who started out as Laemmle's assistant and moved up to head of production at the age of twenty, and was also a lover of classic literature, got the studio to green-light the Victor Hugo story as a "prestige" vehicle for Chaney. Laemmle wasn't sure about more ambitious films, having lost money on Erich von Stroheim's film *Foolish Wives*, which was billed as "the first real million-dollar picture," but *Hunchback* finally went ahead, and it was Universal's biggest hit that year.

Phantom of the Opera was Chaney's tour de force, the deformed appearance of the unmasked Phantom the most incredible achievement in makeup to date, and the scene where he is finally unmasked by Christine, played by Mary Philbin, is still one of the most iconic in cinema history. Rumors abounded that the film was too scary to be shown, and Universal kept the Phantom's unmasked appearance top secret before the movie's release. There were also reports of fainting and ambulances outside the theater, two publicity stunts that were repeated in horror for many years.

But the Universal monsters weren't just about scaring an audience. Having to learn pantomime because his parents were deaf, Chaney brought a great deal of pathos and sympathy to his work. "His parents' condition gave him an early understanding of what it is like to be different and an outsider," said his grandson Ron Chaney. "And it gave him a lifelong sympathy for the outsider that would illuminate his greatest roles."

"I wanted to remind people that the lowest types of humanity have within them the capacity for supreme self-sacrifice," Chaney said. "The dwarfed, misshapen beggar of the streets may have the noblest ideals. Most of my roles since the Hunchback, such as *The Phantom of the Opera, He Who Gets Slapped, The Unholy Three,* have carried the theme of self-sacrifice or renunciation. These are the stories which I wish to do.

"The parts I play point out a moral," Chaney continued. "They show individuals who might have been different if they had been given a different chance."

Next Universal went back to *Dracula,* which was a big hit play in London and on Broadway in 1927. It was still considered a tough project to adapt for the screen, and one Universal reader noted, "It will be a difficult task, and one will run up against the censor continually . . . but there is no doubt as to its making money."

Laemmle, Sr., had his concerns about the project as well, telling his son he didn't believe in horror films, and that people didn't want to see them, while Junior couldn't wait to prove everyone wrong.

Junior overrode his father to make *Dracula,* and directly negotiated with Florence Stoker, Bram's widow, for the rights. The deal to make the big-screen adaptation of *Dracula* closed in the summer of 1930, and director Tod Browning, who directed Chaney at Metro for ten years, came aboard that July.

Dracula was also another "prestige" film for Universal, and it was announced as "A Universal Super Production" in the trades. Laemmle, Sr., wanted Chaney to play Dracula, but he died in 1930, and Lugosi, whom the studio wasn't interested in, had to lobby for the role, and finally got it, albeit at a pittance, $500 a week for seven weeks of production.

"They start to test two dozen fellas for *Dracula*—but not me!" Lugosi recalled. "And who was tested? The cousins and brother-in-laws of the Laemmles," he continued, making fun of the Universal nepotism. "All their pets and the pets of their pets! This goes on for a long time and then old man Laemmle says, 'There's nobody in the family that can play it, so why don't you hire an actor?'"

Universal also had to tighten the film's budget after the market crash, and *Dracula* had the sensibilities of a stage play because a literal translation of the novel would have been too expensive. (*Dracula* ultimately came in at $441,984.90.)

Even with the sound era coming in, *Dracula* also still had the sensibilities of a silent movie. *Dracula* didn't have much music, except for the pieces from Wagner and Tchaikovsky's *Swan Lake,* because it was believed at the time audiences wouldn't understand music seemingly coming out of nowhere, unless it was coming from someplace like an orchestra being shown on-screen. For modern fans, the absence of music makes the film feel even more unsettling. You keep expecting a scary soundtrack to come creeping in, and it isn't there.

Browning liked to work without sound, and had a hard time adjusting with the times. When Browning made the film *Outside the Law,* he was knocked to the floor when he accidentally ran headfirst into a microphone, which then was marked with red warning flags so he wouldn't run into it again. (There was also a silent version of *Dracula* with dialogue cards for theaters that weren't yet equipped for sound.)

It was Lugosi's look and performance in *Dracula* that set the mold for practically every vampire to come, with his trademark cape, slicked-back widow's peak hairstyle, heavily accented line delivery— "I bid you vel-come," and the classic moment where he states, "I never drink . . . wine"—and his hypnotizing stare. (Lugosi's son, Bela Jr., recalled when he misbehaved as a young boy, his father would give him that foreboding look, and it scared him into behaving.) Not to mention Dracula's musty old castle home, which a great deal of the film's budget went to, and was kept standing to shoot on it more Universal productions for years.

When *Dracula* premiered in New York at the Roxy Theater on February 12, 1931, it was a smash hit, selling 50,000 tickets in forty-eight hours. As the film traveled from city to city, the hot streak continued, and twenty-four-hour screenings were set up to meet audience demand. *Time* called *Dracula* "an exciting melodrama, not as good as it ought to be but a cut above the ordinary trapdoor—and winding sheet—mystery." The New York *Daily News* called *Dracula*, "Just plain spooky and blood-thirsty. Brrrrr! We enjoyed it!"

Some *Dracula* reviewers didn't quite know how to critique the film, and in America there truly hadn't been anything like it before. As writer and Universal horror authority Tom Weaver explains, "In most silent 'horror movies,' like *London After Midnight* and *The Cat and the Canary*, the supernatural 'monster' turned out to be human and the whole thing was a hoax. Dracula *was* a vampire, and that was pretty new in 1931."

As horror historian David J. Skal says, "*Dracula* was a unique film because it dealt with a frankly supernatural premise." Because Dracula's existence was treated as real, "it was a truly creepy experience for audiences and critics." There was also an epilogue at the end of *Dracula* with Dr. Van Helsing telling the audience: "There are such things as vampires!" but Universal cut it from the film out of fear of offending religious groups.

Lugosi was lauded by the critics, and as *Variety* noted, "It would be difficult to think of anybody who could quite match the performance." Part of *Dracula*'s success was also attributed to Lugosi's sex appeal, and he claimed that almost all of his fan mail came from women. One actress called him, "probably the most sexually attractive man I have ever known in my life," and Carroll Borland, who starred with Lugosi in 1935's *Mark of the Vampire*, agreed. "He was certainly the most magnetic man I have ever known. We would just sit in a room and all the [women] would go . . . whoom!"

The box-office successes of *Dracula* and *Frankenstein* were even more remarkable considering they were released during the Depression, when money to buy anything was scarce. "People don't often realize what a horrible time the early Depression was," says David J.

Skal. "People eating out of garbage cans, no social safety nets, everything was fear, fear, fear. It's not surprising horror movies struck a chord."

There are moments in the classic Universal horrors that burn into your memories, and the primary image you remember of Dracula is his penetrating stare, as well as how Lugosi's eyes were lit by cameraman Karl Freund to make them stand out so strongly.

Freund also shot the sci-fi masterpiece *Metropolis* and went on to direct *The Mummy* (1932), and there's been speculation about how much Freund may have directed *Dracula* from under Browning, because critics will point out there are significant differences in pacing and camera movement in the film. (Freund also went on to be the director of photography for *I Love Lucy* and invented the three-camera shot, a television standard today.)

Film fans today love to point out all the gaffes and mistakes in movies, and there's quite a few you'll notice in *Dracula* as cinema was finding its feet, but whether *Dracula* holds up well today or not is almost a moot point. It's what *Dracula* represents in the grand scheme of things with Universal horror, with vampire lore, and with Bela Lugosi becoming a star from playing the title role.

And while Lugosi was obviously the star center attraction, Dwight Frye held his own against him, playing Dracula's slave Renfield, with his own blinding stare and his fiendish trademark laugh. And sure enough, after playing the hunchbacked Fritz in *Frankenstein*, Frye was typecast as the maniacal evil assistant doing his master's bidding. (Alice Cooper would write the song "The Ballad of Dwight Frye" because he felt the characters Dwight played in the Universal movies were much scarier than the actual monsters.)

Where *Dracula* was a ground-breaking American first, *Frankenstein* took the genre up another level. Some felt the success of *Dracula* was a one-time thing because it was something new and different for the era, and indeed, the *L.A. Times* called it "a freak picture" that "must be accepted as a curiosity." So when Laemmle, Jr., wanted to make another horror picture, *Frankenstein*, production executives at Universal thought he was "screwy." "I didn't believe in that production either," Laemmle, Sr., recalled. "I knew that most of the studios in town had turned it down."

Again, like *Dracula*, *Frankenstein* was also adapted into a stage play in London, and Laemmle, Jr., bought the rights. And again, because of the market crash, it was hard to raise money to make the picture.

Director James Whale came to Junior's attention after making the 1930 antiwar drama *Journey's End,* and Laemmle offered him a contract with Universal. Whale jumped at the chance to make *Frankenstein*, and chose it out of thirty possible projects. "I thought it would be an amusing thing to try and make what everybody knows to be a physical impossibility into the almost believable for sixty minutes . . . *Frankenstein*, after all, is a great classic of literature, and I soon became absorbed in its possibilities."

Before he jumped on board however, Whale gave the book to his companion, David Lewis, and asked what he thought. "I found it interesting," Lewis recalled, "but, my God, it was so weird." Then Lewis gave Whale the key to how to portray the creature on-screen: "I was sorry for the goddamn monster."

There were two versions of how Karloff was picked for the role of the Monster. Whale recalled asking Karloff to join his table at the Universal commissary, and Karloff immediately got excited because as the actor recalled, "He was the most important director on the lot."

"Your face has startling possibilities," Whale said. "I'd like you to test for the Monster in *Frankenstein*."

"I'd be delighted."

The other version of the story was David Lewis had seen Karloff in the 1931 Howard Hawks film, *The Criminal Code,* and recommended Whale check him out.

"Have you thought of Boris Karloff?" Lewis asked. "I had seen [him] in *The Criminal Code* and he was so good, I cannot tell you. His face—the way he moved, everything about him stuck in my mind. He was powerful, and you have to have a powerful monster." A review of *The Criminal Code* in *Life* magazine also called Karloff "the most quietly terrifying criminal we have ever seen."

Most people with even a passing interest in the classic monsters probably know Lugosi was up for the role of the Monster as well, but Whale didn't think he was physically right for the role, and also thought it would be ridiculous to have Lugosi play both monsters because "there'd be terrible confusion" with audiences. (Lugosi maintained he turned the part down.)

From the outset, Karloff thought *Frankenstein* would be "a fascinating job—he had no speech and hardly any intelligence, yet you had to convey a tragic part." From the get-go, Karloff and Whale also both wanted the creature to be sympathetic. "We had to have some pathos, otherwise our audience just wouldn't think about the film after they'd left the theater," Karloff said. "Whale wanted to make some impact on them. And so did I." Laemmle, Sr., also said the look in Karloff's eyes had "the suffering we needed."

Where Lugosi had a big following with women, Karloff had a big following with children, who understood that the Monster was one of them. He didn't mean to do what he did, he just didn't know any better.

Irene Miracle, who became a bit of a horror star herself in Dario Argento's *Inferno,* says, "Who can't relate to the pain of being a misunderstood child, as the monster is in that tragic interpretation? That film brings me to tears at every viewing."

During the *Bride of Frankenstein* shoot, Karloff had a scene where he's attacked by a village mob, and in the mob were a number of children who gathered around Karloff unafraid, lifting his shoes and pinching his legs to try and see what the Monster was made of. (In addition to performing the voice-over narration for the 1966 animated TV version of *How the Grinch Stole Christmas!* Karloff also narrated a number of children's albums.)

Universal told Whale they wanted *Frankenstein* to be "a very modern, materialistic treatment of this medieval story" and recommended it have elements from *Dr. Caligari*, Poe, as well as the studio's own sensibilities.

Where Lugosi's makeup for *Dracula* was minimal, the Frankenstein Monster required a much more complex design. Enter Jack Pierce, who was considered the makeup man's makeup man, the artist everyone in the business looked up to and respected. Pierce was a Greek immigrant who played minor league baseball, and became a makeup artist after working a variety of odd jobs. After seeing Pierce's work in *The Monkey Talks*, a 1926 Fox film where Jacques Lerner was transformed into an ape, Universal offered him a permanent post as a makeup man at the studio.

In creating his vision of the Monster, Pierce spent three months researching anatomy, surgery, medicine, criminology, and ancient and modern burial customs. The Monster's prominent forehead came from Pierce speculating that Dr. Frankenstein was a scientist, but wasn't a practicing surgeon, so he would make the top of the creature's head a lid, then clamp it down with brackets.

Karloff called Pierce "a genius," and generously gave him major credit for the effectiveness of the Monster. "When you get right down to it, it was Jack Pierce who really created the Frankenstein monster. I was merely the animation in the costume."

When Pierce brought a clay model head of the Frankenstein Monster to Universal, the studio brass was stunned.

"You mean to tell me that you can do this on a human being?"
"Positively."
"All right, we go to the limit."

As it is today, putting on makeup then was a long and tedious process. Karloff would pull his Ford onto the Universal lot every morning at four when the studio was practically deserted. Putting the Monster together took four to six hours a day, and ninety minutes to two hours to take off every day. For *The Bride of Frankenstein*, Karloff made sure he would get a facial massage at six in the morning before his 7:00 A.M. makeup call, and in later years, Robert Englund would get similar facial perks when playing Freddy Krueger.

During the shoot, which took place in the late summer, Karloff was sweating like crazy, and Pierce was at the ready with his makeup kit in case anything fell or melted off the actor's face in the heat. The days were long, hot, and grueling, but Karloff was always a trooper. "There were many days when I thought I would never be able to hold out until the end of the day, but somehow or other I always did," he recalled.

Whale filmed the creation scene first, where the Monster is brought to life, because he felt it was the most important scene to get right. Audiences had to believe that this monster could be brought back to life, or the rest of the picture wouldn't work, and the scene was a great spectacle of electricity and light. Then after the fireworks, Colin Clive delivered one of the classic lines of horror history when the Monster slowly lifts its hand: "It's alive!" The first time you see the Monster, Whale did it in three shots, moving the camera closer and closer every shot, to give the audience a chance to take the Monster in.

In creating Frankenstein's lab, Whale was inspired by the current sci-fi masterpiece *Metropolis* as well as *Dr. Caligari*, which he watched over and over again. Electrical genius Kenneth Strickfaden created the famous lab equipment, and gave names for them like "nucleus analyzer" and "vacuum electrolyzer." Strickfaden made the lab come alive with artificial lightning, photoelectric and gaseous tube effects, lace light and spark spirits, and he also created spark showers and lightning explosions with a gravity neutralizer. (Strickfaden also created effects for *Bride of Frankenstein*, *The Wizard of Oz*, *The Invisible Man*, *War of the Worlds*, and *Young Frankenstein*.)

Once the film was completed and ready to be previewed, Universal was nervous how the public was going to react, and scheduled the first preview far out of town in Santa Barbara, so word of mouth wouldn't spread as quickly if it was a disaster. Laemmle, Jr., was also particularly terrified because he had a lot riding on *Frankenstein*. Even with the success of *Dracula*, *Frankenstein* got made against a lot of resistance at the studio, and if it flopped, he was in deep trouble.

The Santa Barbara premiere was on October 29, 1931, at the Granada Theater at 8:15 P.M. *Frankenstein* was a very stark and strong film for its time, and the preview audience was stunned by what they saw. *The Hollywood Reporter* review stated, "Universal has either the greatest shocker of all time—or a dud. It can be one or the other; there will be no in-between measures."

But by and large, the critics raved, and got the more subtle approach Karloff and Whale brought to the material. *The New York Times* called it "far and away the most effective thing of its kind," and it would make the *Times* ten best of the year at number seven.

The New York *Daily News* called James Whale "an ace megaphoner," and *The Motion Picture Herald* hailed that a horror star was born. "Because of his restraint, his intelligent simplicity of gesture, carriage, voice and makeup, Karloff has truly created a Frankenstein Monster."

Frankenstein was a hit from opening day, breaking house records all over the country, and it was held over in every major city.

Frankenstein was also a bigger hit than *Dracula*, which had to please the Laemmles in that they had proved the doubters wrong.

Frankenstein also came with a lot of controversy. The censors in Kansas and Massachusetts demanded cuts, and newspapers in Providence wouldn't run ads for the film. One of the most notorious scenes that was removed from *Frankenstein*, where the Monster accidentally drowns a little girl, was not restored to the film until the eighties.

Like Lugosi, who finally broke through as an actor at the age of forty-eight, Karloff was also a late bloomer at forty-three years old, after he'd been a struggling actor for years. Universal soon offered Karloff a star contract, and he quipped, "I thought, maybe for once, I'll know where my breakfast is coming from, after more than twenty years of acting!"

"What a pivotal difference that made in my father's life, both professionally and personally," said his daughter Sara Karloff. "You know, it was his eighty-first film, but no one had seen the first eighty!"

On *Frankenstein*, everything came together with the source material, casting, director, and makeup artist. As Sara Karloff adds, "It was inspired by Mary Shelley and you had the magic of James Whale and the absolute genius of makeup artist Jack Pierce and you had my father's interpretation of the creature. It was just a magical marriage of talent."

With the success of *Frankenstein*, the first major horror movie cycle was launched, and the majors all jumped on the bandwagon. MOVIE STUDIOS BUSY WITH NEW HORROR FILMS, read the headline in the *Chicago Sun-Times*. WEIRD TALKIES COME TO FRONT IN HOLLYWOOD, read another. STUDIOS IN A SCRAMBLE TO PRODUCE PICTURES OF MYSTERY AND HORROR.

Dr. Jekyll and Mr. Hyde and *The Island of Lost Souls* (which was remade twice as *The Island of Dr. Moreau*) were both set up at Paramount; *White Zombie*, which was made independently and picked up by United Artists; Warners had *Mystery of the Wax Museum*, which they remade in the fifties as *House of Wax*, and *Doctor X*. At MGM, Irving Thalberg told Tod Browning he wanted the director to "out-horrify *Frankenstein*" with his next film, which was *Freaks* (he should have been careful what he wished for).

"With Universal's *Frankenstein* knocking over all box office records, all the other studios are in a scramble to do likewise," read one report. "When *Dracula* was made it looked like a chance. But its great success encouraged Universal to the extent of launching *Frankenstein* against the advice of all the wise guys, who claimed that the film was 'too horrible' and 'too morbid' to do business."

Soon, like Garbo, Boris would be billed solely as KARLOFF. In *Bride of Frankenstein*, a big hype point of the film was that the Monster finally spoke, which the star wasn't thrilled with. "If the Monster has any impact or charm, it was because he was inarticulate," Karloff said. (Karloff always had a lovely speaking voice.)

James Whale was now a top director at Universal, coming off the success of *Frankenstein*, *The Old Dark House* in 1932, and *The Invisible Man* in 1933. Whale also ventured into comedy with *By Candlelight* in 1933, drama with 1934's *One More River*, and was also going to make a sci-fi flick, *A Trip to Mars,* before committing to *Bride*, which was released in 1935.

As many fans point out today, *Bride of Frankenstein* was the first time a sequel surpassed an original, and it still holds up well today. Even though the Bride, played by Elsa Lanchester, is barely in the film at the end, her presence is unforgettable, with her streaked skyscraper hair offsetting her beautiful face. Lanchester also came up with the idea of hissing in disgust at the Monster's advances, an idea she got from the kind of noises a swan would make.

In *Bride*, the Monster is an even more sympathetic creature, desperately searching for companionship wherever he can, sadly asking, "Friend?" wherever he goes. He becomes friends with a blind man who obviously can't be scared off by the Monster's appearance, and who memorably plays, "Ave Maria" on the violin while the Monster enjoys a smoke. But in the end, with the Monster having to suffer the indignity of a fellow monster rejecting him, it leads to the Monster's classic line, "We belong dead," before he pulls the switch that destroys the castle.

Bride of Frankenstein is considered Whale's masterpiece today, although the director had to endure a lot of backhanded reviews when it came out, calling the film "good entertainment of its kind." Whale will always be best known for horror films, which of course wasn't all he did, or did best, but as history would prove, those not naturally drawn to horror, like William Friedkin with *The Exorcist*, can make some of the best and/or most groundbreaking films in the genre.

From the beginning, the press played the angle that Karloff was as kind and gentle off-screen as he was monstrous on-screen, and by all accounts he was indeed a gentleman. Where Karloff seemed more open, and there was a clear separation between who he was on-screen and off, Lugosi was much more private, which created more of a mystique to the public.

Visiting the sets of his father's films, Lugosi, Jr., remembered his father was "highly respected. He was famous for getting a scene on the first take and he was very nice to everybody, the cast, and grips, and all." Lugosi didn't leave his homeland far behind. He still loved to eat at Hungarian restaurants that had gypsy musicians, who he'd bring home after closing time to play well into the morning.

Lugosi also valued education, would read everything he could get his hands on, and instilled the importance of learning in his son. Lugosi had many times of financial hardship, losing his home and cars at the end of the thirties, and having to go to the Actor's Relief Fund for help. Lugosi would tell his son about his struggles, that he wanted him to achieve, and Bela Jr. grew up to be an attorney. "Acting is too hazardous a career," Lugosi said. "The income is uncertain and it is one field in which very few succeed."

Lugosi was hoping *Dracula* would be a springboard for other roles, but it became a straitjacket. "Where once I had been the master of my professional destinies, with a repertoire embracing all kinds and types of men, I became Dracula's puppet," Lugosi said, adding, "Although I'm afraid I'm typed by now, I'd like to quit the supernatural roles every third time and play just an interesting down-to-earth person. One of these days I may get my wish!"

Where Lugosi cursed being typecast, Karloff accepted it, and wouldn't look at the glass half empty. "The monster? I'm very grateful," Karloff once said. "The monster not only gave me recognition as an actor, but created for me a certain niche, which has given me a career."

"My father could never understand why actors hated to be typecast," said his daughter Sara. "Because it meant he could find work constantly—and what made an actor happier than working all the time? My father was a superb actor—but the world is filled with *hungry* superb actors. *Frankenstein* enabled my father to be a *well-fed* superb actor."

Vincent Price would also make a fine living in horror, and was grateful the genre gave him a career. Price felt that the acting required to make an effective horror film often went unappreciated, and he had no time for actors who felt the genre was beneath them.

There was an unspoken rivalry between Karloff and Lugosi, but Bela always spoke of Karloff with respect in public. "Karloff is a good actor," he said, "and, of course, he has no trouble with English!" referring to the fact that his own English wasn't the best, another thing that kept tying him to *Dracula*. Karloff felt sorry for Lugosi, often calling him "Poor Bela." Karloff once lamented, "Poor Bela. He was worth a lot more than he got."

Karloff would always be identified with the Monster, but he walked away from the role after the third film, *Son of Frankenstein*, in 1939. "He was going downhill," Karloff said. "We had exhausted his possibilities. He was becoming a clown."

By the mid-thirties, there was trouble at Universal. The Laemmles were bought out from Universal, and the company had to take out a bank loan because the studio was in the hole (England had also put a ban on horror films in 1937, which cut into the overseas market 40 percent). Universal tried to bill itself as "The New Universal," and the new regime wanted to concentrate on musicals, comedies, and B pictures, with the classic horror films considered Laemmle's folly.

But without horror, the studio fared poorly. Then a triple bill of *Dracula*, *Frankenstein*, and *Son of Kong* played at the Regina Theater on August 5, 1938, a venue about to go out of business, and it was a smash success. Police had to show up for crowd control, and the theater ran more than twenty hours of screenings. Then Universal struck five hundred new prints of *Dracula* and *Frankenstein*, and brought them back to theaters, where the films did major business, even outgrossing their initial box office takes in many cities.

Once the monsters were officially back, Universal would finally be out of the hole, and they churned out horror movies like a factory. *Son of Frankenstein* was rushed into production with only the title and a release date, and it was on such a tight schedule that the film's composers, Frank Skinner and Hans J. Salter, were practically held hostage at Universal until they finished the music. They would take turns composing music and napping on the couch for a little more than two days straight. Herman Stein, who was a staff composer for Universal who wrote the music for *Creature from the Black Lagoon* and other classic titles, once said, "I still have recurring dreams of not making a deadline."

Son of Frankenstein was finished on January 7, 1939, and premiered nine days later. Similarly, after *The Wolf Man* wrapped on November 25, 1941, it was edited and scored by December 9, and by mid-December, much of the same cast was working on *The Ghost of Frankenstein*. "That's how fast this stuff was being knocked out in those days without much time to really breathe in between pictures," said Universal monsters chronicler Tom Weaver.

With *The Wolf Man*, Universal was now grooming Lon Chaney Jr. to be their next horror star. The son of the makeup great changed his name from Creighton to Lon Jr. after going through a divorce, and having his car and furniture repossessed. "They starved me into it."

The Wolf Man was written by Curt Siodmak. The Universal brass told him, "We have $180,000, we have Lon Chaney Jr., Claude Rains, Ralph Bellamy, Maria Ouspenskaya, Bela Lugosi, a title called *The Wolf Man*, and we shoot in ten weeks. Get going!"

The Wolf Man goes all the way back to Greek mythology when Lycaon, a king, was transformed into a wolf by Zeus. Siodmak also brought a sense of Greek tragedy to the story as well, where Lawrence Talbot couldn't escape his fate.

The key segment that everyone remembers from *The Wolf Man*, even from one viewing, is the transformation, where shot after shot of Chaney growing progressively hairier blends into another until he's a full-blown beast.

Like Dwight Frye playing Renfield, Maria Ouspenskaya gave a very memorable performance as the gypsy Maleva, another secondary character ominously foretelling the legend of the Wolf Man curse, complete with the poem created by screenwriter Curt Sidomak. ("Even a man who is pure at heart, and says his prayers at night, may become a wolf when the wolfbane blooms, and the moon is full and bright.") Like the dignified British actors in the Hammer films, and Donald Pleasence speaking of the nature of evil in *Halloween*, Ouspenskaya's delivery really sold those four lines.

The Wolf Man makeup design was originally going to be for Henry Hull in *Werewolf of London*, but Hull still wanted to be recognizable under the makeup, whereas Lon Jr., in the Chaney family tradition, had no problem being unrecognizable under all that yak hair.

The Wolf Man premiered in December 1941, and many thought people wouldn't want to go to the movies after the bombing of Pearl Harbor, but *The Wolf Man* was another big monster hit for Universal.

Siodmak felt there was a definite parallel between cinematic horror and horrific events in real life. "When the war ended, the bottom fell out of the horror film business," he said. "When they began testing the atom bomb, it all started again. In times of peace of mind, there's no place for horror films."

Universal also wanted *The Wolf Man* in production quick because now the studio wasn't the only game in town for horror. RKO and producer Val Lewton were stealing its thunder, and Lewton's *Cat People* made $4 million on a $134,000 budget, saving the company from bankruptcy. Like many in horror, Lewton drew from what personally scared him, turning his fear of cats (ailurophobia) into one of the great horror classics of the forties.

Lewton was the original master of not seeing is believing, showing the cat people only in shadow instead of trying to create the beasts with the effects and makeup available at the time, which could have been potentially ridiculous. With the success of *Cat People* in 1942, RKO then started their own horror cycle with Lewton producing *I Walked With a Zombie* in 1943, *The Leopard Man* the same year, *The Curse of the Cat People* in 1944, and *The Body Snatcher* in 1945.

Trying to keep up with the Joneses, Universal then started teaming their monsters together like all-star teams for the "monster rally" movies, like 1943's *Frankenstein Meets the Wolf Man* (which Universal billed as "The Battle of the Century!"), then *House of Frankenstein* in 1944 ("The Topper of 'Em All . . . From the Company That Gave You Them All!"), which used sets from *Tower of London* and *Green Hell*. In 1945's *House of Dracula*, both Dracula and the Wolf Man seek cures for their monster afflictions, and although Dracula stays a vampire, Chaney is actually cured of his lycanthropy, but the doctor they call upon to cure them becomes a mad fiend in the process. The story goes Chaney was barely in full-blown Wolf Man mode in the film because there was a yak hair shortage during the war. "One monster would be terrific," the trailer promised, "but here are *five* to bring you five times the thrill!"

With the help of the classic monsters, Universal stayed in profit, but after *House of Dracula*, Universal let their contract players go, and tried to get out of the monster business once more near the end of 1946.

Trying to keep themselves from being typecast, the studio relaunched as Universal International, and dumped horror films, Westerns, and serials, in the hope of concentrating on more high-quality films. But once the studio was flirting with bankruptcy again, they turned to Abbott and Costello and the classic monsters to save them.

Abbott and Costello were big moneymakers for Universal, making twenty hit films for the company, but by the end of the forties their careers needed a boost. With the classic monsters needing a reinvention as well, why not bring them together? Costello initially resisted making a monster comedy, saying, "You don't think I'll do that crap, do you? My five-year-old daughter can write something better than that!" But he finally agreed to make the movie when he got a sweeter financial deal, and it was the movie that brought Abbott and Costello "back with a roar after the war."

It was initially a difficult shoot. Bud and Lou often fought like cats and dogs, would storm off the set, and have lengthy card games that held up the production. Charles Barton, who directed the film, recalled, "All three of the 'monsters' were the nicest. The *real* monsters were Abbott and Costello."

But then once Bud and Lou were in their element, things got much more fun with pie fights and pranks. "The pie bill on a picture like that was $3,800 to $4,800!" Barton said.

Abbott and Costello Meet Frankenstein previewed on June 25, 1948, at the Forum Theater in L.A. *Variety* predicted the "Combination of horror and slapstick should pay off brilliantly," and it did.

When it opened to the public on July 24, 1948, audiences went nuts. A critic for the *L.A. Times* reported one matinee show was "bedlam," and the audience, loaded with kids and teenagers, "shrieked with that fusion of terror and glee which only a motion picture of this sort would have inspired. I wouldn't have missed the show—the one going on around me anyhow—for anything." The *New York Star* also wrote, "It's heart-warming to see all our favorite monsters once more," and indeed, the old gang had a great time working together for the last time.

Abbott and Costello Meet Frankenstein was the most successful Frankenstein film since the 1931 original, and it was not only one of the biggest hits of 1948, but one of the biggest hits in Universal's history up to that point.

Still to this day there are many who don't think horror and comedy should go together, arguing you don't go to a horror film to laugh, and the debate first started with *Abbott and Costello Meet Frankenstein*. Lon Chaney Jr. would later regret the film, saying,

"I used to enjoy horror films when there was thought and sympathy involved. Then they became comedies. Abbott and Costello ruined the horror films; they made buffoons out of the monsters."

As horror historian Greg Mank put it, some horror purists felt the film was "the absolute and final degradation of the once great horror characters," but that many others considered it "an affectionate, polished spoof," and Mank himself found the film "a beautifully mounted, splendidly atmospheric comedy thriller." (Mel Brooks would also wonderfully spoof the Universal classics years later in 1974's *Young Frankenstein*, which also beautifully re-created the look and feel of the monster classics, which greatly enhanced the parody.)

Abbott and Costello Meet Frankenstein also inspired other filmmakers to mash genres together like Quentin Tarantino did in *Pulp Fiction*. As John Landis points out, the horror scenes in the film genuinely scared audiences then, making this mixture of comedy and horror even more bold for the time.

As Landis, who switched genre gears rapidly himself in *An American Werewolf in London*, also mentions, the monsters in *Abbott and Costello Meet Frankenstein* are treated with great respect. For fans of the film, it's a nice send-off to Chaney and Lugosi before their careers slid into schlock.

Karloff also had a great role in 1968 with *Targets*, where he played an old horror star disgusted with the violence of the real world who eventually crosses paths with a mad sniper. Karloff did four more movies before he died, all low-budget junk, but he wanted to keep performing until he gave out.

To cap off the classic monster era in the fifties, Universal would have a sympathetic creature in the Frankenstein mold, 1954's *The Creature from the Black Lagoon*, a monster created from pollution for an era terrified of the bomb. The Creature, which Rick Baker called "the best man in a rubber suit ever," was designed by Bud Westmore, who replaced Jack Pierce when foam latex was coming in and he didn't want to move with the times.

With horror environments like the old dark castle already a cliché, *Creature* was one of the first horror films to take the story out of the expected environment, bringing it into the humid Amazon jungle, where a monster exists among the beauty of nature.

The Creature had the Universal pathos, but this was also a modern movie warning about the dangers of pollution and atomic power, and the company had to rethink its usual monster approach. As Arthur Ross, one of the screenwriters who worked on *Creature*, said, "We're living in another time."

This was now the age of Jacques Cousteau, and instead of a story about a mad scientist, *Creature* now had people who wanted to learn about the forces of nature. Arthur Ross wanted *Creature* to show that nature should be studied, but one needed to be careful not to disturb it.

As Ray Bradbury once pointed out, Lon Chaney's roles tapped into people's fear of being unloved. Like *King Kong*, *Creature* was also a tragic love story. And like Frankenstein, the Creature only gets deadly when threatened by man, and is desperately in need of companionship.

Moving with the times, science fiction was coming in as the hot genre in the early fifties, and *Creature* was also shot in 3-D, although most people today have seen it "flat." With the advent of television in the early fifties, a lot of movies were shot in 3-D with Hollywood hoping it would it bring audiences back to the theaters. Underwater photography was also a fairly new innovation for the time, and director Jack Arnold used it well in the film's most celebrated scene.

Guillermo Del Toro has said his favorite horror film moment was from *Creature from the Black Lagoon*, where the monster is swimming right underneath Julie Adams. "Everything is perfect," Del Toro said. "The white bathing suit, the composition, the hypnotic, balletlike coordination of Beauty and the Beast. The image is a perfect metaphor for their impossible coupling, but also distills the distant longing of the creature. Separated only by a few feet, but so very far apart." Said *Creature* director Jack Arnold, "I was happy that it did turn out poetic." (This scene was also reportedly the inspiration for the first shark attack in *Jaws*, where we see the shark's point of view of a naked swimmer.)

Creature was another big hit for Universal, costing $650,000 and making back $3 million. Two sequels followed, and the third movie, *The Creature Walks Among Us* in 1956, was finally the last gasp of the classic monster days at Universal. The classic films would then debut on television in 1957 as the *Shock Theater* package, where a whole new generation of kids were discovering them, and were inspired by them, for the very first time.

By now the Universal movies were nowhere near as scary as when they first came out. They were sure to scare some kids, but even by the standards of the day they were great fun, almost quaint. Monster movies were now being geared toward kids, showing up on Saturday afternoon TV, or early enough at night that a kid could catch them before bedtime.

As the classic Universal horror films were first debuting on TV, there was one bible on the subject that was mandatory reading for every young "monster kid": *Famous Monsters of Filmland*.

In the world of science fiction, fantasy, and horror, there was one man whose spirit and enthusiasm for fantastic film was stronger than anyone's. With the creation of *Famous Monsters of Filmland*, Forrest J. Ackerman created the ultimate fan guide that inspired generations of kids. The magazine, and the enormous collection of memorabilia Ackerman accumulated throughout the years, was a true testament to his love of fantastic film and literature.

Ackerman was born in 1916, and was an active collector since 1926. When he was in his twenties, he would write to Carl Laemmle, the president of Universal, for movie stills from their classic horror films, and would travel by streetcar to pick up them up (he eventually accumulated 125,000 stills). He had every issue of the old sci-fi pulp magazines like *Weird Tales* and *Amazing Stories*, which he bought when they were new.

Ackerman owned a copy of *Frankenstein* that was autographed by Mary Shelley when she was nineteen. He also had the Creature from the Black Lagoon costume a janitor at Universal took home for his kid to wear on Halloween. Not to mention Bela Lugosi's cape, the model pterodactyl the original King Kong battled, one of the model Martian ships from the original 1953 *War of the Worlds*, and much, much more.

Ackerman's collection never stopped growing, and like a malevolent fifties' science fiction monster, it ended up consuming his house, a four-story, eighteen-room mansion in the hills of Los Feliz, which he dubbed the "Ackermansion." According to one report, the house became so overcrowded with memorabilia that Ackerman and his wife had to park on the street because their garage was too full.

The Ackermansion was open for tours every weekend, and making the pilgrimage to Ackerman's home was a badge of honor for any true monster fan. It's been estimated that more than 50,000 people came to visit when he lived there. When you arrived, he would greet you through the intercom: "Who dares disturb the tomb of the vampire?"

Ackerman also coined the term "sci-fi" and told *GQ* magazine that he would say "science fiction" every night before he went to sleep because if he died before he awoke, he wanted "science fiction" to be his last words.

The first issue of *Famous Monsters* was written in twenty hours in Ackerman's kitchen. *Famous Monsters* would ultimately put out 190 issues in a fantastic run from 1958 to 1983. The very first issue is now a rare collector's item; one reportedly sold on eBay in 2001 for $5,200.

Many of the incredible, richly textured cover paintings for *Famous Monsters* were created by Basil Gogos, who brought the classic monsters to life in full color.

Like many monster fans, Gogos actually felt sorry for the big lugs. "I wasn't trying to capture the ferocity of the monsters," says Gogos. "I was trying to capture the humanity, at least the humanity I could give them. Because I always felt they were kind of vulnerable, and there was pathos to be given to the portraits. I was humane about it because they were so helpless. They were killing people, but in the long run you figured that was their nature, and we just out of fear destroyed them without any feelings, but I had feelings for them in the paintings."

The impact *Famous Monsters* would have on the fantasy, sci-fi, and horror genre was tremendous. Forry Ackerman was the template for the modern film geek, and *Famous Monsters* was the monthly that celebrated all things great about monsters.

Stephen King wrote the introduction to *Mr. Monster's Movie Gold*, one of the many books Ackerman wrote over the years, and in it King recalled the first time he ever picked up the magazine at a local newsstand. "I didn't just read my first issue of *Famous Monsters*," King wrote. "I inhaled it . . . I pored over it . . . I damn near memorized that magazine and it seemed *eons* until the next one."

It wasn't long after King discovered the wonderful world of *Famous Monsters* that he sent Ackerman a story he wrote in 1960. It was the very first time King ever sent anything out in the hopes of being published. Ackerman was also a literary agent, he represented Ray Bradbury, L. Ron Hubbard, and Ed Wood, and he also could have added King to his roster, but unfortunately he rejected the story. Once King grew up and became a literary powerhouse, Ackerman was one of many in line to meet him at a book signing in L.A. Forry brought a one-of-a-kind item that King signed for him: the original copy of the story King wrote and sent out in the early sixties.

Ironically, where King's pubescent writings didn't make the cut, a letter director Joe Dante (*The Howling, Gremlins*) sent in to *Famous Monsters* was molded into an article and published in its pages. "We all tried to get our letters and pictures printed in the magazines," Dante recalls. "It was a badge of honor. It was as if there was this cadre of people out there who had this interest in this material, in these magazines. It was a very small group, it was a whole generation of burgeoning film buffs. They've now been christened 'monster kids' by people in their middle age looking back: 'Oh, I was a monster kid! Were you a monster kid?'"

In Ackerman's massive movie poster collection was a one sheet for *Close Encounters of the Third Kind* autographed in silver marker by Steven Spielberg: "A generation of fantasy lovers thank you for raising us so well." Spielberg also said that reading *Famous Monsters* gave him the "much needed inspiration" to go "scurrying for my father's eight millimeter home-movie camera," and start making his first little films. Growing up in Mexico, Guillermo Del Toro taught himself how to read English by poring over *Famous Monsters*, dying to figure out what it said.

It wasn't only future A-list filmmakers who enjoyed *Famous Monsters*. One of the magazine's biggest fans was Sammy Davis, Jr., who was just as excited to meet Forry as Ackerman was to meet Sammy.

For many years, Ackerman wanted to turn his collection into a museum, but he sadly had no takers. What ultimately happened to the Ackermansion is heartbreaking. According to one estimate, Ackerman's collection at its peak, which had 300,000 pieces, was worth about $10 million. Yet he had to sell pieces of it over the years when he needed money, and sold off most of what he had in 2002 after a costly lawsuit with a former business partner. Ackerman then lived with what was left of his collection in a bungalow in Los Feliz.

Ackerman made it to ninety-two years old, then finally slipped away on December 6, 2008. Knowing the end was near, fans from all over sent in thank-yous and good-byes, and a number of former *Famous Monster* readers, like Peter Jackson and Rick Baker, paid tribute to the original monster kid at geek ground zero, *Ain't It Cool News*.

Rick Baker said that many articles have been written about him over the years, but none of them had the same thrill as reading my own name in *Famous Monsters of Filmland*. Jackson wrote, "He united a generation—more than one generation because whenever you read anybody's tribute to Forry, you only have to substitute names and locations and it pretty much becomes your story."

In Stephen King's memoir *On Writing*, he probably summed it up best: "Ask anyone who has been associated with the fantasy-horror–science fiction genres in the last thirty years about this magazine and you'll get a laugh, a flash of the eyes, and a stream of bright memories—I practically guarantee it."

Launched by renegade comic pioneer William Gaines, the EC Comics, like *Tales from the Crypt,* had a brief life on the newsstands, but like *Famous Monsters* they were a big influence on impressionable young kids who grew up to craft their own horror stories.

Yet EC Comics, which first stood for Educational Comics, and then became Entertaining Comics, tried to provide a moral with their stories for their young, impressionable readers, that bad behavior could meet with disastrous consequences at the hands of a zombie or a lunatic with an ax, and ultimately it was in good, gory fun.

Gaines himself said, "A lot of people have the idea we're a bunch of monsters who sit around drooling and dreaming up horror and filth. That's not true. We try to entertain and educate. That's all there is to it."

In their time, horror comics were blamed for juvenile delinquency, and were eventually shut down by the arbiters of good taste at the same time as the McCarthy hearings, but their influence on the genre proved strong. EC Comics got away with a lot, and it gave many of the leading lights in the future of horror the road map to follow.

"As a kid, I cut my teeth on William Gaines's horror comics," Stephen King recalled. "*Weird Science, Tales from the Crypt*—plus all the Gaines imitators but like a good Elvis record, the Gaines magazines were often imitated, never duplicated."

George Romero would also say the EC Comics had more influence over his movies than the horror films of the time. "I think a great part of my aesthetic in the genre was born out of EC rather than movies," he said. "Horror movies, when I was in my formative years, were generally bad. The effects sucked. The EC's, on the other hand, were nitty-gritty, there was a lot going on in each frame, the stories were great." Not to mention that there was way more gore in an EC comic than you could show on the screen at the time.

Tobe Hooper was also a big fan, and he recalled, "Since I started reading these comics when I was young and impressionable, their overall feeling stayed with me. I'd say they were the single most important influence on *The Texas Chain Saw Massacre*."

Bill's father, Max Gaines, is considered the godfather of the comic book. He had previously tried a variety of professions such as working in a factory, as an elementary school principal, a haberdasher, and then working as a color salesman for Eastern Color Printing.

During the depression, Max was living with his mother in the Bronx with his wife and his two children, Elaine and Bill. Max found a bunch of newspaper comic strips in the attic, and had a great laugh looking through them again. The funnies were printed at Eastern Color Printing because it had a state-of-the-art color press. The press was set up for a newspaper page, but if you folded a standard page twice, you could turn it into a booklet with more pages.

Max then put out *Funnies on Parade*, a thirty-two page comic you could order with a coupon, and Gaines got Procter and Gamble to order a million copies of the issue. Gaines got Dell Publishing to finance 35,000 copies of his next comic, *Famous Funnies*, which sold for ten cents a copy, and all 35,000 copies sold out in a weekend. But Delacorte thought it was a fluke that wouldn't repeat, so Gaines had another publisher print up 250,000 more, and eventually circulation was up to a million copies.

Max's company would eventually print DC Comics, who would soon have the astronomical success of *Superman*, launching the golden age of comics. After Gaines was bought out of DC, he started EC.

Max's son, Bill Gaines, wasn't popular with girls, had asthma, bad eyes, was withdrawn, a nerd, not unlike a lot of the geeks who love comics and horror. He did have a healthy sense of humor, and loved causing the kind of trouble that drove his father nuts.

When Max was killed in a boating accident in 1947, Bill reluctantly took over the family business. "Comics? I hated 'em," Bill recalled. "Never touched the stuff. I wanted to be a chemistry teacher."

EC wasn't doing well after Max Gaines's demise. They were publishing biblical and historical comics that weren't selling, and the company went $100,000 into debt. Bill was determined to get EC back on track, and hired artist Al Feldstein who was adept at drawing sexy, voluptuous women.

EC would now stand for Entertaining instead of Educational, and started putting out crime and Western stories. Horror comics began in 1947 with the first issue of *Eerie*, and EC followed suit, putting horror stories in their *Crime Patrol* and *War on Crime* series. The last issue of *Crime Patrol* had four horror stories, "The Corpse in the Crematorium," "Trapped in the Tomb," "The Graveyard Feet," and a tale told by the Crypt Keeper, "The Spectre in the Castle."

Al and Bill loved the radio thrillers they grew up on as kids, like *Inner Sanctum* and *Lights Out*. *Lights Out* was created by Wyllis Cooper, who wrote the screenplay for *Son of Frankenstein*, and Arch Oboler, who would open the show with a warning every week: "This is Arch Oboler bringing you another of our series of stories of the unusual, and once again we caution you: These *Lights Out* stories are definitely not for the timid soul. So we tell you calmly and very sincerely, if you frighten easily, turn off your radio now."

Lights Out did a lot with sound effects to bring the stories to life. Decapitated heads were sound effects guys chopping cabbage with a cleaver, breaking bones were spare ribs being wacked with pipe wrenches, and people being eaten would be the FX man chomping down on dry spaghetti. Guests on the show included Boris Karloff and Mercedes McCambridge, who would later provide Linda Blair's possessed voice for *The Exorcist*.

Lights Out played on the radio in repeats in the fifties and sixties, which is how Stephen King grew up with the show. King recalled: "Oboler utilized two of radio's great strengths: the first is the mind's innate obedience, its willingness to try to see whatever someone suggests it see, no matter how absurd; the second is the fact that fear and horror are blinding emotions that knock our adult pins from underneath us and leave us groping in the dark like children who cannot find the light switch. Radio is, of course, the 'blind' medium, and only Oboler used it so well or so completely."

Feldstein's parents wouldn't let him to listen to either *Inner Sanctum* or *Lights Out*, but he would sneak out of bed and listen at the top of the stairs when the shows were on in the house. He finally told Bill, "Why don't we put this stuff in the comics?"

Soon Feldstein was soon writing four stories a week and editing seven comic titles that were launched by EC: *Tales from the Crypt*, *The Haunt of Fear*, *Vault of Horror*, *Crime SuspenStories*, *Shock SuspenStories*, *Weird Science*, and *Weird Fantasy*.

The Haunt of Fear, *Tales from the Crypt*, and *Vault of Horror* had a circulation of 400,000, where *Weird Science*, *Weird Fantasy*, *Two-Fisted Tales*, and *Frontline Combat* had a circulation of 225,000 copies for each title. Soon imitations and clones followed to the point where there were 150 or so horror comics on the market.

Max Gaines had his own set of rules when he was comic king, and his son violated every commandment in his horror comics, including, "Never show a coffin, especially with a corpse in it. Don't chop the limbs off anybody. Don't put anybody's eyes out. No blood or bloody daggers, no skeletons or skulls." And, of course, "never show anybody stabbed or shot. Make killings in two panels: In one, the villain approaching with the weapon; in two the villain leaving the body with the smoking gun. Never show the kill."

The "Bill Gaines's Do's and Don'ts of Horror" were as follows:

"We have no ghosts, devils, goblins, or the like. We tolerate vampires and werewolves, if they follow tradition and behave the way respectable vampires and werewolves should. We love walking corpse stories. We'll accept the occasional zombie or mummy. And we relish the *conte cruel* story," or a tale of sadism.

The covers of the EC horror comics were very lurid, featuring severed heads and limbs, rotting zombies rising from the dead, and you couldn't show anything remotely like it in movies for well over a decade. *Tales from the Crypt* was narrated by the Crypt Keeper, who would introduce each story with his trademark "heh, heh" chortle.

One story introduction went: "Heh, heh! Well! So we meet again, dear friends! Welcome! Welcome once more to the crypt of terror! This time I have a really chilling tale from my collection of spine-tinglers to relate to you! Now, lie back in your caskets! Tuck yourselves in with your shrouds! Comfy? Good! Then I'll begin!"

EC tried to take on issues no one in the fifties wanted to talk about like racism and drug abuse, stories that were called "Preachies." The stories tried to teach strong moral lessons for the kids reading them. If the characters did something bad, gory karma would soon follow. "If somebody did something really bad, he usually 'got it,'" said Gaines. "And of course the EC way was he got it the same way he gave it."

The EC Comics were phenomenally successful, selling ten million copies a year. As Lyle Stuart, who was EC's business manager, recalled, "Break-even would be 36 or 37 percent. Our magazines were coming in at 89 percent . . . 93 percent."

But it wasn't long before EC came under fire, and it was the toughest scrutiny horror had come under to date. As early as 1940, the editor of the *Chicago Daily News* Sterling North denounced comic books as "a poisonous mushroom growth" contributing to juvenile

THE FOUNDATIONS OF FEAR ☻ 43

delinquency. J. Edgar Hoover also warned against comic books because of "the glorification of un-American vigilante action, and the deification of the criminal are extremely dangerous in the hands of the unstable child."

The anti-comic campaign was spearheaded by a psychiatrist named Fredric Wertham, and he started campaigning against them in 1948, claiming comics were "definitely and completely harmful and was a distinct influencing factor in every single delinquent or disturbed child we studied." Wertham accused Batman and Robin of being gay lovers and Wonder Woman of being a sadistic lesbian. "As long as the crime comic book industry exists in its present form, no American home is safe," Wertham warned. In Bill Gaines's office he had a picture of Fredric Wertham reading a copy of *Shock SuspenStories* on his wall.

Then the PTA, church groups, and the Catholic Legion of Decency denounced EC comics. The other comic companies were happy their chief rival was taking a beating because EC was outselling them all. Gaines said, "The only way these guys are happy is not if they hear a competitor is dying, but if he's dying particularly painfully."

Then came the Kefauver Hearings, which Gaines called "a headline seeking carnival" providing "fuel to those in our society who want to tar with the censor's brush."

The hearings were launched by Senator Estes Kefauver, who was part of the Senate Subcommittee to Investigate Juvenile Delinquency. He took on organized crime in the famed televised hearings in 1951, and the anti–comic book hearing took place in the same courthouse in New York's Foley Square.

Bill Gaines volunteered to testify, and he was the only one in the comic business who would come forward to stand up against Senator Kefauver.

"Pleasure is what we sell," Gaines testified. "Entertainment. Reading enjoyment. Our American children are, for the most part, normal children. They are bright children. But those who want to prohibit comic magazines seem to see instead dirty, twisted, sneaky, vicious, perverted little monsters who use the comics as blueprints for action. What are we afraid of? Are we afraid of our own children? Do we forget that they are citizens too, and entitled to the essential freedom to read? Or do we think our children so evil, so vicious, so single-minded, that it takes but a comic magazine story of murder to set them to murder—or robbery to set them to robbery?"

Gaines then quoted former New York Mayor Jimmy Walker, who once said he never knew a girl to be ruined by a book. "And no one has ever been ruined by a comic," he added. "As has already been pointed out by previous testimony, no healthy, normal child has ever been made the worse for reading comic magazines . . . I do not believe that anything that has ever been written can make a child hostile, overaggressive, or delinquent. The roots of such characteristics are much deeper. The truth is that delinquency is a product of the real environment in which a child lives—and not of the fiction he reads." (The day after Gaines testified before the Senate, the McCarthy hearings began.)

The boycotts and protests against horror comics continued, and wholesalers were scared to carry them. Within several months, newsstands went from more than a hundred horror comics on the market to practically none.

After the hearings, the Comics Code Authority formed, and comics had to have their seal of approval to be carried in stores. The comics code forbade horror, saying no more "excessive bloodshed, gory or gruesome crimes, depravity, lust, sadism and masochism." Also no more "walking dead, torture, vampires, ghouls, cannibalism and werewolfism."

As usual in situations like this, everybody ran for cover. Gaines went to other comic publishers about forming their own self-regulating group, but they didn't want to fight the Senate, and caved in (we'd also see history repeat itself like this in the future with battles against horror films, violence in mainstream movies, metal and rap lyrics, violent video games, and so on).

Finally word came down on September 14, 1954, that Gaines would no longer publish horror and crime comics. In the last issues ran an editor's note that said, in part: "As a result of the hysterical, injudicious, and unfounded charges leveled at crime and horror comics, many retailers and wholesalers throughout the country have been intimidated into refusing this kind of magazine.

"Although we at EC still believe, as we have in the past, that the charges leveled at crime and horror comics are utter nonsense, there's no point in going into a defense of this kind of literature at the present time. Economically our situation is acute. Magazines that do not get onto the newsstand do not sell. *We give up*. WE'VE HAD IT!

"Naturally, with comic magazine censorship now a fact, we at EC look forward to an immediate drop in the crime and juvenile delinquency rate of the United States."

EC nearly went under, winding up $100,000 in debt, and Gaines and his mother had to put up $50,000 to keep the company alive, but Bill soon bounced back with the success of *Mad*, which survived the comics witch hunt. Now freckled, gap-toothed Alfred E. Newman would replace the decrepit old Crypt Keeper, but the Gaines irreverence would still remain, and once it changed from a comic to a magazine in the twenty-fourth issue, it wouldn't have the Comics Code people breathing down their necks.

By 1959, polls claimed 58 percent of American college kids, and 43 percent of American high school kids were reading *Mad*, and it would have a one million circulation. *Mad* became Gaines's bread and butter for decades to come and its circulation peaked in 1973 at 2.4 million.

In 1989 *Tales from the Crypt* was resurrected as the HBO cable series, which was produced by director Richard Donner (*The Omen*, *Superman*, and *Lethal Weapon*), writer David Giler (*Alien*), director Walter Hill *(The Warriors)*, Joel Silver (producer of the *Die Hard*, *Lethal Weapon*, and *Matrix* films), and Robert Zemeckis *(Back to the Future)*, and lasted until 1996. By this point, it was clear the effect EC comics had on modern horror, and how instead of inspiring juvenile delinquency, they inspired creativity and delight in such readers as Romero and King.

Annie Gaines, Bill's widow, said, "The public may remember Bill best for *Mad*, but *Tales from the Crypt* and the other horror comics always had a very special place in his heart—as did the people who made them. He loved the material, and he loved the fact that there were all these loyal fans who wouldn't let it be forgotten. He was so pleased when it became a successful TV series. It was a great vindication."

First airing on October 2, 1959, *The Twilight Zone* was the creation of Rod Serling, who was often called "television's last angry man." Serling saw television as a medium of change, and like EC Comics, he was able to sneak a lot of important messages past the network censors by coating them in fantasy.

The Twilight Zone's impact is still evident in modern horror. It popularized twist endings, brought a healthy sense of irony to horror and sci-fi, and *The Twilight Zone* also strove to make fantasy believable—just three reasons why the show still holds up and is remembered well.

Says George Clayton Johnson, who wrote for *The Twilight Zone*, "Rod had been shaping the idea of doing half-hour science fiction stories because that way he could escape some of the worst aspects of censorship. If you want to talk about racism in the South, just make them aliens and that's okay."

"Many *Twilight Zone*s address social ills," said Carol Serling, Rod's widow. "I think that's one reason they're still around. It hasn't changed that much and I think that's why they're still popular. People who've never seen them before say, 'Oh, my God, that's great,' because those problems have not gone away. I think some of [Rod's] best work was when he felt the most strongly about what he was writing about."

Rodman Edward Serling was born in Syracuse, New York, on December 25, 1924. His family soon moved to Binghamton, New York. Serling's memories of Binghamton were fond, and he would later re-create idyllic towns like it in episodes of *The Twilight Zone*, particularly for characters who were overworked and dreamed of magical hometowns like the imaginary Willoughby to escape to.

Serling enlisted in the army the day he graduated high school, and being in battle during World War II traumatized him. During one attack, three soldiers that were in his patrol group were killed and Serling himself was badly wounded by shrapnel. While he was overseas, his father passed away, and he was devastated when he couldn't get a leave to attend his funeral.

When Serling came back from the army, he was a changed man. His mother was left shattered and frail from her husband's death and Rod, along with his brother, now had to take care of her. "I was bitter about everything and at loose ends when I got out of the service," said Serling. "I think I turned to writing to get it off my chest."

Serling started writing for radio and would break into television in the early fifties, writing for such shows as *Hallmark Hall of Fame* and *Kraft Television Theatre*. At the beginning of 1955, Serling's big break finally came with "Patterns," which was the seventy-first script he'd written that was aired on television. "Patterns" was the story of a young man who becomes a success in the corporate world, but is disgusted with himself when he sees how ruthless that world is, and how soulless he must become to succeed. The following year, Serling won his first Emmy for "Patterns."

Like many writers after a big success, Serling had to prove, to the media and himself, that he was not a one-hit wonder, that he had more in him besides "Patterns." On October 11, 1956, *Playhouse 90*, the legendary anthology show from the golden age of television, aired "Requiem for a Heavyweight," which was about a washed-up boxer trying to make a new life for himself after his career ends. "Requiem" was a tremendous success and swept the Emmys.

At the age of thirty, Serling was finally a big success, but it was a bittersweet victory. He had important things he wanted to say, but his scripts were heavily censored by the networks so that they wouldn't offend the sponsors. Live drama was also fast becoming an endangered species. The number one show on the air was *Gunsmoke*, and television was soon overrun with Westerns. Serling realized TV would have no place for what he wanted to say, so he created *The Twilight Zone* as a Trojan horse to drive the message through.

"Rod was forever getting into trouble because he wanted to call a spade a spade," says George Clayton Johnson, who wrote the episodes "Nothing in the Dark" and "Kick the Can," among others, for *The Twilight Zone*. "They were forever stopping him, for the pettiest of reasons, which made him even more of a little David against a bunch of Goliaths."

Nobody was sure what Serling was up to at first. "Everybody thought that Rod was taking a big step backward with these little

THE FOUNDATIONS OF FEAR

half-hour plays after having won these Emmys and being the great playwright," says Johnson. "And now here he is off there doing these little science fiction things. So what the hell is he up to here? Is he selling out? No. He was a man who recognized the death of live TV, who saw that everything was becoming film, who was working for several years trying to get this together.

"He had been shaping the idea of doing half-hour science fiction stories because that way he could escape some of the worst aspects of censorship," continues Johnson. As Serling himself once said, "On *The Twilight Zone*, I knew that I could get away with Martians saying things that Republicans and Democrats couldn't."

Carol Serling said *The Twilight Zone* was a labor of love for her husband for this reason. "He was able to do things in the fantasy genre—say things, make points, confront issues—that he couldn't do on straight dramatic TV," she said. "Looking back on it, I think those were probably his happy years on television, because he had the artistic creative control. If he didn't want something, ultimately it didn't happen."

In today's lingo, Serling would be considered a show runner, the guy who created the program and made it all happen, and Serling was one of the first, if not the first show runner, long before the writer was in charge. Back in the fifties, the producer ran the show, and Serling was one of the first writers who changed this, making the key creative decisions for *The Twilight Zone*.

"Rod being a writer did not intrude on us," says Richard Matheson, who wrote numerous episodes of *The Twilight Zone*. "Rod was very respectful of other people's talent. They shot it just the way you wrote it, with the best actors and directors they could get."

"Unlike any other TV show I know of," said George Clayton Johnson, "*The Twilight Zone* was oriented towards the writer. The main people making the decisions were writers. No one else could have ever pulled off *The Twilight Zone* where he could be the creative director and call all the shots."

Each episode of *The Twilight Zone* followed certain dictates. "Buck Houghton, the producer, understood *The Twilight Zone*," said Johnson. "He understood the formula of only one miracle per story. The girl can't read minds and levitate objects too. Also, plain people in plain circumstances, because we have plain sets in the background and we can put those together. If you start asking for a pasha's temple, we haven't got the set."

The Twilight Zone was famous for its twist endings, or "zappers," which many horror filmmakers have tried hard to emulate and outdo since. Says Matheson, "That was part of the structure. You had your teaser, which introduced, hopefully, an intriguing premise. You had your first act curtain, which was the cliff-hanger, and then you had your ending, which hopefully had the twist or surprise. That was the structure of the best *Twilight Zone*s."

For Matheson, the secret to writing a great twist for *The Twilight Zone* was that it had to be inherent to the story. "You can't just tell a regular story and then suddenly tack on what you think is a surprise ending," he says. "It has to be based on what has gone before. There has to be a logic, that's my feeling. Fantasy has to have a logic to it, it can't be far-fetched. It has to be believable."

The Twilight Zone was also a great screenwriting lesson in that the show set up an intriguing premise, got you involved in the characters, and effectively pulled the rug out on you, all in half an hour, and it wasn't a setback to have that tight of a framework to work in, because when *The Twilight Zone* did several one-hour episodes, they didn't work.

"All of these limitations were huge assets for the kind of writer that Serling was," said Marc Scott Zicree, author of *The Twilight*

Zone Companion. "I think Serling had a natural, innate sense of the half-hour structure. He was a master at it. He had in mind those sort of O. Henry twist endings. Those don't really work in an hour-length. You really need the half hour for it to be effective." (William Sydney Porter, aka O. Henry, wrote short stories for *New York World Sunday Magazine* that were famous for their surprise endings.)

The most important element of *The Twilight Zone* were the messages the show conveyed. The heroes and villains usually got what was coming to them, good or bad. "What comes around, goes around, that's one of the big messages," says Johnson. "Be careful what you wish for, you may get it. What you really think you need in your life is just what you don't want in your life, because if you get it, you'll become a spoiled punk instead of the great scientist you might have become."

Many episodes of *The Twilight Zone* reflected the personal fears of the writers themselves, and Serling was certainly no exception. Death, becoming obsolete, and trying to make a mark before leaving the world were all themes he returned to repeatedly. "These are universal human issues," said Zicree, "which is why *Twilight Zone* is so successful around the world."

Like *Star Trek*, *The Twilight Zone*'s cult following would grow much stronger after its initial run. In fact, "it was touch and go whether it was going to be renewed each season," said Matheson. "They even had write-in campaigns by viewers saying, 'Don't cancel it.' That it lasted five years was really miraculous because they were on the verge of canceling it all the time.

"I don't think anybody knows ahead of time that they're working on something immortal," Matheson continued. "If they did, they'd become so self-conscious, it would probably turn into junk. *The*

Twilight Zone is dated and yet it still holds up in today's world. In later years, the only reason some young producers would even know who the hell I was was because when they were kids they would watch *The Twilight Zone*. And here it is, from 1959, it's still showing."

TWO

KENSINGTON GORE

How Hammer reinvented the classic Universal horrors in their own distinctive way

As one monster cycle was ending in the States, horror would get a crucial reinvention from England's Hammer Films. Classics such as *The Curse of Frankenstein* and *Horror of Dracula,* starring Christopher Lee and Peter Cushing, helped keep U.S. distributors Warner Bros. and Universal in business, and kept the British film industry alive as well.

"Speaking purely in economic terms, the returns from Hammer's films brought a vast amount of money into the country," said Christopher Lee. "When everything was starting to fall apart, Hammer kept part of our film industry going." Lee also said Hammer was "probably the most famous independent British production company that ever existed, and undoubtedly the most successful."

"Hammer was different from most studios in that it was a repertory company," says Jimmy Sangster, who directed a number of films for the studio. "In the nine years I worked there as an assistant director and production manager, the studio crew remained essentially the same. Hammer was never considered a major corporation. They were a small production company that needed the big guys to finance and distribute their product."

The Hammer films had their own interpretations of the classic horror creatures, with their own stars like Christopher Lee and Peter Cushing, their own top-notch crews that worked on film after film, and a bevy of beautiful women. Cinematographer Freddie Francis said that Hammer "put beauty in everything, even crypts and coffins."

Hammer worked like American International Pictures (or AIP for short), who were supplying the drive-ins of the United States with films that were made fast, cheap, and furious. Although the Hammer films were much classier movies with higher production values, they were still shot on similarly fast and cheap schedules.

"There's no real difference between what Hammer makes and what a really large studio like Paramount makes, except that Hammer creates far more with far less," said Christopher Lee. "They manage to put on the screen a story, essentially unbelievable, which the actors then make believable, without spending absolute fortunes on script, direction, and cast. Hammer is meeting a far greater challenge than many number one studio prestige productions and winning hands down."

In their time, the Hammer films were considered disreputable, a bloody blot on British culture. "I came away revolted and outraged," wrote one British reviewer of *Horror of Dracula*. "This film disgusts the mind and repels the senses." Another reviewer called a Hammer film "vulgar, stupid, nasty and intolerably tedious business." *Sight and Sound* ranted, "A sane society cannot stand the posters, let alone the films!"

Many years later, the reviews were much different. *The Evening Standard* called *Horror of Dracula* "unimpeachable and unsurpassed," and *The Guardian* called it "brilliantly filmed and acted." No less than Martin Scorsese recalled, "When I went along to the cinema as a teenager with groups of friends, if we saw the logo of Hammer Films we knew it would be a very special picture."

Unlike a lot of horror films in America that were aimed for kiddie matinees, Hammer Films were geared toward adults because they had Britain's X certificate, which meant no one under sixteen could see the film. "The bar was higher for Hammer," Ted Newsom, Hammer historian, says. "They were serious movies that were scary."

"It seemed to me they were striving for something more than a splatter film," Scorsese said. "They set a mood with absolutely striking photography, and you were drawn right into it." (Scorsese would later hire longtime Hammer cinematographer and director Freddie Francis to shoot *Cape Fear.*)

Like AIP, Hammer would come up with the ad campaign for a film first, and if the theater owners and distributors thought it was a good idea and it would sell, the movie got the green light, which is how *The Revenge of Frankenstein* got made. For *The Revenge of Frankenstein,* they made up the poster, and as Jimmy Sangster recalled, Michael Carreras asked him if he'd "please write a movie to fit and hurry it up because he'd promised delivery within an impossibly short space of time."

Producer Brian Clemens pitched an idea for a film to Hammer, *Dr. Jekyll and Sister Hyde,* where the mad doctor turns into an evil, beautiful woman. When Clemens came to the meeting with John (whom everyone called Jimmy) Carreras to discuss the film, he knew he already had a green light because the poster was already drawn up when he came to Carreras's office.

Hammer Films was founded in 1934, and was named after a vaudeville team, Hammer and Smith. Will Hammer's real name was William Hinds, and after vaudeville he worked in music publishing, show promotion, and managing theaters and hotels. Hammer made its first feature in 1935, a comedy, *The Public Life of Henry the Ninth*. The company also made short subjects and one-hour crime movies that could be sold for second bills.

Hammer cofounder Enrique Carreras bought his first movie theater in Hammersmith London in 1913, and eventually owned a chain of theaters. He then went into a partnership with William Hinds, and there would be three generations of Carreras in the company. Carreras looked after the money, Hinds looked after the productions.

Carreras was a great deal-maker who could sell a two-line note or a poster. He was good at selling the idea, but he didn't make profitable decisions, and he sold the company down the river to keep it going. Michael Carreras recalled his father was "a salesman par excellence . . . when I was a child, I think a lot of my energy was drained by just watching my father perform."

Hammer went through several homes where it would make its movies before settling on a seventeenth-century mansion located on the bank of the River Thames they called Bray Studios. Much of the cast and crew of the Hammer films lived in the homes where Hammer made its films. Everyone had their own bedroom, the rooms were all large and fully furnished, and Hammer also hired a cook. In the early days of the company, whoever arrived on the set first had to make coffee.

"Any fan of the old Hammer movies will know what it looks like both inside and out," said Jimmy Sangster. "We rented the place furnished and weren't allowed to move a stick of it. It was said that you could arrive at a cinema in the middle of movie and know it was a Hammer film because you'd seen the same set, furnished the same way, in the last three pictures." Ted Newsom, who directed the Hammer documentary *Flesh and Blood: The Hammer Heritage of Horror,* says, "You watch enough of the Hammer films, you can tell it's the same room. Oh, *there's* the staircase. . . ."

When Hammer's 1955 sci-fi-horror classic *Quatermass Xperiment* was a big hit, the company finally had a success with its forty-third film, and it kept things afloat for a while. Hammer then followed up with *X the Unknown*, where it was decided to have a monster come from inner space, from the middle of the earth, instead of outer space. "Cheaper to dig a hole than construct a rocket ship," director Jimmy Sangster said.

Hammer then started reinventing the classic monsters with *The Curse of Frankenstein*, starring Christopher Lee as the Monster, and Peter Cushing as Frankenstein. *Curse* was originally going to be shot in black-and-white on a three-week schedule, but Carreras liked the script so much, he pushed the schedule up to four weeks and shot the film in color.

Lee had a hard time getting work because of his height (at six five he was the tallest actor in England), but it was also the primary reason he got the role of the Monster. When Lee was approached about playing the Frankenstein monster, "I hesitated only briefly. It was self-evident that this was not the path to glory, but I'd seen the 1931 Karloff film, and it was equally obvious that purely technically it was a tremendous challenge. Besides, my visions of glamour in the business were now totally blown."

Lee didn't care if no one could tell what he looked like under the makeup. He thought, "Well, if I disguise myself to the point where I'm completely unrecognizable, and it works, people will say, 'I wonder what he really looks like,'" which actually happened with audiences.

Lee loved the makeup job Hammer makeup man Phil Leakey did on him. They wanted the Monster to look like a mess, clearly put together from disparate parts, "but we overdid the mess in our hurry." (One critic felt the Monster resembled "a road accident.") Once he played the creature, Lee appreciated the skill Karloff had brought to the role. At one point, Karloff and Lee actually lived next door to each other in England, and both shared a love of cricket.

Sangster said Lee's turns as the Frankenstein Monster and the Mummy were "first-class performances," adding, "It ain't easy to convey emotion from beyond a pound and a half of makeup." *The Mummy* was especially tough because Lee's mask had a tight little mouth line, and he had to breathe through the eyeholes. When the Mummy broke through doors, Lee would curse up a storm under a stiff, bandaged face that never moved, to the hilarity of the crew.

Peter Cushing also had the gift of taking a lot of mad scientist gobbledygook on the page and convincingly selling it on-screen. "So often he got me out of trouble," recalled Freddie Francis. "The luckiest thing that ever happened to Hammer was Peter Cushing. . . . One film I did with Peter, there were three pages of absolute rubbish explaining virtually the whole theme of the movie. I was dreading this, but while we were shooting it, I thought, it's not rubbish at all, it's absolutely true." Cushing and Lee were much better actors than the material required, but as Cushing would say, nobody paid him to play Hamlet, but they paid him to play Frankenstein.

The Curse of Frankenstein premiered on May 2, 1957. It was a smash hit in the UK, and in America, where it was distributed by Warner Bros. Writing to Eliot Hyman, then CEO of Warners, Carreras raved: "England is sweltering in a heat wave and NOTHING is taking any money except *The Curse* [*of Frankenstein*]."

In their time, the Hammer films usually got terrible reviews, but *Variety* got what *The Curse of Frankenstein* was going for: "This British version of the classic shocker well deserves its horrific rating and praise for its more subdued handling of the macabre story. . . . As this is the first time the subject has been depicted in color, all the grim trappings are more vividly impressive. . . . Peter Cushing gets every inch of drama from the leading role, making almost believable the ambitious urge and diabolical accomplishment. . . . Direction and camera work are of a high order."

It's understandable why some were repulsed by *The Curse of Frankenstein*. It had a level of realism that was hard to take in the late fifties, especially showing blood in vibrant Technicolor for the first time. (Hammer called its blood formula "Kensington Gore.")

Next came *Dracula* in 1958, which was Lee's big breakthrough as a horror star, "my *annus mirabus*, or *annus horribilis*." *Dracula* was "the one that made the difference. It brought me a name, a fan club, and a secondhand car, for all of which I was grateful."

For an American studio, Hammer films were a great deal. They were good-looking products that were exploitable, and they cost much less to make overseas than they would have in Hollywood. Universal distributed the film, renamed *Horror of Dracula* in the States, and once again, monsters saved the company from financial ruin. Al Daff, who was president of Universal in New York, pronounced to Lee, "This movie will save us from bankruptcy." (Two years later Universal was sold to MCA, and its primary bread and butter would become television until the movie division turned around in the early seventies).

As Scorsese recalled, "There's nothing like the introduction of Dracula in that picture, in which Christopher Lee just walked down the stairs, and said, 'Hello, I'm Dracula.' Having been reared on Bela Lugosi, with whom you knew you were in trouble, Lee seemed like a very sensible, sophisticated gentleman. So that later on, when one of his brides tries to suck Jonathan Harker's blood and Dracula turns up, eyes bloodshot, in an extreme close-up, it was absolutely terrifying."

Scorsese never outgrew his love of Hammer flicks. When he was making *Alice Doesn't Live Here Anymore* for Warners, he would summon prints from their library, and one day screened *Blood from the*

Mummy's Tomb, claiming it was for research. "Marty got in trouble," says longtime Scorsese friend and former *Time* critic Jay Cocks. "He got a call from [head of production] John Calley wanting to know what bearing *Blood from the Mummy's Tomb* had on *Alice Doesn't Live Here Anymore*!"

The Hammer films, like many horror films, were critic-proof. "Look at the BO returns," says Sangster. Lee certainly learned to have a good laugh at the critical notices, pointing out the reviewers who slammed the movies for being campy and over-the-top were quite campy and over-the-top with their own overheated prose. "Journalists were inclined to write about my eyes as bolt-holes into hell and compare my teeth to a row of tombstones."

The bad reviews didn't faze the powers that be at the company, they were moving too quick to notice. "By the time the reviews came out, I was working on three different films further on," says Sangster. While shooting a film for Hammer, Sangster would have to plan the next one, which would start production two weeks after the first one wrapped. The crew also got paid bonuses if the films finished on time, giving everyone added inceptive to wrap 'em up quick.

Makeup master Roy Ashton, who worked at Hammer for years, recalled, "If I was asked to go on a film a month before it started shooting, that was a long time." Before you were hired as a director, the sets and makeup designs were all picked beforehand, which is not how most directors like to work, but as Freddie Francis recalled, "On their schedules and budgets, there was no time to change these things."

Once the Frankenstein and Dracula films started rolling off the Hammer assembly line, the studio wound up in the same position Universal did in trying to figure out ways to bring the monsters back after they were vanquished in the previous films. For *The Revenge of Frankenstein*, it was pointed out to Carreras that in the previous film, the doctor lost his head by guillotine. Carreras said, "Oh, we sew the head back on again!"

Hammer would make a total of eight Dracula films, eight additional vampire films, seven Frankenstein films, seven prehistoric films, and one werewolf film (*The Curse of the Werewolf* with Oliver Reed). It also made its versions of *The Abominable Snowman*, *Phantom of the Opera*, Jack the Ripper (as *Hands of the Ripper*), Jekyll and Hyde (as *The Two Faces of Dr. Jekyll* and *Dr. Jekyll and Sister Hyde*), *Rasputin, the Mad Monk*, *The Hound of the Baskervilles*, a zombie flick, and several satanic occult films as well. (In the company's life span, Hammer made more than 250 movies and TV shows.)

"Hammer were a wonderful business organization," said Freddie Francis. "Really, they were so efficient, they could have been making anything they wanted." During the *Dracula: Prince of Darkness* shoot, actor Francis Matthews recalled, "There were quite a lot of producers and directors and all the money people dropping in from America. I think they were studying the method of shooting and how Hammer could make them so quickly and for so little money."

Like their American counterparts, Hammer sometimes had fun gimmicks to go with the films. You could apply for fright insurance against "nervous breakdown, heart attacks, fainting spells, loss of voice, or any ills attributed to fright or horror caused by *The Curse of Frankenstein*," and when Lee played Rasputin, theatergoers were given fake beards to wear during the film to disguise themselves against the forces of evil.

Hammer also had a funny way of breaking up its films with humor, in its own droll, British way. In one scene the Monster kills a woman, then the film cuts to a scene where Peter Cushing is at the breakfast table with Hazel Court, asking her to pass the marmalade. "Pass the marmalade" became code for a transition that would make the audience intentionally laugh after a scary scene. "You have to give the audience time to relax before scaring the shit out of them," says Sangster.

Some Hammer films also had social commentary about the class differences in England. In *The Two Faces of Dr. Jekyll*, instead of turning into a monster, Jekyll becomes a handsome, upper-class gentleman. Screenwriter Cyril Wolf Mankowitz remarked, "This is not a horror film; it is a comment on the two-facedness of society. . . . My screenplay exposes the evil of the Victorians, tears off the mask of falseness and hypocrisy."

Yet Sangster said Hammer was primarily in the business of entertaining people, pure and simple. "I read somewhere that Hammer's first Mummy movie dealt with, among other things, the tragedy of colonialism," Sangster said. "I only wish I could go along with that . . . I wrote a simple, straightforward horror movie. . . . Let's face it, neither Hammer or Jimmy Sangster were in the business of moralizing. We were in the business of making a living by entertaining people and we did that by attempting to frighten them."

Like Lugosi, Christopher Lee knew the limitations of the Dracula role, and he once said if he could have changed anything about his career, he wouldn't have played Dracula more than twice (Lee wouldn't play the Frankenstein Monster twice because he felt he brought all he could to the role, and that Karloff did the definitive version).

Hammer needed Lee in their Dracula films so they could get Warner/Seven Arts to cofinance the movies on the strength of the actor's name. Lee wanted to turn more Dracula films down, but then the company would pull a guilt trip on him, telling the actor how many actors and technicians he'd be putting out of work if he didn't do the movie. Hammer would also offer Lee a piece of the action, but it was the producer's net, which meant nothing.

But Lee kept making the Dracula movies because it was his livelihood, and he dreaded every actor's nightmare, being out of work. "I made film after film to get my momentum going," Lee said. "All actors are unhappy while 'resting.'"

From the second Dracula film on, Lee refused to speak because he thought the dialogue "was verging on the absurd." Lee and Cushing used to joke about how bad the scripts were: "I've just been offered a Jimmy Sangster script and there's no dialogue for my character." "Congratulations, old boy!"

Right before making *Taste the Blood of Dracula,* which he hoped would be his last film for Hammer (it wasn't), Lee wrote in his fan club newsletter, "As usual, words fail me, as indeed they will also do in the film."

Sangster countered that Dracula had dialogue in the first movie to introduce himself, and once it was revealed he was a vampire, he never spoke again. In the later films, "we know exactly who he is when he first appears . . . and vampires don't chat. So I didn't write him any dialogue."

Then Hammer went through their prehistoric dinosaur movie cycle, and they had their biggest hit in 1966 with *One Million Years B.C.,* which made $8 million worldwide, and featured the stop-motion magic of Ray Harryhausen, not to mention an even bigger selling point, Raquel Welch sporting a sexy fur bikini.

The Hammer films were shocking for their day, and they got gorier and sexier as time went on. Some of the old guard weren't happy that the films had more violence, nudity, and lesbian vampires in push-up bras. "I did not like the change that came after I left, when it was thought that the films would increase audience appeal by making them soft porn shows," said Anthony Hinds.

With standards and censorship loosening up in Britain, Carreras would say, "God, you can do anything now," where Hinds felt, "Well, I'm not sure that doing everything is what it's all about."

This also didn't guarantee that Hammer would go smoothly into the seventies. The company started falling apart in the late sixties, when they began losing key staff at the end of the decade. Hammer did fairly well in the early seventies with films like *The Vampire Lovers, Lust for a Vampire, Creatures the World Forgot*, and *Blood from the Mummy's Tomb*, but the company soon went off the rails when the country went through a financial crash in 1974 that brought an end to independent filmmaking in England.

International financing soon became tough to come by, and Hammer also made several embarrassing films that tried to be hip to the latest trends, such as *Dracula A.D. 1972*, where Christopher Lee is turned loose in swingin' London, and the silly kung-fu horror film that followed in the wake of *Enter the Dragon, Legend of the Seven Golden Vampires*.

Hammer also found itself unable to catch up with what was going on in American horror, with Carreras believing the success of *The Exorcist* and *Jaws* stole Hammer's thunder. "The American majors were no longer looking to Hammer for a new horror cycle," he said. "I'm not sure Hammer was equipped to throw off the genteel gothic mantle and leap into that new wave. It wasn't our speed. The *Exorcist* type of film was very American. The gothic horror film was much more European."

At one point, trying to catch up to *The Exorcist* and *The Omen*, Hammer made several satanic possession movies and they were also planning a Loch Ness monster film as an answer to *Jaws*, which never got made. Carerras also thought it was a mistake not bringing in younger executives who could pick projects that would appeal to the next generation of horror fans. "We were very busy trying to discover what the new cycle would be," he continued. "I made nearly two dozen films looking for it, but I never found it."

In the last few years of Hammer, Carreras was trying to keep the company alive out of his own pocket, until the company was seized by the banks. Hammer finally went out of business in 1979. There have been a number of attempts to bring Hammer back, and the most recent incarnation of the company produced *Let Me In, The Resident,* and *The Woman in Black,* starring Daniel Radcliffe, but its best movies came from a time and era that can't be replicated.

Still, its influence and fan base continue long after the studio went down, and the quality of what Hammer achieved continues to stand the test of time. In recent years there has also been a major effort in restoring the classic Hammer films, and making sure they'll still be here for future generations to discover and enjoy (many Hammer Films were not available for home viewing or collecting until the late nineties). To celebrate Hammer's fiftieth anniversary in 2007, the British Film Institute restored *Horror of Dracula,* and brought it back to theaters in the UK, including on IMAX screens.

"Hammer Films has been many things to many people," Carreras said. "But in any final analysis, it must be seen to have been very largely responsible for achieving the general public acceptance of British films, in both the American and international markets. . . . It was a major contribution to the history of the British film industry, made by a small independent production company—one that is more often than not overlooked by those critics and historians. . . . Thankfully it has never been overlooked or forgotten by aficionados of the gothic genre and horror fans."

THREE

"THE SIGNPOST THAT EVERYBODY FOLLOWED"

How *Psycho* created the modern horror film

It was a cold November morning in Milwaukee in 1957. Ten-year-old Joseph McBride woke up at 7:00 A.M., opened the front door, and saw the lurid *Milwaukee Sentinel* headline at his feet: MURDER FACTORY IN PLAINFIELD.

Now we know enough to pay attention to the creepy neighbor next door, but back then in Plainfield, Wisconsin, a small, god-fearing community of seven hundred, no one saw the threat in Ed Gein, even when he blathered about his collection of heads, and what he knew about local women who went missing. The locals blew it off as the rantings of an old kook.

Yes, he was an odd neighbor, but in those days it was hard to think he, or anyone else, would be capable of this kind of un-speakable horror. The local people would let him do errands here and there, and babysit their kids. But when police searched his farmhouse with kerosene lamps and flashlights, they found out that Gein was what we now call a hoarder, except along with the piles of old newspapers, cans, and cartons of food, was a hideous collection of death. Gein had a grotesque collection of body parts, chairs upholstered with flesh, a drum made of human skin, faces he would wear like masks and tack to the wall, a soup bowl made of a human skull, and a headless corpse disemboweled like an animal.

McBride says, "One of the reasons Ed Gein seemed so startling was that it was the fifties and people just weren't doing that kind of thing. Ed Gein was truly in a class by himself. No one else could have thought of such horrible and weirdly 'creative' things as he was doing with human bodies. The fact that he otherwise seemed a kindly little man, who was a babysitter for local families, made him seem all the more odd."

Yet many were morbidly amused by Gein, and it seemed that all the kids in Wisconsin knew Ed Gein jokes, like the joke about Gein Beer, lots of body but no head, and Gein covering his furniture with blankets at night so it wouldn't get goose bumps.

Perhaps the jokes were a way to try and deal with something so unspeakably horrible happening right in one's own backyard, or maybe they were a reaction against Gein's own sick sense of humor. What especially bothered the police was that Gein took such ghoulish delight in his crimes, like when the authorities came to his home and found the doorbell was covered by a woman's nipple.

On the McBride family's summer vacation in 1958, McBride persuaded his parents to drive to Plainfield to look at Ed Gein's house. "The town had a creepy aura," McBride recalls. "The people were notably hostile. When I asked one man for directions to the Gein house, he said they had just burned it down because so many tourists were coming by to see it."

Gein's crimes were so hideous, the news would only report so much, but novelist Robert Bloch had to know more. Bloch lived thirty-nine miles away in Weyauwega, Wisconsin, which was close enough to home. "It wasn't considered exactly polite to discuss those sorts of things in newspapers, not to mention fifties mystery fiction." Bloch was especially puzzled how someone could have gotten away with deeds this ghastly in such a small town, and why no one suspected him of anything.

Bloch started writing a fictional story based on Gein, creating the character of Norman Bates, who ran a motel because it was an easy way to get to strangers. Bloch changed the setting from Plainfield into the equally innocuous-sounding Fairvale.

Freudian psychology was starting to become popular at the time, and *Psycho* was a perfect story to include the Oedipus theory of the mother fixation, except here his mother would live on in his mind, and he would become her when he killed. Bloch came up with murder in the shower because there's nowhere you're more defenseless. "Naked, in a confined space, we feel we're alone and a sudden intrusion is a *very* shocking thing."

Bloch wrote a draft in six weeks. "The story basically wrote itself," he recalled. Yet after writing such a disturbing story, he said he would shave with his eyes closed because he had a hard time looking at himself in the mirror.

Psycho was picked up by Simon & Schuster for their Inner Sanctum mystery series for a $750 advance, was published in the summer of 1959 with an initial printing of 10,000 copies, and received good reviews. *The New York Times Book Review* wrote that *Psycho* "demonstrates that a believable history of mental illness can be more icily terrifying than all the arcane horrors summoned up by a collaboration of Poe and Lovecraft."

Bloch didn't think of the possibilities of the novel being turned into a film, the story was too grisly, but in spite of the ghastly nature of the tale, it went to the major studios for consideration in February 1959. A note from a Paramount script reader called it "too repulsive for films and rather shocking even to a hardened reader. . . . Cleverly plotted, quite scary toward the end and actually fairly believable. But impossible for films."

You wouldn't think that this was the kind of material Alfred Hitchcock was looking for, but considering that when you saw his name on the marquee you knew what to expect, he eventually felt trapped. "I'm in competition with myself," he lamented. Now he was looking for something no one would expect, a "typically un-Hitchcock picture."

Because of his successful television show, and his reputation as the master of suspense, Hitchcock was the most recognized director in the world. You looked for his cameo in all of his films, you knew his shadow profile, his theme music ("Funeral March of a Marionette" by Gounod), his trademark greeting ("Good *eve*-ning . . ."), and his trademark suit and tie uniform, which he wore on television and every day on the set of his films.

Because Hitchcock was recognized everywhere, "It was like being with Elvis Presley," his daughter Patricia Hitchcock O'Connell recalled. Once the director went on a Tahiti vacation thinking no one would know who he was on a remote island, but then he was surrounded by a group of small children on the beach who recognized him.

One time, costume designer Rita Riggs drove Hitchcock home in her little VW convertible, and laughing, she recalled, "We almost had accidents because as people were passing us, they'd look over and see that famous profile. There'd be a double take, and they'd swerve in the lane! He enjoyed it."

As Peter Bogdanovich once wrote, "No other (non-acting) director in picture history—with the possible exception of C. B. De Mille— has had such instant audience identity, become an international household word and a marketable commodity." And as François Truffaut once noted, Hitchcock's "genius for publicity was equaled only by that of Salvador Dalí."

Hitchcock's name and persona as a director protected his work from being meddled with. When he was at Universal, his name on the newspaper ads had to be "a size type 100 percent of the title," and as Hitch said, "I have always considered my name and reputation to be the most valuable property right owned by me."

Hitchcock was such a figure of respect that some who worked with him still called him Mr. Hitchcock more than thirty years after his death. When Rita Riggs first met him, she was "a tiny bit in awe. At that time, I don't think I was too much in awe of too many people. He was quiet, a very droll and funny man, with a wry sense of humor."

Truffaut saw Hitchcock as "a deeply vulnerable, sensitive and emotional man who feels with particular intensity the sensations he communicates with his audience," and like many who made scary movies, Hitchcock's being fearful had "a direct bearing on his success."

Hitchcock went to a Jesuit school in London, which was sure to make someone already fearful a nervous wreck. "It was probably during this period with the Jesuits that a strong sense of fear developed— mortal fear—the fear of being involved in anything evil. I always tried to avoid it. Why? Perhaps out of physical fear. I was terrified of physical punishment."

Writing about Hitchcock, *Vanity Fair* columnist James Wolcott felt the system of punishment in Hitchcock's school could have taught him how to structure suspense. You misbehaved or screwed up, you got beaten with a cane. You were called in to see the father, your name would be put in the register, you were told what your punishment would be, and you spent the rest of the day sweating it out until your time came.

At the same time, "The Jesuits taught me organization, control, and, to some degree, analysis," Hitchcock continued. "Their education is very strict, and orderliness is one of the things that came out of that, I suppose."

His father was "a rather nervous man," and the young Hitchcock was a loner without any playmates. "I played by myself inventing my own games," he said, adding, "At family gatherings I would sit quietly in a corner, saying nothing. I looked and observed a great deal." Hitchcock loved to go to the theater and movies opening night, often by himself. "Though I went to the theater very often, I preferred the movies and was more attracted to American films than to the British. I saw the pictures of Chaplin, Griffith, Buster Keaton, Douglas Fairbanks."

In addition to studying at the School of Engineering and Navigation, Hitchcock also studied art at the University of London, going on to create illustrations for an advertising firm. "This work was a first step toward cinema," Hitchcock recalled. Hitchcock also did silent movie titles with illustrations in them.

Of course Hitchcock's movies were heavily illustrated with storyboards before he shot them, and they were his holy tablets that were not to be changed.

"As I worked with Hitchcock, I came to realize that you must deal with him on a photographic level," said Joseph Stefano, screenwriter of *Psycho*. "He must know what's going to be on the screen. The dialogue is your business. The backstory is your business. The characterizations, the reasons why people do what they do are all your business." As Hitchcock himself once said, "When I'm making a movie, the story isn't important to me. What's important is how I tell the story."

Once the writing of the screenplay was done, Hitchcock lamented, "The picture's over. Now I have to go and put it on film." On the first day of a shoot, Hitchcock would joke to the crew, "Well, now you've got to work, my work's all finished!

"The moment the script is finished and the film is visualized, that, as far as I'm concerned, is the end of the creative part," Hitchcock continued. "I'd just as soon not shoot the picture," but Hitchcock wouldn't give it to another filmmaker because "they might screw it up." (Hitchcock also didn't look through the camera when shooting or watch dailies because he knew exactly what he had.)

Bloch felt only two directors could have done *Psycho* justice: Alfred Hitchcock and Henri-Georges Clouzot, the French director who was being called "the Gallic Hitchcock," and who had just given Hitchcock a run for the money with *Les Diaboliques*.

Released in the United States by Seven Arts in 1955, *Les Diaboliques* was a big domestic success, and was the key film that opened up the art house market.

Theaters wouldn't let people in if they turned up late; you had to see the film from the beginning. At the end, viewers were urged not to give away the ending, which wouldn't be hard for filmgoers to predict today because it's been copied so many times, but in terms of scares it still packs a wallop.

The film got rave reviews that must have had Hitch looking over his shoulder. "If director Henri-Georges Clouzot isn't the master of the suspense thriller today, then who is?" asked *The Los Angeles Herald-Examiner*. Now Hitchcock was going to come back with his own variation of the key *Diabolique* elements: shooting in black-and-white, a crucial fright scene in the bathroom, as well as similar policies of making the audience see the movie all the way through, and making a pact with them not to give away the end.

Hitchcock called on his trusty secretary, Pat Robertson, to find the right project he'd respond to. Robertson went through everything that came in to Hitchcock for consideration. In 1959, twenty-four hundred pieces of material came in, out of which only thirty made the cut to be passed on to the boss.

Hitchcock read *Psycho* at his Bel-Air home on Bellagio Drive over a weekend, and immediately saw the shower scene as the foundation, the cornerstone, and the primary reason to make the movie.

At the time, Hitchcock was on the last film of his deal with Paramount. He got a $250,000 director fee, a nice piece of the gross, and had complete control over the film as long as it cost $3 million or less. But even with a deal that any director at the time would kill for, as well as the cachet of Hitchock's name and track record, *Psycho* was not an easy sell.

Hitchcock met with Paramount in June, and they weren't thrilled that he wanted to finish his deal with *Psycho*. The studio threatened not to give him his usual budget to make a picture, and he said he'd make do. In fact, Hitchcock was looking forward to the challenge.

"It was an experiment in that sense," Hitchcock said. "Could I make a feature film under the same conditions as a television show?" Working in television, Hitchcock liked "the challenge of speed. . . . It was a complete change of pace, a different approach."

Psycho would be shot in black-and-white, not just for budgetary reasons and the influence from *Les Diaboliques*, but as Hitch said, "It will have so much more impact in black-and-white." (Chocolate syrup, which now came in a squeeze bottle, would be used for blood.)

Psycho "was made by a TV unit, but that was only a matter of economics really," the director continued. "Speed and economy of shooting, achieved by minimizing the number of setups. We slowed up whenever it became really cinematic."

"He wanted to prove to everyone that a low-budget film could still be a quality one," says Hilton Green. "He was always looking for things that were a little different for him to do, and this was a challenge to him. He was coming off *North by Northwest*, which was one of the most expensive pictures he had made, and he wanted to make a low-budget, quality movie. He had to make it on a very short schedule, and he felt his television crew would be most apt to be able to handle that than the feature crew."

Still, Paramount didn't want the film, and agreed to distribute it only if Hitch financed the film himself through his own company, Shamley Productions. The head of Shamley, Joan Harrison, also turned down points in the film, telling Hitch, "This time you're going too far."

The first screenwriter on the project was James P. Cavanagh, who had previously written for *Alfred Hitchcock Presents,* including an Emmy-winning episode, "Fog Closes In." Many details from Cavanagh's draft made it into the script, but it didn't totally work. Hitchcock then went outside his comfort zone and worked with Joseph Stefano, a songwriter and lyricist who didn't know he could write a screenplay until he did it.

Stefano saw an episode of *Playhouse 90*, and said, "I can do that." He later recalled, "I'd never even read a screenplay. Somebody had to tell me about 'long shots,' 'exterior,' and 'interior.'" Once he started writing, he quickly got a deal with producer Carlo Ponti, and was offered a seven-year deal with Fox.

As Stefano recalls with a laugh, "If you want to know what chutzpah is, I went over to MCA, gave them a list of ten directors I wanted to work with, and I said to the head literary agent, Ned Brown, 'Call me when you get me one of these directors.' " And, of course, Hitchcock was on the list.

A number of people, including Universal chairman Lew Wasserman, were nudging Hitchcock to meet with Stefano, feeling he was what the project needed, because they thought *Psycho* "was a very inferior book, a very sleazy kind of property," Stefano recalled.

Stefano read the book before meeting Hitchcock, and wasn't thrilled with it. Stefano was a Hitchcock fan and was hoping the project would turn into a bigger, classier production like *The 39 Steps* or *North by Northwest*, "not some strange little pulp fiction. [*Psycho*] didn't even ring of a Hitchcock picture."

It's a cliché that screenwriters today hate making characters more sympathetic, but it's what Marion Crane needed in order for the viewer to feel for her dilemma and mourn her loss, and what Norman needed to have to lure her into his trap. "Many murderers are very attractive persons," Hitchcock said. "They have to be in order to attract their victims."

"I wish I knew this girl," Stefano said. "I wish Norman were somebody else. This movie is over unless we get the audience to care about Norman."

Then Hitchcock asked, "How would you feel if Norman were played by Anthony Perkins?"

"Now you're talking."

Perkins could make Norman someone you could pity, as well as give Norman a tenderness and a vulnerability you could hook the audience with. Sympathy was crucial for the scene where Norman is cleaning up the mess of Marion Crane's murder, and the audience thinks he's mopping up his mother's mess. Stefano based the scene on the times he had to clean up his father's puke when he was drunk. "You'd hate your father for making the mess, you hated your mother for making you do such an unpleasant task, and the audience would also feel, 'Oh this poor guy he has to clean up after his homicidal mother.'

"Then the trick of the movie was putting you on the side of someone who was really a criminal, but you didn't know it," says Stefano. "Tony was so brilliant because he was so tense, his teeth were almost chattering as he went about this job. Then after a little while, you realized he'd done this before."

Stefano also suggested opening the story with Marion Crane, and thought the idea of her in a "nooner" appealed to Hitchcock's inner perv. "I think that idea got me the job," Stefano said.

At their second meeting, Hitchcock said, "What if we got a big-name actress to play this girl? Nobody will expect her to die." Stefano also liked the idea that Marion would be killed after she decided to return the money. "To be killed at the moment when you decide to get out of the trap you've set for yourself makes it very interesting."

Once Janet Leigh's name came up, it all started to come together. Like Perkins at the time, Leigh was also against type because she was from the wholesome school of Debbie Reynolds and Doris Day. It was believed that Hitchcock picked her because of her performance in *Touch of Evil*.

When Hitchcock sent the novel to Janet Leigh he told her it was just the basic idea, it wasn't going to be an exact adaptation. It didn't matter. She would have done anything for Hitchcock sight unseen, and Perkins agreed to do it without reading a word of the script.

Anthony Perkins was the highest-paid actor on the film, making $40,000. Janet Leigh usually got $100,000 a picture, but accepted $25,000 to play Marion Crane. "I would have done it for nothing," she said. Hitchcock also assembled his *Psycho* crew for about $62,000, including Bernard Herrmann and Saul Bass.

Hitchcock's antipathy toward actors was well known. He often compared them to children, remarking, "Everyone knows that there are good children, bad children, and stupid children. The majority of actors, though, are stupid children. They're always quarreling, and they give themselves a lot of airs. The less I see of them, the happier I am."

He also couldn't believe how out of control actors' salaries were, and how the integrity of a story could be harmed by a star. "Very often the story line is jeopardized because the star cannot be a villain. You have to clearly spell it out in big letters: 'He is innocent.'"

Now with a major star getting killed so early in the film, and with Anthony Perkins playing Norman Bates instead of re-creating the white-trash slob of the novel, Hitchcock was going to turn the rules of stardom on their head as well.

The first draft of the screenplay was finished in three weeks, dated December 19, 1959, and Stefano passed the most crucial test: Hitchcock's wife, Alma, loved it, which meant no further changes would be made. *Psycho* was a white script, meaning no rewriting, no adding colored pages to the script once it started.

"He just asked me to change one word in it," Stefano said. "When Sam says to Marion, 'We could write each other lurid love letters,' Hitchcock said, 'I don't like the word *lurid*.'" Stefano laughed. "And I thought, Of all the people not to like that word."

Principal photography on *Psycho* began on November 30, 1959. The shoot moved fast, fourteen to eighteen setups a day, no more than three or four takes a scene. Even with Hitchcock doing the first setup when he felt ready, telling stories and holding court, he'd still have half the day's work done by lunch. On Thursdays the crew got to go home early because that was Hitchcock's night out with Alma at Chasen's.

Between setups he would read the London *Times*, pretending to be bored, putting on a show, trying to make it look like making a movie was so easy. Working with Hitchcock, "there was no sense of sweat," Stefano remembers, laughing.

Watching him work and listening to him talk about filmmaking technique in between takes was "like taking a doctorate in filmmaking," says Riggs. "It was a daily learning process."

If it hasn't already been a question on *Jeopardy!* it should be. Seventy camera setups, seven shooting days, forty-five seconds in length: what is the shower scene in *Psycho*?

It goes without saying that the shower scene is one of the most studied, celebrated, and written about scenes in cinema history. Even if you've only seen it once or twice, you can probably still recall it pretty clearly in your mind, or swear you saw more than it really showed. It also goes without saying that secrecy while it was being filmed was mandatory. "It was a closed set, there was a security guard that wouldn't let anybody in," says script supervisor Marshall Schlom. "The shower scene we actually locked the door, *nobody* could come in. Lew Wasserman had to call and say, 'I'm coming,' he couldn't just knock on the door, they wouldn't let him in."

To put Janet Leigh at ease, Alfred Hitchcock showed her the storyboards of every shot, so she'd know exactly where the camera would be. He'd been planning the sequence the month before with a mock-up shower, rehearsing, testing the scene.

Hitchcock wanted to make sure no one involved in the segment would be uncomfortable or embarrassed. Hitch even spared Anthony Perkins from doing the killing himself because it "just wouldn't be nice." Because only a heavily backlit silhouette was shown, they let Perkins go off to a play rehearsal in New York.

The scene was shot on a small set, screens all around to protect Leigh and the secrecy of the shoot. Hitchcock wanted the bathroom to be very clean, with shining white tiles and fixtures, which made it hard to shoot Mother's entrance because of all the reflecting light.

Those who worked on the shower scene didn't recall it being eventful. It took time to shoot, but it was plotted and mapped out so well, if you just followed the plans there wouldn't be any problems.

Word on the Universal lot went around that Hitchcock might have gone too far. Lew Leary, the unit production manager, even said, "He'll never get away with that scene."

Many working on the film didn't know the ending because Hitchcock hid the script pages away. The scripts would also be collected; none of them would be laying around that could potentially get out. Even if you were working on the film it was hard to get a copy.

Stefano wasn't even allowed to bring his wife to a prerelease screening of *Psycho*. "She won't tell anybody," Stefano swore to Hitch. "Joe, somebody will hear about it," Hitchcock said.

Psycho, which cost $806,947.55, wrapped on February 1, 1960. In addition to manipulating audiences and the press, Hitchcock also gleefully looked forward to manipulating the censors. Hitchcock would tell his screenwriters to write bravely and to let him worry about dealing with the censors later.

When he showed them *Psycho*, three on the censorship board saw nudity in the shower scene, two didn't. Hitchcock humbly apologized, promised he'd take out the nudity, then re-sent the exact film, completely uncut. Where the three censors who first saw nudity the day before didn't see it, now the two that didn't see it saw nudity. Hitchcock took it as a compliment to his skills as a director.

After some hemming and hawing there were small dialogue cuts and the movie came down a little in length, but the nooner and the crucial shower scene remained intact. One of Hitchcock's famous

tricks was putting things in he knew the censors would demand removed, then using them as a bargaining chip to keep what he really
wanted. "I'll take the 'goddamns' out if I can keep 'transvestite.'"

It took mere weeks to edit Hitchcock films because there wasn't a
lot of coverage to work with. He'd get exactly what he needed in the
production phase to protect himself. If anyone tried to take the
movie away from him, because everything was so interconnected,
and there was so little material to work with, there'd be no alternate
ways to cut the film. "Hitch planned everything out very well," assistant editor Terry Williams said. "He didn't provide the editor with a
lot of takes. We would have only about a reel and a half on a big day."

In its review, *Variety* noted that Hitchcock "apparently had the
time of his life in putting together *Psycho*," and he was indeed very
proud of the end result because he had a big success with a "pure
film."

"It wasn't a message that stirred the audiences, nor was it a great
performance," said Hitchcock. "They were aroused by pure film. . . .
It's the kind of picture in which the camera takes over."

"It really accomplished what he wanted," says Rita Riggs. "All his
work was so visual. He truly believed that if a scene completely de-
pended on dialogue or sound, it missed its mark in filmmaking."

The musical score is crucial to many horror films, and Bernard
Herrmann was Hitchcock's main man for *The Man Who Knew Too
Much*, *Vertigo*, and *North by Northwest*. He had also scored *Citizen
Kane* and *The Day the Earth Stood Still*, among other films. Hitch had
definite ideas about the music in his films. He would suggest ideas
for music and sound in the screenplays and to what degree sounds
would be heard in the film.

Herrmann was a Juilliard graduate, and a cantankerous perfectionist. Even though he was working with a much smaller budget,

Hitchcock insisted Herrmann score the film. Herrmann wasn't happy about working on a tight budget, but with the score going in a minimalist direction, he used it to his advantage. (Herrmann was paid near scale for the film, but Hitchcock liked the score so much he eventually doubled Herrmann's salary.)

Herrmann decided he would only use strings, violin and cello, on the soundtrack. As John Carpenter says, "I think that using only strings in *Psycho* was the result of, 'Let's score the knife.'"

Terry Williams, who visited the soundstage when Herrmann was conducting, was frightened by the score even then. Williams didn't stay long on the soundstage; he decided to go across the street to Nickodells and have a drink when Herrmann angrily threw his baton at one of the violinists.

Composer Fred Steiner, who knew Herrmann well, said, "Herrmann's selection of a string orchestra deprived him of many tried-and-true musical formulas and effects which until that time had been considered essential for suspense and horror films: cymbal rolls, timpani throbs, muted horn strings, shrieking clarinets, ominous trombones, and dozens of other staples in Hollywood's bag of chilly, scary musical tricks."

When *Psycho* was shown with the music in a crew screening, Hilton Green recalled, "Everybody came off their seats a good six inches!" When people who were working on the film and knew it backward and forward were frightened, he knew it was a hit.

Danny Elfman, who is a big fan of Herrmann's, said of the *Psycho* score, "It's so daring and simple and lean and perfect. No wasted notes, no excess—in short, the exact opposite of me." (Elfman also loved Herrmann's work on *The Day the Earth Stood Still, North by Northwest,* and *Vertigo.*)

Hitchcock was great at building hype by revealing as little as possible. *Newsweek* called it the "well-publicized, in fact noisy, secrecy behind the film." He didn't want Anthony and Janet to do any publicity for the film, just in case they would accidentally give away any plot points or secrets. "It was vital to the success of the movie that it maintain its surprise value." You didn't expect a big star to be killed off this early, and he didn't want moviegoers coming in late and wondering why Janet Leigh hadn't shown up yet. "You can't have blurred thinking in suspense," Hitch explained.

The rule of keeping people out once the movie started was called the S.I.F.T.S. policy, or See It From the Start. There were manuals sent to theater owners called "The Care and Handling of *Psycho*," and theaters who wouldn't go along with the See It From the Start policy wouldn't get the film.

At first, exhibitors were frustrated with this. At one of the first showings of the film the theater was half full while hundreds of people outside were waiting for the next showing, but it clearly paid off once the kinks were ironed out.

A report in *Variety* was headlined COAST OZONERS NOT WARM TO *PSYCHO* WITH TIME CURB, and there were standoffs with a number of L.A. theaters, including the Pacific Drive-In chain, which hadn't agreed to the no-admission-when-it-starts policy, and there had to be negotiations and meetings to straighten things out.

As you waited in line to get into the theater, you'd listen to prerecorded messages from Hitchcock: "How do you do, ladies and gentlemen? I must apologize for inconveniencing you this way. . . . You see, *Psycho* is most enjoyable when viewed at the beginning and proceeding to the end. I realize this is a revolutionary concept, but we have discovered that *Psycho* is unlike most motion pictures. . . . The manager of this theater has been instructed, at the risk of his life, not to admit to the theater any persons after the picture starts. Any spurious attempts to enter by side doors, fire escapes, or ventilating shafts will be met by force. I have been told this is the first time such remarkable measures have been necessary . . . but then this is the first time they've seen a picture like *Psycho*."

His droll sense of humor kicking in, Hitchcock also promised that no one, no matter who they were, would be allowed in after the movie starts, and this included the theater manager's brother, the president of the United States, or the queen of England ("God Bless Her").

Robert Bloch had finally seen the film at a screening, and when he met Hitchcock he told him *Psycho* would either be his biggest hit or his biggest flop. Lew Wasserman wanted to open the film in thousands of theaters at once in case it didn't do well, so they could break even and make money quickly. There would also be no advanced screenings for critics.

On opening day, June 16, theatergoers started lining up at 8:00 A.M. Audiences came out of the film blindsided by what they saw, and those waiting on line asked about the ending, but nobody would spoil it. In one of the advance trailers for *Psycho*, Hitchcock also implored the audience, "Please don't tell the ending. It's the only one we have."

We've seen so many variations on *Psycho* where the supposed good guy and the killer are the same person, but back then it was too big a leap to make that this frail, shy boy's mother is dead and that she lives on and torments him in the insanity of his mind. When *Psycho* was first out, a friend of Stefano's told him, "You know, about halfway through the movie I began to think maybe Norman is the psycho and he's doing the murders. I thought it was so impossible that I didn't even tell my girlfriend I was thinking that."

Psycho was met with gridlock traffic at drive-ins and concession people drove around in golf carts selling snacks to people waiting to get in. At one showing, theater employees had to buy umbrellas for people standing out in the rain waiting to get in.

The *L.A. Times* headlined their review: PSYCHO AS BRILLIANT AS IT IS DISAGREEABLE. "Alfred Hitchcock, who I understand felt piqued when H. G. Clouzot beat him to *Diabolique*, has had his revenge. His *Psycho* is even more diabolique." The *Times* also didn't predict it would typecast Anthony Perkins, "However, it won't exactly further his career. Does Hitchcock still hate actors?"

Time wrote, "Director Hitchcock bears down too heavily in this one, and the delicate illusion of reality, necessary for a creak-and-shriek movie becomes, instead, a spectacle of stomach-churning horror."

Newsweek called *Psycho* "plainly a gimmick movie, whose suspense depends on a single, specific twist. Climatic scenes are rather standardly spooky and contrived." *Variety* wrote their "*Psycho* diagnosis" as "an unusual, good entertainment, indelibly Hitchcock, and on the right kind of box office beam. Campaign backing is fitting and potent. Edict against seating customers after the opening curtain, if respected, may contribute to the intrigue. It all adds up to success."

The Hollywood Reporter called *Psycho*, "Tingling Melodrama Hot Box Office Bet . . . a first-rate mystery thriller . . . certain to be one of the big grossers of this summer . . . Paramount won't let anyone enter theaters where *Psycho* is playing after the picture starts. No one will want to leave before it is over."

In *Esquire*, Dwight Macdonald called *Psycho* the product of "a mean, sly, sadistic little mind," and called the film "third-rate Hitchcock. . . . Merely one of those television shows padded out two hours by adding pointless subplots and realistic details."

The New York *Daily News* wrote, "The suspense builds up slowly but surely to an almost unbearable pitch of excitement. Anthony Perkins's performance is the best of his career . . . Janet Leigh has never been better." *The Village Voice* called *Psycho* the "first American movie since *Touch of Evil* to stand in the same creative rank as the great European films."

Janet Leigh recalled the reviews being 60 percent negative, 40 percent positive. There was speculation some of the bad reviews were because the critics weren't happy about no advance screenings, and they had to see it with the everyday public at regular theaters, even though they were given free tickets to get in.

Hitchcock had seen reviews for his films turn around before, and several years after the initial release of *Psycho*, critics gave it a second look and saw a much different movie. Bosley Crowther in *The New York Times* first called it "a blot on an honorable career," but then changed his opinion and had it on his ten best list for the year. *Time* called the shower scene "one of the messiest, most nauseating murders ever filmed," then in 1966 the magazine called it "superlative" and "masterly."

Psycho made $9.5 million domestic, $6 million overseas (a movie ticket then cost 70 cents). Hitchcock's first check for the film came in at $2.5 million. "Alfred Hitchcock could author a book on how he struck gold with a motion picture," wrote *Variety*.

Rereleased in 1965, *Psycho* made another $5 million, and was also reportedly the most profitable black-and-white film in cinema history. "Only the big color epics surpass it," said Perkins.

Phillip J. Skerry's book, *Psycho in the Shower: The History of Cinema's Most Famous Scene,* gathered memories from filmmakers, critics, and everyday theatergoers about their first time seeing *Psycho*. A theatergoer named Linda Williams remembered seeing it at a Saturday matinee in 1960 with two girlfriends. "We spent much of the screening with our eyes shut listening to the music and to the audience's screams as we tried to guess when we might venture to look again at the screen." A retired college professor recalled his group of friends "tried not to watch, and tried not to miss anything at the same time . . . I remember the silence after the shower scene was over. People were gasping for breath and leaning against each other for support."

Another theatergoer recalled that after the shower scene the audience was dead silent for a split second, then there was an eruption of screaming, people releasing held breaths and saying "Oh, my God."

Like the exodus from the beach after seeing *Jaws*, many felt very uncomfortable and unsafe in the shower after seeing *Psycho*. Sally Carr, a retired college professor recalled, "it was hard to keep clean that summer." (*Psycho* especially struck a nerve with women in its time.)

Another theatergoer recalled how effective the casting of Anthony Perkins was on the first-time viewer. "I was seduced by Anthony Perkins when he appeared. People often speak of the suave charm in Hitchcock's villains, but Norman Bates is the only one who caught me off guard entirely. You can't imagine he's a murderer. You refuse to believe it. . . . No one sees *Psycho* today without knowing who Norman is and what he's going to do. I had seen images from the film all my life, and yet the movie's spell was cast, and I believed the guy was just a victim."

Fred Simon, a documentary filmmaker, told Skerry he hadn't seen *Psycho* since it was in the theaters. "The fact that I have any memory of that first viewing at all is a huge statement about the film." And the trip home was scarier than usual, as it often is after a horror film. "Every shadow was menacing, every person a demon. The landscape had changed. Each darkened doorway a threat."

Future master of horror Wes Craven grew up in a Baptist family where movies were forbidden and he didn't see *Psycho* until years after its initial release. He knew about the shower scene because everyone talked about it and it was cinematic urban legend. Still, he said, "Nothing quite prepares the viewer, not years of references to it, not having tried to imagine it a hundred times in the past. It's simply overwhelming, and the first time that I realized one of the great truths to making frightening movies: that the first monster the audience must fear is the filmmaker himself."

One reason *Psycho* really struck a nerve was that the characters were regular people, like the audience. "Too often, Hitchcock's characters were high society, from a higher economic bracket, and it was more of a fantasy," says Rita Riggs. "I think *Psycho* really did present characters that a bank clerk could relate to."

When *Psycho* became a phenomenon, even Hitchcock himself was bewildered at the film's success. Hitch even tried to conduct research into why the movie did so well, dissect it and condense it down to a formula so that he could repeat it again, which Hollywood tries all the time with market research today. He soon dropped the idea. "Sometimes you make a small picture like *Psycho* and it runs out to be a bonanza," Hitchcock said. "That's an unexpected thing—happens once in a lifetime."

Hitchcock had made so many classy, highly polished thrillers, and with *Psycho* he marveled, "Here's this bloody piece of crap, and the money doesn't stop coming in."

Stefano said, "I think [Hitchcock] was appalled and a little insulted by having made such a low-budget movie and getting a response such as he'd never gotten before, even when he'd spent all that money and done such lavish things. It was like serving people extraordinary feasts time after time, then serving hot dogs and they say, 'This is the best thing I've ever tasted!' What happened to all those great meals I've served?"

Many years after its initial release, *Psycho* was screened in Cleveland, Ohio, and Anthony Perkins joked with the audience, "You know I *have* been in other films." He was also once asked if he knew how his career would go after *Psycho*, would he have starred in the film? Perkins didn't answer right away, but finally said, "Yes, I would've done it, and my reason is that we are in a business to create images. If I was able to give *such* an impression, create such a character, that the audience wouldn't let me be anything else, then I indeed did my job. And yes, I would do it."

When Janet Leigh was asked the same question, she replied, "The best answer I can give you is exactly what Tony Perkins said." After the success of *Psycho*, Hitchcock told Leigh they would never make another movie together again. "Whatever I put you in, the audience would immediately think of *Psycho*. It wouldn't be fair to the picture or the character." (When Leigh died in October 2004, her obituaries in both *The New York Times* and *L.A. Times* ran photos of her screaming in the shower, and *The New York Times* obit was headlined, "Shower Taker of Psycho.")

When Wasserman signed Hitchcock to Universal International, part of the deal was that Hitchcock gave up the rights to *Psycho* and his TV show in exchange for 150,000 shares of MCA stock. "Universal wooed Mr. Hitchcock over and built him a compound," says Rita Riggs. "He was the first director they had really done that for."

And finally at the end of the sixties, with the help of the French, who created the auteur theory, Hitchcock would be taken seriously as an artist. As Peter Bogdanovich recalled, "The conventional wisdom among respectable tastemakers during this period rated Hitchcock as a crafty entertainer at best, a master of suspense, but little else. . . . The U.S. elite have always been terribly snobbish about their most popular stuff. It took Truffaut to make Hitchcock's American period 'respectable.' "

François Truffaut, who wrote the groundbreaking book-length interview with Hitchcock, noted that "American and European critics made him pay for his commercial success by reviewing his work with condescension and by belittling each new film."

As for *Psycho,* the impact it made on cinema, and the modern horror film, still reverberates loud and clear. "*Psycho,* in my humble opinion, is the first modern horror film because it so strikingly took horror out of gothic romanticism," says John Carpenter. "It wasn't a vampire or a werewolf. It wasn't an old castle with cobwebs and costumes. It was a motel. You had the motel in the front, and you had this gothic house in the back. It was like passing the torch from old gothic romanticism into modern horror. The whole thrust of the story was going in one direction, then it took a right turn. The girl stole some money, she's driving along, and gets killed out of nowhere for nothing. It was really shocking. . . . That was the signpost that everybody followed."

FOUR

BUILDING THE MODERN ZOMBIE

How Herschel Gordon Lewis and Dave Friedman created the modern gore film with the Blood Trilogy, how George Romero laid down the ground rules for the undead, and how Roman Polanski gave the devil his due

"Brutal! Evil! Ghastly beyond belief!"
"Nothing so appalling in the annals of horror! More grisly than ever in blood color!"

You can't say they didn't warn you. The Blood trilogy (*Blood Feast, Two Thousand Maniacs*, and *Color Me Blood Red*), created by Herschel Gordon Lewis and Dave Friedman, brought to the screen hideous new levels of violence. They were crudely made, badly acted films, and both Lewis and Friedman knew they weren't making masterpieces, or anything particularly good, but in the annals of horror, they'll always be best known for pushing the envelope with on-screen violence until it exploded.

"We could either do a film that was so loaded with sex as to be almost unfilmable, or we could do a picture that was so loaded with horror as to be equally unfilmable," Lewis said. "And since there was an overabundance of nudie pictures, we opted for the horror angle. . . . There were a whole bunch of taboos that we set out deliberately to violate in order to position our picture."

There was also an overabundance of drive-ins in those days. The drive-ins were built on the outskirts of town where land was cheap, and they went through a huge boom in ten years, going from 820 outdoor screens in 1948 to 4,063 screens in 1958.

The biggest time for drive-ins was the summer, which the major studios ignored for their important films, a complete one-eighty from today. With so many screens across the country, low-budget companies like AIP made two to three times more money playing the drive-ins than the theaters, and with *Blood Feast*, Friedman and Lewis would also make a killing.

The movies certainly weren't on the level of Hitchcock, and Lewis and Friedman would be the first to admit that to you, but as a footnote in cinema history, they paved the way for more graphic screen violence. Said Friedman, "Sean Cunningham, Wes Craven, Tobe Hooper . . . we did it first, they did it more expensively!" Andy Romanoff, who worked assistant camera on *Blood Feast*, says, "Ahead of its time? Sure. It was the first one."

Lewis and Friedman were completely different people, but when they first got together in 1959, they "worked together like macaroni and cheese," according to Friedman. Lewis had an ad agency in Chicago, Creative Communications, and the movie business was a sideline for him. Lewis has a Ph.D. in psychology and an MA in journalism, whereas Friedman once said he had a high school education in making films and a Ph.D. in selling them.

But for this kind of thing, Madison Avenue–style salesmanship wasn't gonna work. Friedman came from the carnival world, and he saw exploitation films growing up in his uncle's theater like *Marijuana—The Devil's Weed*, and *Sex Madness*. "I had a good feeling for carnies, the ol' razzmatazz, and there's a great connection between exploitation and the carnival lot," Friedman says. "I think that *Blood Feast* was basically a freak show."

Friedman heard Lewis had worked in industrials and commercials, and had a small studio on the North Side of Chicago. Lewis already had the equipment, cameras, lights, and editing gear, where Lewis also heard Friedman was the best distributor of low-budget flicks around.

Lewis had enough technical expertise to get the movie done and solve problems with his ingenuity. But even though he came from an advertising background, he didn't know the "hard-boiled rock-'em sock-'em slam-bang advertising" that Friedman was a master of. "Dave taught me campaigning, I taught him how to technically make a film, and the marriage worked out very well."

The nudies they made like *Boiingg!* and *Bell Bare and Beautiful* played a handful of little theaters and weren't a breakout medium. You'd make a few bucks but that was it. How many more nude volleyball documentaries could you make? Not to mention the market was oversaturated with people making 'em, and they knew it would be tough to compete down the road.

Andy Romanoff also feels the gore films Lewis and Friedman made grew out of Herschel's frustration that the serious movies he made didn't go anywhere. "Herschel made a couple of art films in the beginning of his career, *Prime Time* and *Living Venus*," Romanoff says. "Neither of them did very well, and I think it really turned him. 'If you guys don't want to watch that, I'll stick something in your eye.'"

"Herschel had utter disdain for the audience," Romanoff continues. "He used to say, 'If I make a movie with four really gory scenes in it, it doesn't matter what else surrounds it.'" Yet as a person, Romanoff didn't find Lewis a misanthrope. "He was funny, bright, fast, but he certainly was not afraid to pull those levers."

Lewis certainly looked at filmmaking from a cynical point of view, and scoffed at people who took film too seriously. "I'm not a film historian," he said. "I'm the kind of jerk who sits in the theater watching the audience, and if they react, that's all I care about. I don't care about someone who is writing *l'histoire du cinema,* attributing motivations that aren't there."

Lewis certainly didn't believe in the auteur theory, where the director was the star. Lewis felt when making a movie, "You're producing entertainment, not self-promotion." Lewis even gave a crew member writing credit on *Two Thousand Maniacs* "because I didn't feel it looked good to usurp all the credits—that makes it look like a home movie!"

Oddly enough, horror films that have broken new ground, even if, like *Blood Feast,* they weren't particularly good, often came from people like Lewis who didn't like the genre in the first place. "Those who are oversaturated with specifics tend to regurgitate those specifics," Lewis says. "Those who have no gods have an easier time creating gods of their own."

Reports vary, but *Blood Feast* had a fourteen- or twenty-four-page script and was basically an outline. Freidman and Lewis finished the screenplay on the plane ride from Chicago to Miami on a portable typewriter.

Blood Feast also featured Miss June, Playmate of the Year Connie Mason, who Friedman met at the Miami Playboy Club.

"How'd you like to be in a movie?"

"What, a nudie? No way!"

"Who said anything about a nudie? This is a horror film."

"You're Dave Friedman, aren't you? Everyone in Miami knows what kind of movies *you* make."

Ironically, *Blood Feast* couldn't exploit any nudity with Mason because her *Playboy* contract forbid her from getting naked for anyone but the magazine.

The blood came from a company appropriately named Barfred Industries that was a chemical house in Coral Gables, Miami. "Herschel persuaded them to make a custom blood formulation," says Romanoff. "Most fake blood had been developed either for stage or black-and-white photography, and Herschel, knowing he was shooting in color, wanted something that was really going to read in color."

Lewis recalled, "BBF—before *Blood Feast*—there was little need for perfect, floor-correct stage blood. When someone got shot, stabbed, or bludgeoned on film . . . you saw only a drop or two of blood, if any. But now, for the very first time, people were going to die, horribly. . . . It was going to be uncommonly repulsive violence. The blood had to be just right."

The gore effects were very crudely done, and it would have been obvious to a little kid that it was badly faked, but as writer Bob Bankard put it, *Blood Feast* is "extremely disgusting by suggestion. The result is a film that appears far more grotesque than its modern equivalent"—meaning the mad slasher films that followed—"while all the time looking ridiculously staged and unbelievable."

In the editing phase, people looking at the film were completely disgusted and Lewis and Friedman had wondered if they went too far. "The real question was, who was going to play this picture?" Lewis said. "We really began to have second thoughts about the playability of *Blood Feast*." (*Blood Feast* has a lot of jump cuts because Lewis and Friedman didn't shoot enough coverage and was edited by Bob Sinise, Gary Sinise's father.)

Friedman and Lewis worked on the ad copy together, with the

logo and taglines in dripping blood. The poster was done in two colors, black and red, and the cheap process gave it a very lurid, side-show look. "I knew how to sell a freak show," says Friedman. "I en-visioned a campaign more or less like the canvas banners outside one."

"We had two goals," Lewis says. "First to make it clear that this film was over the top, far beyond any horror that ever had been shown on the screen. Second, to eliminate those who might expect the standard Hollywood semishocker." Before the R rating, they also strongly warned parents not to bring their "impressionable ado-lescent" to the film.

Blood Feast premiered in Peoria at the Bel Air Drive-In, and as Lewis recalled, "If we died in Peoria, who would even know about it?" On their way to the Bel Air Drive-In, Lewis and Friedman tried not to get their hopes up in case the film didn't do well. "Two miles from the theater entrance we were suddenly at the ass end of a two hundred car funeral procession," Lewis recalled. "For the next thirty minutes it was go twenty feet, stop, go twenty feet, stop." Then Fried-man realized, "They're going to see *Blood Feast*! It worked! Hot shit, it worked!"

The 1,500-capacity drive-in was packed, and cars were being turned away by the police. Friedman and Lewis talked their way in, and they watched the audience instead of the movie. They recalled the audience heckling the movie, but once the tongue got ripped out of the girl's head, everything fell silent. "All you can see are these white eyeballs staring up at the screen," Lewis recalled. "That one brought 'em up short."

Blood Feast first broke through in the South, then everyone else got interested from there. It broke the house record at the Kohlberg drive-in, then *Blood Feast* headed to North and South Carolina, which had more than 350 drive-ins at that time, where it also cleaned up.

Blood Feast finally made its way to Los Angeles on May 1, 1964, at thirty-four theaters and drive-ins. It also slipped through in New York because the state censorship board had disbanded, and as Friedman recalled, "Exploitation movies were at their zenith in the city at this time."

There were reportedly protests, which low-budget filmmakers would often stage themselves, and one story has it that Friedman put up an injunction against *Blood Feast* himself, then had to fight it in court.

Blood Feast reportedly grossed $6.5 million, obviously an enormous return on a $24,000 investment, and Lewis said they made their money back on one theatrical run. "They got a huge bump out of the controversy," Romanoff says. "If there had been no controversy, *Blood Feast* would have slipped into the night unnoticed. But because they got a lot of flack from the newspapers, and they built on it very cleverly, it became a wildly popular film."

Friedman came up with the idea of handing out barf bags to the theatergoers with the slogan "You May Need This When You See *Blood Feast*," and it was a gimmick many low-budget films would repeat again and again.

The critics were, of course, appalled. In the *L.A. Times*, Kevin Thomas called it "a blot on the American film industry," and the review was headlined: "*Blood Feast* Grisly, Boring Movie Trash" in twenty-four-point type. Friedman loved it, and had the review framed on the wall of his office.

Most of the other reviews also followed suit. *Variety* called it a "totally inept horror shocker . . . a fiasco in all departments." *Newsweek* called it "abominable."

As Friedman put it, "I've always said, 'Say something good or say something bad, but for God's sake, say something.'"

John Waters was heavily influenced by Lewis's movies, and he played a big hand in bringing them back to life at the dawn of the VCR boom. Waters would sit on a hill close to a local drive-in and watch Lewis's films through binoculars. As Waters recalled, "When I saw teenage couples hopping from their cars to vomit, I knew I found a director after my own heart." He also added that Lewis's films were "impossible to defend, thus he automatically becomes one of the great directors in film history."

Waters named his film *Multiple Maniacs* in tribute to Lewis, and also passed out barf bags at *Pink Flamingos* screenings. Lewis was also a fan of Waters, having seen *Pink Flamingos* when he heard so many complaints about it.

After making *Two Thousand Maniacs* and *Color Me Blood Red* together, Lewis and Friedman went their separate ways. Friedman went back to nudies, and founded the X-rated Pussycat Theater chain, while Lewis kept making gore fests until the early seventies, then went back into advertising, where he was extremely successful, with a Rolls and a Ferrari at his Fort Lauderdale home. This time, Lewis went into direct mail marketing working with Omaha Steaks, LensCrafters, and CNA insurance, with many in the ad world having no idea of his sordid cinema past.

Of course in those days there weren't secondary markets like home video, and Lewis's movies were too grisly to play on TV, so no one ever thought they'd have a second life. Romanoff was stunned and amazed that these films lived past their time, "In particular that people would cherish really bad, wretchedly done movies was just beyond my comprehension!" Nor could Lewis believe people were still watching his work years later, and thought the first full book on his films, *The Amazing Herschel Gordon Lewis,* was "*too reverent* a piece of work."

"I guess I'm a footnote in motion picture history," Lewis says. "By now somebody might have cracked the mold showing people dying in blood with their eyes open. That I did it first is an *accident* of history, but it's history . . . and I revel in it!"

Romanoff would eventually go to work for Panavision. He decided he didn't want to work in production anymore when he realized how far horror films *hadn't* come since *Blood Feast.*

"I was working on *Friday the 13th Part 3* in 3-D," Romanoff recalls. "We worked long, long hours on that show. It was the middle of the night, and I believe the scene was a guy sitting on a toilet and he got skewered with a long stake or something like that. I was watching us preparing for the shot and I thought, 'This is what I'm doing with my life?' It had been how many number of years from *Blood Feast* to that picture, I was back doing another really exploitive, terrible kind of movie, and I thought, 'Nah, I gotta find something else to do here.'"

He couldn't have realized it at the time, but when George Romero was making *Night of the Living Dead,* he was setting the template for the modern zombie, much like Lugosi put his stamp on vampires.

"Zombies weren't considered heavyweight fright material like Frankenstein, Dracula, and the Wolf Man," said John Russo, who wrote *Night of the Living Dead* with Romero. "The zombies in old horror movies didn't do much other than walk as if they were in a trance and occasionally strangle somebody or heave somebody against a wall. They moved so slowly you could easily get away from one of them. . . . What we did was give the old zombie legend a new twist. We made our zombies into cannibals—eaters of human flesh.

"Suddenly, they were way more dangerous, way more terrifying," Russo continues. "And in our movie there were lots of them. They were weak and slow—moving as individuals, but they had strength of numbers on their side. Conceptually what we had done was cross the zombie myth with aspects of the vampire and werewolf myths to come up with something new."

"I made them the neighbors," Romero said. "They used to be Caribbean voodoo stuff." With Romero, zombies didn't have to be nocturnal creatures either. As *Dawn of the Dead* proved, they could wander around during the day or in a well-lit environment like a shopping mall and still be scary.

Yet like the classic zombies, Romero's undead would always lurch slowly and would never run, unlike the recent zombies in *28 Days Later*, and the 2004 *Dawn of the Dead* remake. Legendary makeup artist and longtime Romero alumni Tom Savini says, "You'll never see a fast-moving zombie in a Romero film because as far as he's concerned, they're dead and would continue to die. They would continue to rot and get weak, they wouldn't gain superpowers. But to keep it more interesting, that's what they did in the remake of *Dawn of the Dead,* they made them faster, stronger, and more of a threat."

Romero said, "I prefer these plodding, lumbering guys from whom you can easily escape unless you fuck yourself up somehow and are too stupid to do the right thing. That's just more fun for me."

Being based in a working-class environment like Pittsburgh, Romero also called zombies the "blue-collar monster," and they did "all the heavy lifting," while say, Dracula was back at the castle and had a team of fellow vampires that did his dirty work.

While he was making *Night of the Living Dead,* Romero also couldn't have known that in Europe the film would be looked at as an allegory for the Vietnam War and social unrest in America. Nor could he have guessed that his road would lead back to zombies many times over the years, or that *Night of the Living Dead* would wind up in the Museum of Modern Art. Who on earth could have predicted any of this would happen to a bunch of young guys in Pittsburgh just trying to make the scariest movie they could?

Growing up in the Bronx, movies were a refuge for George Romero. "I was a chubby little Spanish kid who was always getting beaten up by Italian guys," he recalled. "I would sneak off to the movies to find a safe place."

Romero would watch *Million Dollar Movie*, which aired on New York's WOR-TV, and it was seeing Michael Powell's classic *Tales of Hoffmann* when he was twelve that inspired him to become a film-maker. Many years later when Martin Scorsese was working on *Raging Bull,* he would borrow a print of *Tales of Hoffmann* from the library, and would often discover if it wasn't available, it was loaned out to Romero.

When Romero was fourteen, he made his first film, *Man from the Meteor,* and was arrested for throwing a flaming dummy off a roof. Romero wailed to the police, "But we're makin' a *movie!*" and one of the cops hauling Romero away told the young filmmaker to grow up.

After attending Carnegie-Mellon, Romero ended up settling in Pittsburgh, and started his own production company, Latent Image, which meant an image that had been photographed but wasn't de-veloped yet, in the early sixties.

The Latent Image offices were located in a $50 a month loft. John Russo, who worked with Romero at Latent Image, recalled they made industrial films about everything from ketchup, corporate presidents, pickles, paint, soda, beer, and more.

The advertising business was often feast or famine. In the winter and spring there wouldn't be any work, then it would all flood in at once. "We were fiercely proud of our work," said John Russo. "But most of the time we were broke, frustrated, and physically and men-tally exhausted." The Latent Image gang would often sleep over at the studio, borrowing money from family and friends to stay afloat. One winter they couldn't afford heat, and had to break the frozen toilet water with an ice pick.

Then the company finally got a commercial gig for Buhl Planetarium, where they re-created a lunar landing with radio-controlled rockets and a clay moon. It cost $1,600, and they lost money making it, but now they finally had something they could show as a demonstration of their abilities.

Soon they got a $30,000 loan, cosigned by Romero's uncle, and moved into a more upscale studio. Latent Image became known as a company that could do a lot for less, and everyone at the company got plenty of hands-on experience under their belts. "Every single person that we worked with at Latent Image could shoot, record sound, they knew lighting, everybody could do it all," Romero says. "We became known as a bunch of young, creative maniacs, bohemians with cameras," Russo said, making "award-winning stuff on ridiculously low budgets."

Whatever money Latent Image made they put back into equipment, and they eventually developed a stockpile of lights, cameras, sound gear, editing and mixing facilities. Once they got a used 35 mm Arrilex for $3,500, Romero and company decided it was time to make their first film.

The Hollywood system was impossible to crack back then, and they didn't want to get piddly industry jobs hoping somebody higher up on the food chain would notice them. Rather than wait around for anyone, they hoped their own movie would be able to help them establish their own stronghold in Pittsburgh.

Everyone was afraid of having to work corporate jobs for the rest of their lives like zombies themselves. Romero huddled everyone in his circle together and told them if they all stuck together, and got a feature-length movie made, they could have a real shot at hitting it big and breaking out.

Russo's original financing idea was to get ten people to chip in $600 a piece and they'd make the movie for $6,000, a ridiculously low and impossible sum. They figured they'd have to give each investor a piece of the film, but they had to work for their pay. Whether acting or doing sound or lighting, each investor had to contribute something to the film.

Many young filmmakers start off making a horror film because you can make one cheaply, and Romero and company also wanted to outscare the competition which, considering what was playing in the drive-ins and on TV then, didn't seem that hard to do.

Russo recalls, "We saw a lot of things with giant grasshoppers, giant caterpillars, they had the same stock plot, and they were always disappointing except for *Invasion of the Body Snatchers,* which knocked me out. I said, 'We need to have people coming out of the theaters wearing the same stunned look on their faces at that I saw on the eight o'clock crowd when I was going in for the ten o'clock show. We wanted to make a movie that would really pay off with horror fans."

Russell Streiner, who played Johnny, said, "Everyone would like to do the great American film, but we found ourselves through a series of what we thought were logical conclusions, making a horror film. Once we adopted that for openers, we then tried to make the best, most realistic horror film with the money we had."

Even in the days before secondary markets like DVD and cable, if the film didn't turn out well, you could still sell it to TV, and it would still have an have an audience. Streiner would see Roger Corman's fifties schlock classic *Attack of the Crab Monsters* on television, and assume that if the film was still being played people were making money on it. Streiner figured if they couldn't at least do something like that, maybe they should stick to making industrials.

Romero was inspired by Richard Matheson's short story, "I Am Legend," which Matheson wrote after he saw *Dracula* at the age of sixteen. With "I Am Legend," Matheson used the famous horror launching point of what-if. Matheson says, "When I left the theater, I thought, 'Gee, one vampire is scary . . . what if the whole world was full of vampires?'" Now with Romero, it'd be full of zombies.

Working on *Night of the Living Dead*, Russo and Romero were working on different typewriters in different rooms. They wanted a story that began in a cemetery because that was an obviously spooky place to start, and it originally started with aliens coming to earth looking for human flesh.

Looking back, Russo believed it was Christmas weekend that Romero came to him with half a story, written in a narrative short story form, that began with people being attacked in a cemetery. At first, it wasn't clear who the attackers were, or what they were after.

"This is pretty good, but who are they?" Romero didn't know. Russo tried, "Well, it seems to me they could be dead people."

"Well, that's good."

"What are they after?"

"Why don't we use my flesh-eater idea? They attack people, they're after flesh."

"Well, that's good."

They couldn't afford to have people coming out of graves, so they decided only the recently dead could come back, or people who had been killed as a result of these attacks.

Once the story was rewritten into screenplay form, Romero read it and said, "I know what it needs, it needs another siege," and they put a group of people in a house warding themselves off from the zombies trying to get in.

"My stories are about humans and how they react, or fail to react, or react stupidly. I'm pointing the finger at *us*, not the zombies." With a laugh, Romero added, "I try to respect and sympathize with the zombies as much as possible."

Casting Duane Jones in the lead role of Ben gave *Night of the Living Dead* an unintentional subtext about race, and Romero says he didn't give casting an African American in the lead role much thought. Jones's audition was very impressive, and everyone voted him for the lead. (Ben was only described in the script as "young, fit, powerful, and cunning.")

"Duane was the best actor from among our friends," Romero says. "We didn't think, at the moment, about the fact that he was black. He did. The scene where he slaps Judy O'Dea, he came to me and said, 'People are gonna hang me on the street somewhere.' He was worried about it, we weren't. Thinking we were bold, we then said, 'We're not gonna change the script because you're a black guy.' And today I think it was wrong. I think we should have made a point of it. That never crossed anyone's mind. The script didn't describe anyone as white or black. We weren't trying to make a racial statement. It was absolute, accidental timing."

Night of the Living Dead was shot in the spring and summer of 1967. There were about thirty shooting days on *Night of the Living Dead* spread over nine months while Romero and company would make commercials at Latent Image to pay the bills.

The farmhouse used in the film was forty miles north of Pittsburgh, and it was rented out to Romero and company for $300 a month. The farmhouse was scheduled to be torn down at the end of the summer and turned into a turf farm, so the owner didn't care what the *Living Dead* crew did to it.

The *Night of the Living Dead* crew made arrangements with a motel several miles away where the actors and crew could shower and clean up because the farmhouse didn't have running water. Those who stayed at the farmhouse slept on cots. Romero, who is six four, was so big that one night his cot ripped open and he fell to the floor.

Friends, relatives, and Goodwill provided furniture, pictures, and props for the interiors. To make sure the film maintained its continuity, the wood that barred the doors and windows had to be nailed in the exact same places, and if you look closely, on one board you can read: "upper left door."

Night of the Living Dead was shot with a single camera, an Arriflex 2C. Romero recalls, "It was a beautiful little camera you could hold in one hand," except "it sounded like a fuckin' Sherman tank" when film was running through it. "So when you needed to shoot dialogue, you had to put it in a blimp. The blimp weighs seventy-five pounds. You have a goddamn umbilical wire running to the tape recorder using thirty-five millimeter tape, not even eight millimeter tape, and the tape recorder was the size of my sofa!"

Romero had to put the camera on sticks when recording with sound, but for the newsreel footage, he went hand-held without sound. "I wanted it to look like newsreel footage, I shot it like run and gun."

Night of the Living Dead cost $114,000, and as with many classic low-budget films, limitations became assets, like the black-and-white cinematography. "It would have cost three times more to do it in color," Russo says. "The makeups were a lot easier because we were working in black and white."

Shooting in black-and-white also helped the production when the cemetery scene was shot in the fall, and you couldn't tell that the leaves changed color. Russo also said that audiences appreciated that *Night of the Living Dead* was shot in black-and-white because of the texture and mood it gave the film.

People often love to play zombies, and *Night of the Living Dead* was no exception. The zombie that attacks Barbara and Johnny in the beginning of the film, Bill Hinzman, was one of the film's investors. John Russo played the zombie who got beaten by Duane Jones with a tire iron, and agreed to perform a stunt where he was lit on fire. Marilyn Eastman, who played Helen Cooper, was also the zombie that ate the live insect off the tree. "We were short on ghouls that day," she recalled.

Playing Johnny, Russ Streiner wore black racing gloves so you could recognize him at the end of the film when he comes back from the dead and drags Barbara into the undead mass. "That's why you notice the positioning as Johnny comes in the door," Streiner says. "The very first thing is his hand with the driving glove on it appears against the white wood framework of the door frame."

Russo says, "I think that strikes a chord with people because everybody's seen loved ones in a casket. You have some grief and revulsion at the same time, and I think that's spookier than some of these decayed or half-decayed monsters."

It may seem tame by today's standards, but *Night of the Living Dead* had a startling level of violence for its time, which was influenced by the classic EC comics. "There was this unwritten law which came over the course of years that you had to stand back and be polite, and just show the shadow, and not show the knife entering flesh," Romero said. "Well, why can't we do that? Why hadn't anyone done it? I didn't think so much we were breaking down barriers, probably my first thought was, 'Why hasn't anyone done it this way?'"

"There was no ratings board then," Russo says. "The movie got released before the ratings kicked in. We did what we wanted to do. We took our chances with whether things had to be cut. We were lucky that the film was able to go out unrated, but on the other hand I still think it would have been successful if you'd taken out some of the gore. That's not what made the film successful. It was a good film in spite of any graphic footage."

Ben getting killed at the end of the film was influenced by the area. Pennsylvania is a big deer hunting state, a large number of deer get killed every year, along with eight to ten hunters by mistake. There was some debate about shooting an alternate ending, because the film having no survivors was obviously a downer, yet Romero and company decided not to shoot a second ending because they didn't want a potential distributor to find out about it and force them to use it.

"The film opens with a situation that has already disintegrated to a point of little hope, and it moves progressively toward absolute despair and ultimate tragedy," said Romero. "Nobody comes riding in at the end with the secret formula that will save us all. The ghouls, in essence, win out." Russo said, "We figured it would shock people and they would hate it, but it would make them keep talking about the picture as they were leaving the theater."

The photomontage at the end of the movie was inspired by Sidney Lumet's *Fail-Safe*. "We were trying to come up with an effective ending that would also save some shooting days," Russo recalled.

AIP was looking at the film to possibly distribute it, and told Romero and company they would take it if Ben lived at the end. Columbia also took a look at it, and turned it down because it was in black-and-white. Through a producer's representative, Budd Rogers, the film got five offers from tiny distributors, and they finally went with Walter Reade Organization, which also put out John Cassavetes's *Faces, David and Lisa,* and *Lord of the Flies.*

Night of the Living Dead premiered in Pittsburgh on October 1, 1968, at the Fulton Theater, and it was billed as PITTSBURGH'S OWN FIRST FEATURE FILM! Romero and company treated it like a real premiere. They took out a big ad in *The Pittsburgh Press*, fancy invitations were printed up, people showed up in tuxes, there were klieg lights and an afterparty at the William Penn hotel. The premiere was packed, and the film received a standing ovation at the end.

The *Night of the Living Dead* gang had a good relationship with the people that owned Associated Theaters, the largest theater chain in Pittsburgh, which is where the film launched on seventeen screens. "We had a really good launching pad from Pittsburgh to get the movie going," Streiner says. "We had the community rooting for us, rooting for the underdogs that finally got their movie finished." It played to turn-away crowds, and quickly grew from there.

Kevin Thomas wrote in the *L.A. Times*, "*Night of the Living Dead* wrings maximum effects from an absolute minimum of means. Indeed, countless far more ambitious movies could benefit from such drive and vitality."

Rex Reed, who has always been a huge horror fan, raved, "If you want to see what turns a B movie into a classic . . . don't miss *Night of the Living Dead*. It is unthinkable for anyone seriously interested in horror movies not to see it."

The fact that *Night of the Living Dead* didn't have any stars in the cast worked in the movie's favor, big-time. One review pointed out, "The fact that the uniformly good cast is completely unknown enhances the movie's basic air of authenticity and throughout there is the feeling that these are real people fighting the nightmarish horror threatening to engulf them."

The Village Voice review of *Night of the Living Dead* wrote that the film "appears to have been made in a state of frenzy," and Russo says, "It *was* shot in a state of frenzy! But it was a controlled frenzy because the film was well put together."

"With *Night of the Living Dead*, we had the passion, we didn't have the skill," says Romero. "But you could tell we were trying.

Every work of art, every meal you cook, every relationship you have, everything comes down to sincerity."

Night of the Living Dead played for a year in theaters and drive-ins, then it got revived by a review in the French film journal *Cahiers du Cinéma*, which drew parallels to Vietnam and social unrest in the film. "It wasn't until two years later that critics in France started to write about the film as though it was a political statement," says Romero.

"We weren't thinking anything like that," Russo says. "Our whole goal was to make a film that would really pay off for horror fans. I read an interview one time where I think George in a moment of weakness said, 'Yeah, that's what we were doing,' but it wasn't. It was a horror film, and it did what horror films are supposed to do—it scared people. Then people look for all these reasons because they have to have something to write about. I mean, most critics are full of shit really." Streiner agrees. "We didn't set out to make a political statement," he says. "We set out to make the best zombie movie ever made."

Romero says, "It's there, but it's unconscious. I think it creeped in. *Night* really reflected our thoughts at the time, it reflects a period of time. What we were trying to do was make a horror movie that might go out and make a few dollars, but in the meantime, we didn't want it to be a piece of shit. We set out to make a horror movie, and we wanted to sell tickets, but we tried not to sell our souls."

Another horror film, Bob Clark's *Deathdream*, released in 1972, also used the living dead as a metaphor for the Vietnam War, and because of the genre, indie horror films were able to criticize the war, where mainstream Hollywood didn't touch Vietnam until several years after the war was over.

"I think it would have been very difficult to get a major distributor for the film," said Clark. "We had the autonomy to make a film about Vietnam." Making the film independently, "we weren't censored or second-guessed by anyone," says *Deathdream* screenwriter Alan Ormsby.

Like a lot of filmmakers their first time out, Romero and company signed a bad deal that took forever to try and resolve. Russo says, "The distributor later tried to say it didn't make any money until it became a cult phenomenon, but that's totally false. It was a success from the start, and they were pocketing millions of dollars that belonged to us.

"We hired an attorney, we hired a producer's representative with forty years experience, we used the right accountants, and we still got screwed. We knew where we needed advice and help, and we got the wrong kind of help. We had people that wanted to screw us, and in this business, they can."

"We were very naïve in terms of trusting a distributor," Streiner says. "Extremely naïve. I take principal responsibility for that because that was part of my job. We knew we were going to get some money stolen from us, that goes with the turf."

Everyone figured by hiring a wily, older producer's representative who'd been around a while that they'd be protected, but they didn't know he was on the distributor's payroll. "We were being fed false information from the get-go," Streiner said.

Romero and company filed suit against the Walter Reade Organization in the early seventies, and it took forever to wind its way through the court system. The case was supposed to go to trial in the late seventies, but once the case came on the trial docket, Walter Reade filed for Chapter 11, and by then, everyone wanted to just recover their property, and walked away learning a very costly lesson.

How much money did the *Night of the Living Dead* gang get cheated out of? "Nobody can ever figure it out because its too enormous, and it's gone on for too long," says Russo. "It's millions, and millions, and millions of dollars. We don't dwell on it, we went on to other things."

"The experts and auditors we had hired were willing to testify that at a very bare minimum at least three million dollars had been stolen from us," says Streiner. "That's what they were willing to testify to. Our general speculation was probably more like $15 million. That was their best guess as experts, but they were willing to testify to $3 million underreported and underpaid." According to one report, *Night of the Living Dead* made $12 million domestic, $20 million worldwide.

In spite of having to learn a tough lesson financially, "*Night of the Living Dead* was an unvarnished independent success," Streiner says. "It was highly rewarding in that sense. Filmmakers have looked at that as a guidepost to how their careers could get started, and they figure if these guys in Pittsburgh can do it, we can do it here in Texas, we can do it here in New York, and we can do it here in Iowa."

Romero is certainly flattered that *Night of the Living Dead* is still remembered and revered, especially considering he built a career around it. Yet he also feels, "It doesn't quite deserve all that credit. When I look at that movie, all I see are the flaws in it. I wish I had a better control of the medium when I made the movie, but there's something under there, some emotional thread that people latch onto, and I'm happy for that.

"When I go to these horror conventions, people will rip their shirts off, show me tattoos of Bub from *Day of the Dead* on their chests, raise their firsts and say, 'Gore lives!' I feel to some extent that there's an audience out there that's all they care about, but that's not all I care about, and I also don't think the shit would survive if that's all it was. It wouldn't be on the shelf over forty years later."

Published in 1967, Ira Levin's *Rosemary's Baby* was the acclaimed bestseller that Truman Capote called "a darkly brilliant tale of modern deviltry that induces the reader to believe the unbelievable. I believed it and was altogether enthralled." In 2003, Stephen King called Levin "the Swiss watchmaker of suspense novels, [he] makes what the rest of us do look like cheap watchmakers in drugstores."

As a young filmmaker, Roman Polanski was looking for a *Rosemary's Baby* for a long time, meaning a big American vehicle that could fit his sensibilities and could break him out of the art house circuit. Famed B-movie producer William Castle was also hoping *Rosemary's Baby* would be his breakthrough to legitimacy, and shed his reputation as a schlockmeister.

Like Hitchcock, William Castle was inspired by *Les Diaboliques*. He saw it on a stormy, rainy night with his wife Ellen. Castle saw a lot of teenagers in line waiting to see it, and as he recalled in his autobiography, "It was an amazing phenomenon—hundreds of youngster waiting patiently to have the shit scared out of them."

Castle bought a novel called *The Marble Forest,* and he wanted a punchier title, a single word that would sum the movie up. Castle finally came up with *Macabre,* which sounded great no matter how you pronounced it.

Castle was driven to make a scarier movie than *Les Diaboliques,* and he obviously fell short, but he had a few tricks up his sleeve to make up for it. Castle came up with the idea of offering life insurance to everyone who came to the movie in case they died of fright. "It was a crazy scheme, but that's exactly what the movie needed—a sales gimmick," he recalled.

Castle struck a deal with Lloyds of London, and a large copy of the insurance policy loomed over the theater marquee where nurses were on duty inside the lobby, and an ambulance was parked outside the theater.

Released in 1958, *Macabre* was a big hit, and Stephen King recalled it was the "gotta see" movie when he was in grade school. King's parents and the parents of his classmates wouldn't take them to see it because of its ad campaign, but King told his mother he went to see *Davy Crockett*, and he felt he could repeat the plot back to her well enough because he owned the trading cards, which clearly told much of the story.

After the success of *Macabre*, the films, and the gimmicks, kept on coming. *House on Haunted Hill*, starring Vincent Price and released in 1959, had an inflatable skeleton floating over the audience on a track. The skeleton once fell into the audience, who threw it around like a beach ball, and at another screening, kids in the audience threw trash at the inflatable for target practice.

1959's *The Tingler* had buzzers in the seats that lightly jolted the audience, an idea Castle said he came up with when he got zapped changing a lightbulb. *Homicidal*, a blatant take-off on *Psycho* with a transvestite killer released in 1961, gave the audiences a fright break five minutes before the end, and also provided a "coward's corner" for those who couldn't take it. 1964's *Strait-Jacket* also had the tagline later reused and made famous by *Last House on the Left*: "Just keep saying to yourself, it's only a movie—it's only a movie . . ."

In the old days when movies didn't open at thousands of theaters at once, they usually traveled from city to city. Castle would personally appear at the openings of his films to greet his fans across the country. "It would be like a big Hollywood premiere for that small town," says Jeffrey Schwarz, who directed the William Castle documentary *Spine Tingler*. "It was the most exciting thing that happened in that given town in forever." When Castle's daughter Terry was born, he went to a theater in San Francisco that was showing *House on Haunted Hill* and gave a cigar to everyone standing on line.

At the end of the sixties, Castle's pictures were fading out at the box office, and he was tired of his rep as a schlockmeister whose films were only successful because of their gimmicks.

Castle then received the galleys for Ira Levin's *Rosemary's Baby* from literary agent Marvin Birdt. Castle loved it and, like Hitchcock with Alma, Castle often double-checked with Ellen. She loved the book too, but predicted it would catch heat from the church, free publicity that Castle would certainly welcome. "Even if they ban it, Catholics will go," he said. Castle bought the rights for $100,000 and got an additional $50,000 when the book became a bestseller.

Castle then took *Rosemary's Baby* to Paramount, and was soon locked in negotiations with the famously vitriolic Charles Bluhdorn, who ran the studio. Bluhdorn wanted to bypass all the lawyers and bullshit and insisted on dealing with Castle one on one. Even a legendary hustler like Castle knew that with Bluhdorn he'd met his match. "His eyes looked into mine and I felt he saw right through me."

After Bluhdorn and Castle came to terms and shook hands on the deal, the Paramount head then mentioned he wanted Roman Polanski to direct. Castle fumed. Bluhdorn tried to explain that the money would be the same if he accepted only a producer credit, but Castle also desperately wanted to direct.

Polanski was given the galley proofs for *Rosemary's Baby* by Bob "The Kid Stays in the Picture" Evans. Polanski went back to the Beverly Hills Hotel, where he was staying, and was going to read the novel the next day by the pool because he was tired from jet lag, but he started leafing through it. The first few pages Polanski wondered to himself, "Hey, what is this, some kind of soap opera?" But he kept reading, and was still reading it at four in the morning. He found

Rosemary's Baby "an outstandingly well-constructed thriller," and told Paramount he was in.

"The reason I decided to make *Rosemary's Baby* was simply because I adored the novel," Polanski recalled. "For a filmmaker like myself it's a very seductive book and made me want to film it. This is quite normal—it's like when you want to make love to a woman even though you know she's a prostitute. I told myself I really had no choice in the matter, even though the ideas behind the story are quite foreign to me."

Bluhdorn persuaded Castle to at least have a meeting with Polanski. At first Castle wasn't immediately impressed with the director, finding him "cocky and vain," and noticing he kept staring at himself in the mirror. But once they got down to business, it was clear they were on the same page about where they wanted the movie to go.

Polanski loved the book and told Castle, "I have been looking a long time for a *Rosemary's Baby*." He wanted his adaptation to be faithful to the novel, and wanted the movie to be "honest. Like peeping through the keyhole of life."

Polanski told Paramount he would do the film only on the condition it stayed close to the novel "and they don't try to improve it. That's what they also do in Hollywood—try to improve great scripts that then turn out terribly."

Polanski also made sure the film took place in 1965, three years before the film's 1968 release, obviously not a big stretch of time to go backward, but Roman kept it in '65 because it was the year the pope visited America. "Roman found the irony of Satan siring a child right under the pope's nose too delicious to give up," says Anthea Sylbert, who was the costume designer on the film. "It would have been cheaper to set the film at the time we were making it, but he was able to convince the studio it was worth the extra money."

Anthea, her brother-in-law Richard Sylbert, who was the production designer, and her husband at the time, Paul Sylbert, also a production designer, were all fond of William Castle. "Bill was a very nice guy and a great old Hollywood type with the big cigar," Paul says. "He made a lot of crap movies, but he wasn't the least bit embarrassed by it. It was showmanship, he loved all that." Anthea liked and respected Castle a great deal, and recalled he was a large, sweet man who reminded her of FDR.

Castle was there during the shoot, but Polanski was clearly in charge. Paul Sylbert recalled that at the start of the movie, "Bill was . . . hurt is not quite the expression. He felt he'd been pushed aside and he was very frustrated. We were on the East Side of New York where the doctor's office was, and we would walk around that building frequently because he had all this energy. He would go on about how he wanted to direct it, 'I'm sure I could have done it,' but he began to live with it.

"*Rosemary's Baby* was a big bestseller," Paul continues. "They were set to have a movie that was as big as the book, and Bill was known as a schlock artist. It was bigger than anything Castle could handle. I mean, it just wasn't gonna happen."

Castle put a good public face on it, telling the press he was making four films for Paramount that year and "simply didn't have the time to direct 'em all. Besides, Polanski is the greatest talent I've ever seen and an absolute perfectionist technically. 'Gadge' Kazan even came up to watch him work and was very impressed."

Although Polanski wasn't a fan of Castle's previous films, he acknowledged that Bill and Bob Evans protected him from the studio to make the movie he wanted. As Polanski said, "[Castle] never pretended he was making masterpieces, but he's an excellent technician who understands filmmakers' problems and doesn't have the usual worries other producers have. He made a constant effort to make me happy in my work. I can't think of a better producer."

Polanski also added that Evans "was resolute and always believed in me, even allowing me to go overbudget, which is inexcusable in Hollywood. It's thanks to those two men that I was able to make exactly the film I wanted to."

Just as Polanski first thought he was initially reading a soap opera, the look of *Rosemary's Baby* would also be deceptive. Anthea Sylbert says that Roman's goal with *Rosemary's Baby* was to make "a classy horror film. He wanted to avoid any of the easy scares. He thought anyone could scare you when the lights are off and it's dark. He wanted to do it with all the lights blazing." William Fraker, who was the film's director of photography, says, "All of Polanski's films aren't darkly lit. That's his whole approach. He'd say, 'No, Billy, I want to see this, I want to see that . . . ' "

The costumes Anthea picked for the elderly coven were also similarly deceptive, dressing them as gaudily as possible with mismatching outfits, loud, tacky colors, and cheap, junky jewelry.

"*Rosemary's Baby* opens like a Doris Day movie, that's the whole point," said Richard Sylbert, the film's production designer. "There was nothing about the lighting or the mood that suggested a horror film," adds Paul Sylbert. "It starts off like a little domestic comedy, or a little domestic drama. You have to want to deceive the audience, you want to suck 'em in. You don't start out with the horror, you start out deceptively. Roman understood that you have to ground fantasies, including horror films, because if they're not grounded, they get no resistance, and they never get up in the air. What makes it work is everything is just as it should be, except there's something weird going on."

Paramount still kept actors under contract and they sent all the contract actresses to Roman in the hopes of finding Rosemary. Tuesday Weld and Jane Fonda were considered, but once Polanski met Mia Farrow, he was sold, and he cast her without a screen test.

Everyone's first choice for Guy Woodhouse, Rosemary's husband, was Robert Redford, the perfect clean-cut, all-American actor you'd least expect to play a villain but he couldn't do the role because he was in litigation with Paramount at the time over dropping out of the Western *Blue*. Jack Nicholson tried out, but Polanski never seriously considered him because you would have suspected him from the first frame.

John Cassavetes could also be considered too on the nose, but Polanski recalled without Redford or Beatty "we lowered our sights," and by all accounts, they had a contentious relationship throughout the shoot.

"Everybody was kind of reluctant to have him cast because he was not a very good actor," says Paul Sylbert. "The story that went around was you can't make a movie with Roman and have a leading man, because he wants to be a leading man. So he always took guys who wouldn't take your breath away. And he does tell actors what to do, no question about it, 'cause he's done a lot of acting himself. He loves to act, loves to be the center of attention. He will really crowd you out if you're getting more attention than him."

Cassavetes would take major studio roles to finance his own independent films, and he reportedly financed *Faces* with his *Rosemary's Baby* salary. When Cassavetes performed in Brian De Palma's 1978 film *The Fury*, he was finishing postproduction on his film *Opening Night*. When De Palma needed to shoot an extra ten days of exteriors in Israel, Cassavetes demanded an extra $10,000, which was money he needed to get *Opening Night* out of the lab.

Ruth Gordon got into the film because Garson Kanin, her husband, was an old Castle friend. Everyone adored Gordon. "She was a great lady, very original," says Fraker. Anthea Sylbert says, "Ruth was what used to be described as a 'great dame.' She was smart, funny, eccentric, and at seventy-two had the kind of energy that even a teenager would envy." Sylbert also recalled Gordon danced a mean twist. (Gordon won Best Supporting Actress for *Rosemary's Baby*.)

The novel was published in April 1967, and the film began shooting on August 21, 1967. *Rosemary's Baby* had a fourteen-week production with a $3.2 million budget.

The setting, as it was in the novel, was the famous New York apartment building, the Dakota, and Richard Sylbert re-created the interiors exactly on a soundstage. David Walsh, the camera operator on *Rosemary's Baby*, recalled that Polanski wanted the interiors to be "big and frightening, almost overwhelming," and one reviewer noted the massive walls of the Dakota set "seem to lean inward, *Cabinet of Dr. Caligari*–style."

As Paul Sylbert says, "Here's these little newlyweds in their new apartment with not a lot in it. They kept the camera low so he'd get a lot of the floor and get a sense of the bareness of it. They could only have so much, they just got started in life. Nobody who gets started in life where the husband is barely making a living is gonna have a lot of stuff in the apartment." Polanski also achieved a similar effect in his 1965 masterpiece of terror, *Repulsion*, where he wanted Catherine Deneuve's apartment to feel as if it was getting bigger and bigger and she was getting lost in the middle of it.

Where Castle worked fast and furious, Polanski was slow and meticulous, and the producer couldn't believe that on the first day, six hours went by without Polanski getting a shot. In one scene, Polanski sent a red cab back, insisting on a yellow one, causing Charlie Bluhdorn to constantly cackle, "Zat crazy Polack didn't like ze color of ze cab." Polanski recalled the studio telling him, "What you are doing is great, but can you do it cheaper and faster?"

It wouldn't be saying anything out of school to call Polanski arrogant or a dictator on the set. When asked in *Vanity Fair*'s Proust Questionnaire which historical figure he most identified with, Polanski answered, "Napoleon." When asked what he valued most in his friends, his response was, "the guts to tell me when I'm wrong—if I ever am!"

But watching Roman work, it was clear to everyone he knew exactly what he was doing. "Other than Hitchcock, he could take any director I've worked with to school, any of them," says Paul Sylbert.

"*Rosemary's Baby* was a tremendous experience for me because I really grew up as a cameraman on that picture," said William Fraker. "In all aspects, from really realizing what contribution you can make to understanding the complete marriage of a cameraman and director."

William Castle also managed to slip in a gimmick for the film, Mia Farrow getting her hair cut short by Vidal Sassoon, which happened at Stage 13 at Paramount. Red carpet was rolled out to Vidal's haircutting station, which was also blocked off by velvet ropes, and bleachers were set up for the press and photographers.

It was also during the *Rosemary's Baby* shoot that Farrow's marriage to Frank Sinatra finally came apart. Polanski, echoing the sentiments of many, had remarked, "I couldn't quite fathom the Mia-Sinatra relationship." During a lunch break, the stage door opened, and a squat little man came in to hand her divorce papers. Polanski, when he came back to the set, told Mia, "You can go home. We'll shoot something else," but she said, "No, I'm not gonna hurt the picture." The film was behind schedule, and Farrow didn't want it to go further because of her.

"Mia was devastated, but within hours she pulled herself together and was back on the set performing magnificently," Anthea Sylbert recalled. "She had a wonderful spirit and great inner courage and strength."

One of Farrow's best moments in *Rosemary's Baby* comes at the end, when she finally sees her child in the crib. Without dialogue, her facial expressions showed what was expressed in the book. At first she looks at her baby in horror, then we see the tenderness and love in her face looking over her newborn, the unconditional love mothers have for their children. It's a range of facial expressions done very well, and Farrow blended them together seamlessly.

Until the day they shot the ending, Fraker didn't know the baby would never be shown. "I just assumed we would," he says. Incredulous, he asked Polanski, "You mean we got a picture that's two hours long, it's called *Rosemary's Baby,* and you never see the baby?" "Exactly," Polanski replied.

"It was always conceived that you would never see the baby," Anthea Sylbert recalls. "Allowing the audience to imagine for themselves what this horned, goat-footed, tailed child looked like, was bound to be more chilling than actually seeing it."

Polanski's decision not to show the baby came from the book, *Eye and Brain: The Psychology of Seeing,* by Professor R. L. Gregory. "One of Gregory's contentions is that our perceptions are shaped by the sum of our visual experiences," Polanski explained. "We see far less than we think because of past impressions already stored in our minds."

William Castle was certain the audience would feel burned if they didn't see the baby, and Polanski told him, "Of course, but I don't think we should ever let them [see it]. On the contrary, everyone will have his own personal image. If we show our version—no matter what we do—it'll spoil that illusion. If I do my job right, people will actually believe they've seen the baby."

"Polanski was right," Castle said. "Many people leaving the theater believed they had seen Him. Imagination plays strange tricks. When *Rosemary* was shown on TV, columnists reported that 'due to censorship,' ABC had cut the scenes where the 'baby' was shown. Rosemary's 'baby' was never photographed."

Today a lot of filmmakers would have to fight for not showing the baby at the end, or resign themselves to it being voted out of the test screening process, but to the best of anyone's recollection, there were no problems or battles with the powers that be at Paramount over not showing the baby at the end. Where the *Rosemary's Baby* shoot went slowly, editor Sam O'Steen, who also cut *Chinatown* for Polanski, rushed to finish editing the film because Castle bet him a grand.

Lists of the greatest movie posters and ad campaigns have always included horror films, and *Rosemary's Baby* often makes those lists along with *Jaws, Alien, The Omen,* and *The Silence of the Lambs.*

The classic ad campaign for *Rosemary's Baby* was created by Steve Frankfurt, who was creative director and president at the legendary advertising firm Young and Rubicam. One ad campaign that was created on Frankfurt's watch at the firm included "Betcha Can't Eat Just One" for Lay's potato chips, as well as campaigns for Excedrin, Eastern Airlines, Johnson and Johnson, and Bristol-Myers.

Frankfurt did his first film work on *To Kill a Mockingbird.* Frankfurt got a call from Peter Bart, who was then vice president of production at Paramount, to put together the *Rosemary's Baby* campaign. (*Rosemary's Baby* was also one of the first big projects new production head Bob Evans took on.)

The photo of the black baby carriage was shot in Central Park on Seventy-second Street, and Frankfurt created the classic tagline, "Pray for Rosemary's Baby." It was a different approach to movie advertising, catchy and economical, that Frankfurt brought with him from Madison Avenue. "When we did the campaign for Lay's potato chips, 'Betcha Can't Eat Just One,' that's all we said and it became part of the lingo of the country," Frankfurt says. "My philosophy was make it a tease, make it something that will get them involved. To me, involvement is the first step to persuasion."

Frankfurt thought of a number of different ways to advertise the film, including running ads in the birth announcements of the paper with the "Pray for Rosemary's Baby" tagline, and spray-painting it with a stencil all over New York. "We stenciled it on the steps of St. Patrick's Cathedral, for which we almost got in trouble!" Frankfurt says. Johnny Carson was also ending *The Tonight Show* by saying, "And remember folks, pray for Rosemary's baby."

Frankfurt would later be told by people in the industry that *Rosemary's Baby* was the breakthrough movie ad campaign of its time, creating a whole new way that the studios looked at movie ads as they tried to learn the so-called science of the marketing world. (Frankfurt went on to create the campaigns for *Catch-22*, *Downhill Racer*, and *Goodbye Columbus*, among others, for Paramount.)

When *Rosemary's Baby* was a big hit, "Castle went into shock," says Paul Sylbert. "He never had anything like that in his life, and suddenly he became a legitimate producer."

The film broke the house records at the Crest Theater in Westwood, California, and as Polanski recalled, "Bill Castle couldn't resist touring Westwood Village and feasting his producer's eyes on the crowd that wound its way around the block. He used to stand and stare and add up the receipts in his head." As the film let out, Castle stood outside, chomping his trademark cigar, asking moviegoers as they were leaving, "Well, whadda'ya think of the picture?"

The film got mostly good reviews. Michael Korda, who went on to be a top editor at Simon & Schuster, reviewed it for *Glamour*, calling it "absolutely faithful to the book but *better* . . . a faultless, lawless motion picture, slick, chilling, beautiful, convincing and thoroughly entertaining."

Farrow also got strong reviews for her work. *Variety* wrote that with *Rosemary's Baby* "Farrow becomes a genuine, above-title star." *Time* wrote, "Even those who read the book are in for a shock: the very real acting talent of Mia Farrow."

Many years after the initial release of *Rosemary's Baby*, David Thomson wrote, "That visceral, erotic and frightening film owes so much to her: not just because of her daintiness and the sense of her life being sucked away from her as it grows inside her, but in her exceptional interest in what it is like to be pregnant. . . ." Thomson wrote that since *Rosemary's Baby* she rose to every acting challenge, though she has not recaptured "the piercingly tragic figure she had been for Polanski." Thomson has also written that to him, nothing dates worse than horror films, "but *Rosemary's Baby* is very disturbing still."

As Hollywood lore goes, in the late sixties Paramount was in deep financial trouble after a series of flops like *Darling Lili, The Molly Maguires,* and most notoriously, *Paint Your Wagon. Rosemary's Baby* didn't completely bring Paramount back from the brink, *The Godfather* and *Love Story* did, but *Rosemary's Baby* definitely helped the studio when it desperately needed a hit. "I think *Rosemary's Baby* helped enormously," says former Paramount advertising executive Charles Glenn. "I think it went a long way to help Paramount turn around."

Frankfurt also says that with the success of *Rosemary's Baby,* "Suddenly, people were taking Bob Evans seriously. That was the big factor. Before that, he wasn't taken seriously as head of production. Bluhdorn really rolled the dice on this one, then lo and behold all of the sudden he starts cranking hits out, one after another, and suddenly Paramount was a very different company."

"*Rosemary's Baby* was the foothold of bringing the studio back dollar wise," says Fraker. "The success of *Rosemary's Baby* helped bring Paramount back. It was a major, major help to the studio at the time, and it made Bob Evans a big hero because he really stood behind the film."

Many point to *The Exorcist* as the film where people started taking horror seriously, but *Rosemary's Baby* also brought respect to the genre as well. "It kicked it upstairs, no question," says Paul Sylbert. "It opened the door for class A productions of horror films. The money spent on *The Exorcist* was pretty steep, but it paid off. *Rosemary's Baby* opened the door. It took it out of the schlock genre and put it up there with the other big successful movies."

FIVE

IT'S ONLY A MOVIE

How Wes Craven and Sean Cunningham launched their careers with *The Last House on the Left,* and how William Friedkin created a horror masterpiece with *The Exorcist*

As *Night of the Living Dead* and *Halloween* would prove, many critics try to examine the subtext of horror films, even if it's unintentional or what they bring to the films themselves. Released in 1972, *Last House on the Left* wasn't overtly about the failure of the sixties or the horror of the Vietnam War, but Wes Craven did see it as a protest film, and the anger that came at the end of the decade clearly seeped into the film.

"People who were educated who were watching the war in Vietnam, and the way the government consistently lied," Craven says. "There were so many big-time lies that were promoted by our government during Vietnam. 'We're not bombing there, we don't have any troops over here . . .' One after another it was revealed as lies. When I was a college teacher, I was involved in the protest movement, and we'd get a lot of raw footage from Vietnam. People would literally send around 16 mm footage, various antiwar groups, that showed real violence, unedited footage."

Craven continues, "When I made *Last House,* my feeling was, 'I'm going to do a film where I don't cut away, I won't make it look operatic and balletic like Peckinpah. Someone isn't going to get shot, clutch their chest, and fall down dead. They're gonna get shot and scream and crawl, because that's what I'd seen, and that's when I realized that's what violence is. It's horrendously messy and it has a perverted sexual side to it of the incredible power of one person over another. Most American cinema that I was familiar with showed violence that was really a lie. So it was like, 'Okay, we're gonna put it in your face.' It was almost like an entrapment and a bait and switch with the audience. We were kind of saying, 'Okay, we're gonna make a film that's a scary movie, come watch it and you'll be entertained.' Then we will expose you to this horrendous violence and you'll sort of be disgusted at yourself. Really what happened, of course, was people were disgusted with us, but I just feel like for one time, and I think we only did it once, we showed violence the way it is."

Like *Halloween, Last House on the Left* has a fairly simple story line. A Mansonesque gang of scum kidnap two girls hitchhiking their way to a concert. They are raped, humiliated, and killed, and the parents seek bloody revenge. *Last House* is one dark and ugly movie, and the sociopolitical context of the time it came from gave the film even more power.

Like many who made classic horror, or horror films that broke new ground, neither Wes Craven nor his good friend Sean Cunningham, who would later create the *Friday the 13th* series, were initially fans of the genre or had seen many horror films. "To be fresh, a horror movie has to get under people's skin in unexpected ways, with things that make them profoundly uneasy," Craven said. "Horror movies have to show us something that hasn't been shown before so that the audience is completely taken aback. You see, it's not just that people want to be scared; people *are* scared."

Because of his repressive upbringing, Craven didn't even see his first movie until he was seventeen. "We weren't allowed to do much of anything," he recalled. "Drink, smoke, play cards, have sex, or go to the movies. I was the quirky kid who read books all the time, painted, and read poetry. So when I began to find my own way, I was very separated from my whole family."

Once Craven started going to the movies, he saw *Night of the Living Dead* in a theater and was fascinated by the reaction of the audience a horror film can inspire. It was when Craven was teaching at Clarkson College in Potsdam, New York, where he saw what became the inspiration for *Last House on the Left*, Ingmar Bergman's *The Virgin Spring*, which was playing at a nearby art house theater.

"The late sixties was not a successful time for me," Craven continued. "I think at that point in my life I was still trying to please my parents, unconsciously trying to be the good boy that went off to school then became a teacher. This was an acceptable profession and very respectable. But about four or five years into teaching I just realized I was profoundly bored and out of place. It just wasn't me, and so I just made one of those big leaps. I said, 'I'm just gonna take a shot at doing something that I would really enjoy.' So I just quit and went to New York to work in filmmaking."

For a year and a half, Craven did everything from sweeping floors to working as a postproduction manager to synching dailies. Craven learned how to be a film editor from Harry Chapin, the songwriter of "Taxi" and "Cat's in the Cradle." Harry's older brother Steve was one of Craven's college students, and Harry was then cutting and producing industrial films for IBM. Harry told Craven, "Look, I can't give you a job but I can teach you what I'm doing."

It wasn't long before Craven was synching dailies on documentaries, which is how he came in contact with Cunningham. After graduating from Stanford, Cunningham was a stage director and stage manager on Broadway, and was trying to plot his way into the movies. He started out making industrial films and commercials in New York, and used to believe that all you needed to be a movie producer was a phone and stationery.

Cunningham was making X-rated movies before *Deep Throat* brought dirty movies into the public consciousness in 1972. "Porn chic came later," Cunningham said. "That's when censorship came, and everything changed at that point."

First was *The Art of Marriage* in 1970, which played on Forty-second Street for twenty-seven weeks, and made Cunningham more than $100,000. The first film Wes and Sean Cunningham worked on was *Together*, released in 1971, which was another adult film that featured Marilyn Chambers a year before she became a porn superstar with *Behind the Green Door*. Rushing to finish the film with little money or sleep bonded Craven and Cunningham together as friends. "We really became war buddies at the end of that process," Cunningham said.

Cunningham went to Hallmark Releasing about potentially distributing *Together*. Hallmark Releasing grew out of Esquire Theaters, a chain of about a hundred screens. George Mansour booked their theaters when he worked at Warner Brothers, and joined the company when they decided to make their own movies. Hallmark was owned by three partners, Phil Scuderi, Steve Minasian, and Robert Barsamain.

Mansour said the Hallmark guys were "a little shady and shaky—but they also had a lot of good movie houses." Ron Kurz, who wrote the second *Friday the 13th*, called Scuderi a cross between Roger Corman and Michael Corleone.

Years down the road, Hallmark would put up the money for *Friday the 13th* before it was picked up for distribution by Paramount. Betsy Palmer remembered two of the Hallmark partners on the *Friday the 13th* set who "were like the men in black . . . these strange men lurking around on the set . . . all they told us was that these were the moneymen from Boston."

When Mansour watched *Together*, he told Cunningham: "It's pretty crude and stupid, but I think that people would pay to see this." The movie also had a black actor with a big schlong, and Mansour added, "You know, Phil, there's a big group of people out there who have never seen a big black dick before. We can exploit this."

After *Together,* Hallmark then told Wes and Sean they'd love a really violent, scary movie, and offered them $90,000 to make one. When Craven and Cunningham were making *Last House on the Left,* their attitude was that they were making a tiny little film for a company in Boston, it would only be shown in a few theaters up there, no one would see it or know that they did it. Let's be as bad boys as we can, they thought. We're going to show things that people have never seen before on a movie screen, we'll pull out all the stops and just do whatever the hell we want.

"Exploitation films, a term I hate, but it will have to do, are made by relatively disenfranchised people," Craven said. "Exploitation writers, directors, and producers tend to be younger people, people more on the outside. Often they have very little to lose by telling the truth, and they're speaking to an audience that will accept the truth more readily than entrenched adults with all sorts of illusions and political obligations and whatever."

The screenplay that Craven wrote was way more brutal than the finished movie, which is really saying something. Fred Lincoln, who played Weasel, recalled, "I read the script, and it was absolutely the most disgusting thing I'd ever seen . . . I mean it was *really* hideous."

Lucy Grantham was also uneasy about the project, but when she met Wes and Sean she knew they were decent people. "I could see from meeting them they were bright and intelligent, and I immediately recognized they were ambitious . . . I had no idea—and I'm not sure that *anybody* did—that this was breaking ground. I wish I had been prescient enough to know that."

Last House also marked the first time in horror the chain saw was used as a weapon, and it may have directly influenced *The Texas Chain Saw Massacre.* Krug and the father's last battle was originally going to have the father fight him with a scalpel because he was a doctor, and would know where to make a bunch of little incisions that would add up and eventually bleed Krug to death. "We noticed there was some movie out that had a bunch of guys fighting with chain saws," Craven recalled. "I remember seeing the poster on Times Square, it was kind of a cheap low-budget action film. So Sean said, 'Fuck the scalpel, let's get a chain saw going!'"

Another key scene that fans repeatedly brought up to Craven as their favorite was the nightmare segment, where the victim's parents knock gang member Weasel's teeth with a hammer and chisel, and it planted the seed for *A Nightmare on Elm Street* years later. "I realized the power of dream imagery, and I went back to it as I made more films," Craven said.

The shoot began on October 2, 1971, and ran about four weeks with some make-up days. "*Last House* introduced me to the fact that you don't sleep for five weeks when you're shooting a film," Craven said. "But it was also a lot of fun, especially shooting the outdoor scenes, with all that running around, falling and screaming . . . it was great."

Although Craven had the burning ambition to go out and make a movie, he later admitted he knew "precious little" about making movies. "I didn't know how to plan a film. I didn't know how to shoot a master shot. I didn't understand the concept of coverage, and I didn't know a great deal about film direction . . . I literally did not know any of the rules or techniques of film . . . we simply went out to make a movie without knowing how to do it."

Sean Cunningham would recall years later, "The fact is that if any of us knew what we were doing, we never would have gotten the picture made . . . because we would have said, 'This is impossible!'

"Shortly after *Last House* was edited, I went out to Los Angeles to watch a movie being made," Cunningham continued. "I noticed that there was a person on the set of this movie that was in charge of continuity, making sure things matched in consecutive shots. The reason we didn't have somebody like that on the set of *Last House* was not because of budgetary restrictions, or because I refused to hire somebody, but simply because we really didn't know there was such a thing as continuity!"

Like with *Night of the Living Dead* and *The Texas Chain Saw Massacre, Last House* was blown up from 16 mm to 35 mm, and horror fans often like the realism the grain brings to a horror film. One of the sickest scenes in the film, where one of the kidnapped girls, Phyllis, is stabbed repeatedly and disemboweled, was shot with a very fast film stock that's been used in documentaries in low light conditions. "That gave a grainy look to it," Craven said. "It was almost like old footage from World War II, with the light burned out and the darks very grainy and black. It turned out to be very powerful."

Cunningham said, "I think one of the things that was effective about *Last House on the Left,* and Wes did this on purpose, he shot it in a style—it was meant to be a hand-held documentary style so that it would kind of look like newsreel footage. It wasn't like you were watching a regular movie, it was like you were watching something awful. At least that's the impression it had on me and that was sort of what messed around with people's heads."

After the scene where Phyllis was stabbed, there was a distinct feeling things went too far. Craven recalled, "We all just sort of sat around and laid out staring at the sky in this beautiful, sylvan setting and just thought, 'What the hell have we just done?'" Everyone broke for lunch after shooting the scene, but no one felt like eating. "I was so grossed-out," said costar Jeremy Rain. "I thought, 'I'll never eat meat again . . . I'm ruined!'"

Craven didn't realize the overall effect of the film until he showed it to an audience. "That was like, 'Wow, it hit like a sledgehammer,'" he says. "I realized I had done something very powerful kind of behind my own back."

Last House wrapped in November 1971, and David Hess, who played Krug, went to every prerelease screening. Usually the audience was dead silent at the end, and outside the theater heated debates and fights would start. Some would say they were going to protest it once it came out, while others would say, "Finally, we see a movie that shows horror in all its graphic reality." Hess even took his parents to see it, and his mother wouldn't speak to him for a week. "I remember her saying, 'What's a nice Jewish boy like you making a film like this for?'"

When *Last House* was released in late 1972, controversy over the film was immediate. People protested the theaters, and Craven started hearing stories of people fainting, fistfights breaking out, projectionists cutting up the movie, and angry audiences wanting to break into the projection booth and hack up the movie themselves.

One of the only positive reviews the film got came from Roger Ebert, who called it "a tough, bitter little sleeper of a movie that's about four times as good as you'd expect." David Szulkin, who wrote the behind-the-scenes account of the film, *Last House on the Left: The Making of a Cult Classic*, called it "the Altamont of horror films."

Years after its initial release, in the book *The Psychotronic Encyclopedia*, Michael Weldon was right on target about *Last House*: "Is it a remake of Bergman's *Virgin Spring* illustrating the sickness of life in modern-day America? Is it a coarse, repulsive exploitation film for sickos? It's both. . . . No matter what you think about it, *Last House* is effective and disturbing."

While Craven was working on an editing gig, he was hoping to make enough money to live on, and he called Sean to ask how the movie was doing. "Are you sitting down?" Cunningham asked. "It's a hit!"

The *Last House* budget came in at under $100,000, and it made $3 to 4 million in rentals. Not to mention that, unlike a lot of neophyte filmmakers, Craven and company didn't get screwed by the distributors.

"I didn't even carry a wallet," Craven recalled. "I didn't have a credit card, I didn't drive a car, I didn't have anything. I just disappeared from the radar screen for like three years. When *Last House* came out and we started getting checks, I went to the bank and they said, 'Do you have an account?' 'No.' 'Can we see your driver's license?' 'Well, I don't really have one.' I had to go into a reintroduction to society."

In the year following *Last House's* release, Craven made close to $100,000 from the film. The most he made in a year teaching college was $11,000. "Suddenly, I was making all of this cash, and I had to figure out how to pay taxes. And after about two years of trying to write other kinds of scripts, I was essentially broke again. So at that point, I was saying to myself, 'Did all that really happen?' "

The fallout from making such a vicious movie lingered over the participants for years. Craven hoped that people would see the film "as this brilliant, breakthrough film," instead, "there was this powerful feeling that we had done something unspeakable. That sort of ostracism was very difficult to deal with personally."

"No agent would touch me," Hess said. "And *Last House* was a stone-cold smash! People really believed that I *was* that character. They gave me no credit for being an actor."

Ten years after its initial release, Cunningham saw *Last House* again at a midnight show in Connecticut. "It just wasn't the movie that I remember," he lamented. "I thought we were getting away with all this stuff, but we weren't getting away with anything. Jesus, this is terrible!" During the scene where Lucy Grantham is forced into pissing herself by Krug and company, Cunningham thought, "Oh, jeez, I really don't want to be here," and he got up and left.

Last House was indeed "deeply offensive," Craven said. "It was intended to be. I did not want to entertain with violence, with rape, or shooting, or terror. And I did not want to show killing as a heroic action, even on the part of the parents at the end."

Once Craven and Cunningham got *Last House* out of their systems, they never went back to the same level of intensity with violence again. "I know when I went on to other films I consciously backed away from doing that again," Craven says. "But then you're in the quandary of saying, 'Well, am I making it more entertaining and less real, and am I participating in a lie?' I try to keep an element of the fact that violence taints everyone."

It was an important lesson for both Craven and Cunningham. Horror was clearly a lucrative genre, and they both wanted to make something more entertaining, less punishing, and there'd be a lot more money to be made.

When Richard LaGravenese, screenwriter of *The Fisher King* and *The Bridges of Madison County,* was putting together a documentary about the great films of the seventies, *A Decade Under the Influence,* among the directors included in the documentary was William Friedkin. Friedkin had two huge hits back-to-back in that fabled filmmaking decade, *The French Connection* in 1971, which would win Oscars for Best Picture and Best Director, and, of course, *The Exorcist* in 1973.

While working on the documentary, LaGravenese's editor told him she had never seen it because she was too afraid to watch it, and it brought back Richard's memories of seeing the film the first time himself.

"I saw *The Exorcist* when I was fourteen," he recalls. "I wasn't allowed to see it, and I snuck into the city on a train." LaGravenese had to take a train into the city because back in the seventies major movies played the big cities first, then branched out to the smaller cities when they went wide.

"I got this old couple to take me into the theater," he continues. "I was by myself in New York and I *freaked* out! I felt punished for it because I was shakin' when I came out of the theater! I just remember the whole theater would all scream, then the next scene everyone would break into nervous laughter and talk to each other, then get back into the film. It was such a communal experience."

The Exorcist "became a social phenomenon in itself," wrote Stephen King. "Lines stretched around the block in every major city where it played, and even in towns which normally rolled up their sidewalks promptly at 7:30 P.M., midnight shows were scheduled. Church groups picketed; sociologists with pipes pontificated; newscasters did 'back of the book' segments for their programs on slow nights. The country, in fact, went on a two-month possession jag."

Julia Phillips, producer of *The Sting*, which opened on the same day as *The Exorcist*, wrote that after the movie you were "unsure whether to hit a church or a bar," and one of the big reasons it shook people up so badly is it made them confront issues of faith and belief. As *Exorcist* creator William Peter Blatty recalls, "A couple of Jesuit priests at Loyola University told me that after the publication of the novel they'd never seen such a stampede of students to the confessional box."

Says Father William O'Malley, a Catholic priest who was an advisor on *The Exorcist* and also had a role in the film, "*The Exorcist* wasn't just a horror movie the way other horror movies are that don't probe the human psyche. Even now, more and more we develop a tolerance for evil so that we no longer see it. I think what Blatty was trying to say is at its most basic level evil is ugly."

The Exorcist was realistic enough that people believed they themselves were possessed. As Father O'Malley recalled, "People were constantly calling me to exorcise their house, their cat, their daughter. I told people, 'If you think I'm going to take the devil out of your cat and jump out the window, you're crazy.'"

Friedkin said, "After the film opened, Jason and I were living in New York and we'd be walking down the street and people would come up and grab him by the arms, 'Father, it's my son, you have to help me.' He would have to tear himself away. 'I'm not a priest, I'm just an actor.' He went into seclusion for a while. He couldn't walk the streets."

As a novelist and screenwriter, William Peter Blatty's forte was comedy. His credits included *A Shot in the Dark*, *What Did You Do in the War, Daddy?*; *John Goldfarb, Please Come Home*; *Promise Her Anything*, and *The Great Bank Robbery*. Blatty met up with Marc Jaffee, who was the editorial director at Bantam, at a New Year's Eve party on the last day of 1968, a modest get-together in the San Fernando Valley, when Blatty had an idea he wanted to pitch.

"I had no story," Blatty recalls. "Only the theme of demonic possession, and whatever I told Marc took me no more than three minutes to do so." Blatty's brief pitch sounded intriguing to Jaffee, it was strange and interesting territory. "Sounds like the making of a terrific suspense novel," he said, and they made a deal.

Blatty took a year off from screenwriting and started writing *The Exorcist* in a cabin in Lake Tahoe in the summer of 1969. He wrote the book chapter by chapter, "building each new scene on everything that preceded it, and praying to God that I wouldn't paint myself into a corner."

Once the book was turned into Bantam, they were very happy with the end results. "The book more than met our expectations, and I learned how a really great suspense story was told," Jaffee says. "*The Exorcist* grew out of a very serious and distinctive aspect of Catholic practice, real religious life in a way, then it slowly but surely became a horror story."

Like Father Karras, Blatty, a devout Catholic, was questioning his faith, and writing *The Exorcist* brought him back in touch with it, and he would also call the novel his "350-page thank-you note to the Jesuits."

But the novel didn't take off until fate intervened. Blatty recalls that *The Exorcist* was out for seven weeks, "and was being returned to Harper & Row by the trainload. It was a disaster." When his book tour ended, Harper offered Blatty any number of copies he wanted to buy for fifty cents each.

Then Blatty and a publishing company representative were having lunch when Harper and Row called them at the restaurant. It was right before showtime on *The Dick Cavett Show*. One of the guests had called in sick, and they wanted Blatty to come in to fill the gap, so he ran the three blocks to Cavett's studio.

Blatty continues, "I came out, Cavett said, 'Mr. Blatty, I'm sorry but I haven't read your book.' 'Okay, would you like me to tell you about it?' 'Oh, please do!' and I got to do a forty-one minute monologue about my novel. In less than three weeks, *The Exorcist* had gone from 'Better luck next time, kid,' to number one on the *New York Times* fiction (Best Seller) list, where it stayed at that position for seventeen weeks, and fifty-seven weeks overall." *The Exorcist* would sell 400,000 to 500,000 copies in hardcover, four million in paperback, and another four million with the success of the movie.

Blatty recalled the book going out to all the majors, and all of them turning it down. Then John Calley, who was head of production at Warner Bros. read it lying in bed. "John told me he was alone in his home reading *The Exorcist* in bed on a windy night with lots of tree branches rustling and sighing against the roof," Blatty says. "At a certain point in his reading, he got so spooked that he called for his German shepherd to get up on the bed with him. The dog had previously been forbidden to ever do so, so there ensued a titanic struggle with John trying to drag the dog up onto the bed by his collar, and the dog whining and digging his claws into the wood pine floor. John said to himself, 'My God, if it's this scary, we've got to make it!'"

Eventually Warner Bros. bought the movie rights for $641,000. When Blatty appeared on *The Tonight Show*, Johnny Carson asked, "Why six forty-*one*, why not six-forty or six forty-five?" "They wanted to make the figure look honest," Blatty answered.

Mike Nichols, John Boorman, and Arthur Penn, who were all favorite directors at Warner Bros., turned it down, as well as Peter Bogdanovich, who was hot from *The Last Picture Show* and *What's Up Doc?* and was about to have another hit with *Paper Moon*. Then William Friedkin, who had just won Oscars for best picture and best director for *The French Connection*, sat down to read it for "relaxation," and like the old cliché goes he couldn't put it down.

For Friedkin to take on a project, he had to have a "gut-level reaction" with it. "If It doesn't get me viscerally, I'm out." From the first time Friedkin read *The Exorcist*, he had a clear vision of how he wanted to make it, and after seeing *The French Connection,* Blatty felt, "The pace, excitement, and look of documentary realism were what *The Exorcist* needed."

As it turns out, they couldn't have picked a better director for the job. Nessa Hyams, who was head of casting at Warner Bros., and also cast *The Exorcist* with Juliet Taylor, recalled Friedkin was "intense, very strong, very opinionated, very tough, but fun. He knew exactly what he was doing as far as I could tell. He was pretty fearless about a lot of things, and you knew you were working on something that was going to be controversial and good."

Blatty liked the fact that Friedkin wasn't scared of anybody, and once he was on the film, he became the Terminator in making it. Richard Lederer, who was vice president of advertising and publicity at Warners, said, "Until he got it he wouldn't quit."

The Exorcist was clearly steeped in Blatty's Catholicism. But Friedkin, who is Jewish and agnostic, tried to make the film more of a litmus test about how the audience views faith, and let the audience draw its own conclusions about what the film meant.

Blatty and Friedkin certainly had their battles, but Friedkin always praised the book, feeling it was as good as anything he'd read from Kafka, and Blatty recalled Billy "always wanted to stay as close to the novel as he could."

Except for a rare genre classic here and there, like *Psycho* or *Alien,* Friedkin has never been a horror film fan, and nobody involved in *The Exorcist* dared call it the H word.

Terence Donnelly, who was Friedkin's assistant director on *The Exorcist* says, "I don't recall that Warner Brothers ever referred to the film in the horror genre, although, of course, it turned out to fit that description very well. It was more of an enormously popular novel as far as they were concerned. I can't speak for Billy, but I would imagine that if the script had been presented to him as a pure 'horror' play, I think he would have tossed it straight away. The cachet of the horror genre was schlock at best." (Many years later, Friedkin still wouldn't call it a horror film, but "a theological thriller" instead.)

It made sense, especially considering the horror genre still wasn't taken seriously by the majors. As Calley recalled, "It was like when Stanley Kubrick took *2001* to Wasserman, Lew said, 'Kid, you don't spend over a million dollars on science fiction movies. You just don't do that.' And this was about, you don't spend over a million bucks on a horror movie.

"When we did *The Exorcist* with Friedkin, we knew that it was a terrifying book, but you always kinda low rated horror movies," Calley continued. "And we decided we wanted to do it as wonderfully as possible."

"John Calley was the one directors liked," recalled Nessa Hyams. "John was smart, charming, witty, seductive, and he believed in these people [the filmmakers]. He really trusted them."

Still, Friedkin kept the film far away from Hollywood, shooting in New York, Washington, and Iraq. "One of the reasons that Billy chose to do the picture on the East Coast instead of Hollywood was he felt Warner Brothers would be breathing down his neck if we were shooting in the studio's backyard," says Terence Donnelly.

Like many great horror films, realism was crucial, and there was no middle ground with *The Exorcist*. When Marcel Vercoutere, who would do the special effects for *The Exorcist*, met with the Warner brass, he was told, "You're flirting right on the borderline. If you go a little bit one way or the other, it'll be a laughingstock."

Before filming began, Friedkin laid down the law that there would be no optical effects on *The Exorcist*, everything had to happen in front of the camera. "If I was making *The Exorcist* today, I still wouldn't use much CGI," he said years later. He also insisted on no flashbacks, freeze frames, or flash forwards, nothing that would call attention to the fact that you were watching a movie. Decades after the fact, Friedkin was pleased at how well the effects held up. "Even when I went back to the film for a DVD release in 2000, I didn't have to digitally erase any wires."

When talking about *Jaws,* Spielberg mentioned the baggage actors bring to the screen, and it usually takes a reel for that to disappear, which is why the film worked so well without big-name stars. Hyams says that for *The Exorcist*, "The idea was not to cast anybody well known. It was much more effective. Warner Brothers didn't insist we hire movie stars, they were good at letting us do that. Once we got the leads for *The Exorcist,* nobody was a big star really, but Billy was a star because he had done *The French Connection.* The book was a star, and Billy won every award that year. Once the studio had something they could hang the movie on and sell it, they left the directors alone."

Having worked with Peter Bogdanovich, Hyams had seen Ellen Burstyn in *The Last Picture Show*, and thought she was spectacular. "She was probably only forty at the time, but it was very hard to find a mature woman who was so brilliant that nobody knew."

"It was very challenging and I have always loved a challenge," Burstyn said. "There was nothing about it I didn't like, except I was afraid of it. The film was dealing with dark forces . . . I didn't specify my feelings, I just felt that we all had to be very careful, cleanse ourselves psychically at the end of the day, pray a lot." ·

For Father Karras, Friedkin wanted an actor who had Catholic schooling, and Jason Miller went to a Catholic University for three years. When he saw Miller's renowned play, *That Championship Season*, "I thought he had an inherent sensitivity that I could photograph," and that the play "just reeked of lapsed Catholicism." Jack Nicholson had just finished *The King of Marvin Gardens* with Ellen Burstyn, and also went to Friedkin about playing Father Damien, but Friedkin told him, "Jack, if I saw you in a priest's collar, I would burst out laughing."

Linda Blair was cast by Juliet Taylor in New York (Taylor's credits include *Taxi Driver*, many Woody Allen films including *Annie Hall*, *Close Encounters of the Third Kind, Schindler's List*, and more). "We saw so many kids, I couldn't find anybody in L.A.," Nessa Hyams recalls. "Billy and I used to have dinner, and he would make me get up and ask people with little girls at their table, 'Hello, you don't know me, but I'm doing a movie.' Most people would look at me like I was some horrible pervert or something!"

Another reason why *The Exorcist* was primarily shot back east was New York's child labor laws weren't anywhere near as restrictive as California's at the time. Also, because *The Exorcist* was such a long shoot, Blair was no longer a kid by the end of it. "The picture took so long, Linda finally became a woman during the course of the shooting," Hyams continues. "So in the dailies she kept getting more and more developed, and more and more a young woman than she was a kid."

Friedkin and *The Exorcist*'s makeup wizard Dick Smith both felt protective of Linda as if she were their daughter, and were concerned about her psyche being harmed from acting in the movie, which thankfully didn't happen.

One day when she came back to the makeup room, Smith asked her, "Linda, how do you feel when you have to say these awful things?" "It's Regan," she replied, not her doing it. Smith suspected that Ellen Burstyn may have taught Blair how to divorce herself from her character, and it worked. "She was fine when she left the film, she wasn't disturbed in any way," he says. (After the shoot, Friedkin and Blatty also put their money together and bought Linda a pony for Christmas.)

Donnelly says, "If there was one consistency about the making of the film it was that the actors were as professional a team as I have ever had the pleasure of working with during my career. I thank the Lord that we didn't ever have one egomaniac or difficult actor to deal with. All the actors and crew alike were like foot soldiers in some combat zone, leaning on each other to survive the rigors of war. They were a class act."

Like a number of seventies films, *The Exorcist* also had nonactors. "They were looking for authenticity more than anything else," says Father William O'Malley. "The woman who played Karras's mother was a cashier at a Greek restaurant and somebody found her there, she wasn't a trained actress at all. We didn't have to be told how a real priest would act. I was credited as a technical advisor, that's just because I showed Jason Miller how to say mass, that's all. I would say things like, 'Priests wouldn't wear that, priest wouldn't do that,' that kind of thing."

The special effects in the film, especially with the effects technology of the early seventies, were a case of reinventing the wheel and trial and error. To turn a sweet twelve-year-old girl into a monster, as well as make a forty-two-year-old Max von Sydow look ancient, the makeup skills of Dick Smith were crucial.

Smith began in television right as the medium was getting started, working for NBC in 1945. Working in live TV, Smith had to move fast. He once made actress Claire Bloom age sixty years in the space of an hour and a half for a live TV drama, and had to do it during the short commercial breaks. He also had an assistant who counted down how many seconds they had left before they had to go back on the air.

In the early seventies, Smith broke major ground with his makeup work on *The Godfather* and *Little Big Man*, where he made Dustin Hoffman a hundred-and-twenty-one years old. "I had one of the best aging makeups to date on Max von Sydow in *The Exorcist*," says

Smith. "Most people thought he was an old man and never realized he was forty-two."

John Chambers, the makeup artist for *Planet of the Apes*, was the pioneer of using foam latex. Where in *Planet of the Apes* the masks didn't move very well when the actors spoke, Smith's innovation was to break the latex into individual pieces so that the makeup had more flexibility, the actors could be expressive with their makeup on, and would also look more realistic.

"Dick Smith is the greatest living makeup artist on the planet," says Tom Savini. "He's invented all the techniques that every makeup artist uses today. They might improve on it, they might make it better, but it all begins with his techniques."

As Smith recalls, "The number of makeup artists who did character makeup appliances back then was very limited, and when I did the first *Godfather*, I didn't get another job for six months after that. So then comes *The Exorcist*, and in it I had a lot of true special makeup effects. When I did *The Exorcist*, I worked in my little house in Larchmont, New York. I had a basement with a couple of rooms, a single car garage, which I took over, and sometimes I borrowed one of my neighbor's basements when I needed the room."

Halfway through *The Exorcist* shoot, Friedkin decided to change Linda Blair's makeup design, and Smith then had to set up new makeup tests on top of his daily workload. Rick Baker was a huge fan of Smith's, would write him fan letters and send along photos of his work. Smith was very impressed with what he saw, invited Baker to his home, and graciously shared many of his makeup techniques with him. When Smith needed help, he called on Baker to be his assistant. "He was the best one I could think of," Smith says. "There was no one around me I could use, and I could already see that Baker was extraordinarily talented."

"Of course I lit up and said I'd be right there," Baker recalled.

"For me, it was like a dream come true. Every day I was learning how the master did his stuff. I actually lived at Dick's house. Dick would knock out sculptures and I'd knock out molds, and I'd be running three or four batches of foam a day so we could build up a stock. Sometimes I'd pull a piece out of a mold, and he'd almost literally slap it right onto Linda Blair's face."

"No other film that I'd ever done had been so loaded with makeup creativity, and it's amazing I was able to do this with one assistant," Smith said.

Without traffic, it was a forty-five-minute commute from Smith's home in Larchmont to New York City. He would head home usually after 7:00 P.M., sit in terrible rush-hour traffic on the West Side Highway, get home, eat dinner, go to bed, then get up again at four or five in the morning, and get back to work.

Still, Smith recalls, "It was an enormously exciting, exhilarating time in spite of all the hardships and difficulties. When I think of what my life was like then, the hard work, the stress, the pressure, the exhaustion, I look back and say, 'Jesus, did I really like this stuff? I must have been crazy!' But that's just it, it was just one of those things that carries you along because it's so exciting, you put up with all the bad things."

Smith took the Linda Blair dummy home with him every night, he didn't dare leave it in the studio storage room, and would put it in the passenger side going up the West Side Highway. The head of the dummy was loose, and whenever Smith would stop and start the car, the momentum would make the dummy's head turn.

Driving home, the traffic was usually stop and go, and as Smith recalls, "There'd be someone right alongside me who would suddenly see this weird face looking at them, and I'd go ahead. I'd look in my rearview mirror and I could see these people trying to catch up with me. Of course the traffic wouldn't let them, they were trapped way back there and they couldn't get a second look! It was great fun."

Probably the most basic special effect was Regan's puke, and reports vary as to what the exact ingredients were. Primarily it was Anderson's pea soup, supposedly mixed with oatmeal and other ingredients for consistency. Linda Blair hated vegetables at the time; ironically, she's a staunch vegetarian today.

For Regan's bedroom, Friedkin had a "cold room" made, putting a big restaurant air conditioner on top of the set, running it all night, and in the morning the set would be forty below.

"The 'cold room,' what an understatement," says Terence Donnelly. "Picture this . . . it's ninety degrees outside the stage on the streets of New York. We come to work and immediately suit up in Eddie Bauer's finest quality arctic cold weather gear." Sweat froze on people's bodies, and the cold filled the air with moisture, causing a light snowfall on the set.

Like Hitchcock and Kubrick on their films, Friedkin was extremely secretive throughout the shoot. He wouldn't let anyone into the screening rooms, and sometimes he'd bolt out of his chair, and look in the hallway to see if anyone was peeping through the door.

If you know your *Exorcist* or Friedkin folklore, you know the director liked to fire guns on the set to startle the actors, and get the reactions he wanted out of them. "I wanted to create chaos on the set to produce a chaotic reaction," the director said. One day Friedkin was trying to get the right reaction from Max von Sydow and it just wasn't coming, so he fired off a gun, and a member of the crew dropped a dead chicken from the rafters. "I will never reveal the perpetrator's name but suffice to say, the set was never again the same!" says Donnelly.

One of the priests working on the film told Friedkin that in a case of real-life possession, the obscenities spewing out of someone's mouth would be even worse than what was already written. Blatty recalled Friedkin telling him, "I want the most steaming, horrendous obscenities that you can give me."

"I sat down and wrote the ugliest stuff I could possibly think of," Blatty said. "I never knew how far I should take it." Dick Smith recalled that when Blair yelled "Your mother sucks cocks in hell" during the shoot, the stagehands cringed.

Years later, Blatty saw the film after the soundtrack was redone digitally. "When I heard it I was shocked. In the past, the dialogue was always muddled and muddy, but now every word was crisp and right in your face and I wanted to sink down in my seat. The fact that my son was sitting next to me made it much worse." Mercedes McCambridge, who provided the possessed voice of Linda Blair, was considered "the world's greatest radio actress" by Orson Welles. McCambridge had chronic bronchitis, which also created the wheezing noises that split into octaves onto the soundtrack.

The Exorcist, and later *The Omen*, had religious advisors on the film. Father William O'Malley taught English and drama at McQuaid Jesuit High School in Rochester, New York, and there were several other priests on the film as well.

"I think they not only enjoyed our being there, but were also incredibly puzzled because we were happy," O'Malley says. "We didn't have anything that they believed was essential to human life: money, fame, sex, power."

One day Friedkin said to O'Malley, "Can I ask you a personal question?"

"Sure."

"Do you mean to tell me you don't get laid."

"No, Billy, we don't get laid."

"Then why are you happier than me?"

As *The Omen* would also do, several incidents around the *Exorcist* shoot were played up to the press, including the set mysteriously burning down and several deaths that occurred during the shoot. As for whether these things happened because the film was playing around with dark forces, O'Malley said, "Nah, it was a bunch of crap. It was all hype. Jack McGowan died, but he was an alcoholic who had emphysema, so there was no surprise there."

O'Malley became the subject of *Exorcist* folklore himself when he was infamously slapped by Friedkin to get the right performance at the end of the film. It happened at about three in the morning after a very long day. Donnelly recalled, "The O'Malley slap was a shock not only to this Irish Catholic-bred kid but to the entire crew."

Friedkin would signal Donnelly to roll camera and sound so the actors wouldn't know. They would also slate takes at the end of a scene so the actors wouldn't be aware they were rolling. Donnelly thought Friedkin was going to cue the gunfire to get a reaction out of O'Malley, instead he lurched on to the set and slapped him.

"He belted me to get my adrenaline going, and I'm eternally grateful to him," O'Malley says. "He made all the difference in the world. It's awfully difficult to spill your guts with all those people standing around smoking at two in the morning, looking at their watches, hoping they'll get to bed. You give your best friend the last rites fifteen times in a row, you're just doing it by the numbers, and all of the sudden he rocked me to my heels, got out of the way, and I knew instinctively what I was supposed to do."

After Friedkin called cut, he bounded over to O'Malley and gave him a big kiss, then a stagehand offered the father an inch of Scotch. "Billy was not the kind of guy who could rationally explain to you what he wanted," O'Malley says. "He's a gut director. And at least in my case his gut was right on . . . he had drawn out of me more than I thought I had to give."

The most difficult shot of the film was the light coming through the window as Max von Sydow arrives to perform the exorcism, an image that was also used in the film's ad campaign. The shot was inspired by René Magritte's painting *The Empire of Light*, and Friedkin wanted the light to come through Regan's window with the shade down. "You can't make a shaft of light through a shade," director of photography Owen Roizman said. "You have to have a sharp source of light."

Finally, when they got what they wanted and rehearsed it with fog, it looked great. But when they started shooting, a wind came and blew a lot of the fog away. Roizman suggested another take, but Friedkin loved the imperfection, which probably made it look even more realistic. "Great. Print it. Let's move on."

"That shot was an ordeal to get," says Donnelly. "It took us two full nights just to get it right." Roizman would also say, "That was the biggest challenge of the movie, no question about it." They used six huge Ritter fans to direct the machine-generated fog, which was churning out several blocks away, onto the set. "There was so much smoke blowing around Georgetown, a neighbor called the fire department," Donnelly says.

The Exorcist was a difficult enough shoot when Friedkin decided to shoot the film's introduction in Iraq. Friedkin felt the beginning of the film would "set the mythological underpinning that would set the rest of the film. I felt that was very important to tell the audience that this is a timeless battle of good and evil."

"At the end of the prologue you can see the antagonist and the protagonist on each side of the screen," says Father O'Malley. "Pazuzu is on one side of the screen, Merrin is on the other, the little girl is just the battlefield. The demon doesn't want the little girl, he wants the priest, and he wants Merrin because he apparently had a conflict with Merrin before which he lost."

The Iraq shoot was very difficult and dangerous. As Donnelly recalls, "Due to the fact that we were so behind schedule at the end of our New York and Washington schedules, our Iraq adventure came not in the spring, when the desert temperatures would have been tolerable, but in July, when you could fry an egg on the tailgate of the camera truck. The British camera crew had a thermometer on their truck that read the centigrade equivalent of 140 degrees during midday, and that was the highest temperature that it could show! It was so brutal that it became dangerous, so it was decided that we'd venture out to shoot at dawn for a couple of hours, retire to the relative comfort of our spartan accommodations until the worst of the heat had dissipated, then return to the set for a couple of hours at the end of the day. Every day you would wake up and have good light by 7:00 A.M., and by eleven, it was 130 degrees in the shade. We'd have to go into our tents, shut down, and resume at 8:00 P.M."

As if all of this wasn't enough, during the shoot a coup was under way to try and unseat the sitting president of Iraq. It ended quickly, and forty-two perpetrators were publicly hung in Baghdad. The crew was anxious, to say the least, and Jean Louis D'Carme, the French soundman, had a shortwave radio and listened for developments from Radio Paris.

For the Iraq shoot, "Warners didn't want to let me go," Friedkin recalled. "The United States had no diplomatic ties with Iraq. Iraq was at war with Syria, Iran, and Kuwait. We were detained for three days while there was a coup in the country. I went to Iraq because I thought it would be wonderful for the movie. But I endangered people's lives. I was a schmuck. Today I would shoot the opening in the Mojave Desert with a lot of guys in bedsheets."

The Exorcist shoot was scheduled for 105 days, but ended up totaling 200 days, ending in March 1973, where by comparison, *The French Connection* was shot in fifty days.

Hyams recalls the studio reaction to the budget and schedule overruns as "panic. It was very hard, but it was like its own monster. It was like the James Cameron thing years later with *Titanic*. He's got control over the beast, and nobody else does. I don't think anybody else could have finished it. I think people wanted to kill Billy Friedkin, but I don't think they ever would have thought of taking him off the movie. There was nothing they could do, they just had to get it done."

Friedkin has been well known for his explosive behavior on set, his nuclear temper tantrums, his dark moodiness. There are many horror stories about working with him, most of them are already in other books, and many who survived the experience of working with him have . . . ah . . . complicated feelings toward him, to put it mildly.

Bud Smith, one of the editors who worked on *The Exorcist* who also worked with Friedkin on a number of films, recalled, "Billy from the first time I met him in Chicago was no different than he was during *The Exorcist* or *Sorcerer* or *The Brink's Job* or *Cruising* or *To Live and Die in L.A.* He is the same character. He has no respect for authority at all."

Years later when Smith tried to get Warner Bros. to do a documentary for a *Cruising* DVD, the response from the studio was, "Number one, we hate the fucking movie, and number two, we hate Billy Friedkin."

"Billy's style is often perceived as manic, unfair, and generally obnoxious," says Donnelly. "Those of us who survived as many adventures with him as I, learned early on that the way to keep Billy on your side was to deliver exactly what was asked of you. Certainly no less, and hopefully a bit more. On occasion he would practically reduce me to tears with his bombastic temper, but I realized at some point during the making of *The Exorcist* that I was being used as a sounding board (or as a substitute for a punching bag). When it was awkward for him to express his frustration with an actor's performance, he would take it out on his closest supporters. Once I was able to rationalize these attacks in that way, it was an easier cross to bear for sure. I never did like it, but it became a part of the job for me."

Donnelly worked with Friedkin on a number of films, and like many who worked with Billy, had a falling-out with him. Friedkin wanted Donnelly to be the unit production manager on his 2000 film, *The Rules of Engagement*, but Donnelly went to produce an ABC miniseries instead. Donnelly saw it as a career choice, where Friedkin saw it as a breach of loyalty. Still, Donnelly says, "When I pass on, he will come to my funeral and deliver a tribute to me that I would cherish, I'm sure. If he predeceases me, I will do the same for him. The concept of love-hate originated on a Billy Friedkin set I'm sure."

Owen Roizman recalled, "There were times on *The Exorcist*—many times—when I just thought, 'This isn't worth it.' But in my case, it was early in my career and I figured I could use another good credit. I couldn't survive on just *The French Connection*. So I stuck it out and I'm glad I did. I'm probably the only cinematographer who's done two films with Billy!"

The Exorcist had a dense sound mix with a lot of great little aural tricks and subtleties. Lalo Schifrin (whose innumerable great scores include *Cool Hand Luke, Bullitt,* the theme for *Mission: Impossible,* and many others) was going to compose the original score for *The Exorcist,* and was recording it on a soundstage with a 110-piece orchestra. Friedkin didn't like what he heard, "I fucking hate this," and told Schifrin in front of everyone, "It's over, you're out of here." (Schifrin did use some of the music he wrote for *The Exorcist* in 1979's *The Amityville Horror.*)

Then taking a cue from Kubrick, Friedkin decided to use source music instead, and he received a bunch of music from people who wanted to score film. "In those days, it wasn't CDs or tapes, it was LPs," he recalled. Friedkin grabbed a hundred records, would drop the needle on one, listen to a few notes, then move on to the next. But when he dropped the needle on an LP labeled "Tubular Bells," written by Mike Oldfield, he found what he was looking for.

Just watching it on a Moviola, Blatty thought *The Exorcist* was a masterpiece. Nessa Hyams has only seen *The Exorcist* twice in her life, "and I can still see the movie in my mind," she says. "I can still see shots from the movie, they stay in my mind forever and ever."

To the surprise of just about everyone, when *The Exorcist* went to the MPAA, it received an R rating without any cuts. " 'Your mother sucks cocks in hell' raised some hackles, but otherwise I don't recall even being asked to shoot alternate dialogue," says Donnelly.

Father O'Malley says, "When you get nitpickers like that over-looking the crucifix scene, the language, all the terrifyingly ugly things in that film because they thought it fit into the context, that is an achievement." As Blatty said, "*The Exorcist* isn't a pointless rambling demonic visitation. It's about the struggle for a man's soul."

Like Kubrick, Friedkin was anal about the theaters *The Exorcist* played in, the quality of projectors, sound systems, and so on. Dave Slaven, the film's associate producer, recalled, "We had a crew go around to the twenty-six theaters *The Exorcist* was going to open at to examine their production and sound facilities, and a couple of places had to make changes or we weren't going to give them a print."

"I knew the names of all the projectionists," Friedkin said. "I had them replace the screen at the Mann Theater in Minneapolis. I told them I wouldn't send the print if they didn't fix it, and they believed me. I sent guys from Warners to check the light on the screen. I called every theater every day for six months to check to make sure the sound levels were right. I loved it. I could control the way audiences saw it."

Richard Lederer recalled the awareness and tracking on *The Exorcist* was through the roof, but Warner Bros. was cautious in releasing it. "Once they had the book they were scared to death they had it," Lederer says with a laugh. "There was tremendous interest, more interest than ever before on any movie in my time. There was very little for me to worry about it in the marketing because it was gonna go bang."

When the studio asked Lederer what the marketing plan for the film should be, he said, "I can recite it in about a dozen words. We open the theater doors and get the fuck out of the way." Lederer felt the movie should open in a hundred theaters, and told the Warners brass, "I don't understand you people. They're dying out there to come and see this movie."

The Exorcist and *The Sting* opened on the same day, December 23, 1973, and *The Exorcist* first opened in twenty-four theaters. Once *The Exorcist* exploded, Warners scrambled to get as many new screens as it could. *The Exorcist* grossed $160 million, $89 million in rentals in its initial run, and for a time *The Exorcist* was the biggest-grossing film in Warners history. (With rereleases *The Exorcist* has grossed $232 million domestic, $441 million worldwide.)

Opinion in the religious community was mixed. In the Catholic community, "It was very positive," said Father O'Malley, "especially the conservative Catholics who you think would be completely put off by a child saying, 'Your mother sucks cocks in hell.' I think it's because they're more against evil than they're against a few bad words."

Blatty was especially pleased to find *The Exorcist* was bringing people to God, just as writing the novel brought him back in touch with his own faith. "There was a significant increase in vocations to the Jesuit priesthood," Blatty says.

Yet Billy Graham denounced the film, and Reverend Juan Cortes, a Jesuit at Georgetown University, said, "You can't bring people to God by scaring them," a ludicrous statement considering that's what many religions have done since the dawn of time. Fundamentalist Hal Lindsey said the film "sets the stage for an attack by Satan."

The Exorcist was nominated for nine Academy Awards and won two, best screenplay adaptation and best sound. *The Exorcist* was beaten out for best picture by *The Sting*, and Friedkin felt he got the shaft because George Cukor, the director of *My Fair Lady*, bad-mouthed the film, calling it a disgrace. During the Oscar ceremony, Candice Bergen and the famous mime Marcel Marceau presented the best sound award, and when Bergen announced *The Exorcist*, Marceau mimed throwing up.

The Exorcist has been seen by many as a major turning point where Hollywood took horror films seriously, and it continues to enjoy a long second life.

Both Blatty and Friedkin have mixed feelings that *The Exorcist* is what they'll be best known for. "You know what it's gonna say on my tombstone? It's going to say 'The man who directed *The Exorcist*,'" Friedkin said. Ellen Burstyn is more amazed she's remembered for the film than anything else she's ever been in. "It had an enormous impact way beyond anything we could have imagined," she said.

The Exorcist also marked the beginning of the golden age of makeup artists, which would soon fulfill its promise with Rick Baker's innovative work in *An American Werewolf in London* in 1981, Rob Bottin's tour-de-force effects in *The Thing* in 1982, and Tom Savini's breakthrough with *Dawn of the Dead* in 1979.

With horror being taken much more seriously as a genre, there was now more money going to makeup and special effects. "This kind of stuff was always in B movies that had B movie budgets," Baker says. "You had very little time and money to make a monster. You did the best you could in the time, but you can't do a masterpiece, you're lucky to get something done. When movies like *The Exorcist*, which was an A movie and a horror movie, were being made by great directors with a budget, you could just do better work. It definitely made a big difference."

SIX

JUST WHEN YOU THOUGHT IT WAS SAFE

How Tobe Hooper brought cinema verité realism to horror with *The Texas Chain Saw Massacre,* and how Steven Spielberg scared everyone off the beach with *Jaws*

Orson Welles said, "The enemy of art is the absence of limitations," and horror is a genre where a low budget often can work to a movie's advantage. "There were certain qualities that low-budget horror movies had that work to their advantage in terms of unnerving an audience," says *Alien* screenwriter Dan O'Bannon. "I noticed that with *Night of the Living Dead* and *The Texas Chain Saw Massacre,* these films were crudely made, and they were clearly not made by any established studio, but by a bunch of guys somewhere. Right away that gave you the feeling that there were no civilized restraints on the people making this film. If they follow that by slapping you in the face with some horror that you've never seen before, then you're completely disarmed because you're now convinced that the people making this movie are psychos and they'll show you anything!"

This is certainly how many people besides O'Bannon felt about *The Texas Chain Saw Massacre*. As Joe Bob Briggs, "world's foremost drive-in critic," has noted, newcomers to *Texas Chain Saw* are "inevitably stricken with a vaguely uneasy feeling, as though the film might have actually been made by a maniac."

Even the director of *Last House on the Left* was shaken. "It looked like someone stole a camera and started killing people," said Wes Craven, who saw the film in Times Square. "It had a wild, feral energy that I had never seen before, with none of the Band-Aids that soften things. I was scared shitless."

Bill Mosely, who went on to star in *Texas Chain Saw* sequels, saw the first *Texas Chain Saw* on a double bill with *Return of the Dragon* in Boston in 1974. The audience was cheering Bruce Lee on, whooping and hollering, but once *Texas Chain Saw* started, "it sucked the air right out of the auditorium."

Mosely saw the first *Texas Chain Saw* a number of times after that, hoping the low budget would start to show through and it wouldn't feel as realistic. "Finally I'd see the zipper in the costume, I'd be able to say, 'It's only a movie'—but it never happened!"

Castle of Frankenstein magazine, which along with *The Monster Times* was one of the celebrated horror fanzines of the day, even wrote that *Texas Chain Saw* "extends the boundaries of cinematic terror and revulsion to the point where we are now forced to redefine the term 'horror film.'"

Alison Macor, author of *Chainsaws, Slackers, and Spy Kids: 30 Years of Filmmaking in Austin, Texas*, says, "As often happens with some independently made films, the conditions of *The Texas Chain Saw Massacre*'s production—low budget, tight shooting schedule, lack of resources—actually made the film more convincing and realistic. Its realism and gritty look, even the awkwardness on-screen

of some of its principal actors, create a very effective tension throughout. As a viewer, you feel as hot and tired as Pam and Kirk by the
time the characters find the Leatherface house."

And as with many low-budget horror films, enthusiasm went a
long way. As production designer Bob Burns recalled, "There was an
enormous amount of raw energy that helped carry it."

"It was our energy and enthusiasm," says makeup artist Dorothy
Pearl. "We were really up to the challenge of it, and determined to
make it really good. It has a lot to do with one's youthfulness and
gaining experience. We were so young that we got through it. I can't
imagine doing it in your forties and fifties, I think you'd get so
tired."

When many filmmakers make their first horror movie, it's often
after they've seen a lot of crap in the marketplace, and know they
can do better. "The horror genre had gotten kind of boring," Hooper
said. "I loved the genre and I wanted to see something that gave me
my money's worth. I figured I was paying two dollars, dollar and a
half a ticket, and I was getting about ten cents worth of scare."

Hooper often told a story that the inspiration for *Texas Chain
Saw* came to him when he was stuck in a department store, a Mont-
gomery Ward, during the Christmas rush in 1972. Tobe was frustrated and tired, and he spotted a rack of chain saws in the hardware
department. "Immediately the idea occurred of how to get out of
this crowd." Either he'd rip through everyone or they'd get out of
the way real quick.

Bob Burns scoffed at this story, and believed Hooper probably
got the idea from the ending of *Last House*. Another story went
that a friend of Tobe's who was living out in the woods, Lou Per-
ryman, had a chain saw in his home, and Hooper was scared to be
around it.

After making a number of short films, and a feature called *Egg-*

shells, Hooper and Kim Henkel went to work on a horror screenplay. They went back to the fairy-tale roots of horror because they were originally going to update Hansel and Gretel, and they also researched cannibals and serial killers when it wasn't easy to find material on them. Also needless to say, the legend of Ed Gein loomed large over the story.

As with many first time, low-budget horror films, Hooper and Henkel wanted to go all out. "I needed to build a fire big enough that it would get noticed all the way out [in Hollywood]," Hooper said. Hooper would also tell people that with *Texas Chain Saw,* he and Hinkel wanted to take everything that ever scared them in a movie, and put it into the film. Another time, he simply said he wanted to do a horror film right.

The film was tentatively titled *Leatherface,* and other titles included *Head Cheese* and *Scum of the Earth.* Then Warren Skaaren, who was head of the Texas Film Commission and sold the film when it was finished, had a stroke of genius: "I've got it," he told Ron Bozman, who would be the production manager on the film, "*The Texas Chain Saw Massacre.*" Home run, Bozman thought.

"We could have had the lousiest movie in the world and everyone would have watched it because of the title," said Marilyn Burns, who played Sally. At one point E! claimed that *The Texas Chain Saw Massacre* was the most recognized film title in the world, even beating out *Gone with the Wind* and *Debbie Does Dallas,* and this probably still holds true. Skaaren went on from the Texas Film Commission to become one of Hollywood's top screenwriters and script doctors, his credits including *Top Gun, Beetlejuice, Batman, Beverly Hills Cop II,* and *Days of Thunder.*

Henkel and Hooper went around trying to raise funds the usual way, hitting up "anybody with a buttonhole" for money, as Kim put it. A former Texas legislator, an attorney, even an alleged marijuana smuggler helped finance the film. Ron Bozman, who was the production manager on *Texas Chain Saw*, and later went on to work on a number of films with Jonathan Demme, recalled the budget ended up at $100,000 in cash, and $40,000 deferred.

Principal photography began on July 15, 1973, and the shoot went about thirty-two days. Hooper and company were fortunate to shoot during the summer because they could make the film with borrowed cameras from the University of Texas that weren't being used while school was out. The crew had just come out of the University of Texas, were a pretty capable group, and were willing to work for the credit and experience.

It was also unfortunate to shoot during the summer because of the heat, and there was no air-conditioning in sight. Every day was 95 to 100 degrees, one report said the heat got as high as 110. For the opening sequence in the van, it was Tobe, Daniel Pearl, an assistant, and the soundman all crammed together with the actors, and the windows were rolled up so the whistling wind wouldn't ruin the dialogue. One day the heat got so bad, the actors were rolling cold beer cans over their bodies, and poured the cold brew on themselves instead of drinking it.

The *Texas Chain Saw* gang worked twelve to sixteen hour days for three weeks with only one day off per week. Everybody wore the same clothes because the movie takes place in less than a twenty-four-hour period, which as you can imagine, got pretty smelly during a long, hot Texas summer.

The *Texas Chain Saw* family were all a group of dirty, Mansonesque freaks, but Leatherface couldn't help but stand out and become the focal point of the movie. Gunnar Hansen, the man who would be Leatherface, was a giant, three-hundred-pound Icelandic American who edited a poetry journal named *Lucille*, and was working as a carpenter in Austin. He ran into a friend who said some guys were in town making a movie, and he'd be perfect to play the killer. When Hansen came up to meet Hooper, and Tobe saw him lumbering across the street, he had the part right there.

When Hansen took the Leatherface gig, he figured, "Well, it's just a summer job, I'll be able to tell my grandchildren about it." Years after the fact he remarked, "I'm happy I did it, but they'll probably put 'Gunnar Hansen—He Was Leatherface' on my gravestone."

For the Leatherface mask, Burns wanted a material that was the right consistency and translucency of human skin, and it was a combination of thin fiberglass insulation and latex. In the screenplay, it would be determined later whether Leatherface would be shown unmasked, but they made the right decision not showing who was underneath. The less human Leatherface seems, the better, and taking off the mask to reveal a Norwegian hippie would have brought the film to a screeching halt. There was also a scene where Leatherface spoke that was later eliminated, because Hooper felt, "It doesn't work, there's too much intelligence in the character."

Texas Chain Saw has been called "the quintessential Austin film," and it opened the door for other filmmakers from the area like Richard Linklatter (*Dazed and Confused*), and Robert Rodriguez (*Spy Kids*). Hooper wanted someone from Texas to shoot the movie, yet he ultimately went with Daniel Pearl, who was from New Jersey, but considered Texas "his adopted home."

With some exceptions, Hooper primarily wanted *Texas Chain Saw* to be shot hand-held. Pearl had shot a lot of hand-held camerawork before, and he knew Hooper "wanted that sort of fluid movement and tension."

"I had little knowledge about lighting," Pearl says. "I had to be efficient with light, and the little that I knew about lighting had me lighting in a very documentary vérité style." The technology he had to work with, and the equipment, forced him to light it that way. The film was also pretty much shot in sequence with a few exceptions. "I don't know why it was scheduled that way, but it kinda made sense. It's a journey, they go to the house . . . I don't think it was illogical to shoot it in order."

The crew didn't have much equipment to work with, most of the sound was recorded with one boom mike, there were a few lights, and one chain saw. Bozman was the mechanic, although they got lucky because the chain saw never broke down on the shoot. "We tried to get McCulloch to promote it or give us some free chain sws," Bozman continues with a chuckle. "But needless to say, they were not amused. It wasn't a great product placement opportunity."

To make sure no one got hurt, the blade was dulled down, and Bozman took out the clutch so the motor couldn't engage the blade. Only in certain scenes, like when Leatherface cuts the door open, was the live clutch put back in.

"It was generally pretty safe, but not because we were smart enough to be safe, we were just lucky nobody got hurt," Bozman says. He adds that things did get "a little scary" the night everyone ate the pot brownies.

Someone on the crew made brownies for everyone without disclosing the secret ingredient, and when Hansen got the munchies, he went back to the brownie stack for more. Hansen was chasing Marilyn up the stairs with the chain saw when the brownies kicked in, and was still high when he kicked down the door, making it hard to really concentrate because they only had the one door and he didn't want to screw up the shot. "I trust Gunnar 100 percent," Marilyn Burns said. "But not Gunnar on brownies, with a chain saw, running up the steps, take forty-four, oh, no."

"Everybody was completely stoned, certainly things went into a warped reality, I mean seriously out there," Bozman continues. "But we were lucky nobody got hurt. I can recall a Band-Aid but nothing more." (Long after the shoot, Marilyn Burns could still hear the buzzing of a chain saw in her sleep.)

The family lived in a house in Quick Hill, Austin, that was built in the 1890s and was occupied by a bunch of hippies. Burns called it, "A nice old Victorian place." The *Texas Chain Saw* crew arrived, and promised "We're not going to mess up your house," like famous last words in a Three Stooges short.

For the home décor, the bones in the film were real, and a girlfriend of a friend in dental school sent in teeth. Dorothy Pearl worked for a vet part-time, and knew there was a landfill of animal carcasses outside of Austin where they did a "two week clean out" at the pound. Dorothy says, "I was able to turn Bobby Burns on to it, he went out and collected all those bones, and it was unbelievable how he was able to turn those into furniture."

The animal corpses were shot up with formaldehyde to preserve them. Because of the hot weather, Dorothy wore shorts every day, and once accidentally shot herself with embalming fluid. "I just screamed," she says. "I was so worried it was gonna kill me, but it didn't do anything. I just tried to push it out through the little hole that it made. I didn't inject myself with that much, it was just enough to be afraid. I never had any reactions from it, but it was very, very scary when it happened."

Eventually a bunch of embalmed Dobermans were stacked in a pile and burned, and they melted down like plastic. The smoke and stench blew back into the house, causing many to lose their lunch. Marilyn Burns became a vegetarian for years after the *Texas Chain Saw* experience, and Guillermo del Toro also became "a total vegetarian" for four years after seeing the movie.

At first, Hooper was hoping for a PG rating, although past a certain point he wondered if they could even get an R rating. Hooper recalled, "I put in a lot of telephone calls to the MPAA asking their advice. 'How do I get a PG rating and hang someone on a meat hook?'"

Still, *Texas Chain Saw* never showed as much gore as people thought it did, and got a lot of mileage out of the audience's imagination. "We never considered having a chain saw come through flesh," Bozman says. "You could've pulled that off somehow with prosthetics and things, but it was never planned to see the blood and all that."

With the chain saw as your weapon, and with "chain saw" in the title, knowing the horrible damage one can do, the movie got a lot of mileage out of theatergoers' personal fears they brought into the theaters. "We realized even back then what whatever you can leave the mind to imagine can be much more horrific than what you can show," says Daniel Pearl. "Tobe was well aware of that. That was definitely part of our MO, our credo. When your brain fills in the blanks, your brain will fill it in with something much scarier than you can show."

"Sometimes when you put too much blood in a movie, it gets boring," Dorothy Pearl says. "It doesn't shock you. We wanted to use the amount we did, and when we used it, it would come across very strong."

The scene where Pam is hung on the meat hook was going to have a hook appliance coming out of her chest, and Burns talked Hooper out of it. "That scene is still one of the most memorably gut-wrenching in filmdom without a single drop of blood," said Bob Burns.

The worst part of the shoot hands down was the dinner table sequence, which was shot in twenty-six grueling, endless hours. Instead of getting an old man to play Grandpa, they got a young actor heavily made up to look ancient. The makeup took forever to apply, he swore he wouldn't go through it again, so they shot straight through.

The crew had to use blackout curtains when shooting day for

night, and the temperature rose more than 100 degrees inside. Add headcheese, body odor, and rotting chicken bones to that, and you can only imagine how horrible the stench was to endure. (The house later had to be fumigated.)

It was during this part of the shoot that it finally hit Dorothy Pearl: "We are truly living this thing. We aren't making it anymore." Years after the fact, the cast and crew of *Texas Chain Saw* would recall the shoot like war veterans. "I moved troops through the jungles of Vietnam, and it wasn't as bad as making this film," said Edwin Neal. "A lot of people ask if it was fun," said Hansen. "Fun was the one word that never came to mind."

"Grueling?" asked Paul Partain, who played Franklin. "Surely you jest. I am a native Texan. I thrive on rolling around the state in hundred-degree temperatures in an unair-conditioned econovan with seven other sweating persons, chewing on raw sausage because some twit of a production assistant didn't know she was supposed to buy the cooked kind. Add thousands of watts of light to an already hot, dry, windless set filled with decaying chicken bones and other pleasant set decorations and you have gonzo filmmaking!" With the film being shot in continuity, the last shot with Leatherface spinning around in circles, then finally hurling the chain saw away, seemed a fitting end to it all.

The Texas Chain Saw Massacre premiered in Austin, Texas, right before Halloween in 1974. "I just thought it would make a couple hundred thousand, which to me was a lot of money," says Dorothy Pearl. "The fact that it made so much more was so great and surprising."

Jim Siedow, who played the head of the family, thought, "It would be a pretty good class B drive-in movie, and that's all we thought it would be. Hell, what happened to that thing is just amazing. There was no doubt in all our minds that the thing would show at about three drive-ins in south Texas, and that would be the end of it, and we'd all have a laugh about it when we got old. When it went crazy, we were totally astounded."

AIP and Bryanston, the company that made $100 million from releasing *Deep Throat* and was owned by Joseph and Louis "Butchie" Peraino (aka the Piranha brothers), were both interested in the film, where Fox, Warner Bros., Columbia, and Universal all passed on it.

The Peraino brothers were allegedly connected to the Colombo crime family. Allen Danziger, who played Jerry, recalled that the Perainos "made the Sopranos look like Boy Scouts," and looking back on the situation, the *Texas Chain Saw* gang had to have been smacking themselves in the heads: we entrusted this movie to *the Piranha brothers*?

Adding to the audience's unease, Bryanston Pictures also created the myth it was based on a true story, and this may have happened by accident because the Piranhas may have misunderstood the introductory speech in the film, and believed it was indeed based on real events.

Reviews were all over the board from praise to absolute disgust. Rex Reed called it "the *Jaws* of the midnight movie," the *L.A. Times* called it "despicable . . . ugly and obscene . . . a degrading, senseless misuse of film and time," *The Los Angeles Herald-Examiner* called it "gory and horrible," and *Harper's* called it "a vile little piece of sick crap . . . with literally nothing to recommend it."

Leonard Maltin gave it three stars and called it a "sweat-inducing, claustrophobic, unrelenting suspense-comic-horror film. Classic and influential—and nowhere nearly as violent as it's reputed to be." Stephen King also called *Texas Chain Saw*, "Still the all-time champeen when it comes to pure fright."

Over the years, *The Texas Chain Saw Massacre* would get serious critical acclaim, and praise from filmmakers such as Steven Spielberg and Ridley Scott, but it also was a big hit on the grindhouse circuit. Television writer Fred Rappaport saw *Texas Chain Saw* at a run-down theater on Forty-second Street, long before one of New York's sleaziest areas was cleaned up. Usually the Forty-second Street audiences would yell back at the screen, whooping and hollering throughout, turning up their ghetto blasters when they got bored, but *Texas Chain Saw* was so intense, the theater was very quiet, which was pretty unusual.

"I remember there were rats running under my seat at one point," Rappaport says. "I was really into the movie, and all of the sudden I saw rats. I jumped so high! But it didn't dissuade me from watching the rest of the film, it was just a momentary setback."

The Texas Chain Saw Massacre reportedly made more than $20 million dollars when it was first released, not that anyone involved in the film saw any of that money. After nine months a check for $47.07 came in (one report claimed the check was for $28.45). Some who had points only made a few hundred dollars.

When Robert Kuhn, who had invested in the film, and Warren Skaaren went to confront the Piranhas in their office, Louis Peraino was sitting at his desk, with two big palookas on each side of him. He told Kuhn and Skaaren that Bryanston's accountant was out sick, and wouldn't be back for a week or two. When Kuhn demanded to see the books, Peraino said, "You ain't got the balls to sue me."

The Piranhas eventually went to jail for transporting obscene materials across state lines (a print of *Deep Throat*), and the company went under in 1976. Like Romero and company with *Night of the Living Dead*, the *Texas Chain Saw* gang had to learn a hard lesson from signing a bad deal.

Billy Kelly, a special agent for the FBI who went after gangsters working in porno, recalled that when he taught police recruits, he'd ask them how many had seen *The Texas Chain Saw Massacre*. After

75 percent of the classroom raised their hands, he'd say, "Congratulations. You sent two and a half million dollars of your money to the Colombo family in Fort Lauderdale."

It took years to hack through the jungle of red tape, but the legal wrangling over the film was finally resolved in 1982, and New Line rereleased the film in 1983, where it grossed another $6 million, which was pretty good for a film that was nine years old, and already available on home video.

In 2004, Gunnar Hansen and Marilyn Burns found themselves in London promoting *The Texas Chain Saw Massacre*'s DVD release, and had a laugh about it at the local pub. Who could have predicted they'd be having a beer in London thirty years later thanks to the film? Hansen also marveled that there were even Leatherface action figures, bobblehead dolls, and *Texas Chain Saw* lunch boxes.

Where something like the shower scene in *Psycho* has been studied to death, it's been harder to pick apart what made *The Texas Chain Saw Massacre* so horrifying, but there's certainly more than filmmaking technique that creeped in and seeped out of it.

When the entire movie was finally cut and mixed, editor Sallye Richardson recalled, "I got really scared, because it became something other than what it was. It went into another dimension, it was like a spirit went into it. It became that entity that people now look at."

"It's just potently made," says Bozman. "The terror, the shock, it just remains strong throughout, and never lets up. Tobe knew exactly what he was doing."

Al Ebner was head of TV publicity at Universal when one day he got a call from Sid Sheinberg, who was then head of Universal Television. "I got a new kid directing a segment of *Night Gallery*. Would you keep an eye on him?"

The kid was directing two cagey old veterans, Joan Crawford and Barry Sullivan, so Ebner dropped by the set and just observed. Ebner called Sheinberg back and told him he was needlessly worried. "They're both respectful of him, they're listening to him, and they're doing what he says he wants done."

A kid in his twenties directing on the lot was unusual, but after all this was the period after *Easy Rider* in 1969, where young film-makers were finally getting their break, even at conservative companies like Universal.

"There weren't that many young directors at the time," says Carl Gottlieb, who wrote the screenplay adaptation for Peter Benchley's *Jaws*. "There were notable exceptions like Truffaut and Orson Welles making *Citizen Kane* when he was twenty-five, yet for the most part it wasn't a place where kids worked. But Steven was never a kid. He was always like a little adult when it came to making movies."

Says William S. Gilmore, who was the production manager for Spielberg's first theatrical feature *The Sugarland Express* and *Jaws*, "He was twenty-five when he directed *Sugarland*, he was twenty-seven when he directed *Jaws*, but you put a camera in Steven's hand, he was forty-eight! He was a very skilled man with a camera, and he had a great eye." John Stacy, who worked on *Jaws* in the sound department, says, "We also learned from Steven. Just being around him we learned things we thought we could never do."

During the *Jaws* shoot, Gottlieb recalled being amused that Spielberg, at the ripe old age of twenty-seven, told him, "I'm over it with lenses, I went through my experimental phase already."

Until Universal turned its feature division around, the company's primary bread and butter was television. If you were shopping a movie, it was usually your last resort if you couldn't sell it anywhere else, until the company realized they couldn't keep making *Airport* sequels forever.

"In the early seventies, Lew Wasserman decided it was time to turn the creative engine of the motion picture side of the company around," says former Universal president Thom Mount. "Wasserman organized a resurgent attack on motion pictures, and we quickly got reorganized as a motion picture division. Wasserman really felt there couldn't be a future for the motion picture side of the company unless we went very young, and built up something fresh."

Universal would finally turn the movie division around with *The Sting,* the company's first Best Picture win since *All Quiet on the Western Front,* and would cement its power with *Jaws,* not that anyone knew it would be a major milestone for the movie business at the time. "Universal was not excited about this picture," said Roy Arbogast, who was Bob Mattey's right-hand man working on the mechanical shark. "*The Hindenburg* was the one they put everything into. They left us out there to die."

When everyone came back from the long, arduous shoot, production designer Joe Alves recalled, "We were really looked down upon as those guys out there making this dumb shark movie."

But when a bunch of information about *Jaws* was fed into the mainframe computer at Universal, it calculated the film would make $65 million in the States. Gottlieb recalled, "They felt it needed to be reprogrammed, because it just wasn't logical."

Born in Cincinnati, Steven Spielberg decided he wanted to be a filmmaker when he was twelve and his family had settled in Arizona. His father Arnold had a twenty-dollar Brownie 8 mm camera, and when Steven would critique his father's shaky camera moves and bad film exposures, his father let him direct the home movies from there on out.

When making movies, Spielberg went from nerd to local super-star. For his 8 mm film *Fighter Squad*, he was able to convince the local airport to let him film there and use their fighter and bomber planes. He'd also completed a feature-length, two-hour-plus science fiction film before he was eighteen, *Firelight*, which helped pave the way for *Close Encounters of the Third Kind* down the road.

Spielberg came to Sid Sheinberg's attention with his short subject *Amblin'*, and he left college for a seven-year deal directing television for Universal at $275 a week. After directing the *Night Gallery* episode, his next big step up was the TV movie *Duel*, which aired on ABC on November 13, 1971.

Duel was based on a real incident where Richard Matheson and fellow *Twilight Zone* and *Outer Limits* writer Jerry Sohl were playing golf on November 22, 1963, and heard about the Kennedy assassination. When they left the golf course, a truck was speeding on their tail. They yelled at the driver to slow down, but he couldn't hear them, and they had to run off the road to escape.

"A lot of people have told me the same thing happened to them," Matheson says. "It's probably still going on because truck drivers take pills, uppers, in order to stay awake so they can make more money, and I think it drives 'em a little over the edge."

Spielberg could make a scary movie because he knew fear very well when he was young. "I was born a nervous wreck, and I think movies were one way of transferring my own private horrors to every-one else's lives," he said. "It was less of an escape and more of an exorcism. I was really able to alleviate those fears by making movies."

A great white shark was a natural for a movie villain. They can range from seventeen to thirty-six feet in length with three-inch teeth, they have skin that feels like sandpaper, and they're man-eaters.

Jaws was inspired by several real-life shark attacks. Benchley based the story on an incident that happened in 1965, where a seventeen-foot, 4,500-pound shark was caught off Montauk, Long Island. The fisherman, Frank Mundus, was the initial inspiration for Quint.

Peter Benchley was the son of Nathaniel Benchley, who wrote a number of children's books, and the grandson of Robert Benchley, the famed humorist who wrote for *The New Yorker* and *Vanity Fair.* He would spend summers on Nantucket as a boy and loved the ocean. When Benchley was fifteen, his father paid him every day to write for the entire summer, and when he was older he worked at *The Washington Post, Newsweek,* and *National Geographic* as a journalist. (Benchley was also a speechwriter for Lyndon B. Johnson).

Peter Benchley was reportedly down to his last six hundred dollars when he made the deal to write *Jaws* with Doubleday senior editor Tom Congdon in 1971. Benchley couldn't come up with a title, and his father Nathaniel reportedly suggested *Jaws* twenty minutes before the book went to press.

When the galley copies for *Jaws* went around in 1973, producers Richard Zanuck and David Brown read the coverage by a studio reader and wanted in. Universal paid Benchley $175,000 for the rights and for him to write a screenplay.

Zanuck and Brown knew it would be an exciting movie from galley stage, and at first, they figured they'd make the movie for about $750,000 to $1,000,000. They also thought of hiring a more experienced director, but then realized they didn't want rear screen projection, and actors sitting in a tank. The producing team had previously worked with Spielberg on *The Sugarland Express,* and although it wasn't a hit, they were happy with the film, and said, "Let's do another picture together."

Production designer Joe Alves first got the galley sheets for *Jaws* in June 1973. The book wasn't out yet, and the biggest thing about it was the Zanuck and Brown name. They were about to win the Academy Award for producing *The Sting* with Julia and Michael Phillips.

Alves was thrilled to get the assignment because he thought *Jaws* would be a big movie. But Alves also recalled that the studio didn't think it would be a big film, otherwise they would have hired a bigger art director. Alves was the youngest person in the art department, and he and Spielberg had worked together before on the TV show *The Psychiatrist*, as well as on *The Sugarland Express*.

"He always had a clear direction about his career and he wanted to make the right moves," Alves said. "He was being cautious about taking on a picture like *Jaws*."

Alves recalled the movie was stopped four times. "They didn't have the confidence in it and didn't want to spend six million dollars." Alves had a big meeting with Universal and the special effects department. Alves said what he wanted for the movie, and he was told it was too expensive and would take too long.

"This is ridiculous—we just bought this book, now you're saying it's impossible? I think it *can* be done."

"Do it. You go out and make the shark."

Not realizing the grief they were in for, it was decreed that there would be no miniatures and no tanks, it would be filmed on the ocean with a full-sized mechanical shark. Spielberg also insisted on shooting on the water, which would heighten the movie's realism. If they shot it on the ocean, it would make the shoot a difficult, expensive proposition in the long run, but Alves, Zanuck, and production manager Bill Gilmore all agreed as well.

"I can't tell you how many times that came back and bit us on the ass," Gilmore recalled. But "despite all the problems it caused us, ultimately it's why the picture was so incredibly successful, because everybody was *there*. It was a real sea and a real boat."

Alves did research on sharks at the Scripps Institute and an ichthyologist loaned him a big set of shark jaws. Alves used it in the film, putting it in Quint's window, which nicely framed the boat as it set off to get the shark.

To build the mechanical sharks, Alves called on Bob Mattey, who was head of the Disney mechanical special effects department. Mattey had created the squid from *20,000 Leagues Under the Sea*, and had also worked on *The Absent-Minded Professor, Mary Poppins,* and *The Love Bug*. Alves recalled that Mattey was "the most optimistic guy in the world. He convinced me he could do it . . . I sold the studio on the idea that he could do it."

Mattey came out of retirement to do *Jaws,* and although he was much older than the rest of the crew, he still had a lot of pep and excitement in him. When the crew was exhausted from the long hours they had to work, Mattey would jump up in the air, click his heels, and say, "Come on, boys, we got work to do!"

Three sharks were built for *Jaws* that cost $150,000 each, and the requirements were that it had to move its head and tail, and that its mouth could open and close. The sharks were made of polyurethane rubber, and their skeletons were made of tubular steel. Two of them were "half sharks," where one side was the shark, the other side hydraulics. Chopped walnuts, sand, and dust were used in the paint for the shark's skin texture. The shark was also covered in zinc, to keep it from wearing away in the water.

Of course, if *Jaws* were made today, it would probably be done with a CGI-animated shark. "They could make anything happen, and it would be better technically," said Bill Butler, the film's director of photography. "[But] there's a certain feeling of reality that comes through the camera lens that the audience can feel . . . CG images are harsher and crisper; they lack the mellowness of film. It's the same with motion control cameras. They're precise, but [camera operator] Michael Chapman hand-holding a camera was more artful."

For a long time, it was just Steven and Joe Alves working on the movie, but Spielberg, knowing full well *Jaws* wasn't going to be an easy shoot, started to get cold feet, and tried to leave the film three times. "I stayed up at night fantasizing about how I could get myself off this picture short of dying," Spielberg said, "how I could drag myself, break my leg or shoot myself in the foot, fall down a flight of stairs and hurt my arm and maybe feign, Oh I can't direct this movie, my arm doesn't work. I was out of my mind for a while." When legendary producer Jennings Lang, who helped develop *The Sugarland Express* for Steven at the studio, found out Spielberg was going to quit *Jaws*, he called the director and yelled at him, "You're going to stay with the movie. You're going to do a great job."

When it was clear that the *Jaws* script needed work, Carl Gottlieb got a call on a Sunday from Spielberg. "My whole involvement on *Jaws* came from the fact that it was Sunday and they couldn't find a writer!" he recalled. "Where do you get a writer on Sunday?" Two days later, Gottlieb flew out to Boston to rewrite the script and act in the film as Meadows.

"I was brought aboard *Jaws* to add humor and humanity to the story," Gottlieb says. "The characters were somewhat cardboard, they spoke in a kind of standard moviespeak. When you add humanity to a scary movie, what you do is create enormous sympathy and empathy with the characters on-screen, so when they're killed they're not Soldier One or Teenager Two. They're human beings. You mourn their loss, you're stunned by the violence of it."

Gottlieb was a comedy writer, and good scares, like good comedy, depend on timing, structure, and execution. "A shock moment in a horror film is like the punch line to a joke," Gottlieb says. "If it's not set up properly, it doesn't work well. If it's handled clumsily or bobbled, it doesn't work at all."

To play Chief Brody, Spielberg turned down Charlton Heston, who let it be known that he wanted the role, because you'd know from the first frame he'd save the day. At first Spielberg was resistant to casting Roy Scheider because he didn't want a tough guy playing the role. During the shoot, Spielberg told Scheider, "I don't want to ever feel you could kill that shark," and at the end of the film when the shark is blown to hell, Scheider gives a great reaction of exhilaration and surprise that he actually pulled it off.

Gottlieb recalls, "There was a tension on the set between Steven and Roy Scheider because Roy was coming off *The French Connection* where he played a tough guy, a broken-nosed New Yorker who could handle himself. And Steven made him wear glasses right up until the two-barreled chase. The moment where Scheider loses the glasses and goes into his bag for his gun, we postponed that as late as possible. It was also somebody's idea to make him fearful of the water, and it adds to his vulnerability."

"I wanted somewhat anonymous actors to be in [*Jaws*] so you could believe this was happening to you and me," Spielberg said. "Stars bring a lot of baggage with them, and those memories can sometimes, at least in the first ten minutes of the movie, corrupt the story."

Says Gottlieb, "One of the reasons some of the best horror films had unknown casts or leads who got their fame and notoriety from being in the film is that the audience had no expectations. They had to accept the characters at face value."

In the novel, Brody's wife was cheating with Hooper, but Spielberg kept that out of the film. "You can't have three people on a boat being pursued by a killer shark where one of them would like to see the other dead," he said. "I wanted you to care so much for the characters you wouldn't want to see them get eaten."

Spielberg debated whether Hooper would live or not until late. Gottlieb said, "Aw, let him live." And considering they cut out the affair with Brody's wife from the novel, "We don't have to punish him for having sex!" Gottlieb said, referring to what later became a notorious rule of horror. However Quint was always destined for Davy Jones's locker. "Had to die," Gottlieb said. "Too big. Too 'marked by fate.'" Says James Fargo, who was the unit production manager on *Jaws*, "In a way you knew going in that he was gonna get it, because he spent all of his life going after the big one, like in *Moby-Dick*."

Robert Shaw took the role of Quint because his wife, Mary Ure, urged him to do it. Spielberg initially worried that Shaw would be over the top like in his other performances, then he realized the role should be played that way.

It was also Shaw who finalized the famous *Indianapolis* speech, which Gottlieb said "was always planned as a very big moment in the film. It's the last dialogue scene in the movie, and it's followed by forty-five minutes of hard action. Steven and I always referred to that scene in our outlines as the 'just before the battle mother' speech."

Howard Sackler, who wrote *The Great White Hope*, did some work on the *Jaws* script, and the *Indianapolis* scene was his initial idea. "In the book, Quint was an enigmatic shark hater, so Sackler tried to give him some sort of backstory," Gottlieb says. "Sackler was in the U.S. Navy, and was a sailor and yachtsman himself, so it was natural he would come up with that. Because it was a pivotal speech, and inherently a cornerstone of the character, we gave it a great deal of thought and effort. Steven was asking everyone for help and suggestions, and every writer he knew was calling and sending ideas."

John Milius, screenwriter of *Apocalypse Now*, was one of the writers who contributed, and he also wrote the Quint line, "I'll find him for three, but I'll catch him, and kill him, for ten." Gottlieb gave all the materials to Robert Shaw not long before the scene was going to shoot. Shaw came to dinner, which he didn't do often, and after dinner he said, "I think I got that speech licked."

The housekeeper dimmed the lights, Shaw performed the scene, and it was "an unforgettable and powerful reading." The room was silent when he finished, then Spielberg broke the silence by saying, "That's it. That's what we're going to shoot." Gottlieb recalled it was "almost exactly as it appears in the movie."

Patrick Jankiewicz, author of the *Jaws* companion book, *Just When You Thought It Was Safe,* says, "The *Indianapolis* scene is what propels *Jaws* into true greatness. It's the scene where our heroes all truly bond and it gives Quint a horrifying backstory that explains his motivations. With just the actor Robert Shaw's description, the sharks he conjures in our mind's eye are far scarier."

When Joe Alves went location scouting, he drew up a map of tide tables. The seas were rough in Nantucket, and he had to turn back, but on his journey he discovered Martha's Vineyard and it felt like the perfect location for the film.

The *Jaws* shoot arrived in Martha's Vineyard in May, and Spielberg and company were hoping to get out by the first of July, or the summer crunch, when people came out to their summer homes and the population went from 5 to 8,000. The local papers were reporting that *Jaws* was coming to town, and people started coming down to see "that shark movie" getting made.

Universal hoped the film would wrap in the summer of 1974, which gave Universal the option of opening the film for Christmas.

At first, everyone on the film stayed in hotels, but as the shoot dragged on into mid-July and August, the rooms were all booked, and they still hadn't gotten to the shark yet, so everyone found small houses to live in on the backstreets of Edgartown.

The house Spielberg lived in, where the nightly script meetings took place, had six bedrooms, was up on a hill, and overlooked the ocean. One guest there recalled it feeling like a rustic log cabin. Spielberg's parents also visited the set, and Jeffrey Kramer, who played Deputy Hendricks, helped carry their luggage up to their room.

When the sharks arrived on trucks from California, Kevin Pike, a crew member, naïvely asked Roy Arborgast, "Did you test these in the Pacific Ocean?"

"We haven't even had them in the water yet."

Pike had never worked on a movie before, but he knew right there it was gonna be a long shoot.

Spielberg hired Bill Butler to shoot *Jaws* because they had previously worked together on Steven's TV movies *Savage* and *Something Evil*. "A lot of what a director looks for is just to have a good time while they make their picture," Butler said. One day they ran into each other in the studio parking lot where Butler mentioned, "I hear you're making a movie about a fish."

When Butler told Spielberg he wanted to shoot hand-held on the boat, "he just about fainted," Butler recalled with a laugh. Spielberg didn't think it could be done, and wanted the boat scenes shot on a tripod, but Butler showed him hand-held could work, and it was the first time a film at sea was shot that way. To keep the audience from getting seasick, Butler and Spielberg made sure to keep the horizon level.

Butler shot second unit on *Deliverance,* and that's where he got the idea to shoot at water level for *Jaws.* "Regardless of what was on top of the water, or what was happening in the scene, the fact that the water was right on the bottom of the edge of the picture told you, 'There's something down there.'"

Butler knew *Jaws* would be a hit the first week it went overschedule. Universal's policy was that directors didn't go overschedule. You got a warning the first day you fell behind, the second day you were replaced. When *Jaws* went over the first week, Butler told Spielberg, "It's been a week and we're still here. You have nothing to worry about. They must think we've got a great project going here or we would be gone, because we're over further than any picture at Universal has ever gone over!"

When George Lucas got a look at the shark in the North Hollywood hangar, he told Spielberg, "If you can get half of this on film you will have the biggest hit of all time." As it turns out, Spielberg was able to get only a third of their planned storyboards into the movie. Anyone who has even a passing interest in *Jaws* knows the shark often broke down and wouldn't work, which turned out to be a blessing in disguise because it added great character development to the film. Dreyfuss, Gottlieb, Shaw, Scheider, and Spielberg would meet at the house, and work out scenes together that were to be shot the next day when they couldn't shoot the shark.

"Everyone was focused on the story, and whenever we made changes, we really talked them through," Gottlieb says. "Every change was very carefully examined before it became reality so we didn't create problems for ourselves later."

In addition to its top-notch action and terror, Spielberg biographer Joseph McBride also says that *Jaws* "stands out as a superb and intimate character study of three men under pressure. That wasn't much recognized at the time, and indeed Spielberg's skills as a director of actors are still not fully understood. The fact that the film is mostly about a flawed father figure, Roy Scheider's Chief Brody, coming to terms with his responsibilities was also largely lost in the shuffle."

"Steven and I were both impressed by *The Thing* as young movie-goers, and we knew [hiding the monster] was a valuable device," says Gottlieb. "We couldn't show the monster, we didn't have a monster! If we had a full budget for the shark and the shark was working, you would have seen much more of it. It may have been problematic in that it wouldn't have been as effective of a movie, but I would give Steven credit enough that if we had a shark for all the shots we needed a shark for, I think he would have created an equally terrifying movie, we just would have gone about it a different way."

Yet in the early scenes of the film where nude swimmer Susan Backline is attacked, and the scene on the pier where two local townspeople try to catch the shark with a pot roast, you were never going to see the shark, whether it was working or not (the first time the shark was originally going to be revealed was when the Kinter boy on the raft gets eaten). Backline said, "They never, ever consid-ered showing the shark" in those scenes. "That's exactly how Steve wanted it filmed."

"There was always at least some of that in the script that they were not going to see it for a while," says Michael Chapman, who was the camera operator on *Jaws*. "It was just lurking and lurking."

"The scenes early in the film were written to show the power of the shark without revealing it," says Gottlieb. "If you reveal the shark, then it has to bite. By having the shark off camera, that was deliber-ate, to give it more menace. That's why there's very little of the shark eating the guy at the pond, and why you never see it at the beach."

Says Bill Gilmore, "We got only maybe two, maybe three shots a day with the shark because it took so long to get it in position, and get it to work, it was a painstaking process, but you only need a little bit of the shark, a few feet here, a few feet there, and it works. The rest is reactions and long shots. Every usable frame that we shot is in that picture! We didn't have much, but what we have and the way it was presented was extremely effective."

Thankfully, the scenes involving humans moved much faster. "When we were shooting on land, everything went well," says James Fargo. "As soon as you got out on that boat, you had problems." Jeffrey Kramer, who played Deputy Hendricks, recalled Spielberg shooting three takes per scene "tops" without the shark. "Steven knows what he wants," he said. "He gets it and moves on."

Spielberg acknowledged that today's audiences would want more shark, but *Jaws* didn't overstuff the turkey. It showed the shark just enough, and when they were able to show it, the scenes delivered.

Of course this begs the question how successful *Jaws* would have been if Spielberg was able to show the shark as much as originally planned, and he would later say, "I think the film would have made half the money had the shark worked."

It was also hard to keep the shark hidden before the movie came out. One night a young reporter from *The Washington Post* came up to the hangar where the shark was kept when it wasn't shooting. The time was post-Watergate when *The Washington Post*, and Woodward and Bernstein, were household names. At the mention of *The Washington Post*, the security guard got starstruck, and let the photographer in to take pictures. When Al Ebner, who was the unit publicist on *Jaws,* found out, he went through the roof, and had to call Ben Bradlee, the legendary editor of the *Post*, and plead his case. "Ben, come on, what's this kid doin'? We're only tryin' to protect this thing for the public so they can see it and enjoy it."

The Washington Post did run a picture, a very close headshot that didn't give away too much, but then the law came down that the shark had to be covered whenever it wasn't shooting. Bruce was kept hidden under a giant canvas sheet where you could only see the rear fin sticking out.

Jaws wasn't just a difficult shoot because of Spielberg's youth or relative inexperience, it would have been a nightmare shoot for any director. Arbogast recalled working five months straight with one day off, and twelve-hour days were the minimum.

"I don't think anybody really understands what it is to shoot on water until they do it," says Ebner. "It's just impossible. Anyone who's never shot on water and thinks they'll be in command . . . it's a very humbling experience." Ebner also said trying to get the shark to work in those conditions "was like trying to build a thatch hut in a snow-storm."

"It was certainly the most difficult shoot I ever did," says production manager Bill Gilmore. "No one had ever taken on the Atlantic Ocean in a small, thirty-foot boat, and we had to fight tooth and nail to get that film in the camera."

During the *Jaws* shoot, "Steve was a very scared young man," Ebner remembers. "On the weekends, we'd wrap on Saturday night. Some people would take a plane just to get away, we were very close to New York, or they'd fly to Boston. I said to Steven, 'You've never left the island, why don't you get away?' He said, 'I'm afraid I won't come back.'"

However, the *Jaws* shoot wasn't drudgery for everyone involved. Scheider loved to lay out and work on his tan, but then notes started coming in to the camera department asking to keep him out of the sun because he kept changing color from shot to shot. On *Jaws 2*, Scheider spent so much time in the sun, and his tan got so progressively dark, that he had to be color-corrected in the film lab.

"My memory of it was it was enormous fun," says Michael Chapman, who was Bill Butler's camera operator on *Jaws,* and would go on to be the director of photography of *Taxi Driver* and *Raging Bull.*

"I had a wonderful time. It was Martha's Vineyard in the summer. People pay thousands of dollars a week to be there, and they were paying us! We were on the water, I've been a water person my entire life, so it was wonderful for me."

The *Jaws* shoot ultimately went 159 days. Even being in a wonderful location like Martha's Vineyard, Dreyfuss felt like Papillon, who was trapped on Devil's Island. The Martha's Vineyard residents got sick of the production being there. It got to the point where some put up JAWS GO HOME signs in their windows, and some locals slashed tires and put sugar in the gas tanks of the production boats.

Jaws was originally budgeted at $3.5 million, but with the production delays it went up to $8.5 million, and overhead brought it to $10 million. There was definitely a lot of tension and stress over the budget and production problems, "But it wasn't *Waterworld*," said Zanuck. "Dick and I had been hardened to that kind of thing before," Brown recalled, referring to when they both worked at 20th Century-Fox, and a number of big movies on their slate like *Star! Hello, Dolly!* and *Tora! Tora! Tora!* all went in the toilet.

Verna Fields was not only a great editor, but she was also one of Spielberg's buffers protecting him from the studio when *Jaws* went overbudget and overschedule. Fields is fondly recalled today by many who knew her and worked with her. Film journalist Gerald Perry, who interviewed Fields for a publication called *The Real Paper*, called her "a nice, approachable, call-me-by-my-first-name Jewish lady." (Several *Jaws* alumni also grew teary when recalling Verna.)

Jim Troutman, who worked as a sound editor on *Jaws*, says, "Verna was always open to the people down below her. She felt everyone should get the credit they deserve. Everything was straight up, no crap, straightforward. On her tombstone it should have said, 'I'm an Honest Broad.'"

Spielberg was introduced to Fields by screenwriter-director Matthew Robbins (*The Sugarland Express, Dragonslayer*), who knew Verna from his USC days, and felt they'd make a good match. Fields let USC alumni like Walter Murch and Caleb Deschanel use her home Moviola, and was very generous with advice.

Fields was also a big inspiration and groundbreaker for women in the industry. Nikki Rocco, president of distribution for Universal, says, "In my early days with the company, it was very rare that a woman held an executive position. Verna was the one who gave me the encouragement to seek a career and not just push a pencil, and as a result, I became brave under her guidance." Before *Jaws* was released, Verna Fields was named executive consultant on all Universal films, and became vice president of feature production in 1976.

Most involved in the *Jaws* shoot don't believe the urban legend that Fields "saved" the film. "But Verna Fields did a hell of a lot," said Zanuck. "She was really brilliant." Troutman says, "I think Verna taught Steve what editing can do."

The last lines of the film, Scheider saying, "I used to hate the water," and Dreyfuss saying, "I can't imagine why," were written by Gottlieb and added into the film when it was in ADR (automated dialogue replacement). "In the script, there were a few places that were actually marked 'dialogue to be added during looping,'" said Gottlieb, "and it was at that time, when we were looking for a way to finally end the movie, that I wrote those two lines." Says James Fargo, "It's a *Casablanca* ending."

The sound department also saved the day when they needed to extend the "you're gonna need a bigger boat" scene, because the screaming in the audience at the first preview still hadn't died down when Scheider said the classic line. A cut was added to the scene, and when Scheider moved his foot, Troutman added a creak in the floor to cover the cut.

When the shark suddenly jumps out of the water, Spielberg wanted it as loud as it could go on the sound mix. "It was loud by the standards we had then," says George Fredrick, who also worked as a sound editor on *Jaws*. "We tried to push the maximum limits that we had to work within. Steven would say, 'I want to hear it louder,' the mixer would tell him, 'We can't give you any more, it won't go on film.' In other words, it would go into distortion. I think the first time you actually saw the shark in the film, Steven wanted that as big as you could make it."

When the shark jumps out of the water, a sound effect is used called "hizz and fizz," which is created by shaking up a soda bottle, hurling it through the air, and when it hits the cement, it explodes and is propelled by carbonation, making the fizz as it's flying away.

John Williams's score was also great icing on the cake, and Spielberg would also credit 50 percent of the film's success to Williams's music. Like when Warren Skaaren came up with the title *The Texas Chain Saw Massacre*, or the first time Led Zeppelin jammed together, it was a no-brainer this was gonna knock it out of the park, but initially Spielberg needed a little convincing.

The first time Williams played the *Jaws* theme for Spielberg, the director laughed.

"You're joking."

"No, I think this could be fun. What do you think of this?"

Spielberg thought it was too primitive, wanted something more melodic for the shark theme, then Williams explained he hadn't made a serious drama like *The L-Shaped Room*. "You made yourself a popcorn movie."

The iconic *Jaws* artwork that appeared on both the paperback edition and the film's poster was created by Roger Kastel. Kastel came up in the great age of illustration doing a lot of work for paperbacks, and magazine ads. "It was a wonderful time," Kastel says. "Paperback covers were such a great market for artwork then." Kastel did a number of paperback covers a month, because the top price you'd get for one was $1,000, although Kastel did get a $10,000 bonus for the *Jaws* painting.

The shark on the cover of the hardcover edition looked like a sock puppet, and Kastel took the cover concept much further, with greater, more realistic detail. Bantam loved the initial sketches, their only comments were about making the shark bigger, and they weren't sure about the shark's teeth, but Kastel did his research at a museum, and assured them it was an accurate representation of a shark's jaws. From sketch to the final painting, the artwork took two or three weeks (it was a thirty-by-forty oil painting on a masonite panel).

Spielberg loved the artwork, and he told several people at Bantam it influenced his approach to the movie. "Spielberg was very strongly impressed with it," says Oscar Dystel, who was president at Bantam for the *Jaws* paperback. "He told me it made a major impact on his approach to the movie."

Then David Brown decided to use the paperback cover illustration, and also use it for the movie poster so there would be a consistency with the image representing the film and the book. Without carefully reading the fine print, Bantam signed away the rights to the illustration, and then you saw the rising shark everywhere on beach towels, toys, and T-shirts. Dystel felt great about seeing that illustration everywhere, "except they somehow secured more rights than we thought we gave them!" (Len Leone, who was Bantam's art director and also oversaw the cover for *The Exorcist,* says Bantam lost out on $2.5 million from the merchandising of the *Jaws* illustration.)

The first sneak preview of *Jaws* was in Dallas at the Medallion

Theater on March 28, 1975, scheduled for 5:30 P.M. Ads didn't have the title, just the cover art from the paperback, and driving by the theater at three in the afternoon, there was already a big line waiting to get in.

The shark was everyone's biggest worry. If the audience laughed at it, it was all over. But once Zanuck and Brown heard the first scream, they knew they were in. When the shark popped out and scared Roy Scheider, the first time we see the shark clearly, "It was at that moment that we knew we had a giant hit," said Zanuck. "They bought it! They bought that dummy shark!"

During the screening, Ebner looked away from two people sitting in front of him for a moment, and when his head turned back, their chairs were empty. "They all slid so far in their seats they were practically on the floor!" he says.

"The studio was in shock seeing the audience reaction, then they're looking at the cards, which just confirmed what they'd seen," Ebner continues. "But you didn't have to read the cards once you saw the audience react. You knew you had a big movie."

A second show was added at 11:00 P.M. that night, and after the screenings, there was a big champagne celebration in the Registry Hotel penthouse that went until four in the morning with Spielberg, Sid Sheinberg, Bill Gilmore, Verna Fields, and John Williams. Says Gilmore, "For those of us who went through all of the pain of trying to get it on the screen, it was a welcome reward."

Then *Jaws* previewed on March 28 at the Lakewood Theater in Long Beach, California, where the movie got a standing ovation. Gottlieb says, "When *Jaws* previewed in Long Beach, it was an extraordinary reaction, I've only seen it a couple of times. I was at a sneak preview of *M*A*S*H,* and that was the only other time until then I'd seen an audience go nuts like they did. The minute the lights came up and the movie was over, everybody knew it was gonna be big. Nobody knew how big, but you could not argue that it wasn't gonna be a hit, that it wasn't gonna be an audience picture. It was quite clear."

Joseph McBride, who wrote the definitive biographies of Frank Capra and Steven Spielberg, was a reporter at *Daily Variety* when he attended the third and final *Jaws* screening at the Cinerama Dome on Sunset Boulevard on April 24, 1975.

"As a press screening almost two months before the film's opening, the Dome screening was unusually early," McBride recalls. "In those days, studios would usually screen their pictures for the press a week or so before the opening. In retrospect, showing it so early was clearly an expression of unusual confidence and a great way of building further industry buzz. There was great anticipation at the screening. The buzz was out that the film was good and that it might be a hit."

McBride recalls the moment he knew the movie would be a smash hit was when Susan Backline was yanked underwater and dragged back and forth by the shark underneath. "That was a startling shock that literally caused the audience to jump. You could see the audience moving in a wave and you could hear a collective gasp. I remember thinking then that the film would surely be a major box office hit."

Right before the release of *Jaws*, the June 2 headline of *Variety* read, WITH ADVANCES BUILDING UP, 'JAWS' $8 MIL TAB LOOKS LESS WORRISOME. The article also called the advances for the film "record, or near record." Theater owners weren't happy about a ninety/ten split for a twelve-week run on a movie, until they actually saw the film. One theater owner wouldn't give in to Universal's terms until he saw the film, then wired the studio the next day: "Hell has just frozen."

Another telltale sign the movie was going to be big was when

Robert Shaw saw an early cut of the film, and wanted to exchange his salary for 1 percent of the profits (he was turned down).

The trade review in *Variety* two days before the film's release was even more promising: "Excellent filmization of the book. Smash b.o. outlook. Getting right to the point, *Jaws* is an artistic and commercial smash. Producers Richard D. Zanuck and David Brown, and director Steven Spielberg, have the satisfaction of a production problem-plagued film turning out beautifully."

The *Variety* review also made it clear that hiding the shark really paid off: "The creature is not even seen for about fifty-two minutes, and a subjective camera technique makes his earlier forays excruciatingly terrifying all the more for the invisibility."

The rest is Hollywood history. *Jaws* made $7,061,513 opening weekend, which today would be $70,000,000, almost twice what *The Dark Knight* made opening weekend. On September 5, sixty-four days after the movie opened, it became the most successful film in motion picture history, in its time. Final gross was $260 million domestic, $210,653,000 foreign, $470,653,000 total.

"*Jaws* changed the landscape," says Mount. "No one understood how much money there was in the movie business before *Jaws*. Not only was it the first blockbuster by any reasonable definition, it was the first wide release picture, and what we now see as a standard pattern. It set new standards at the company for what we had to do, and how we had to do it.

"The picture really is a horror film, and it would have been made by Universal in the fifties in the classic pantheon of classic Universal monster horror pictures. But by broadening the public accessibility of the story, making it a kind of everyman's story, the picture really worked in the same way that no monster movie had worked in American filmmaking since *King Kong*."

Jaws, like *Alien,* was also considered one of the first B movies done the A way. Greydon Clark, who starred in, wrote, and directed a number of B movies throughout the sixties, seventies, and eighties (*Satan's Sadists, Dracula vs. Frankenstein*), says, "From *Jaws* forward, the majors have been making exploitation films and making them very well. *Jaws* is a great picture by a great director, but it's an exploitation film. It's a monster that comes out of the water and chews people up. It used to be that those kinds of films were not made by the majors, which is why the independents then kind of had that genre to itself."

Zanuck and Brown said they could tell what scene was playing in the film by the sounds coming out of the theater, and Gottlieb says, "After the movie opened, my wife, Steven, and I would be out having dinner, we'd look at our watches and say, "Oh, 8:37 the head's gonna be poppin' out of the boat in Westwood!" So we'd go to the theater, the manager would let us in, and we'd stand in the back and watch the entire audience levitate out of their seats when the head popped out. That's the highest form of involvement in a film, what they call a kinetic response, where your body responds to something you know is just a flat image on a screen."

Jaws also raised hackles with the fact that it got away with a PG rating. The studio did add a disclaimer—MAY BE TOO INTENSE FOR YOUNGER VIEWERS—on the poster, and it's believed several frames were cut from the scene where the guy loses his leg in the pond to avoid an R.

Paul Heller, one of the producers of *Enter the Dragon,* starring Bruce Lee, complained about *Jaws* getting a PG to *The Hollywood Reporter.* Heller said, "I can't seem to find consistency in terms of attitudes towards violence by the ratings board," to which Jack Valenti responded, "In the view of the rating board, *Jaws* involved nature's violence rather than man's violence against man. . . . If this were a man or a woman committing violence as seen in *Jaws,* it would definitely go in the R category. But it's a shark, and I don't think people will go around pretending they're a shark." (Heller found this ludicrous. "Violence is violence. The emotional impact on a child, whatever it is, is what's involved.")

Eric Pleskow, who was then president and CEO of United Artists, also brought up *Jaws* in arguing with Richard Heffner, chairman of the ratings board, about the futuristic sci-fi film *Rollerball* receiving the R.

"I don't understand. In *Jaws,* there's a severed leg floating down and that gets a PG, and you're giving *Rollerball* an R."

"Well, that's because of imitative violence."

"You're absolutely right," Pleskow replied facetiously. "In New Jersey, they built a couple of these arenas, and a few people have been killed."

"Really?"

Of course people avoided the beach in droves that summer, but as it was also reported in *Time,* "Vacationers are in fact flocking in ever greater numbers to the seashore." A lifeguard at Jones Beach said he was getting hundreds of questions a day about sharks, and some beachgoers just stayed on the shore, watching the horizon for fins.

With the unprecedented success of the film came the later spin that *Jaws* and *Star Wars* ruined movies by creating the blockbuster, a debate that still comes up more than three decades after the movie's release. David Brown said, "We have been accused of creating the blockbuster, (but) people forget that it was a darn good movie."

On the thirty-fifth anniversary of *Jaws, New York* magazine film critic David Edelstein wrote, "I've never blamed *Jaws* for what happened: It's the best summer movie ever made. People forget how real it seemed. It was shot in a beach resort (Martha's Vineyard) in the days when Steven Spielberg was forced to use the world as he found it instead of building one from scratch. I loved the tension between the texture of life and his smooth, beautifully modulated, movie-ish technique."

On the film's thirtieth anniversary in 2005, there was Jawsfest, which was held from June 3 to June 5 in Edgartown, Massachusetts, the real Amity Island of the movie. Spielberg sent a taped message where he said: "I think it's amazing the shelf life this film has had and that's only because fans like yourselves have kept this film alive and [in] people's consciousness and I only have to thank you for that." He also apologized for blocking people's driveways for seven months.

The buoy Susan Backline clinged to in the beginning was there, and she embraced it for the first time in thirty years. Greg Nicotero, of the modern-day makeup masters KNB, also made a replica of the shark's head from Joe Alves's designs. Some who came to Jawsfest hadn't seen one another since working on the movie, and Joe Alves recalled, "Last time we were here, we couldn't wait to get off this island!"

Looking back on *Jaws*, fans and critics alike agree it's held up very well. *The New York Times* wrote on the film's thirtieth anniversary: "Without any of the Cuisinart editing, whipping camera movements or computer-generated effects that have rendered today's commercial blockbusters visually incoherent, using only camera placement, perspective and editing, Spielberg succeeds in completely shredding any sense of safety in the viewer. His craft dovetails beautifully with that of his heroes, who defeat the shark through brains and not brawn."

When asked what it would take to make a scarier film than *Jaws*, Gottlieb said, "A scarier movie than *Jaws* would be one in which greater fears would be raised, even more interesting characters would be put in jeopardy, the plot could not be guessed, the surprises would be even more unexpected, and the ending even more cathartic. Good luck."

SEVEN

GIVING THE DEVIL HIS DUE

How *The Omen* tried to one-up *The Exorcist*, how Stephen King launched his career by giving a tormented nerd psychic powers, and how the Italian troika of Dario Argento, Mario Bava, and Lucio Fulci brought a new foreign flavor to fear

You have been warned. If something frightening happens to you today, think about it. It may be The Omen.

The Omen began with producer Harvey Bernhard, who had previously produced TV documentaries, as well as the blaxploitation classic *The Mack*, about the rise and fall of an Oakland pimp. David Seltzer, who wrote the screenplay for *The Omen*, says, "Harvey had seen *The Exorcist*, and I credit him with being smart in having a sense as an entrepreneur that the marketplace could take another one of them."

Seltzer had previously written an adaption of *Willy Wonka and the Chocolate Factory*, *The Hellstrom Chronicle*, a well-received science fiction film, and *The Other Side of the Mountain*, a true story about a champion skier triumphing over becoming paralyzed. When Bernhard approached Seltzer about writing *The Omen*, he was initially resistant.

"I frankly don't do things I can't learn from," Seltzer says. "Well, how naïve I was, because I'd never read a Bible. In the course of my research I became a fan of the Bible. I'm fascinated with mythology, and the characters and the narrative of it. Whoever was writing those books had a fantastic imagination."

Seltzer was struck by a passage in the Book of Revelation that says the unholy one will rise from the eternal sea. One of the interpretive texts Seltzer consulted said that the eternal sea is metaphoric for revolution and turmoil, which sparked the idea of the Antichrist being adopted into the world of wealth and politics, because revolution is usually political. Then Seltzer thought, "Well, what if you were born to somebody whose ascension would be toward the White House?"

"I had the Antichrist being born into a political family, usurping their power," Seltzer says. "When George W. Bush became president, I said, 'That's my story! The Antichrist made it to the White House!'"

In his research, Seltzer also learned about the number of the beast, 666, and decided to make it a birthmark on the young Antichrist's head. The film was originally called *Birthmark*, and also went under the title of *The Antichrist* before it finally was called *The Omen*. In addition to his biblical research, Seltzer was also a fan of *Rosemary's Baby*, saying, "I never forgot being electrified by it."

Some of the best-remembered elements of *The Omen* are its disturbing set pieces that are hard to get out of your mind: the nanny hanging herself at the birthday party, the priest being impaled by the lightning rod, David Warner losing his head when the brakes on the glass truck give way.

"I was following the structure of *Jaws*," Seltzer says. "*Jaws* was very inspirational to me, because I watched the movie knowing full well a fish can't eat a boat, yet it did, and I jumped out of my seat. So I knew you could lift something like that off the ground and make it believable. The structure of *Jaws* was a dialogue scene, then horror, and occasionally he'd break it up a little bit with two dialogue scenes, but that would only build up your expectation for what kind of ungodly thing was about to happen. It's like reeling in a fish: you pull 'em, then you reel, you pull 'em, then you reel."

Seltzer named his Antichrist Damien after Father Damien, who was one of his idols. Father Damien started the first leper colony in the Hawaiian Islands, and caught leprosy on purpose so he could become one of the people he was serving.

Father Damien was one of Seltzer's idols, he loved the name Damien, but at first he wasn't going to give that name to the Antichrist. He was first going to call him Domlin, after the son of a friend, "just a total obnoxious brat," and Seltzer thought it would serve him right, but his wife scolded him, saying, "You can not do that to that kid." (Seltzer also says he didn't realize at the time there was also a Father Damien in *The Exorcist*.)

Another interesting idea at the core of *The Omen* is that Damien's too young to understand that he's the Antichrist, or the terrible things he's doing. "That was completely the idea, he had no clue," Seltzer says. "He inherited the heaviest mantle that any person born to this earth did. He's controlled by evil, and he doesn't know it. There was a lot of innocent characters in that movie. Everybody was innocent. The most guilty person was Gregory Peck for trying to do a good thing for his wife, but that became his primal sin."

It took about six weeks for Seltzer to finish the script, and Bernhard sent it out to all the studios, who all turned it down, the consensus from everyone was that it was too frightening. With the help of producer Mace Neufeld (*The Hunt for Red October*) the script was eventually optioned to Warner Bros. in the fall of 1974, but when *Exorcist II* went into development, the studio thought *The Omen* would be too similar, and it was stuck in limbo for a year.

If Warner didn't start the film in a year, the project would be free again, so Mace sent the script to director Richard Donner, who then called his agent, Alan Ladd Jr., and implored him to read it. "I think the potential's phenomenal," Donner said. "You've *gotta* read it."

Ladd was due for dinner at Ian McShane's house, but was half an hour late because he couldn't put the *Omen* script down. The option ran out that Monday, and *The Omen* was now at 20th Century-Fox, where Ladd would soon become head of production.

Before *The Omen*, Donner was an assistant director in live television, commercials, and documentaries. He then directed episodes of many of the well-known TV shows of the sixties and seventies including *Route 66, The Rifleman, The Twilight Zone* (Donner helmed the classic "Nightmare at 20,000 Feet" episode), *Perry Mason, The Man From U.N.C.L.E., Get Smart, Gilligan's Island, The Fugitive, Ironside, Kojak,* and *The Streets of San Francisco.*

Donner had also done two feature films prior to *The Omen, X-15* and *Salt and Pepper*, starring Sammy Davis, Jr., and Peter Lawford, but they usually brought him right back into television instead of launching a feature career. "I've always taken a film because I wanted to make that specific film," Donner said "But every project has the potential to be the turning point of your career."

Originally the script showed covens and creatures with cloven hooves, but eventually everyone came to the conclusion that it would be best to make the script as realistic as possible, so that all of the terrible events in the film could be weird coincidences until they reach critical mass.

"Dick Donner said to me there must be nothing in this movie

that you can't believe is actual," Seltzer recalled. "The whole force of this movie was going to be the critical mass of a man's paranoia coming to be realized as actual. Every single event, every single death could be seen as the kind of freak accident that could occur in the world. By the time Gregory Peck's eyebrows go up, you realize something's happening here."

For the most part, Donner and Seltzer were on the same page about the script, and Donner flattered Seltzer by telling him, "This puts *The Exorcist* to shame, it's brilliant shit. All I have to do is not fuck it up."

The only disagreement Donner and Seltzer had was over British actress Billie Whitelaw, who played Damien's nanny, and who was hip to the fact he was the Antichrist from the beginning. Whitelaw made up her own dialogue, and Seltzer says, "She was the only one who was in a different movie. 'Oh, little one, be not afraid.' She was effective because she was creepy, but she wasn't in the same movie as everyone else. I complained about it to Dick, 'You're throwing away this character, please,' and Dick said, 'No, she's brilliant, she's the greatest.'" Seltzer let it go, and Donner otherwise stayed close to the script.

At the time Fox made *The Omen*, a low-budget movie didn't cost an average of $60 million, and the stakes for success and failure weren't so dangerously high. When Ladd was head of Fox, he would green-light smaller movies if they could be made for $3 million or less. If the movie was a hit within that budget range, like *The Omen*, it was a great coup, and if a movie flopped in that budget range, it wasn't the end of the world or the end of the studio.

And along with making a movie for $3 million or less came more freedom for the filmmakers, as long as they stayed on budget and on schedule. "Ladd chose the right people to entrust the movie with,"

Seltzer says. "He was the old-fashioned studio executive who loved movies, loved moviemakers, and let them do their thing."

Charlton Heston, William Holden, and Roy Scheider had all turned down the role of Ambassador Thorn, and the studio was apphrensive about approaching Gregory Peck because his son, Jonathan, had recently committed suicide. But Peck's agent told the studio it was okay to send him the script. Peck liked it, thought it would be a fun movie to work on, and quickly committed. After losing his son, Peck just wanted to get back to work.

Seltzer says, "I think there may have been some connection in his exorcising his own sense of . . . I lost a kid, and when you lose a child, there's no way not to feel at fault."

Donner felt that casting Peck in the lead validated the film, "it raised it tenfold," and everyone else involved in *The Omen* agreed. "Putting Gregory Peck and Lee Remick in it, you're saying to people right off the bat this is not a normal horror picture," says Ladd. "It was scary, but it was classy scary."

"Frankly, without Gregory Peck straight-facing his way through it, without the authority his body of work brought to it, this movie would have been preposterous," Seltzer says.

Gregory Peck taking a starring turn in a horror film was also one of the reasons *The Omen* was heavily previewed before it came out. "It was a different kind of movie than you'd expect to find Gregory Peck playing in," says Gareth Wigan, a former production executive at Fox. "That was very intriguing, but it was also risky. The Gregory Peck audience wouldn't want to see this kind of movie, and vice versa. It was to build it up into something special and unique."

For the Antichrist himself, four kids were auditioned every ten minutes for two days when along came Harvey Stevens. A cute little boy with blond hair and blue eyes, Donner wanted to test Stevens for the scene where Damien throws a violent fit in the car when his adoptive parents try to take him to church. "I'm gonna fight with you," Donner told him. "Even though I say stop, don't stop." Stevens then proceeded to beat the shit out of Donner, and his family had to come in and tear him off. "Take him, dye his hair black," Donner said. "He's the Antichrist." Damien's hair was dyed dark so his eyes would stand out more, and he doesn't talk for most of the film because Stephens was from London's West End, and had a thick accent that wouldn't have come from a well-off family.

Donner also hired Gilbert Taylor, director of photography of *Repulsion, Dr. Strangelove*, and *A Hard Day's Night*, to shoot the film. Taylor came out of retirement, where he was milking cows on his farm, to shoot the film, and once the shoot was completed, George Lucas was shown some footage and hired Gilbert to shoot *Star Wars*.

The Omen was a three-month shoot that began in October 1975, filming in London, Jerusalem, and Rome, and ended at the beginning of January. The film ultimately cost $2.8 million, including its large saturation advertising campaign.

Although *The Omen* was made on a tight budget, Ladd put up $25,000 to bring aboard Jerry Goldsmith to compose the film's soundtrack, and it was money well spent. Using a Gregorian chant for the foundation, Goldsmith's music was terrifying icing on the cake, and it would be the only soundtrack he would win an Academy Award for in his entire career of incredible scores, including those for *Planet of the Apes, Patton, Chinatown, Alien*, and many others.

In reviewing the film for *The Hollywood Reporter*, Todd McCarthy called Goldsmith's score "a major one and [it] represents an indispensable contribution to the impact of the film." Says Seltzer, "I would have to say Jerry Goldsmith kicked it up 50 percent with that score. I thought it was brilliant, and everybody fell over it."

Before *The Omen*'s release, Fox had had a recent run of box office flops like *Lucky Lady*, which starred Liza Minnelli, Burt Reynolds, and Gene Hackman, and the remake of *The Blue Bird*.

The Wall Street analysts were predicting a bad year for the studio, but then the headlines in *Variety* offered a much different forecast: FOX HOPES ANTICHRIST IS SAVIOR. *The Wall Street Journal* also ran the headline, FOX IS COUNTING ON RESCUE BY 2 NEW FILMS, which in addition to *The Omen* also included Mel Brooks's *Silent Movie*, which was released the same month.

Bernhard and Donner were against *The Omen* being marketed as a typical horror film, and Fox brought in an outside advertising agency based in New York, Smolen, Smith and Connelly, to create *The Omen* campaign. (Smolen, Smith and Connelly also handled the advertising for a number of James Bond movies, *Close Encounters of the Third Kind*, and *Star Wars*.) *The Omen* had a great advance poster campaign, and mysterious warnings of doom soon began appearing everywhere.

"Good morning. You are one day closer to the end of the world."
"Remember . . . you have been warned."
"It is the greatest mystery of all because no human being will ever solve it.
It is the highest suspense because no man can bear it.
It is the greatest fear because it is the ancient fear of the unknown.
It is a warning foretold for thousands of years.
It is our final warning.
It is The Omen."

"*The Omen* lent itself to a teaser campaign," says David Forbes, who was in charge of special projects at Fox at the time. "We focused on creating materials that would be classy, scary, and would create some anticipation for the movie. We brought in some outside industry consultants, and that was really a time when it was important to step up and have a better understanding of what you were doing in the marketplace with advertising, testing, research from screening the pictures. We didn't see *The Omen* as a low-entry, quick in-and-out horror film. We thought it was a well-crafted, well-cast, high-quality movie. I don't mean to put it in too high a category either, but clearly *The Omen* and *The Exorcist* were not low-end films."

The publicity for *The Omen* also tried to play up incidents that happened during the shoot, implying it may have been the work of Satan, including stuntmen getting bitten by attack dogs, Gregory Peck's and David Seltzer's flights getting struck by lightning, Richard Donner getting into a car accident, the crew almost taking a plane that went down, and so on. Lance Hendrickson, who had a role in *Damien: Omen II*, recalled, "Everybody seemed to have gotten a memo that said, 'We are gonna look for anything strange going on. Flat tires, car accidents for no reason. Come and tell us, because we want to get that in the paper right away.'"

There was also another funny mishap that happened during the film's release. With *The Godfather* bringing in a new era of darker cinematography, the studios usually had to make two prints of a film: a lighter one that could be seen outdoors at night in drive-ins, and a darker one for theaters. But on *The Omen*, the dark prints accidentally went to the drive-ins, and the lighter ones went to the theaters.

The Omen opened on 526 screens on June 25, 1976, and the critics who liked it saw it as a slick, well-made commercial movie, a harrowing roller-coaster ride.

In the *L.A. Times*, Kevin Thomas wrote, "There's no getting around it. No matter how much you may dislike *The Omen*, there's just no denying that it is an absolutely riveting, thoroughly scary experience, a triumph of sleek film craftsmanship that will inevitably but not necessarily unfavorably be compared to *The Exorcist*."

In *Time*, Richard Schickel wrote, "*The Omen* is like *Jaws*, a brisk, highly professional thriller, in which an implausible tale is rendered believable by the total conviction with which it is told . . . farfetched in subject matter, but not far out in its handling of it, *The Omen* speaks well of the Devil—and of the virtues of solid commercial craftsmanship." Schickel felt for the audience to believe in the film, they needed to take "a slightly greater leap of faith in these secular times to believe in a brainily malevolent shark, all concerned make the jump quite a manageable one." Donner "has a smooth way of burying absurdity in atmospherics and does well with his set pieces, which include many gory, shocking and thoroughly entertaining deaths by special effects." Schickel also pointed out "the use of a sweetly innocent-appearing child as the principal menace is a stroke of pop genius, reversing all generic conventions and audience expectations while avoiding through understatement the kind of queasy excesses of *The Exorcist*."

Rex Reed gave *The Omen* three stars in *Vogue*, calling it "sophisticated, spleen-churning horror in the tradition of *The Exorcist* and *Rosemary's Baby*. . . . Some of the religious mumbo jumbo seems preposterous, but the film is imaginative, riveting, and—ultimately—shatteringly scary."

"Richard Donner's direction fully meets the demands of the material and then some," wrote Todd McCarthy, who was then writing film reviews for *The Hollywood Reporter*. "Long a top television director, Donner's set-ups and camera moves are judicious and often arresting and he pulls off two chilling horror set pieces magnificently, the death of the soothsaying priest in a sudden daytime storm, all the more astonishing and beautiful for having been shot on location, and the investigation of two graves by Peck and Warner and their subsequent attack by killer dogs on a superbly designed studio cemetery set. Donner is clearly in command of his medium."

The Omen, of course, had its detractors and Gene Shalit of *The Today Show* was especially appalled a major studio would spend so much money advertising a film, which today is par for the course: "When a producer spends as much money on ads and commercials for a movie as he spends on making the movie itself, perhaps audiences have a right to suspect that they are being sucked into seeing a piece of junk. And that piece of junk is called *The Omen*."

As with most horror films, the reviews didn't mean a damn thing to the fans, and they didn't stop *The Omen* from becoming one of the biggest hits of the year, grossing $60 million. "It was a huge return on investment," Ladd says. "In those days, it didn't cost you that much money to advertise. Marketing costs have gone up five, six times from what they were at that time. We spent for the entire run of the movie as much on advertising as they spend on one day for films these days."

Not to mention this was in the days of $2 to $3 tickets, which Donner said would put *The Omen* on the level of "a $400 million movie [today]." The success of *The Omen* also gave Fox the money to complete Lucas's upcoming space epic, *Star Wars*.

Inspired by *Love Story*, a huge novelization that made author Erich Segal a fortune, Seltzer also wrote a novelization of the film. It made *The Omen* a number one bestselling paperback about six weeks in advance of the movie, and it stayed on the bestseller lists for several months.

At Academy Awards time, Jerry Goldsmith won the Oscar for *The Omen* score, beating out Bernard Herrmann who was nominated twice, posthumously no less, for composing the scores for *Taxi Driver* and Brian De Palma's *Obsession*.

Jerry Goldsmith was nominated for the Oscar seventeen times in his career, and he didn't want to go to the Academy Awards ceremony when he was nominated for *The Omen* because he didn't think he could handle being rejected again. But Harvey Bernhard and Mace Neufeld were both convinced Goldsmith would win, so he braved the ceremony one more time. Goldsmith was so nervous at the Academy Awards, he was smoking three cigarettes at a time, but he won as Bernhard predicted.

Less than two months after *The Omen* exploded at the box office, *Damien: Omen II* was announced. There were going to be four *Omen* movies total, but the series was cut short when *Omen II* didn't perform as well as expected in the summer of 1978, so Harvey Bernhard decided to settle for three, ending the series in 1981 with *The Final Conflict*. "We had to kill him sometime," he said.

In the wake of the success of *The Exorcist* and *The Omen*, there were many imitations from the majors and the drive-in companies. Warner Bros. had *Exorcist II* in the works, there was the TV sequel to *Rosemary's Baby*, Universal had *The Sentinel*, AIP had *The Devil Within Her, J.D.'s Revenge*, and *The Chosen* (aka *Holocaust 2000*), and Dimension Pictures (not the Weinstein's Dimension, but a seventies low-budget company that also released the *Dolemite* movies) had *The Redeemer*, to name a few, before the "devil movie" trend, as *The Wall Street Journal* called it, got old. "The genre that began with *The Exorcist* and *The Omen* fell into trash very quickly," Seltzer says.

The Omen was finally the film that launched Richard Donner into the big time as a feature director, and he followed up with the enormous success of *Superman* in 1978, and continued to hit pay dirt in the eighties with the highly lucrative *Lethal Weapon* series.

"*The Omen* changed my life," Donner said. "*The Omen* opened up my career. I will be obligated to Alan Ladd, Jr., for the rest of my life. He gave me that opportunity, he believed I could make that picture and could do something with it. From that came the rest of my career. Everything that I hold near and dear all followed because of *The Omen*."

Seltzer went on to write such films as *Table for Five, Punchline*, and he also wrote and directed the high school drama *Lucas*, but when asked if he felt *The Omen* was his legacy as a screenwriter, he said, "Umm, sure." He laughed and added, "Yeah, I don't mind, I think it's a really good piece of work.

"When someone says what have you written, be it anybody, my dentist, and I start going through my credits, I know I better start with *The Omen* and stop there. Everybody remembers *The Omen*, everybody knows it, everybody was scared by it as a kid."

Before the publication of *Carrie*, Stephen King worked at New Franklin Laundry during the summer, making $1.60 an hour, and his wife Tabitha worked at Dunkin' Donuts. King wrote for adult magazines that still ran fiction, like *Adam, Cavalier, Dude,* and *Swank*, and what little money King made selling short stories in the winter of 1973 and 1974 was "just enough to create a rough sliding margin between us and the welfare office."

When King wrote *Carrie*, he was also teaching English in Hampden, making $6,400 a year. King and Tabitha were living in a trailer in Hermon, west of Bangor, and they couldn't afford a phone. It was hard for King to write, because at the end of the week, his brain was fried from teaching.

Carrie was created out of a composite of several girls. "I had been teaching school, and I had seen a number of these unfortunate bottom-of-the-pecking-order children, and I remembered kids like that from my own time in high school. It was hell. High school is hell. The further down the ladder you are, the more like hell it becomes. And for kids like Carrie, it's really like the ninth circle of hell."

When creating Carrie, King thought, "Wouldn't it be fantastic to give her powers that would allow her to get back at the kids who torment her?"

Carrie was going to be a short story for one of the adult magazines King wrote for, but before Carrie's explosion, "I saw that I'd have to lay a longer fuse than that."

King's wife Tabitha made a big difference with *Carrie*, giving Stephen insight into women, and she was a big supporter of his work when he was struggling. King recalled in his autobiography *On Writing* that Tabitha "never voiced a single doubt" that he would get somewhere. "Her support was a constant, one of the few good things I could take as a given. . . . Writing is a lonely job. Having someone who believes in you makes a lot of difference."

King thought it would be a good story for *Cavalier*, or even *Playboy*, which paid up to two grand for a good fiction piece. "Two thousand bucks would buy a new transmission for the Buick with plenty left over for groceries."

King sent the manuscript for *Carrie* to William Thompson, a friend he had at Doubleday who later went on to discover John Grisham. During period five at school, King's free period, he was paged on the intercom. Tabitha was calling. She got a telegram from Thompson:

CONGRATULATIONS, CARRIE OFFICIALLY A DOUBLEDAY BOOK. IS $2500 ADVANCE OKAY. THE FUTURE LIES AHEAD. LOVE, BILL.

Carrie was accepted for publication in late March, early April 1973 and was scheduled for release in the spring of 1974. King still wasn't ready to quit teaching. How much could they make if the paperback rights sold? King had just read in the paper that Mario

Puzo scored $400,000 for the paperback rights to *The Godfather*, but King didn't think *Carrie* would get anywhere near that, if it even made it to paperback at all.

Still, King thought the chances it would get to paperback were good, and even with the deal he had signed giving Doubleday half the profits, maybe he could ultimately make somewhere between $10 to $60 grand.

King bought a new car with the advance money, he and Tabitha were also renting a place for $90 a month, and now the King family also had a phone. King went back to teach for the 1973–1974 school year, and he also started writing his next novel, *Salem's Lot*, which he called a combination of "*Peyton Place* and *Dracula*," and vampires in *Our Town*.

He had almost forgotten about *Carrie* when Bill Thompson called one day. "Are you sitting down?" he asked. "The paperback rights to *Carrie* went to Signet for four hundred thousand dollars." King couldn't believe it. He was speechless. Thompson laughed and asked if he was still there.

"Did you say it went for forty thousand dollars?"

"Four *hundred thousand* dollars. Under the rules of the road two hundred K of it's yours. Congratulations, Steve."

"Are you sure?"

King asked Thompson to say the number again, slowly and clearly, to make sure he heard correctly. A four followed by five zeros, Thompson explained, then a decimal point and two zeros after that.

When Tabitha came home, King told her the good news. She was similarly stunned, and Stephen had to repeat it twice for her as well to make sure she heard it right. When it finally sunk in, tears of joy streamed down her face.

The movie rights for *Carrie* ended up at United Artists, and Mike Medavoy and Eric Pleskow wanted Brian De Palma to direct. King knew De Palma's work, he was a big fan of his film *Sisters*, and King thought he would be a great director to bring *Carrie* to life.

Alfred Hitchcock was a revelation to Brian De Palma, and the movie that made him want to be a director was *Vertigo*. "It's like when you see things the same way [as someone else], you find a writer who writes how you think and you say, 'This guy is speaking to me,'" De Palma says. "Hitchcock always spoke to me right from the beginning, and I took many of his techniques, like the use of the point of view shot, which is seen in *Rear Window* in the umpteenth degree, where you convey information directly to the audience. The character sees something, the audience sees something, and there's no other form in which the character and the audience sees the same information but the movies. It's an essential building block that is completely unique to cinema.

"I was always very open about my use of Hitchcock's language when I made the movie," De Palma continued. "They're the best that exist. If you're working in this genre, Hitchcock's done it all, so if you're gonna be good, you're gonna use some of his ideas."

De Palma first broke through with *Sisters*, which producer George Litto sold to AIP. Litto eventually became De Palma's agent and produced *Obsession, Dressed to Kill,* and *Blow Out* with him. Litto liked De Palma's work because he was a big Hitchcock fan, and he saw that they shared the same sensibilities.

"What I saw in *Sisters* was somebody who had the ability to tell a story with the same visual sense and tempo that Hitchcock had," Litto says. "You judge a director by his ability to tell the story visually, and that's what I saw in De Palma, his visual sense. I vividly remember the day that Hitchcock passed away. Brian called me up, shaken. 'George . . . the master died.' To Brian it was a great personal tragedy."

De Palma also had a mischievous, bad boy streak, a director who liked to cause trouble, and Litto also wasn't afraid of trouble. As an agent and producer, he'd taken on a number of controversial films and filmmakers, representing Robert Altman, Melvin Van Peebles, and blacklisted screenwriters Dalton Trumbo, Ring Lardner Jr., and Waldo Salt. Litto also sold Van Peebles controversial *Sweet Sweetback's Badasssss Song* ("Rated X by an All White Jury"), and Trumbo's *Johnny Got His Gun,* another hot-button film no one wanted to touch.

Litto says with Bob Altman, his bad boy streak was clearly overt. In contrast, "Brian was shy, but inside the motor was always running," Litto continues. "The anger was there. They showed it differently."

"Brian is wily, sardonic, takes no bullshit from anybody, and will say whatever comes into his head," says Jay Cocks, a longtime friend. "He doesn't edit himself at all, he can't be bothered." But Cocks also says that "Brian has a side that is more vulnerable, even sentimental. Brian's [emotions] are more deeply hidden, but perhaps more deeply felt. One of the most personal movies Brian has ever made is *Phantom of the Paradise.* You want to know about Brian, you can imagine him as both the Paul Williams character and as this hidden self. Imagine him as the character that William Finley plays. That's Brian, the guy who does this great work who is totally smashed and exploited by this cunning, satanic force."

De Palma's peer group had big hit movies. Lucas had *American Graffiti*, Spielberg had *Jaws*, and De Palma wanted that kind of success, but he clearly couldn't make a movie like *Star Wars*. After seeing Lucas's space opera, De Palma told him it wasn't his kind of thing because "there's no blood in it."

Then *Carrie* was recommended to De Palma by a friend. Buying a copy in hardback, "I immediately saw all kinds of possibilities," De Palma recalled. "I saw *Carrie* as my way of getting back into the system while still doing what I wanted to do cinematically."

And unlike Lucas, De Palma certainly couldn't do a nostalgic look back at his teen years. Paul Hirsch, who edited a number of films for De Palma including *Carrie*, recalled, "I think that Brian felt that *American Graffiti*, for all its success, didn't represent what he remembered as high school. *Carrie* was much closer to that."

Daphna Krim, daughter of legendary United Artists president Arthur Krim, was close to the age group coming to see *Carrie* in the seventies, and when she first saw the film, it struck her "as being not too far off" from the "tortuous nature" of high school. Marcia Nasatir, who was vice president and head of production at United Artists, says, "I never thought of *Carrie* as a horror film. It's a film about teenage angst."

Carrie was certainly different from the kind of film Krim usually made at United Artists, it wasn't his kind of thing, but as Daphna continues, "He had a great knack, a gift of envisioning a project. He thought a lot of De Palma and Sissy Spacek. I think he was proud of it for those reasons. Spacek was an important new actress, she did a great job, that kind of redeemed it."

Sissy Spacek had worked with De Palma before because her boyfriend and soon-to-be husband, production designer Jack Fisk, worked on *Phantom of the Paradise*. Spacek, who originally wanted to be a rock star when she grew up, wanted to be Phoenix in *Phantom*, which was played by Jessica Harper, but Spacek was a set decorator on the film instead.

At first De Palma had someone else in mind for *Carrie,* but Spacek already liked the book, lobbied him for the role, and De Palma was finally sold on her once she did a screen test.

Spacek was waiting in the car while the United Artists brass were checking out her screen test. Then Jack Fisk ran out of the building, jumped in the car, and told her, "You got it!" Spacek later recalled, "We sped off before anyone could change his mind."

Another actress who auditioned for the role "played Carrie as someone you could hate," recalled Fisk. "You could understand why everyone made fun of her. You didn't really care about her as much as yourself. Sissy, you felt hope for. You could almost fall in love with Carrie White when she played her, and it made the film twice as effective."

"In the book, she was just a complete loser," Spacek said. "And I felt like there needed to be some little ray of hope. It would make it sadder to think that Carrie *could have been* the prom queen. The possibilities of all of it, if you could have believed it, and she could have pulled it off, then it would be sadder when the walls came tumbling down. And I think that it really was that little ray of hope that is what got me the part."

Spacek remembered a girl who was an outcast she went to high school with and who helped her shape her performance. "She was beautiful, but she was poor and didn't have money for clothes. So she wore antiques and the kids were really brutal with her. I remember always loving her clothes, baggy and old-fashioned. She was barefoot most of the time."

When the rest of the cast were having fun together, Spacek kept to herself to stay in character as someone with no friends. "I sort of lurked in dark corners of the soundstage, and peered out from behind things," she said. Spacek also recalled, "I worked hard at being a nerd."

According to Harriet B. Helberg, who cast *Carrie,* Piper Laurie was suggested by Mike Medavoy to play Carrie's lunatic, Holy Roller mother. Helberg also recalled that Louise Fletcher was up for the role, and she and De Palma saw *One Flew Over the Cuckoo's Nest* together to check out her performance. But when Piper Laurie showed up for the audition wearing all black, with her wild, flaming red hair, De Palma was sold. He didn't want Carrie's mother to be a dried-up old prune, but someone sexy.

John Travolta was just coming into stardom with *Welcome Back, Kotter* while *Carrie* was shooting, and the film provided a good bridge from his television career into features. Travolta had just bought a brand-new Mercedes, but had to check the owner's manual to learn how to take the top down. By the end of the shoot, he'd become a superstar.

De Palma wanted Travolta from the get-go. "I don't know if it was deliberate, but Brian went against type with someone that charismatic," Helberg says. "He wasn't a mean or scary-looking or monstrous guy. John came in and he nailed it."

Carrie was clearly a big breakthrough film for much of the cast, and as Helberg says, "We got some fabulous people. We felt very strongly about the choices that we made. Brian had impeccable taste in actors."

Because *Carrie* was low budget, Laurie and Spacek were the only two actors on the film who worked above scale. It was hard to get actors willing to work for scale, and it was also hard to get people to do nudity. (Amy Irving wouldn't do any nude scenes, which is why you don't see her naked in the opening shower scene.)

Carrie was the film that De Palma first worked on with his future wife, Nancy Allen, but they didn't connect until after work because of De Palma's laser beam focus when making a movie. "I think [Brian] likes planning movies more than shooting them," Allen said. "People just get in the way of his vision." Yet off the set, they went out to dinner and she found him "a completely different person: funny, sociable, a great conversationalist. I was like, I've never met this man before."

De Palma and Allen married in 1979, and when Brian cast her in two hooker roles back to back in *Dressed to Kill* and *Blow Out*, Allen's mother asked her, "When is Brian going to write a nice romantic part for you?"

Carrie was shot in fifty days on a $1.8 million budget. In the film, De Palma utilized two important Hitchcock principles. The first was doing something horrible in the first reel, leaving the audience dreading that something bad could happen again, and the second was the bomb-under-the-table theory of suspense, except here it was a bucket of blood up in the rafters.

"The biggest problem was the menstruation scene," Nasatir recalls. "I don't know how Brian convinced them. People were very concerned about it, but it was very important to the story."

For the menstruation scene, De Palma told Spacek he wanted her to feel like she'd been hit by a truck, and she could actually tap into that because Fisk had been hit by a car when he was a kid. Before he realized what was happening, the car hit him, which is how Spacek played the scene.

"That shower scene, I've never seen anything like it before or since in terms of cold-blooded nudity," says Donald Heitzer, who was first assistant director on *Carrie*. "You think we've got everyone's interest? I think so!" Heitzer also recalled during the filming of the scene, the girls yelled, "Don! More steam! More steam!" hoping it would cut down on their exposure. (It obviously didn't.)

School was bad enough for Carrie, then she had to come home to a virtual prison at the hands of her wacked-out, religious fanatic mother. De Palma asked production designer Polly Platt (*The Last Picture Show*) for advice, and she thought Carrie should live in a modern, suburban home, but Fisk recalled, "Brian wanted a Victorian type of Munster house." Fisk himself was looking for something in between.

Fisk drove all over L.A. until he found an asymmetrically designed home in Piru, California. "There was a dormer on top, and a
front porch, but they didn't line up," he said. "It was weird by being
just a little bit off." He also put a picket fence on the house "to separate it from the rest of the neighborhood."

"The closet was designed to be the most horrible part of the house,"
Fisk said. "We put it in the center to act as the core of the whole house
and made the space really small. Putting it under the steps gave some
jagged angles and roughness to it." Fisk also wanted something horrible in the closet that terrified Carrie, so he made a plaster crucified
Jesus with glass eyes, put a light behind the eyes to make them glow,
and arrows in him to make him look like Saint Sebastian.

As mentioned before, the bucket of blood prank at the prom did
a great job of utilizing the Hitchcock metaphor of the bomb under
the table for suspense, where you show there's a bomb that's going to
go off in ten minutes under the table, but the people sitting there
don't know it. Instead of the bomb going off, and jolting the audience for fifteen seconds, now its working for ten minutes.

In *Carrie,* you see the bucket of blood, you know it's going to be
dumped within a certain amount of time, and the inevitability of it is
agonizing. "I tried to make it even more uncomfortable for the audience by shooting it in slow motion," De Palma says. "I really made it
just the worst kind of thing when you know it's going to happen. The
bomb starts ticking extremely slowly, and I have many balls in the air
at the same time. You need all this parallel action going on, because
if slow motions are not cut very well, they can be very boring, so you
have to find a way to drive it with all kinds of counteraction."

Hitchcock said about suspense, "There is no terror in a bang, only
in the anticipation of it," and De Palma also felt the important part
of suspense is "the anticipation, the waiting for something that's going to happen. The dread, that's where the artistry is involved."

Editor Paul Hirsch said, "Suspense is created in an audience by presenting them with the threat of something awful happening within a given time. You can't have suspense unless you are working within a limited time framework. The famous example of that is *High Noon* where they had a picture without any tension that was made very tense by the introduction of periodic cuts to a clock getting closer and closer to noon. So in a sense, in all suspense sequences, you have to have a 'clock' going."

De Palma also used one of his trademark techniques, split screen, in the segment. He had first used it in his documentary *Dionysus in '69*, where he showed the narrative of the play on one side, and the audience reactions on the other.

The blood was dumped on Spacek twice, and fifteen to twenty gallons were mixed for the scene. The blood that covered Spacek was the usual formula of clear Karo syrup and food coloring. "It was incredibly sticky," Spacek said. "If I sat in a chair I got stuck in it. If my arms went down to my sides they were stuck. If my chin went down it was stuck. Someone with a little spritz bottle would be unsticking me all the time." The syrup also would heat up because Spacek was close to the fire in the gym, and as De Palma recalled, "She smelled like some kind of gummy candy left on a radiator for days."

P. J. Soles, who played Norma Watson, one of the mean girls in the film, recalled Spacek slept in her blood-soaked prom dress in her trailer, laying completely still. "I thought, that's tremendous dedication," Soles says. "I never forgot that. Sissy was really zen, she was really into the role." Spacek wanted the blood to look exactly the same in every scene, and if any of the blood coagulated and fell off, the area would be easy to fill back in. "She was fanatical about things matching," Soles continues.

The coda at the end of the film with Carrie's hand coming out of the grave was De Palma's idea. It was influenced by the end of

Deliverance where the hand with the shotgun comes out of a river in a dream. Paul Hirsch and De Palma saw *Deliverance* together, and Hirsch remembered DePalma saying, "That's a great idea, but I could do it so much better."

The idea was that even though Amy Irving became Carrie's friend and tried to stop the terrible prank from happening, she shouldn't have gotten off scot-free. When it came time for the hand coming out of the grave, Spacek grabbed Irving herself, and didn't want another actor or stand-in to do it because she was worried someone else's hand performance wouldn't look right. "Besides, how often do you get to be buried alive and know that it's going to be okay?" she said. Fisk buried Spacek for the scene, and although the rocks were pumice, which scraped and cut her arm, and she understandably got a little claustrophobic, "it was still exciting."

George Lucas loved the fact that De Palma saved the best scare for last. "The people standing in line for the ten o'clock show hear this shriek, and twenty seconds later the doors open and everyone comes out," said Hirsch. "So you go into the theater thinking, 'What the hell was that?'"

When *Carrie* was first screened for the cast, crew, and UA executives, the audience of people who'd worked on the film freaked at the end. "I didn't know it was coming either," Helberg says, and she didn't recall reading it in the script. According to Lou Stroller, who was associate producer on *Carrie*, the ending was never scripted, another trick De Palma would have taken from Hitchcock, who hid the end of the *Psycho* script from people working on the film.

Stephen King saw the film for the first time at a sneak preview in Boston on a double bill with a Redd Foxx comedy called *Norman . . . Is That You?* where the star of *Sanford and Son* discovers his son is a homosexual. There would be many King adaptations to come, "but this was the first one, and it's like sex—you never forget your first time."

King and Tabitha were the only two white people in the theater, and they thought, "Oh, this is going to be really bad. These people are gonna laugh and throw things at the screen. They're not gonna have any sympathy at all for this little white girl and her menstrual problems." But the audience was with the film, and went nuts when Carrie finally got her revenge and burned down the gym.

King recalled that he and Tabitha had no idea the great last scare scene was coming, all he knew was screenwriter Lawrence Cohen wrote him a letter promising, "Watch out for the ending. It'll kick your ass." "And it did," King said years later. When the ending hit, two huge, two-hundred-pound-plus African American men that were sitting in front of King and Tabitha completely lost it, and grabbed each other in fear.

When *Premiere* magazine did a retrospective on *Carrie* in their August 2001 issue it drew parallels to Columbine, which had happened two years previously, and the film is still relevant in an age where society is trying to eliminate school bullying. To King, *Carrie* was "a cautionary tale" and the idea at the core of the story is "the worm turns. That if you push somebody hard enough, they will turn around and bring the house down on you. And in a sense, we know it to be true. And we only have to look as far as Columbine High School to know that: If you bully enough, push enough, and hurt enough, sooner or later there will be trouble."

Carrie was released on November 3, 1976, and it received mostly good reviews. Kevin Thomas, then the main film critic for the *L.A. Times*, wrote, "Any of us who, for whatever reason, were outsiders in school identify with Carrie and recognize how accurate is De Palma's depiction of teenage life—a depiction that allows the kids' cruelty to suggest that a primitive savagery lingering in mankind is older than time and ever lurking just beneath pathetically vulnerable civilized surfaces."

Frank Rich, then writing for *The New York Post*, felt the plot was predictable enough that you could trace the whole movie from the beginning, but he was impressed with how De Palma told the story. "De Palma makes a point of revealing his hand early: He knows that expected shocks, if executed properly, can be more frightening than unexpected ones. . . . [De Palma] works steadily to deepen the meaning—and with that the impact of the material." Rich also called Carrie White "one of the most sympathetic characters ever to grace a horror movie" and "a girl who should be familiar to anyone who's ever attended an American high school."

Carrie made more than $15 million, a big return on its $1.8 million budget, but De Palma felt it could have done much better. "I was very unhappy with the way the studio sold *Carrie*," he said. "They dumped it in Halloween and treated it like a B picture. . . . When the picture did so well, they were startled."

The following month, United Artists had a huge, runaway low-budget smash with *Rocky*. Lou Stroller remembered Stallone walking his bulldogs around the MGM lot when they were making *Carrie*, and nobody knowing who the hell he was.

"When we tested *Carrie*, it was incredible to see people react to it the way they did," Stroller says. "We really had high expectations. We were running neck and neck with *Rocky* and they were like our next-door neighbor. But I always thought we were going to be the breakout movie."

Sissy Spacek and Piper Laurie were both nominated for Best Actress and Best Supporting respectively, and *Cinefantastique* magazine also felt that with *Carrie*, De Palma gave new life to horror when it was stuck in a demonic possession rut post-*Exorcist* and *The*

Omen. Carrie also enjoys a strong second life with today's generation of fans, and in its time it was the right film De Palma needed to take him up to the next level as a filmmaker. "It launched me into my next round in the Hollywood system, and I was now a respected guy in the club again."

At the end of the seventies going into the eighties, Italian horror directors Dario Argento and Lucio Fulci started making a big impact in the States with *Suspiria* and *Zombie,* and Italy's impact and influence on horror would continue to grow strong in the coming decades.

"I believe Italy is a fertile ground for more than just horror directors," says Barbara Magnolfi, who had a role in *Suspiria.* "Just take a look at the long list of artists, singers, actors, directors, writers, painters, sculptors, cooks, photographers, fashion designers, and more throughout Italian history. Seems that we are more passionate and creative people."

"Italians are the most superstitious people in the world!" says Antonella Fulci, Lucio Fulci's daughter. "If a black cat crosses a street, you'll probably see more than one car turning back and taking an alternative road not to cross its path. My father kept a piece of garlic near the telephone, I'm not kidding, just in case someone well known for bringing bad luck would call. It was his placebo, and no one ever reminded him that garlic only works with vampires, 'cause it worked with him.

"We are genetically 'hyperemotional' people, growing up in a country where almost every place has its own ghosts," Fulci continues. "Next time you look at the magnificence of the coliseum, think of how much blood had been spread over those stones, and how many restless souls must be around such an old town."

Antonella also adds, "Another source of our primal fears is the Catholic education we all have received, willing or not. As a kid, you grow up believing that the wrath of God may fall on you if you're no good in math, and I still remember how scared and somehow fascinated I was by the stories of the saints' martyrdoms I learned at school. Actually, the harmless nun that taught religion in my school told me more horror tales than Clive Barker, and was way more graphic describing horrible ways to die than my dad in *The Beyond*."

Today, thanks to the efforts of fans like *Video Watchdog*'s Tim Lucas and Martin Scorsese, the work of Mario Bava, the godfather of Italian horror, is more popular than ever.

As a young filmgoer, Joe Dante was a huge fan of Mario Bava's work, first getting hooked on his black-and-white classic *Black Sunday*, which had a big American release. "It didn't look like the other pictures that were around at the time," Dante says. "*Black Sabbath* came out next, and it was quite apparent that this guy's work didn't look like anybody else's. I really sparked to his use of color and design. I started writing reviews extolling him in *Castle of Frankenstein* magazine hopefully trying to raise awareness of him."

It often wasn't easy to catch Bava's work in the States. Dante continues, "Except for the movies he made for American International, they had very spotty releases, and then when he got into the sadism genre, it was hard for kids to even get in and see the movies. *Blood and Black Lace* was his big introduction to that kind of picture in America, and it was a fabulously photographed movie. It wasn't just unusual, it was electrifying to see this thing."

Not to mention Dante often had to go to some sleazy theaters to see Bava's films. "They'd basically play inner-city markets, outlying drive-ins, except when the picture was released by AIP, who had access to theaters. The smaller companies were never able to book their pictures into the big city theaters. They also didn't make very many prints, so there wasn't that many choices of places to go. So you'd have to get on the subway, and go to see these pictures. You didn't even want to touch the seats. This was in the days when theaters operated twenty-four hours. The lights literally never came on, and the grindhouse showings of these pictures never stopped, so the theaters were never cleaned." (Dante also recalled people would pee off the balcony, but thankfully he never was rained on personally.)

Bava's popularity has grown tremendously in recent years, with fans and critics clearly seeing the artistic flourish, vibrant color, ingenuity on a budget, and style he brought to his films. As *New York Times* critic David Kehr noted, whether working in color or black-and-white, the man certainly knew lighting and texture, "projecting pools of hot, electric colors onto his sets—great washes of golden yellow, emerald green, inky blue . . . Bava added a level of compulsive visual refinement, complex in-depth compositions, full of varying textures and insinuating shadows."

Paul Malcolm of *L.A. Weekly* noted that "the glory of [Bava's] Grand Guignol remains his use of color . . . the purples, greens and yellows of his palette are the sinister stained glass of his expressionist horror cathedrals."

As Bava biographer Tim Lucas wrote, "*Black Sunday* is a stylish and relentlessly visual film, clearly the work of a man who once studied to be a painter, and its graphic horrors are steeped in a tradition of Roman Catholic art with their vivid attention to martyrdom and suffering."

"I like Mario Bava's films very much," said Martin Scorsese. "Hardly any story, just atmosphere with all that fog and ladies walking down corridors—a kind of Italian gothic. I would just put them on loops and have one going in one room in my house, one going on in another, as I have many televisions around. I do that sometimes, put different tapes on and just walk around, creating a whole mood."

Both Fellini and Scorsese have borrowed from Bava's film *Kill Baby Kill*, using his idea of Satan appearing as a little girl in the "Toby Dammit" segment of *Spirits of the Dead* and *The Last Temptation of Christ*. Bava was respected by his filmmaking peers in Italy— Visconti reportedly gave *Kill Baby Kill* a standing ovation when he saw it, and one day Vittorio De Sica came by the set of *Planet of the Vampires* to see what "Mario Bava could invent this time."

Mario's son Lamberto Bava says, "My father was very happy when he saw Fellini's 'Toby Dammit' with more than a quotation from *Kill Baby Kill*, but Federico was a huge friend of my family."

No matter the genre of movies you made, the Italian film community was very close-knit, and there weren't tons of barriers around directors no one could penetrate. As Antonella Fulci recalls, "It wasn't hard to meet Fellini. If you used to take the A train that connects Via Margutta, where he lived, to Cinecittà, I once sat two seats from him on the train. I watched him reading his newspaper behind his huge glasses. No passengers bothered him. Someone approached him to politely say hello, and he was kind with everyone. He was one of us, and the best of us."

Mario looked up to his father, Eugenio Bava, who he called "a real artist, an incredibly gifted and sensible man. I grew up following his footsteps, I learnt all his secrets and skills." Eugenio was a cinematographer who shot *Quo Vadis* and was also an assistant on *Cabiria*. Eugenio was also a master of special effects, and he could also create art in a number of mediums, as a painter, sculptor, photographer, chemist, electrician, and inventor.

Mario recalled his father was "an alchemist, and his workshop seemed like Aladdin's cave to a little boy like me." Years later, Eugenio would create the mask of Satan that was nailed to Barbara Steele's face in *Black Sunday*, as well as the hideous mask for the "Drop of Water" segment in *Black Sabbath*.

Mario originally wanted to be a painter, then realized he couldn't make money that way. "I ended up helping my father, then I eventually found my way behind the camera."

Once he became a full-fledged director of photography, Bava worked with Roberto Rossellini, G. W. Pabst, Raoul Walsh, and took over and finished several movies directed by Riccardo Freda, like *I Vampiri* and *Caltiki—The Immortal Monster*, without credit. Bava didn't finally direct his first movie until he was forty-six.

"I think my father was more than ready when he directed *Black Sunday*," says Mario's son Lamberto. "Everybody agreed with that in the cinema industry here. Even when he was just a cinematographer, he used to have a lot of ideas, most of all practical ones, on the set, so the smart directors loved him. On the set of *Black Sunday*, the crew loved my father because they understood that he really knew how the camera worked. I think he could have started directing at least ten years before."

Black Sunday was shot in beautifully textured black-and-white, and although it wasn't easy to shoot a color film then, "my father's choice was conditioned by the conviction that horror cinema was deeply connected in the mind of the audience in black-and-white," Lamberto continues.

"My aim is to scare people, but I'm a fainthearted coward," Bava said. "Maybe that's why my movies turn out to be so good at scaring people, since I identify myself with my characters . . . their fears are mine too." He also said making horror films was "a way of taking revenge on my fears." As Lamberto recalled, "If we had to use a coffin on the set, my father used to enter it in order to exorcise his fear of death."

Bava shot *Black Sunday* himself, and his films had great visual flair because he knew cinematography so well. Bava would bring his father's old Mitchell with him to the set, and would use it several times on each film in his father's memory.

For *Blood and Black Lace*, Bava used a little red children's wagon for a camera dolly, and a seesaw for a crane, with members of the crew sitting on one end to keep Bava up in the air.

Black Sunday and *Black Sabbath* were distributed by AIP in the States (AIP also later distributed Bava's *Planet of the Vampires*, the Austin Powersesque comedy *Dr. Goldfoot and the Girl Bombs*, and *Baron Blood*). AIP founders Sam Arkoff and Jim Nicholson were in Rome looking for inexpensive movies they could bring to the States and they thought *Black Sunday* was "first class," adding, "We knew that we were in the presence of a real picture maker."

AIP picked up *Black Sunday* for U.S. distribution for about $100,000. It was also a fairly risky movie for the company at the time, and they had to cut out several minutes of violence and suggested sex.

Black Sunday did very well for AIP, and next came *Black Sabbath*, the anthology horror film starring Boris Karloff. (It was also the film that the legendary heavy metal band took their name from.) Arkoff wanted Bava to make movies for AIP in the United Kingdom, and producer Alfredo Leone wanted him to come to America, but he always declined offers to leave Rome.

If Bava were alive today and knew the following he currently enjoys, "He'd be proud," Leone says, "but he was very humble. He was not a braggart. He'd feel undeserving. That's the way he was."

Bava often playfully downplayed his work. "In my entire career, I only made big bullshits," he'd say, and when told people liked his films, he replied, "Nowadays people lack culture. You're being generous. I'm just a craftsman. A romantic craftsman."

Yet one time looking back on his career, he said, "You never managed to make money, but you were proud of your work, of the beautiful inventions you managed to create."

Bava worked cheap and fast, making movies in fifteen to twenty days. "We had to do everything by ourselves, and to solve problems using only our brain and enthusiasm," Mario said. "It was the result that mattered, not the money."

On Bava's *Planet of the Vampires,* which many consider a big influence on *Alien,* "I had nothing, literally," Mario recalled. "There was only an empty soundstage, really squalid, because we had no money. And this had to look like an alien planet! I took a couple of papier-mâché rocks from the nearby studio, probably leftovers from some sword and sandal flick, then I put them in the middle of the set, covered the ground with smoke and dry ice, darkened the background. Then I shifted those two rocks here and there and this way I shot the whole film. Can you imagine it?"

For the credit sequence of *Hatchet for the Honeymoon,* Bava devised more clever, low-cost, do-it-yourself effects ingenuity, such as animating colored sand, an idea that went back to his childhood. As a kid, Bava would fool around with chemicals in his father's lab, and loved to play with potassium cyanide because of its red color, mixing it with white hyposulfite, shifting the colors together like finger painting.

One can speculate what Bava could have done in America with a lot of money, but lower budgets meant independence, which he liked. "Considering his original way in making cinema, I think a low budget could allow him to have complete control of the movie," says Lamberto. "Big-budget productions don't allow that. He did the best he could and I don't think bigger budgets could have improved the quality of his films. Then, of course, if you're a smart director and you also have the money, who knows."

Both Bava and Dario Argento were called the Italian Hitchcocks, but Argento would usually brush off the comparison. "While I would be delighted that people felt my body of work was as important and influential as his, I think there are marked differences in our films," he said. "Mine are more passionate and hysterical while his are always so controlled and remote. Plus I'm a hot-blooded Latin and he isn't!"

Argento's father Salvatore helped popularize Italian cinema. He was a PR executive for Unitalia, a company that imported films and was funded by the government, and he also worked as a line producer for legendary Italian producer Dino De Laurentiis. Being born into the business, Argento grew up knowing everyone, and one of his earliest memories was sitting on Sophia Loren's knee. Once Dario was up and running as a filmmaker, Salvatore devoted himself to promoting his son's work.

Argento's mother was a celebrity photographer in the forties and fifties, which gave Dario an appreciation for beauty, composition, and the fine points of a woman's face. Argento's uncle was also a photographer, and as Dario said, "My films have such a distinctive look because of my mother's and uncle's influences. I was always fascinated by the way they used light and contrasts."

Argento started reading the works of Shakespeare and Edgar Allan Poe at a young age, "my first awe-filled introduction to the worlds of death, the occult, strange thoughts and absurd ideas."

Then Argento saw the 1943 Technicolor remake of *The Phantom of the Opera* starring Claude Rains at an open-air cinema. "It made a strong impression on me because I discovered a whole world I had never seen before—one filled with color, gothic romance, Grand Guignol imagery and terror."

Where Argento's brother Claudio was popular and had a lot of friends at school, Dario was a loner who lived in a dream world.

Argento loved fantasy, and he looked forward to going to bed and taking off on incredible adventures in his mind. "So naturally I gravitated towards the cinema because it was exactly like dreaming adventures in the dark."

Argento was first a film critic, and met with Sergio Leone on a writing assignment. "Even though I started out as a film critic, it is no exaggeration to say that Sergio introduced me to the full wonder of the cinema medium. I owe him a great deal in firing up my enthusiasm on all creative cylinders."

Argento and Bernardo Bertolucci worked on the treatment for *Once Upon a Time in the West,* and were paid $800 each by Leone for their efforts. "We couldn't believe that was it!" Argento said. "It was such a tiny amount for so much hard work. But at least we could justify it as valuable work experience. And, of course, I loved the completed film. I do feel I picked up many of my distinctive methods from Sergio as he was a master filmmaker."

At first he didn't want to direct his first thriller, *The Bird with the Crystal Plumage,* but his father told him, "If you really can't stand anyone else doing it, you have to direct it yourself."

"The idea was a hazardous one because I had never directed before," Dario recalled. "Most people start out making short films and I hadn't even done that. The only thought I clung to was, if I knew cinema in theory through being a film critic, all I had to do was apply myself. What did I have to lose?

"I had no idea what I was doing. I know I made mistakes that people took as style. . . . When you make your first picture, you invent stuff that isn't rigidly page one textbook. . . . The secret is to keep reinventing and pretend you know what you're doing." Although he initially resisted directing, he realized it was in his blood. "From the moment I stepped behind the camera lens, I knew I had some instinct for directing."

232 ⚑ REEL TERROR

It took eighteen months to raise the $500,000 budget. "It wasn't a good period for Italian cinema at the time and the bottom was falling out of the spaghetti Western boom," Argento recalled. Salvatore was there for Dario, overlooking the production, and brother Claudio would eventually become his producer. There was a lot of drama in Argento's family. He had a stormy relationship with his father, and they used to fight over the usual production stuff like money, scheduling, and redoing shots.

Dario and Claudio were also yin and yang as siblings. Claudio was easygoing and even-tempered, Dario more explosive. Dario's marriage to actress Daria Nicolodi was also operatically dramatic, with a lot of wild ups and downs.

"What can I tell you that hasn't already been said a billion times before about the mysteries of love," said Dario. "Daria is as schizophrenic as I am, yet we seemed to connect on so many different levels. It was a stormy relationship containing as many lows as incredible highs."

Daria did wonder if their relationship would have been better if they didn't work together. "Yet I'm very proud of Dario's success and my part in it," she said. "When I first met him, I really loved his cinema, his imagination, and his great technical skill. That remains and I can't cancel it. He deserves the success he has found all around the world. And, after all these years and everything we've been through, I still love him in so many ways."

Daria would recall that the movies they made together, beginning with *Deep Red*, often reflected where their relationship was. "I'm truly happy in *Deep Red* and it clearly shows," she said. "In *Inferno*, as our relationship declined, I get killed off by cats."

"They lived together, loved each other, and screamed at each other endlessly," Claudio said. "Both have very strong personalities and neither would give an inch. From an artistic point of view their union was very positive on the creative front. From the domestic point of view, it was a nightmare."

Mario Bava once advised Daria not to work with someone she loved, it would cause her a lot of heartache, and she obviously didn't listen to his advice. Still, "despite all the arguments, bickering, recriminations, and lies, I wouldn't change what happened between us," she said. "The ultimate testament is the work we did and the daughter we raised."

Argento said that after the success of *Deep Red*, he wanted to take a quantum leap into the unknown. "I knew my core audience would follow my lead if I took a step in another direction so I started thinking about a subject with occult fixtures and fittings."

The Italian directors became known for "giallo," the term for Italian pulp mystery paperbacks with yellow covers (*giallo* is yellow in Italian), but giallo later came to define stylish and bloody Italian horror films. Daria suggested to Dario to leave giallo films behind for a bit. "He had nothing left to prove in that arena," she said. Primarily, Argento wanted to make a damn scary movie. He said fear in the body is 370 degrees, and he wanted *Suspiria* to be 400 degrees.

Deep Red was also the beginning of Argento's relationship with the Italian progressive rock band Goblin, who also provided the score for *Suspiria*. Argento wanted Deep Purple to score *Four Flies on Grey Velvet* and Pink Floyd to score *Deep Red* before he heard Goblin's music.

The band had never thought of writing soundtracks before, but as Goblin guitarist Massimo Morante relates, "I also liked the giallo and horror films before knowing Argento, therefore I was already prepared to make music of that kind. Argento had pointed out to me the atmosphere that he wanted in the films, Goblin and I immediately realized them, and two beautiful sonorous columns were born."

In *Suspiria*, the soundtrack is overbearingly loud and Goblin created the music to be a protagonist in the film. Goblin initially wrote a different score for the film, then started over. "Before, the music was only a comment to the images," Massimo says.

Daria came up with the story for Dario's masterpiece, *Suspiria*. Daria's grandmother practiced witchcraft, was a "white magician," and used to tell Daria bedtime stories of going to school near Basle on the border of Germany and Switzerland. The teachers were showing the kids black magic, and were awarding prizes to the students who performed it best. On the night of the award ceremonies, she would hear strange, slow rhythmic noises, "like a slow samba," and she eventually fled the school.

Suspiria is a visually challenging, experimental movie, and probably the only time a horror film was directly inspired by Disney's *Snow White and the Seven Dwarfs*. Argento showed *Snow White* to cinematographers as an example of what he wanted, and one cameraman told him, "Too heavy. Impossible to achieve."

Luciano Tovoli stepped up to the challenge, and the film was shot with an outdated Technicolor stock without filters, making the primary colors in the film vibrant and strong. Argento was also a big fan of German expressionism, and you can see its influence in how he frames the film's architecture.

Like a nightmare, the film has surreal moments, such as a woman falling into a room full of razor wire, and a blind man being mauled by his Seeing Eye dog in a German square where Hitler used to give speeches. "You must view the entire film as an escalating experimental nightmare," Argento said. "It was always meant to be a real magical acid trip."

Jessica Harper added, "*Suspiria* was a groundbreaking film in another area aside from being such a shocker, and it's something Dario is never given credit for. It was completely dominated by women. That was very unusual at the time."

Argento cast Jessica Harper after seeing her in *Phantom of the Paradise,* which was a hit in Italy. "Brian and Dario are very different, and I admire them both tremendously," Harper says. "Both have incredible vision and an identifiable style, and I enjoyed both of them personally. They are both brilliant, eccentric, humorous, and, well, amazing."

Harper got the *Suspiria* script and thought it would be fun to make a movie in Italy. She watched Argento's previous films, liked them, and wanted to work with him because he "seemed like a fascinating man to work for. I'm always drawn to projects that are a little out of the mainstream—for better or worse sometimes."

Harper had also recently been in *Inserts,* where Richard Dreyfuss played a reclusive porno director who was allegedly based on Ed Wood, and Woody Allen's parody of Russian literature, *Love and Death.* "I think I'm becoming known as an actress who appears in obscure films by auteurs of apparently eccentric tastes," she said at the time. (Other Harper credits include *Stardust Memories, Pennies from Heaven,* and *My Favorite Year.*)

Harper adds, "I'm not, in general, a fan of the [horror] genre. I hate sitting in a movie theater feeling terrified. That said, I think it's a great genre, and when a horror film is made by someone with the talent of Argento, it's a real artistic event that can have an impact on film, regardless of the genre."

Although Argento is slight in frame, he can have a quietly intense vibe, with a penetrating stare as if he's studying you or trying to look into you. Jessica Harper recalled, "I remembered being impressed by his presence in the room. He had a remarkable kind of . . . thing about him, where you look at him and wonder what could possibly be going on [in his head]."

Irene Miracle, who starred in Argento's *Inferno,* recalled when she auditioned for the role, "A lanky, dark-haired, intensely shy man stepped into the room. We were only very curtly introduced to one another, 'Dario, this is Irene, Irene, this is . . .' and the man edged toward me, examining my hair, gingerly walking around me as I sat there, gently touching my shirt, looking at my face, my legs, my arms, my hands, my body. Amused, and somewhat intrigued, I waited and waited for him to say something, anything. Once he'd made the tour around me, he cocked his head, and the corner of his mouth began to curl in what seemed like an attempt to smile, leaned over to whisper something to his associate, and then, gave me another quick 'look over' again. It was the look of a mad scientist who was trying to work out some complicated formula. I smiled. 'Would I do?' I wondered. Finally, he nodded to his associate, and was gone. Poof! The meeting left me feeling very strange. I had no idea what he thought of me until a couple of days later when my agent called, 'They've made you an offer, you've got the part.' I was over the moon. I was off to Rome, off to make another feature."

Working with Argento, "I recall his perfectionism and wanting to get exactly what was in his mind," says Magnolfi. "He was almost like an artist painting a canvas in this manner. Those huge gothic sets were almost intimidating, the colors very vivid. Dario was very passionate and excited on set, he would not settle for less than perfection, but he was kind and gentle with actors, and took as long as needed to get the exact, fitting performance. The actors were left freedom in their interpretation as long as the result was satisfying to Dario."

Argento recalled it being a happy shoot, but his fondest memory was when people saw *Suspiria* and were screaming and running from the theater when it premiered in Rome, just as he saw audiences fleeing from the theater when he saw *Night of the Living Dead*. Similarly, on a Saturday night in August 1977, Harper went to see *Suspriria* in a Hollywood Boulevard theater, and "the audience went bananas."

Suspiria had the best U.S. distribution of any Argento film, and it was released by 20th Century-Fox in the States. It had a great ad campaign ("Once You've Seen It You Will Never Again Feel Safe in the Dark") but it clearly wasn't an easy film to market because of its nonlinear, experimental nature. The pressbook called it, "A Terrifying Challenge to the Imagination," and promised, "More than a movie to see, *Suspiria* is a film to experience."

"Dario was attempting something entirely new and vivid," said Claudio. "I was surprised at how well *Suspriria* did internationally actually as I was convinced it was such a typically Italian product. But when I think about it, that's exactly why it did work. The genre was changing worldwide and audiences were hungry for something more vibrant, violent, and shocking."

"A good song never dies," says Magnolfi. "You can listen to it years and decades later, and it's still a great song. I believe the same is true for a movie. There are some movies that are timeless and will appeal to every new generation. Sometimes *Suspiria*'s fans are very young. *Suspriria* was a magical experience, and maybe the magic carries on."

"It's odd to have *Suspiria* keep sneaking up on you after all these years and still have so much attention paid to something I did so long ago," Harper says, "but that's Dario's artistry for you."

Lucio Fulci was always an icon with the gorehounds, and out of the Italian troika that is comprised of him, Argento, and Bava, the violence in Fulci's films was always the most nihilistic and angry, like Argento's murder set pieces on PCP.

When Fulci came to an American Fangoria convention in early 1996, he was hailed like a rock star, and was seemingly the last to know about his American following. When he arrived in New York during a hideous blizzard, some fans even hitchhiked to meet him.

"He was never told by anybody that he was worth a damn," says

Howard Berger, a filmmaker who spent time with Fulci near the end of his life in 1996. "That was the Italian film industry's game, that you don't let your talent know they're worth something, just keep employing them because they need the work. And don't ever let them know about international success. He was really in the dark about that. He knew that people had seen his films, but he had no idea there was literally a following. He was actually really shocked."

Right before *Zombie,* Fulci got some notice in the States for *The Psychic,* which was released by a low-budget company, Group One, in 1979. Along with the political film *Beatrice Cenci, The Psychic* was Fulci's favorite of the films he made, and although it appeared in the States in a cut-down version, it actually received decent reviews. The *L.A. Times* called it "scary, claustrophobic . . . a tacky treat." *The Hollywood Reporter* also liked "Fulci's hypnotically eerie vision," calling the film "a tense, moody chiller hauntingly directed by Lucio Fulci," with a "mezmerizing, understated" performance from Jennifer O'Neil in the lead role.

Fabrizio De Angelis, the producer of *Zombie,* clearly tried to cash in on the success of *Dawn of the Dead,* which was a big hit overseas. *Dawn of the Dead* was titled *Zombi* overseas and he even released Fulci's film as *Zombi 2* to fool people into thinking it was a sequel. "My father used to say that directors are 'call girls,'" says Antonella. "Someone called asking for a zombie film, and since it paid well, he ran for it."

Zombie was shot in eight weeks on a budget of about $250,000. Fulci enjoyed the shoot because it took place in two of his favorite locales, New York and the Caribbean Islands. Fulci shot films in New York, Boston, Massachusetts, and Louisiana, "cities that he thought were culturally interesting to him," says Berger. "That was a big thing that was important to him, creating a locale." Fulci also shot most of

The Beyond in New Orleans. (Toward the end of the shoot they couldn't afford extras to play corpses, so they rounded up a bunch of winos they paid off in hooch.)

Although *Zombie* came hot on the heels of *Dawn of the Dead*, Fulci denied any similarities, or that it was ripped off from Romero's work, saying *Zombie* was more of an homage to the classic undead of yesteryear.

"I believe my father saw *Dawn of the Dead* right after finishing *Zombie*, and I remember he liked it, but the film is mostly an homage to Jacques Tourneur's *I Walked with a Zombie*," Antonella says.

"I feel that *Zombie* is an authentic zombie film," Fulci said. "I wanted to send them back to their origins; this is why we shot the film in Santo Domingo. My inspiration comes from Jacques Tourneur, not from Romero." Fulci said Romero's zombies "are alienated creatures who live on the fringes of society. I truly think that *Dawn of the Dead* is a political movie, a great movie, but different from my *Zombie*."

Zombie was released in the States by legendary exploitation producer Jerry Gross, whose Jerry Gross Organization distributed many controversial films like *Sweet Sweetback's Baadasssss Song*, *I Drink Your Blood* (the first film in cinema history to be rated X for violence), *Fritz the Cat*, and *I Spit on Your Grave*, a movie Siskel and Ebert loved to hate. Gross was never afraid of the MPAA's scarlet letter, and released many X or unrated films.

Zombie also had the time-honored horror tradition of providing theatergoers with barf bags in case the movie made them lose their lunch. Looking back fondly on *Zombie*, Guillermo Del Toro said, "This movie is definitely worth the barf bag that was given in the theater at the time!"

Fulci's legacy would be his gorefests, yet he was not a horror film fan, although one of his all-time favorite films was Tod Browning's *Freaks*. "He was literally locked up in the role of horror director, and there was no escape," says Antonella Fulci. "I guess that my father was a bit frustrated for the limited role he had to play because he was a wonderful filmmaker, but that's life, and we were a family who loved to live well!"

Fulci usually didn't have any participation in his films when they were released in America. "My father used to leave the fate of his movies in the hands of the producers after the movie was done," Antonella says. She isn't exactly sure how much *Zombie* made in the States, it may never be known for sure, "but I wish I had a penny for every official, pirated, or half-pirated copy of the film that's been sold in the U.S.A.," she says with a laugh.

In addition to the extremity of the gore and violence in his films, Fulci had a reputation for volatility, to say the least. "He was a strong misogynist and was also something of a sadist," said Dardano Sachetti, who wrote *The Psychic, Zombie,* and others for Fulci. "What I want to say is Lucio was very sweet, very well-mannered, very proper, but he was also quite fragile and hid his fragility behind a proverbial meanness. He was mean in his relationships with other people, ask anybody, they will tell you that talking with Lucio was impossible, that he mistreated them, et cetera. But this was a form of protection, it was like a shield. This meanness comes through in his films in the form of sadism."

"If you wanted to live with Dad, you had to stop trying to understand him," says Antonella. "You just had to accept him. He hated whoever tried to put some order in his life. . . . If he thought you were trying to take control of his life, he rebelled against you and treated you as badly as he could."

"Fulci was an extremely volatile person and the business he was in was not pleasant," says Howard Berger. "There's a lot of two-faced people and not a lot of trust. There's a lot of anger represented in the films that I think was thoroughly acceptable to him."

Berger didn't know what to expect before he met Fulci, and he approached him with caution. They first met at the Fanta Film Festival in Rome where Berger's film *Original Sins* was playing and where Fulci was a juror. "Everyone was telling us he was a madman," Berger recalls. "He's insane, he's nuts, he flies off the handle at the drop of a hat, he doesn't make any sense, he's crazy. We didn't know what to do because we were still kind of starstruck."

Then Berger ran into Fulci in the lobby, and he expressed his admiration for Fulci's *Lizard in a Woman's Skin*, which they showed at the festival. "It's not just a good horror movie," Berger told him. "There's portions of it that are really great cinema." Fulci stood silent, hadn't said a word. Then he reached out and gave Berger a hug.

From that point on, they started talking, and as Berger discovered, "He was absolutely not a madman, he was not crazy. He just didn't suffer fools gladly and what I found out from being in his company after a while is when certain people would make appearances, he would put on an act which was to be an intolerant screamer, and he did it to push the other intolerant screamers away, to alienate people. That's what he would do, that was his big game. But he was really one of the most coherent, smart, cultured people I've ever met."

Fan Shawn "Smith" Lewis made $800 in phone calls over two months arranging a Fulci appearance at the rival Chiller Theater convention, which took place in New Jersey, then *Fangoria* magazine found out, and snagged him for a Fango Weekend of Horrors instead in January 1996. "At first I was pissed, but then I realized the whole point was to get Fulci *here*."

Fulci was frail and weak, but once he got onstage and the crowd went nuts, he jumped back to life. Howard Berger also put together a ten-minute "Fulci's Greatest Hits" highlight reel. Once Fulci appeared, "It was as if Hitchcock were in the room," Berger recalled. "He was really touched by it all. He also seemed totally shocked that the American people gave a shit."

"Fulci was on top of the world," said *Fangoria* editor Tony Timpone. "Fans followed him everywhere. When he returned to Italy, he boasted that 'they'd thrown a special convention in America just for *him*."

As fans were lining up to meet Fulci and get his autograph, he was constantly shaking his head in disbelief, like it was all an elaborate prank someone was pulling on him.

"Lucio was right there as the respect for his work was just becoming vocal, and then he died, which was a terrible tragedy because if you knew him, it was a revelation to him," says Berger.

As fans lined up to meet him and ask for his autograph, he said, "You are all too kind, you treat me like a king." When a fan gave him a handmade shirt that read, "Lucio Fulci: Godfather of Gore," he started to cry.

With horror being more fan-oriented than any other genre, it's the fans that have kept Bava and Fulci's work alive and thriving so many years after they have passed away.

And again, like many involved in foreign horror films, Al Cliver, who starred in *Zombie*, had no idea of the film's following in the States until he came to America for *Zombie's* thirtieth anniversary. "It was when I truly realized the impact that *Zombie* had throughout the cinematic world," he says. "What I also find amazing is how much the new generation loves *Zombie*. The majority of my fans are so young.

"Fulci was born like a small genius, and he continued all his life," Cliver continues. "As a director, he knew exactly what he wanted. The only difference was he was limited to medium-budget films, and he could never make high-budget movies. What I personally really miss is that we don't have a Lucio Fulci film with a really high budget. He never had the chance to realize such a dream. We cannot imagine what kind of amazing masterpiece or legacy that he would have left us if this were the case."

EIGHT

THE NIGHT HE CAME HOME

How John Carpenter raised a B drive-in movie horror story to the level of art, and accidentally launched the slasher film, while George Romero created an epic with *Dawn of the Dead*

Right before the end of 2006, John Carpenter's *Halloween* was put in the National Film Registry by the Library of Congress. The 2006 selection was picked from more than a thousand titles. Steve Leggett, staff coordinator for the registry, said, "*Halloween* launched Carpenter's career and started the slasher genre. Some people may say that's good or bad, but it's really a good film."

It's safe to say that *Halloween* will in all likelihood be the only mad slasher film to reside in the Library of Congress. *Halloween* has been imitated many times over, but what will always separate it from its numerous pale imitations is Carpenter's skill as a filmmaker. Unlike a lot of low-budget films cinematographer Dean Cundey had worked on previously, "It was obvious everybody was aiming higher on *Halloween*," he says.

Carpenter has said he always looked at *Halloween* as a stylistic exercise. "That's all we had!" Carpenter recalls today with a laugh.

"We only had the style because we had a very slim plot: an escaped lunatic comes back to this town and starts killing these babysitters. A lot of horror can live and die on visual flourish. Horror requires mood and tempo, it's a little trickier, and usually you're suspending some sort of ridiculous premise that you have to make people believe in."

In terms of independent cinema, *Halloween* was the *Pulp Fiction* of horror films, an indie film that became a phenomenon, and established Carpenter's name as a major new talent in filmmaking. But unlike *Pulp Fiction*, which was released under a major studio umbrella, *Halloween* was released through a true independent company that had no ties to the major studios.

"It's almost hard to track how influential *Halloween* was to the horror genre," said Rob Zombie. "Not since *Psycho* had there been a horror movie *that* powerful. John basically reinvented the wheel."

John Howard Carpenter was born on January 16, 1948, in Carthage, New York, and his family moved to Bowling Green, Kentucky, in 1956. Carpenter's epiphany with film came when his mother took him to see *It Came from Outer Space* when he was four years old. The movie was in 3-D, and he sat down in front with his mother wearing the red and blue glasses. "This meteor came out of the screen and blew up right in my face," Carpenter recalled. "I got up and ran down the aisle, completely terrified. But by the time I reached the lobby, I knew that this was the greatest thing that ever happened to me."

Carpenter first made movies with his father's 8 mm camera, like *Revenge of the Colossal Beasts* and *Gorgon the Space Monster*. He also learned pacing, and Hitchcock's rule of suspense, that the anticipation is more important than the zapper, from fun houses when he was a kid. "I realized the fun of it all was not the moment of the jolt, but the whole waiting for it to happen while I was finding my way down the corridor."

Carpenter put together several fanzines with names like *Fantastic Film Illustrated*, *King Kong Journal*, and *Phantasm*. Tommy Lee Wallace, who grew up with Carpenter in Kentucky, said, "This was a man writing stories and music, songs, creating art, sculpture, and drawing comic books, writing a column for a wrestling magazine, he was a dynamo in terms of self-motivated, creative endeavors. I was just in awe of his energy, his originality, and his drive."

By 1964, Carpenter had a Beatle haircut, and was playing Rolling Stones songs on guitar in the back of the school bus. John and Tommy would also form a psychedelic rock band called Kaleidoscope, and during their concerts they projected Charlie Chaplin movies on the bass drum.

Carpenter moved to L.A. in 1968 and attended USC. Also attending at the same time were Dan O'Bannon, who wrote *Dark Star*, and Nick Castle, who cowrote *Escape from New York* with Carpenter in 1974, and would play the shape in *Halloween*.

Where a lot of directors of his generation wanted to experiment and be self-indulgent, Carpenter admired the classic old-school directors like Ford, Hawks, and Hitchcock, "products of the studio system," said Wallace. "Highly disciplined master craftsmen, no-bullshit artists, unpretentious men who might even scoff at any label smacking of 'art.' John modeled himself after them."

"If I had three wishes, one of them would be send me back to the forties and the studio system and let me direct movies,'" Carpenter said. "Because I would have been happiest there. I feel I am a little bit out of time. I have much more of a kinship for older-style films."

Carpenter said one of the benefits of film school was, "They actually require you to make a lot of films, and so you get to work out a lot of foolish excesses. Once you've masturbated with the camera, you've got it out of your system. Eventually you learn what works and what doesn't. You also get a solid grasp of technique: how the camera works, how the sound works, and so on."

"The lore that revolved around film school was that UCLA was kind of an art school, and USC was kind of a trade school," says Wallace. "At UCLA you could work on one film for several semesters, it was very artsy-fartsy and you could follow your creative muse. At USC you were expected to crank out stuff, and turn it in on time at the end of the semester. So it taught John the kind of discipline his heroes had. John's heroes were workmen like directors who fit right into the Hollywood system, and knew how to deliver the goods on a schedule and budget."

John knew how he wanted to express himself, he knew the art, he wanted USC to teach him the craft. There were indeed film theory classes that endlessly talked about film as art, but Carpenter and Wallace were looking for the same thing: show me how to do this, show me how the camera works, show me the secrets of editing, help me learn how to manage a budget, learn script structure, give me some discipline.

In 1970, Carpenter made a short film, *The Resurrection of Bronco Billy,* that won the Academy Award for best short subject. Carpenter's first feature, *Dark Star,* a takeoff on *2001,* started as a 16 mm student film the same year. Once it became a feature, the budget went from six to sixty thousand dollars. Carpenter was raising money for *Dark Star,* trying to get it finished and released. Then Jack H. Harris, who produced *The Astro Zombies,* John Landis's *Schlock!, The Blob,* and *Beware the Blob* came in.

Carpenter had forty-five minutes of footage, and in addition to expanding it to feature-length, Harris also wanted reshoots, cuts, and new special effects. "He saw something in it, and he wanted a space movie, said Carpenter. Harris was known for picking up movies for cheap, movies that were abandoned. He would take them over and remake them." According to Harris, Carpenter shot the space crew snoring in their bunks for five minutes to fill up time.

Harris had a rep for being a shyster B-movie producer, and Dan O'Bannon, who wrote the screenplay, hated his guts. In one scene, he got "Fuck Harris" to flash by quickly on one of the ship's video screens. But Carpenter always credited Harris with getting the movie out there and into theaters. "He was the only distributor in Hollywood who was willing to take the movie on."

Dark Star, which was released in fifty theaters on Carpenter's twenty-seventh birthday, January 16, 1975, came and went, and it did nothing for Carpenter's career, although it did eventually develop a cult following. (Ridley Scott is a fan.) Carpenter was hoping the struggles he went through would translate to the audience, who would feel how much work and effort he put into his first feature, but he learned the hard way that audiences care about the final result. "I expected to be offered a directing job after *Dark Star* and I got shit. I couldn't get hired. It was the first big depression of my life. I was like, 'What am I going to do?' It truly was a swift kick in the ass. It was a wake-up call and I had to start all over again."

Dark Star was entered into the Filmex film festival, which got him an agent, and he starting writing a lot of screenplays. Carpenter sold *The Eyes of Laura Mars* as an original idea, and he got $19,000 for writing the treatment and the screenplay. "Wow! This is a great living," he joked years later. "I'd usually get two or three months, sometimes less, to write a screenplay, so I'd sit down for the first couple of weeks and do a treatment. Then I'd party for about two months and, when the deadline was coming up, I'd spend about a week banging it out and turn it in. Once I had to do one in a night. That was the toughest."

Carpenter "got battered a bit" by legendary lunatic producer Jon

Peters, but "one gets lured by the big money." Peters would go through four more writers, as well as hire and fire a director before settling with Irvin Kershner (*The Empire Strikes Back*). Peters obviously didn't have the foresight to think Carpenter would be a hot writer and director, and maybe he could have saved *The Eyes of Laura Mars* from being a mediocre thriller that opened to mediocre business in August 1978.

Carpenter had much better luck when he met the late Debra Hill in 1975. Hill was recommended to Carpenter as a script supervisor for *Assault on Precinct 13*, and they also became a couple. *Assault* was the second film Hill ever worked on, the first was *Goodbye Norma Jean*, a low-budget Marilyn Monroe biopic directed by Larry Buchanan, the man who gave us *Zontar, The Thing From Venus*. Carpenter also encouraged Hill to write, and they wrote the screenplays for *Halloween* and *The Fog* together.

"Unlike many producers, she came from the crew ranks," Carpenter said. "I think they're the most underappreciated people, and they work the hardest. She had experienced the ins and the outs and had a thorough understanding of what it took to make a picture."

Hill came up in an era when women weren't taken seriously in executive positions in Hollywood, and is today considered a major pioneer for the women who came after her. "The ground that she trailblazed can now be followed by anyone," Carpenter said.

"Women in powerful positions were perceived in a sexist way," Hill said. "They did love stories. For a woman to come and do a film like *Halloween* really paved the way for other women to be viewed as filmmakers and good storytellers first, as opposed to just being women producers."

And as anyone who's read the book *Easy Riders, Raging Bulls* knows, a lot of women behind famous men in Hollywood often got left behind by their mates when they got famous, whereas Carpenter and Hill would do interviews together with Carpenter telling the press, "We're a team."

As a producer, Debra Hill ran a tight ship. Jamie Lee Curtis recalled that Hill was the only producer she'd ever seen check all the petty cash receipts, and if money was missing without a good explanation, there was trouble. "She was a tough gal and you didn't cross her without some consequences."

Kim Gottlieb-Walker, who was the still photographer on *Halloween*, said Hill was "efficient, smart, and tough when she had to be. She always got the job done on time, and usually under budget. John and Debra were a fabulous creative team, I adored them both. She took care of business, and he took care of the shooting."

Carpenter loved Westerns, he had a GOD BLESS JOHN WAYNE bumper sticker on his car, but by the time he got to Hollywood the Western was a dead genre, so he moved his screenplay, *The Anderson Alamo*, to the urban jungle, and retitled it *Assault on Precinct 13*. (*Assault* has also been called "*Rio Bravo* in a ghetto.")

Assault on Precinct 13 was shot in November 1975 in about twenty-five days or so on a budget in the neighborhood of two to three million dollars. Carpenter didn't have much money to spare with *Assault,* but instead of going cheap and shooting on 16 mm like a lot of low-budget filmmakers, he put every cent into paying for the best resources available.

"Everybody was working almost for free," Tommy Lee Wallace recalled. "What money there was was going to film stock and MGM Film Labs, postproduction sound at Goldwyn Studios, the mix at Goldwyn, the best in town. And it was Panavision, it was wide screen, it looked like a real movie." No matter how low the budget, Carpenter told Wallace, "The movie will be here long after we're gone. Do whatever it takes to make it look and sound its best."

Wallace worked on the film as the art director, sound effects editor, and he also edited the action sequences. Carpenter showed dailies to Wallace on a bedsheet that wasn't big enough for the whole picture, but Tommy was blown away. "This looked like a real movie," he recalled. "*Assault on Precinct 13* didn't look remotely like its tiny budget. We were going to fool everyone!"

Carpenter was cutting *Assault* himself because they couldn't afford to hire an editor, and Wallace volunteered to help out. "Ask anyone, anywhere, who has tried to do that, that's a very difficult and lonely job," says Wallace. Wallace had no idea what sound effects entailed, but Carpenter quickly taught Wallace how to edit and off he went.

"I don't know if Orson Welles said it, but it's a famous quote that the techniques of filmmaking can be learned in an afternoon," Wallace continues. "Then it's a matter of adding inspiration and hard work, and perhaps genius into the formula in order to make a great movie. I think John took that to heart because he taught me how to edit film in an hour one afternoon in that cutting room. So the technique of sticking the film shots together and making it match up to the film was no big deal. It's what you do with it that counts."

Carpenter also scored the film with a Moog synthesizer because, as he said, "I was the cheapest and best person I could get for the money." Like many kids of his generation, he was forced to take music lessons, and like many kids forced to do it, he initially hated it, "but I did pick up an ear for music."

And the opening of *Assault on Precinct 13*, much like the music for *Halloween*, had a great, simple, and memorable theme. Austin Stoker, star of *Assault on Precinct 13*, was once at the doctor and when a nurse recognized him from the film, she ran into the room and started singing the movie theme, "Dum Duh-Duh-Da-Dum!"

Assault on Precinct 13 opened in September 1976. In its initial release, *Assault* didn't do well in the States, but audiences went crazy for it at the London Film Festival, where Carpenter and Hill raised the funding for *Halloween*. *Assault* then became a cult hit in London, where Stanley Kubrick caught the film and enjoyed it.

Where *Dark Star* and *Assault* later became cult hits in the States, the British knew right away Carpenter was a good filmmaker. Britain's *Time Out* magazine profiled Carpenter, and encouraged the readers to, "Check out for yourself what America doesn't know it's missing." After *Assault on Precinct 13,* Carpenter also worked in TV, writing the screenplay for the TV movie *Zuma Beach,* and writing and directing *Someone's Watching Me,* a thriller for Warner Bros. Television. Carpenter made it in about seventeen days, and it starred Lauren Hutton, David Birney, and Adrienne Barbeau, his future wife. Carpenter couldn't stay for postproduction on *Someone Is Watching Me,* because he had to start his next film, *Halloween,* three weeks later in May 1978.

Irwin Yablans was the executive producer of *Halloween*, and his company, Compass International Pictures, released *Assault on Precinct 13* overseas. *Halloween* was Yablans's idea. He wanted to make a horror film for a low budget. Something with babysitters was a sellable concept because everyone had babysitters when they were kids or had been a babysitter themselves, and a story putting teenagers and kids in jeopardy could make a scary movie.

Yablans thought, "What if we made a film in one night? We could probably do it real cheap because we'd use one set, we'd do it all in a couple of days or a couple of weeks." Then Yablans realized no one had ever made a movie about Halloween.

Yablans came up with the idea while flying home from a film festival in Milan. He called John Carpenter when he landed, and pitched the idea. "Don't tell me any more," Carpenter said. "I know exactly what to do." Then Yablans asked, "Would it be too on the nose if we called it *Halloween?*"

Carpenter said as soon as he heard the title, "the whole movie took shape for me." He also felt the title raised the film to a new level because it could then encompass all kinds of fear, unlike the original title he was going to use, *The Babysitter Murders*, which would indicate a schlockier kind of movie.

John agreed to make the movie if he had final cut and his name above the title. If Carpenter could bring the film in on that schedule and budget, Yablans promised he could have whatever he wanted, and he kept his word. Yablans came to the set a few times, but it was to support Carpenter and the film, and he never meddled or interfered.

Carpenter wanted his name above the title like his favorite old-school directors such as Ford, Hawks, and Hitchcock, and Wallace also says, "Branding is all the rage now, and I just think John was working very hard to set himself apart and create a brand for himself."

Carpenter and Hill wrote the *Halloween* screenplay in three weeks on an IBM Selectric typewriter, and they shot the first draft. "I always compared us to Dashiell Hammett and Lillian Hellman," said Hill.

For *Halloween*'s setting, Debra Hill drew on her hometown of Haddenfield, New Jersey, which was transformed into Haddenfield, Illinois. "I wanted a Midwest, sleepy town," she said. "What's so interesting to me about horror movies is they take place in small towns where they don't have a huge police force. You put the story in a sleepy town, really beautiful homes, nice full trees, it seems safe. You think nothing could go wrong there and nothing could be further from the truth. Every town has a secret, every town has that lore of something that went horribly wrong with it. What inspired me was *Rear Window* where you pull off the veneer and have a peek inside each of the apartments. The idea of pulling off the veneer and seeing what lies beneath has always intrigued me."

"It could be any place in the Midwest," Carpenter said. "Most small towns have a kind of haunted house story of one kind or another, at least that's what teenagers believe. There's always a house down the lane somebody was killed in or somebody went crazy in."

Shooting *Halloween* outdoors in Southern California, cinematographer Dean Cundey had to use tight framing to keep out the palm trees out of shots and make it look more like suburbia. Fake leaves were also used to resemble autumn, then gathered up in a pile and reused.

Carpenter loved strong women characters, a major influence from Howard Hawks, and unlike the mad slasher films that followed in the wake of *Halloween*, the lead character of Laurie Strode wasn't a cardboard victim set up for slaughter or a weakling waiting for a man to rescue her. "You can't separate the political milieu from the movies," Wallace says. "This was a time that women were asserting their rights like never before, and Debra was a very assertive woman. She was not going to have a weeping violet type as her heroine, no way."

Jamie Lee Curtis was Debra Hill's casting decision. "It was between two girls and I really loved Jamie," Hill recalled. "From a creative standpoint I thought she was a perfect young actress who had a huge career ahead of her, and I thought she was the best one for the part. From a financial, business point of view I thought, 'Well, it doesn't hurt that she's Janet Leigh's and Tony Curtis's daughter.' I realized even back then, even as independent and naïve as we were, I did realize there was a business aspect to selling the movie and that could get us some publicity."

Hill felt Jamie was very much like Laurie, an introspective, complicated, multifaceted woman. Curtis asked Carpenter, "Are you going to cast me as the smart aleck, or the quiet, repressed, brainiac virgin?" and later remarked, "The fact that they wanted me for the virgin really made me feel like an actor."

P. J. Soles exclaimed "Totally!" throughout the film, which several years later became a big Valley Girl phrase, yet Hill said she hadn't heard anyone say it before. "I made it up, I created that!" she said. "I don't think of it as a Valley Girl saying. I gave her a speech pattern that was consistent with who the character was. The movie's about three girls, and I had to make them three separate personalities so they'd separate themselves. A lot of times people write movies about friends but don't give them individual personalities. Laurie Strode was the bookish do-right girl, P. J. Soles character was kind of the ditsy girl, and Nancy Loomis's character was the know-it-all."

Carpenter and Hill went after British actors to play Dr. Loomis, and both Peter Cushing and Christopher Lee turned it down (Lee later told Hill it was the biggest mistake he'd ever made). Yablans thought of Donald Pleasance, having enjoyed his performance in the Western *Will Penny*, thinking he would bring a "touch of class" to the film. Donald's daughter Angela was also a fan of Carpenter's music, and helped convince her father to take the role.

Hill recalled Pleasance "was wonderful to work with, very odd, quiet sense of humor. We liked him so much, we made him the president of the United States in *Escape From New York*!"

As seen with Cushing in the Hammer films, British actors can really sell dialogue, even if they really think what they're saying is nonsense. "I think because of his wonderful use of the English language he gave extra importance to John's writing about the personification of evil," said Hill.

Another smart decision Hill made was hooking Carpenter up with cinematographer Dean Cundey, thinking they'd make a good team.

Like most people getting started in moviemaking in the seventies, Cundey, and his longtime camera operator Ray Stella, started out in the B-movie drive-in world. Cundey had been working with a lot of low-budget movie directors who thought the camera wasn't much more than a device to record actors talking, and he also felt the term "exploitation films" meant exploiting the crews, who usually worked inhuman hours for no money. Stella recalled on a lot of B movies, "We had to shoot twenty-four hours a day for fifty dollars a day. That came out to about two dollars an hour."

Cundey found out working with Carpenter was a much different experience right off the bat. "Working with John was a revelation because suddenly here was a guy who was interested in using the camera in a creative way, drawing the audience in, where suddenly the camera is contributing, where you're telling the story with visuals." Stella says, "John was very innovative, I thought me and Dean moved up the ladder as soon as we hooked up with him. You knew that he had it together."

In addition to shooting future Carpenter films such as *The Fog, Escape from New York, The Thing*, and *Big Trouble in Little China*, Cundey and Stella were also the director of photography and camera operator team on *Back to the Future, Who Framed Roger Rabbit, Jurassic Park, Apollo 13,* and more.

Halloween opens with an elaborate, long take that follows young Michael Myers in and out of his house when he commits his first kill. "I'd always admired long tracking shots in the opening of movies," Carpenter says. "*Touch of Evil* immediately comes to mind, and there's one in the original *Scarface*. An acquaintance of mine had done a short film that was all one take, and it was really an engrossing way of moving the camera through an environment."

Cundey feels what Carpenter wanted was to "make the statement the audience was the point of view of somebody. John wanted to create the illusion, the feeling that we were a person watching. And in real life, our life is one continuous shot, except when we sleep. I think he wanted to be sure the audience understood that that's what we were seeing, that we were this mysterious presence. He wanted to take the audience through this event, the first cut is when we see who we are, which is this child, Michael Myers.

"It was written to be one fluid shot," continues Cundey. "We didn't have a lot of time or money. How do you tell three pages of a story, one shooting day, that has no dialogue? We couldn't have done it without the Steadicam. There was no other piece of equipment that would have been able to go across the street, look into the house, go into the kitchen, up the steps, into a bedroom, and back down again."

Carpenter didn't storyboard the film, he had it all in his head, and he walked Cundey through the opening shot, where he wanted him to start, where he wanted him to go, what he wanted the audience to see. The late Moustapha Akkad, who was *Halloween*'s executive producer, recalled when Carpenter pitched the film, he could explain it to you "almost frame for frame."

Halloween was another horror film done deceptively without blood, and while it may not have informed the direction of *Halloween*, Carpenter did learn a lesson about losing the audience from *Assault on Precinct 13* in a scene where cute little Disney star Kim Richards is killed by a gang member. Carpenter wanted a random killing in the film because "it's scarier when it's random," but "killing that little girl turned off an enormous amount of the audience. They hated me for it because it really upset them."

Cundey says the no blood approach in *Halloween* was intentional because even before the mad slasher craze, the feeling was that too much gore and special effects can call too much attention to itself, take the audience out of the movie, and make the story less realistic. "We actually spoke specifically about it," says Cundey. "I think part of what was so effective about *Halloween* is you could say any of this could happen."

Carpenter says, "The treatment of that in *Halloween* was the result of me just having done a very fast TV movie, *Somebody's Watching Me,* where there was a great deal of censorship on what you couldn't show. So that was my mind-set and I took it along with me. It wasn't that conscious of a decision."

Unlike horror films that try to explain everything, Myers is like evil itself in that he just exists without reason, and he earned the nickname "the Shape," adding to his mythical stature, like the bogeyman.

"I think John was really playing with the supernatural," says Tommy Lee Wallace. "It was a knife movie and therefore it was grounded in the real world. But Michael Myers did have slightly supernatural powers, he would be able to be in more than one place at the same time, seemed to disappear almost at will, seemed to be unstoppable, unkillable. John skated along the very edge of that, physically creating a myth."

Wallace bought two masks for Michael, a Captain Kirk mask and an Emmett Kelly clown mask. "I believe I wound up finding what I was looking for at a mask shop in Westwood. We talked at length about what would be scariest. There were two concepts floating around, one was a kind of a blank mask, a sort of anything mask. John is someone who if he goes to one place and it strikes his fancy, there's no more looking. My working approach is more about choices and options. It may have been at my insistence that we had at least two choices on this mask thing. I just needed to find a neutral face, and something that was odd and compelling in some strange way. After all, who would just put on a mask of a regular-looking guy?"

The masks cost about $5.95 a piece or something in there, definitely under ten dollars each. Wallace then spray-painted the Shatner mask white, cut the eyeholes a little bigger, took off the sideburns, and messed up the hair. They tried both masks, and the Emmett

Kelly mask definitely would have been scary, "But there was no question once the Captain Kirk mask came out, it was really unsettling and scary, and we knew we had what we needed. I think all you had to do was look at that mask and say, 'Something is desperately wrong here and I am scared.'"

Nick Castle would play the grown-up Michael Myers, or the Shape as he came to be known. Many like to think anyone can play a monster in a mask, but the grace and agility of Castle was clearly missing in the *Halloween* sequels. Castle's father was a dancer, so he understood movement and pacing. "Plus they got the mask all wrong in *Halloween II*," Wallace adds. "It's a typical story of Hollywood. They got a fancy mask guy to look at the original movie, and spend a bunch of money casting and sculpting trying to re-create that."

Halloween started out with wide shots and, then the camera moved in closer and tighter, subconsciously creating anxiety and fear in the audience until you feel as if you're trapped in the closet with Jamie.

"Everything is closing in on you and all of the sudden you are in a closet and he is two inches away from you," said Carpenter. "There is no place to go; there is no place to get out anymore. So that was purely intentional."

Halloween unconsciously left things open for a sequel with the ending. Wallace recalls, "Almost as an afterthought we had him just get up and walk away and shot some extra footage of the blank ground. Then the other empty street shots were stolen from other sequences. That was not planned on film. It think it was just a good way of drawing the curtain and saying, 'Okay, this was a story, but now it's in your face, it's on your street, it's everywhere. That's a nice way to end a horror movie."

As with many of the best horror films, the enthusiasm Carpenter and company brought to the proceedings transferred a lot to the final product. "We were proving ourselves, and you got a tremendous jolt of energy off the screen," says Tommy Lee Wallace. "We didn't know how hard it was, how crazy it was, or what a far-fetched dream it was to pull this thing off, so we just went out and did it."

"We were young, hungry, and not yet jaded or cynical about the industry," said Debra Hill. "The industry was very different then. Now students of filmmaking want to be writers, directors, producers, they're very calculating about the business, and they're more business-oriented than we were. We were kids playing in the most exciting sandbox on the planet."

"*Halloween* was a blast," says Carpenter, looking back on the experience. "It was just a bunch of kids making a movie. It was absolute fun, no pressure whatsoever. When you're doing a horror film, it's the most fun you can ever have. People just love putting on makeup and getting killed, it's just so much fun on the set."

Carpenter and company probably didn't know it at the time, but *Halloween* was an experience where the planets aligned, and things went better than anyone could have expected, which doesn't happen often. It was a last moment of innocence before everyone moved up the ladder in Hollywood, and would have to deal with the bullshit that came with it.

Carpenter recorded the music for *Halloween* in a three-day session after the film wrapped. "I had the theme already written for years," Carpenter says. "It was just something I'd tinkered out on the piano. I played 5/4 time on an octave on a piano, that's all it was. I hadn't necessarily applied it to *Halloween,* it was just sitting there and I thought, 'Oh, I'll use this. That works okay.' I'm not an accomplished composer of symphonies, I just do basic, straight-ahead, riff-driven music."

The first time Tommy Lee Wallace heard the *Halloween* theme,

"It made me smile," he said. "It was so John, nobody else composes music like him."

5/4 is an odd time signature to write music in, and the five is the accent, the sticking point. "It was never a peaceful or restful rhythm or melody," says Cundey.

Carpenter also used the music to jolt the audience when Michael would jump out of nowhere, and in some scenes the music was so frightening, Yablans recalled people in the audience covering their ears in terror.

Debra Hill believed Carpenter had the music in his head while he was making the movie, and shot and paced the film to the rhythms in his mind, but Carpenter says he doesn't think of music while he's shooting. "It's a separate task," he says.

As for *Halloween*'s prospects before it was about to go out into the world, "I felt from the get-go that it was a winner," says Wallace. "There was no question in my mind it would find an audience, I had no clue it would turn into the phenomenon it turned out to be."

At first Yablans tried to get *Halloween* set up at a major studio, then decided to distribute the movie through Compass International. *Halloween* was released in October 1978 and was expanded to major cities on Halloween night. "At first we had to fight for theaters," Yablans recalled. It opened at ninety-eight theaters in Southern California and seventy-two theaters in New York.

Halloween wasn't a hit right away, it took about three or four months to build. "Low-budget horror films, genre films were dormant, slightly sleeping at the time," Carpenter says. "*Halloween* revived this 'Let's go to the movies and have fun' idea. Lots of screaming, lots of grabbing your date, lots of laughter afterwards."

Halloween was a word-of-mouth phenomenon that kept the movie in theaters and drive-ins for months before it finally became a hit. "That's the amazing thing," Carpenter says. "It started as a regional release, prints were bicycled from city to city, and word of mouth just kinda grew as people saw it. It was a very, very limited release, so in that sense it was amazing. The last one like that I can remember is *My Big Fat Greek Wedding*. That built from people talking about it: 'You gotta see this because blah, blah, blah,' and the word spread."

"The audience recognized the value of the film," Cundey says. "The fact that they empathized with the characters, and even subconsciously appreciated the visual storytelling. It was very rewarding to see that happen as opposed to a lot of the films we worked on, which were sort of projector fodder for drive-ins that would be released, and after two or three weeks would disappear. I started getting phone calls from everybody who had a cheap horror film, and the feeling was if they hired me it could be the next *Halloween* because somehow it would rub off from me." (Cundey's camerawork was such a key element to *Halloween* that the producers of *Halloween II* insisted Dean shoot it because they wanted the sequel to have the same look.)

Right after the release of *Halloween*, Carpenter plunged ahead with the TV movie *Elvis*, a project Carpenter was excited about because he was a big fan of the King, and it was the first time he and Kurt Russell worked together in what became a long actor-director collaboration and friendship.

Carpenter didn't even know *Halloween* was a hit until he was approached on the set of *Elvis* by Bob Rehme, the head of Avco Embassy, which was about to become a major horror powerhouse. Rehme wanted Carpenter to come to Embassy, and they soon struck a deal to make his next two movies, *The Fog* and *Escape from New York,* for the company. "Apparently while I was busy at work, the movie had gained some momentum," Carpenter says.

Halloween made $40 million in the States, $70 million worldwide, which in today's money would be about $200 million. When it finally sunk in that *Halloween* was a big hit, Hill's reaction was "shock . . . surprise . . . delight! We were just kids."

Halloween also received raves from the serious critics. *Newsweek* called it, "A superb exercise in the act of suspense . . . the most frightening flick in years," and Roger Ebert called it, "An absolutely merciless thriller."

"I've often compared *Halloween* to *Psycho*," Ebert said. "I think it's a fair comparison because, with *Halloween*, it's such a terrifying experience to watch that film and you also feel a real joy with the director in the way that he's toying with the audience."

"I was just happy that somebody liked it," Carpenter says. "I didn't know who Roger Ebert was at the time, so it was just nice to get a good review. Joe Schwartz from Pacoima could have given me a good review and I would have been happy."

Debra Hill was also amazed by Pauline Kael's *Halloween* review, and although she didn't like everything about it, like many critics Kael did appreciate Carpenter's strengths as a filmmaker.

"[Carpenter] quickly sets up an atmosphere of fear, and his blue night tones have a fine, chilling ambience," Kael wrote in *The New Yorker*. "The film is largely just a matter of the camera tracking subjectively from the mad killer's point of view, leading you to expect something awful to happen . . . in fact, there's so much subjective tracking you begin to think everybody in the movie has his own camera . . . Carpenter also wrote the score himself—all four bars—and he's devoted to it."

Kael concluded her review with, "A lot of people seem to be convinced that *Halloween* is something special—a classic. Maybe when a horror film is stripped of everything but dumb scariness—when it isn't ashamed to revive the stalest device of the genre (the escaped lunatic)—it satisfies part of the audience in a more basic, childish way than sophisticated horror pictures do."

And, of course, many pointed out what eventually became a rule of horror in the *Scream* series, that if you had sex in a horror film, you'd get killed. Carpenter first read the "have sex you die" observation in an essay by respected film critic Robin Wood called "Revenge of the Repressed," and Kael also made reference to it in her review, that Michael Myers "has no trouble picking off the teenagers who 'fool around'; only Laurie has the virginal strength to fight back."

"I read 'Revenge of the Repressed' at the time and I said, 'What the fuck is this?'" Carpenter says. "It's not so bad now that I look back on it, but at the time I thought, 'That's not what it's all about.' I just hadn't thought of it. It wasn't my intention to make a moral point. The other girls were busy on their boyfriends, they were busy on other things. Laurie had the perception because she's not involved in anything. She's lonely, she's looking out the window."

"They missed the point," Carpenter told *Rolling Stone*. "Sure, the other girls who are sexually active are the ones who get killed. But Laurie is the virgin with all this repressed sexual energy. And she stabs him with the knife again and again. It's a backward twist. She's the one who sticks it in."

"It was never a conscious decision," Hill said. "The people who mentioned that in reviews applied their own morality to it. I thought they were being ridiculously introspective about a film that was meant to have no social statements. There wasn't any cerebral thinking about making this movie." However, in another interview Hill said her Catholic schoolgirl education may have crept into the script a bit.

Laurie Strode wasn't picked to be the survivor because she hadn't gone all the way yet. "We wanted to make Laurie Strode a strong character who was very willful and feared nothing," Hill continued. "Here was a woman who didn't run from danger but stepped up to it. We thought of her as a Lauren Bacall–Howard Hawksian character, someone who was quiet yet defiant and faced the enemy. P. J. Soles's character tends to flirt with everything, 'Oh I don't care, totally,' you know? Nancy Loomis tries to explain everything. The Laurie Strode character was someone with an inner strength you didn't see on the outside."

As with Romero's zombies, the critics often read too much into great horror films, and perhaps they feel they have to give them more depth in order to like them, just as many different readings were brought to Hitchcock's work, many of which were probably the farthest thing from his mind when making the movies in the first place.

"To me, the zombies have *always* just been zombies," Romero said, invoking a famous Freud saying. "They've always been a cigar." Romero adds, "Now people start *over*analyzing it. I've read articles about when Scott Reiniger dies in *Dawn of the Dead* and when Ken Foree pops that champagne cork, it's absolute proof they were gay for each other!"

When asked by a writer if the success of *The Exorcist* reflected any disillusionment in America at the time of Vietnam and Watergate, reflecting Father Karras's crisis of faith, William Peter Blatty said, "I think all such speculation—and there is much of this kind—is academic foolishness primarily designed to either denigrate the work or to come up with something new that you can get into print. Why not simply accept what nearly every heavyweight reviewer has said about the novel, namely that it's so gripping that you can't put it down."

With the enormous success of *Halloween*, it was inevitable that the majors and indies alike would rush imitations into production, and mad slasher films would be the dominant force in horror for the first half of the eighties.

266 👁 REEL TERROR

"*Halloween* sent a powerful message to the major studios," says Tommy Lee Wallace. "They figured it out right quick, and started cloning *Halloween* as quickly as they could."

Steve Miner, who was one of the producers on the first *Friday the 13th* and went on to direct the second *Friday* film, said *Halloween* was "a breakthrough for American cinema really. It pioneered several concepts, of the independent film having mainstream success, and of a certain type of horror film as a genre. And it was really well done, a really terrific film. It relied on classic suspense and situations and not gore. With *Friday the 13th,* we tried to copy the success of *Halloween,* clearly. We did it to break into the movies."

After *Night of the Living Dead,* Romero did a variety of different films, including the *Graduate*-esque comedy *There's Always Vanilla, Jack's Wife* (aka *Season of the Witch*) about a suburban housewife messing with the occult with disastrous consequences, *The Crazies,* now a cult classic about the leak of a deadly virus, as well as a series of sports documentaries called *The Winners,* but then the government stopped funding films as tax shelters, and the money dried up.

Romero and his producing partner Richard Rubinstein then tried to finance another low-budget horror film. Romero had the first half of *Dawn of the Dead* already written, and he and Rubinstein raised $100,000 from a group of Pittsburgh investors, which wasn't anywhere near enough money to make *Dawn,* but they figured they could make a movie within that budget, which became *Martin.*

Romero had the basic idea for the movie when the financing came together, and he came up with it in the middle of the night. At first it was going to be more comedic, about a vampire trying to get along in the modern world. Like the scene in the blaxploitation spoof *I'm Gonna Git You Sucka*, where the pimp gets out of jail in the eighties wearing a wide-brim hat and transparent platform shoes with goldfish swimming inside to hoots of laughter, nobody takes vampires seriously anymore either, and he doesn't scare anybody. Then he has to move to New York because the Dracula family went broke and had to sell the castle, and he gets into gambling and selling drugs to survive. In addition, Romero also heard about a serial killer in L.A. that drank the blood of his victims from a goblet he'd bring with him to the scene of his crimes. As these story ideas started piling up, the movie went in a lot of different directions, and Romero got confused himself, which formed the conceit of the film. Was Martin really a vampire, or did he just think he was one?

The audience is left to decide for itself, but during the shoot, Romero and John Amplas, who played the title role, didn't believe Martin was really a vampire. "Martin, from my point of view, was alienated, isolated, and troubled," says Amplas. "As most actors do, I was able to use some of my own personal experience because I didn't grow up with my parents, so I had a sense of what it was like, and what Martin may have felt like in terms of being abandoned or orphaned. We never sat down and discussed the whole vampire issue. For me, and George has said this too, Martin's probably just a mixed-up kid. The flashbacks in the film could be memories of his previous life, but I think they were probably just delusions."

Martin was also Romero's first film with Tom Savini providing the makeup effects, including custom vampire teeth made from dental molds instead of the silly plastic ones, and director of photography Michael Gornick, who shot many films for George afterward. In the film, Martin is a regular caller on a late-night Pittsburgh talk show, and Gornick also plays the radio host who dubs his frequent guest "the Count."

"There are all these dead towns, but people still live there, waiting for the mills to open up again," Romero said. "When you listen to late-night radio, all these devastated, lonely people call up, half of them drunk out of their minds, and it's all they talk about. 'We gotta rebuild this town!' "

Many young filmmaking hopefuls in Pennsylvania sought out George Romero because he was a local legend, and working for him was the closest anyone locally could get to a film school, and get hands-on experience.

Pasquale Buba, who went on to become the editor of *Knightriders, Day of the Dead,* and Michael Mann's *Heat,* and his brother both worked for Romero, and the interiors of *Martin* were shot in the Buba family home. Martin's bedroom was the room Pasquale grew up in, and all the religious iconography belonged to his eighty-two-year-old grandmother, who loved Romero and had no problem with a horror film being shot in her home.

When they shot the end of the film, where Martin is killed the traditional vampire way with a stake through his heart, Buba's grandmother was downstairs saying a rosary to make sure John Amplas didn't get hurt. "Savini was very good about cleaning up all the blood splatters," Buba says.

Romero also gave Buba's grandmother a 3-D picture of Jesus to add to the collection, which she absolutely adored. When anyone came to the house, she would bring them over to the picture and say, "George gave me this. Even the priests don't have a Jesus like this one!"

Shot on 16 mm and blown up to 35, *Martin* cost less than $100,000, but Rubinstein inflated the film's budget in the press so he and Romero wouldn't get less money for their next movie.

Martin was picked up by Libra, a distribution company run by

Ben Barenholtz, who pioneered the midnight movie. When it was released in July 1978, *Martin* also played the midnight circuit, where it stayed at the Waverly Theater in New York for nearly a year. (At the same time, *Martin* was also competing with David Lynch's *Eraserhead,* which was also released by Libra and was burning up the midnight circuit.)

Romero could usually count on the critics to be in his corner, and *Martin* received rave reviews, including one from *Newsweek*'s Jack Kroll they quoted in the ads: "One of the most original horror movies in years . . . a scary, ironic variation of the Dracula theme . . . Romero has become a dazzling stylist . . . his balance of wit and horror is the best since Hitchcock."

Although it wasn't a hit, *Martin*'s cult kept growing when many fans sought it out on video in the early eighties, and with the help of home video, the film finally broke even for its investors in 1983.

Romero thought about making a sequel to *Night of the Living Dead* for a long time, "but I resisted it because I didn't want to get trapped in the horror genre." He took stock of his career in 1977, and said to himself, "Well, okay, let's see if I can come up with a continuation."

Legendary producer Irvin Shapiro, who worked on a number of films for Laurel and would go on to work with Sam Raimi on *The Evil Dead*, sent the unfinished *Dawn of the Dead* screenplay to a producer in Italy, Alfredo Cuomo, hoping someone overseas would cofinance the movie. Cuomo passed the script on to Dario Argento, who loved it. Argento called Rubinstein, asking where the rest of the script was. The truth was there was no rest of the script yet, but Rubinstein told Argento he couldn't see the second half until they got down to business.

Argento flew out to the States and a deal was struck. Dario, his producer brother Claudio, and Cuomo would put up half the budget in exchange for all foreign rights in non-English-speaking territories except South America, which Romero got the rights for. Argento and Romero also had a handshake agreement that Dario had final cut on every non-English version, and George had final cut on all English-language markets. Romero liked the fact that there would be two different versions, and when he was making the film, Rubinstein said Argento stayed hands-off out of "director-to-director respect."

Back when Romero was looking for financing for *Martin,* he met with an entrepreneur who showed him the Monroeville shopping mall, located in Monroeville, Pennsylvania. It was a $50-million-dollar complex that was built by Oxford Development, and Romero knew it would be a great place to make a movie. "There were all these walkways above the shops, dark little shelters, and loads of places for people to hide," Romero recalled. The mall had 143 stores and 130 of them agreed to be used in the film. Some of the store owners even gave Romero and company the keys without interference.

In the scene where the living survivors go to the bank and take out money, which now that the world has ended is worthless, Rubinstein wrote a check for $20,000, which the bank traded for cash. Once the scene was done filming, they scooped up all the cash off the floor, gave it back to the bank, and got their check back. The bank didn't know it then, but Rubinstein didn't have enough in the bank to cover the $20,000.

The screenplay for *Dawn of the Dead* was extremely long—253 pages—but Romero wrote everything out in great detail because he didn't have time to make storyboards. "I was just trying to communicate the film to all the different departments," he said.

At first, *Dawn of the Dead* would be like *Night of the Living Dead* in that there were would be no survivors at the end, but Romero ended up letting two of the human survivors live at the end because he liked the characters too much to kill them all off.

Dawn of the Dead was shot on a four-month schedule from November 13, 1977, to February 1978. Romero was able to rent the mall for a reasonable price—$40,000 plus a small cut of the profits—but had to shoot from 10:00 P.M. to 8:00 A.M. The shoot usually went from midnight to 7:00 A.M. When the Muzak came on, it was the signal everyone had to clear out of the mall before the customers came in at eight.

Romero said the gore in his films was "the fun part, the payoff, the downhill dip of the roller coaster," and *Dawn of the Dead* was the first major makeup tour de force for Tom Savini. He was working on a play when he got a telegram from Romero: "We have another gig. Start thinking of ways to kill people."

Savini did the effects in *Dawn of the Dead* for $15,000, which included materials, help, and assistants. "The budget didn't matter," Savini says. "What the script said I had to do was for it to look as realistic as possible. The fun was inventing this stuff, how to do it. *Martin* and *Dawn of the Dead* were really low budget, and we had so much freedom. Sometimes the more money you have, there's pressure, there's deadlines, you second-guess yourself constantly, and back then we weren't doing that. We were havin' a ball, it was Halloween every day."

"Tom Savini is a force on the set," Romero says. "You get there and he comes up with a solution. It may be a soda straw painted silver so it looks like a screwdriver. In two minutes, he's got some sort of solution. It's just not the same process [today]. 'We'll paint it in later.' In the old days, we had to solve it. We had to figure out,

'Okay, here we are, we have four dollars and a soda straw.' People tell me that's one of the best sequences I've ever done, the screwdriver in the ear, I'm tellin' ya, two minutes, done."

In the second half of *Dawn of the Dead*, 40 to 50 percent of the gags and effects were improvised. "George left stuff open for that," says Savini. "He had the Francis Coppola mind where part of making movie is what happens while you're making it. He certainly planned the damn thing, but having a plan becomes a great foundation that you can build on and you can accommodate improvisations."

"I was casting director on *Dawn of the Dead*," says John Amplas, "which meant I was mostly casting zombies. Fans would come in, we'd line 'em up, find a costume, put makeup on 'em, and send them out to the mall to roam around."

Approximately 1,600 extras came in to be zombies through an open call. In the screenplay, Romero didn't give the zombies specific characters or costumes that you saw later like the nun zombie, the Hare Krishna zombie, the nurse zombie, and so on. The open call for zombies told people to come as you are. Romero wouldn't direct actors how to move, he'd let them find their own zombie movements, just telling them, "Do your best dead."

"On *Dawn of the Dead*, George really came to have a strong affection for the zombies he created," Amplas continues. "I think he was becoming more and more attached to his zombies." Romero decided not to kill the nun zombie, because he couldn't bring himself to kill a nun.

"For me personally, the appeal of the zombie is essentially they're us," John Harrison says. "George Romero's zombies have been particularly effective because he's always made sure that the zombies in his movie are not simply extras with funny makeup that are just killing machines. He's given them characters, you can identify them in all his movies, 'Oh, there's the nurse zombie,' 'There's the Hare Krishna zombie.'"

Harrison was the zombie who met his end by a screwdriver in his ear. Harrison showed up to the mall at about eight o'clock, and Savini went to work making him up. Eight turns to ten, ten turns to twelve, twelve becomes two in the morning.

"Finally they get to me, and I'm okay with this because it's fun," Harrison says. They do the scene, Harrison rushes home and has enough time for a shower and a forty-five-minute nap before he has to go to downtown Pittsburgh to meet with the vice president of Equibank.

Harrison threw on his jacket, rushed down to the bank and made his pitch. The vice president of Equibank kept staring at Harrison during his pitch and finally said, "Are you okay?"

"Well, yeah, is something wrong?"

"Well, you got blood comin' out of your ear."

"Aw, man . . ."

"I hadn't gotten all the makeup off and I was still bleeding out of my ear," Harrison said. But Harrison explained the whole spiel, which the vice president enjoyed listening to, and Harrison got the job.

Several years later, Harrison was living in Los Angeles and bowling with friends at the alley next to Jerry's Deli in Studio City. A woman three or four alleys down kept staring at Harrison. "What's this all about?" he wondered. Finally she walked by Harrison and told her friend, "See, I told you, I knew it was him. You were *the screwdriver zombie!*"

By March 1978, Romero had a two-and-a-half-hour rough cut of *Dawn* completed, and it was clear the movie wouldn't get an R rating. Warner Bros. and AIP were both considering picking up the film, but neither would put out an X-rated film. Warner's corporate policy wouldn't allow it, and Larry Gordon, who was then AIP's vice president of production and went on to become the producer of *48 Hours* and *Die Hard*, wanted AIP to move away from exploitation films, and releasing an unrated gorefest wouldn't bring the company mainstream respect.

"We felt that to cut the picture to get an R rating, we'd destroy it," said Rubinstein. "While we might get broader distribution, we felt we wouldn't have a picture people wanted to see . . . we felt that *Dawn* was strong enough to make up for the business problems of going without a rating by doing well at the box office."

Out of the three distributors that were interested in *Dawn of the Dead*, AIP, Warner Bros., and United Film Distribution, UFD offered the lowest bid, but they promised they wouldn't tamper with the film.

"When United Film Distribution released *Dawn* and *Day of the Dead*, Salah Hassanein [head of UFD] went without a rating," Romero says. "He absolutely refused to take a rating. He said, 'No, man, I think we're better off without one.' If you don't take a rating, you can't advertise in some newspapers, you can't advertise on prime-time TV, but this private maverick distributor made the decision that we might even score a little *better* if we don't take a rating."

Janet Maslin of *The New York Times* left the movie five minutes in, but the critics who stayed loved it. "An ultimate horror film!" Roger Ebert raved. "*Dawn* is a comic apocalypse that has come to maul the becalmed seventies," wrote *The Village Voice*.

Dawn of the Dead, which cost $1.5 million, reportedly made $55 million, and ultimately only one theater chain wouldn't carry the film because it was unrated. In 1983, UFD cut *Dawn of the Dead* down to an R so it could play on double bills with *Creepshow,* but the fans revolted and the R-rated cut of *Dawn* was quickly yanked from theaters. UFD begged for the fans' forgiveness in a press release: "Due to radical rejection from the longtime cult followers of *Dawn of the Dead,* United Film Distribution Company has taken the position of surrendering the R-rating certificate to the MPAA, and will in the future release *Dawn of the Dead* in its original state, as an unrated picture."

Laurel became a public company in 1980, and everyone's financial panic subsided for the time being. "The controversy surrounding *Dawn,* and its success worldwide made me 'hot' again, though on a small scale," Romero said. "I was only a 'cult' figure, after all; a mysterious guy who made movies in . . . where was it, Philadelphia? I was happy. It looked like I was going to be able to keep working for a while."

As often happens after you have a big hit movie, you have a shot to make the smaller, personal film you've always wanted to make, and that movie for Romero was *Knightriders.* "Because of prior successes, I was able to make *Knightriders,*" Romero said. "Had it been a success, I would have been able to make some other nonhorror. Happy thing that I love scare shows!"

The idea for *Knightriders* started coming together around 1976 and 1977 as Romero and Rubinstein were making sports documentaries and were trying to get a feature made.

Romero and Rubinstein wanted to make a realistic film about the age of King Arthur before John Boorman made *Excalibur.* One version of the story went Romero pitched the idea to AIP's Sam Arkoff, who sat at his desk with his big cigar and said, "I'd like it better if you put 'em on motorcycles and I'd buy it." Then Romero thought, "You know, that's not a bad idea." Others Romero pitched the idea to wanted to make it more like a *Death Race 2000* kind of film, but Romero wouldn't let the concept be corrupted.

Both Romero and Rubinstein had been working with United Artists, who distributed *Dawn of the Dead* in South America,

Australia, and New Zealand. UA offered to put up half the money for the European rights to *Knightriders,* and Rubinstein got UFD to cover the other half of the budget.

Knightriders dealt with a group of bikers dressed up as knights who run a traveling Renaissance fair, and like the knights of the round table, they try to keep their integrity and honor. There's pressure on the troupe to go more commercial, like the Medieval Knights theme park, because they can barely cover their overhead as they are. The leader of the group, Billy, played by Ed Harris, is the most fanatical about living by the code, and when he says, "I'm fighting the dragon!" he means modern-day society.

Ed Harris was recommended to George by a friend who represented the actor, and Romero knew he was the guy three lines into his audition. "That was a pretty good little movie," Harris recalled. "Everybody worked really hard and it was a really good time. I was always a fan of Camelot, and when George asked me to do it, I was really excited about it. Any moments where we were talking about the soul of the piece or the ideas of it, George took them pretty seriously and gently just like a play."

Previously Harris had a tiny part in *Coma*, and he also had a role in the Charles Bronson movie *Borderline*, but this was his first starring role, and he was featured prominently in the ad campaign. "I was twenty-nine years old man, I was excited." (Romero also brought Harris back for *Creepshow*.)

Savini had a featured role, playing Morgan, and he recalled the *Knightriders* shoot was "the best summer of my life. I was a knight in shining armor on a motorcycle in the bright summer heat. People I know who've seen it say, 'We still want to see you act sometime,' because I was basically just being me." Stephen King and his wife Tabitha also visited the set, and had cameos in the film.

Like *Dawn of the Dead, Knightriders* was another epic, and

Romero and Pat Buba edited down 300,000 feet of film. Pat started in September, and they needed a cut by December, so Buba started the first half, George started the second, "and we met in the center!" Romero says. The first cut was close to three hours, but it was cut down to a more reasonable two hours and twenty minutes.

Romero could usually count on the critics to be in his corner, and the film got great reviews. "*Knightriders* has a startling sweetness, warmth, and humor," wrote Jack Kroll in *Newsweek*. So when *Knightriders* did no business, Romero and the executives at UFD, who loved the film, were dumbfounded.

Audiences didn't know what genre the movie fit into, and unlike a zombie film, which is pretty cut-and-dried marketing-wise, *Knightriders* didn't have any obvious marketing hooks to hang the film on. It was also a longer film than average, but Romero didn't think that was a factor in the film flopping at the box office.

Famed fantasy artist Boris Vallejo did the *Knightriders* poster with Ed Harris in a suit of armor on a motorcycle, and both Laurel and UFD later felt it was the wrong campaign, looked too much like the campaign for *Rollerball*. Romero also felt the movie had a "timid" release pattern, and word of mouth on the film was strong, but it wasn't traveling fast enough.

In many cases when a movie doesn't take off, there's usually no easy answers why. John Harrison, who worked with Romero as a composer and assistant director, speculates, "I don't think UFD really believed in it. They put it out but I don't think they put enough money behind it. *Excalibur* came out at almost the same time, and I think the audience was confused about the idea of knights on motorcycles. The whole Renaissance fair thing, while it was big in certain parts of the country, it was not a major national phenomenon. I think both of those things contributed to it. Sometimes you do everything right and an audience doesn't respond."

Still, Romero was very proud of the film, and it proved he could do more than zombies. Of course there's been talk of a *Knightriders* remake, along with talk of remaking Romero's other favorite, *Martin*, to which Romero said, "Those are sort of particularly mine, and you can't have that party without me."

Celebrating Alfred Hitchcock's *Psycho,* which has been widely considered the first modern horror film. "That was the signpost that everybody followed," said John Carpenter. *(Courtesy of Rue Morgue Magazine)*

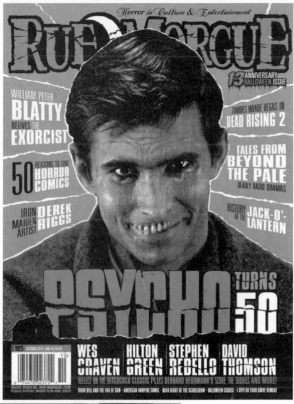

Herschel Gordon Lewis (left), who created the "Blood Trilogy" with veteran exploitation producer David Friedman, which gave the world the first gore films. Here Lewis is photographed with Lee Christian, who provided a number of photographs for this book. *(Courtesy of Lee Christian)*

John Landis (left), who reinvented the werewolf with *An American Werewolf in London,* with George Romero, who godfathered the modern zombie as we know it today. *(Courtesy of Lee Christian)*

George Romero surrounded by some old pals. *(Courtesy of Lee Christian)*

Starting off with the brutal *Last House on the Left*, Wes Craven was later able to reinvent himself with *The Hills Have Eyes, A Nightmare on Elm Street,* and the *Scream* series. *(Courtesy of Lee Christian)*

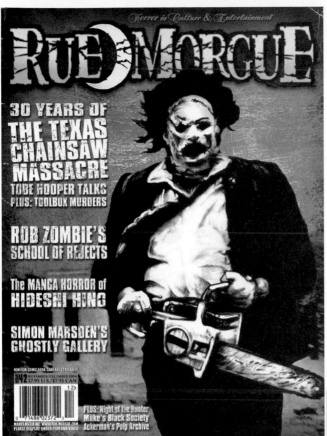

Texas Chain Saw director Tobe Hooper. As famed drive-in critic Joe Bob Briggs noted, newcomers to *Chain Saw* are "inevitably stricken with a vaguely uneasy feeling, as though the film might have actually been made by a maniac." Wes Craven, speaking for many, recalled, "I was scared shitless."

(Courtesy of Lee Christian)

Although William Friedkin (right) hates horror films, he made one of the greatest in the genre's history with *The Exorcist,* which he preferred to call "a theological thriller." Friedkin is pictured here with Josh Olsen, the screenwriter of David Cronenberg's *A History of Violence. (Courtesy of Lee Christian)*

Halloween may have launched the slasher film, but it was always much more than a low-budget stalk-and-stab flick. It was repeatedly imitated, but John Carpenter's masterful style and execution could never be duplicated. *(Courtesy of Kim Gottlieb-Walker)*

John Carpenter at a screening
of his work in Los Angeles.
(Courtesy of Lee Christian)

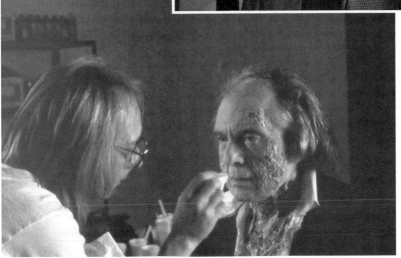

Makeup artist Mark Shostrom working on Angus Scrimm, *Phantasm*'s Tall
Man. After the success of *Phantasm*, fans on the street would plead for
him to yell out, "BOOOOYYYYY!!!" *(Courtesy of Mark Shostrom)*

Sean Cunningham followed the *Halloween* roadmap very closely in creating *Friday the 13th*, making a pile of money and launching an endless horror franchise. "The person who calls *Friday the 13th* a film is pretentious." *(Courtesy of Sean Cunningham)*

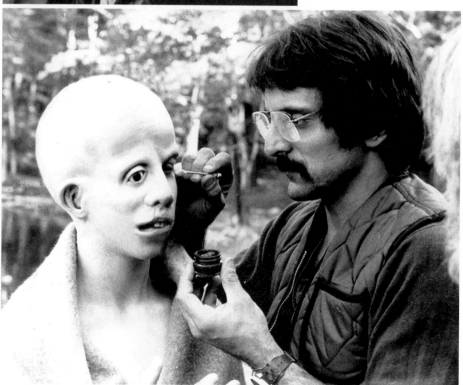

Makeup master Tom Savini giving Jason Voorhees a touch-up. *(Courtesy of Tom Savini)*

Lucio Fulci's gore masterpiece *Zombie*. As part of the Italian troika of terror—Dario Argento's best-known classic *Suspiria* was a surreal visual and aural nightmare, and Mario Bava's work had the most style—Fulci's work was always the most balls-out. *(Zombie theatrical poster artwork: @2011 Blue Underground, Inc. All rights reserved)*

Clive Barker once said of David Cronenberg, "He was so massively calm, so massively in control of himself, I thought if this guy was dangerous, I'd be scared! I'm just glad he's a good guy." *(Courtesy of Ashlea Wessel/Rue Morgue Magazine/ Marrs Media Inc.)*

Like Boris Karloff when playing the Frankenstein monster, Robert Englund had a provision in his contract for a facial after wearing the grueling Freddy Krueger makeup. *(Courtesy of David B. Miller)*

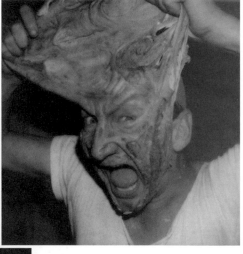

Sam Raimi couldn't come up with a better way to torture his brother Ted than by making him Henrietta in *Evil Dead 2. (Courtesy of* Rue Morgue Magazine/ *Marrs Media Inc.)*

NINE

NO ONE CAN HEAR YOU SCREAM

How Don Coscarelli created a unique, homemade horror gem with *Phantasm*, while *Alien* brought sci-fi and horror together in a terrifying crossover, and *Fangoria* became the new horror manual for young genre fans

There's a line in *Phantasm* that every "phan" of the film knows well: "I do know one thing, something weird is going on up there." Up there meaning the Sunnyside Cemetery and Mausoleum, where an old mortician known only as the Tall Man is lurching about.

Also, there are malevolent hooded dwarves running around that used to be full-sized people. The Tall Man scrunched them down to be his slaves in another dimension. Not to mention *Phantasm* has one of the most incredible weapons in horror history, a deadly flying silver sphere with retractable blades and a drill that bores through one victim's skull, sending his brains flying.

Okay, got all that? Thankfully, like *Suspiria,* a horror film like *Phantasm* can get away with wild, nightmarish tangents, and one of the most perceptive reviews of the film came from Vincent Canby in *The New York Times:* "If you've ever listened to a bright, imaginative eight-year-old child make up a ghost story, you'll have some idea of what it's like to watch *Phantasm*. What happens next is never more logical than what happened before, but at least something is happening, which often necessitates that characters and facts be suddenly introduced (or dropped) with the kind of heedless enthusiasm that only eight-year-old raconteurs can muster." He also called the film, "thoroughly silly and endearing."

The phans of *Phantasm* often became attached to the film as kids, and in addition to being a wonderfully unique horror film, *Phantasm* is also a coming-of-age story. Director Don Coscarelli and Angus "the Tall Man" Scrimm were well aware a lot of fans are in the ten to thirteen year age range, and as Scrimm said, "It seemed to give expression to all their insecurities and fears."

Coscarelli himself was a young wunderkind director, and his first two feature films were dramas about kids: *Jim the World's Greatest* and *Kenny and Company*. Both had major studio distribution in 1976 with *Jim* being released by Universal, and *Kenny* coming out through Fox.

Coscarelli made *Jim* when he was eighteen, "which was extremely young to make what was a very sophisticated family melodrama with very intelligent adult themes," says Robert Del Valle, who was the unit production manager on *Phantasm*. "It was a very mature picture for someone who was eighteen."

"I did get an early start," Coscarelli said. "In my naïve and youthful exuberance, I swore that I'd make a feature film while I was in my early teens, and to my amazement I actually pulled it off."

Don Coscarelli is from Tripoli, Libya, and grew up in Long Beach, California. Coscarelli's father, Dac, was an investment broker who helped bring the financing for Don's movies together. "I believe *Jim* was pretty much financed by Dac with successful investors who thought it was kind of cool to invest in their friend's son's movie," says Reggie Bannister, who plays Reggie in *Phantasm*.

Coscarelli was a hands-on filmmaker who was the writer, producer, cinematographer, and editor on his movies. "It's not an ego thing," he said at the time. "I simply don't know any other way to put my ideas on-screen. The more hands a movie goes through, the more it changes from the original concept of the writer or director. This way, at least, if the picture bombs, I have only one person to blame. Me. And if it succeeds, I get to take the bows.

"I never went to film school," Coscarelli continued. "My first year at UCLA they told me I'd have to wait two years to enter the film program. I'd been making small movies, documentaries, and even TV commercials with my neighborhood gang of friends all through high school. There was no way I was going to wait around at college for two years just to be in their program. So I left college and convinced my father to stake me in a microbudget feature. That film was my college! It took four years, and it was certainly 'learn by doing.'"

Coscarelli went by the motto "self-taught is best taught," and his productions also made a great makeshift film school for friends like Del Valle, who went to UCLA with Don and worked on *Jim* every weekend for six months down in Long Beach.

To make his movies, Coscarelli did the time-honored indie trick of renting the camera, grip, and electrical equipment on a Friday and returning it on Monday, so you could get a three-day weekend by paying for one day.

Making movies himself, Coscarelli felt his independence was very important. He once said, "There's nothing more heartbreaking than having a film come out with your name on it loaded with mistakes made by other people," and would later work for the major studios, like he did with *Phantasm II* at Universal, begrudgingly.

One scene in *Kenny and Company* takes place on Halloween night, where someone in a costume jumps out of nowhere and scares the kids in the film. The audience screamed and jumped out of their seats, and Coscarelli loved it. "For a young filmmaker to be able to make several hundred people jump in the air on cue was rather phenomenal. So I decided that in my next film I would go for screams, the more the better."

"There was a through line in both *Jim* and *Kenny*, and it had to do with kids," says Reggie Bannister. "Since Don wasn't much more than a kid, he really understood the angst of growing up, the little pitfalls of trying to figure out who you are. Those three films, *Jim, Kenny* and *Phantasm*, all gave birth to one another."

Phantasm was also thematically similar to another terror tale told from a child's perspective, *Something Wicked This Way Comes*, written by Ray Bradbury. In *Something Wicked*, a kid finds out about an evil that's going to envelop the town, and at first nobody believes him, then his father comes in to support the fight, like Jody's brother in *Phantasm*.

Bannister told Don about *Something Wicked*, Don read it, loved it, and wanted to make it, but Michael Douglas owned the rights at the time, so the themes of *Something Wicked* seeped into *Phantasm*. (*Something Wicked This Way Comes* was finally adapted into a film in 1983 for Disney and it flopped.)

Angus Scrimm appeared in Coscarelli's previous movies under his real name, Lawrence Rory Guy. "In my first horror role, I felt a new identity was called for," Scrimm said. "William Henry Pratt, Bela Blasko, and Laszlo Lowenstein all did the same at a similar stage in their careers," he said, referring to Boris, Bela, and Peter Lorre. And like Karloff, off-screen Scrimm was "a very intelligent gentleman," says Robert Del Valle. "A very gentle, literate person, not in the least what you see in *Phantasm*."

Don Coscarelli also said that *Phantasm* came out of the idea of "the American way of death," or how American culture handles death. "The wicked embalming tools, the sealed caskets, and the sleek black funeral coaches are just amazing props. I knew this subject would make for a great horror movie."

Like *Suspiria, Phantasm* takes a lot of wild, unpredictable turns, making it one of the most unique horror films in the history of the genre. "I was searching for a way to surprise audiences, to take them off the beaten track to a point where they feel they're losing control," Coscarelli said. "Good horror films do that. You have to create a reality of the unexpected and veering off into sci-fi and fantasy was a great way to do it."

Phantasm had elements of science fiction because Coscarelli is a big fan of the genre, and the film also had unintentional similarities to *Star Wars*, especially the hooded dwarves.

"Before we got to the dwarves, the idea was trying to come up with something weird the tall man would do," Coscarelli said. "This idea came to me, 'Well, what if he took a human and shrunk it down?' We couldn't really afford to do that kind of an effect on our budget, so we got the cloaks and there were these kids next door to the house we were filming, and we recruited them to come over and play the dwarf creatures. These kids were made like rubber. They would jump off boxes, they would fight Reggie, they had a good ol' time.

"We were filming the movie, we shot for about three months, and somebody came in and said, 'We saw a trailer for a movie called *Star Wars* and your little guys are in it!' So we went and saw the trailer and thought about changing the color of their robes, but it was just too much of a hassle on a small-budget movie, so we just decided, 'Ah, that movie will come and go, we'll just go ahead with this.'"

Phantasm's silver sphere was also originally going to have a needle sticking out of it that would drain its victims, instead of blades and a drill, and again, someone saw the black floating ball with a needle coming after Princess Leia in the *Star Wars* trailer, so they changed it.

The idea of the sphere, or the orb as it's often called, came to Coscarelli in a dream. He had a nightmare with the silver ball chasing him through corridor after corridor endlessly. "Unlike most dreams, this one stuck with me. And while writing *Phantasm*, it seemed like a perfect device with which to arm the Tall Man.

"I really didn't have any idea that he would take it to the level he did," Coscarelli continued. "His hair was combed back and his cheeks were hollowed out and he glared at me in the mirror and did the raised eyebrow thing, I could see it was going to be a very powerful character. It's one of the coolest things about directing, really. You're like the first audience for elements of the movie and when something wonderful like a performance is evolving you're the first one to see it."

Coscarelli also wouldn't "demystify" the character, meaning no stupid backstory to explain how he became the Tall Man.

Don's mother designed the Tall Man's costume, shortening his jacket sleeves to make his arms longer, a trick they did with Karloff playing the Frankenstein Monster. Scrimm, already over six feet, also wore two-inch lifts in his shoes.

The Tall Man was a man of few words, but when he spoke in his craggy voice, it was very effective. "The Tall Man, I counted, I think he had about six or seven very terse lines throughout the picture," Scrimm recalled. Fans also approach Scrimm all the time and ask him to utter his trademark line, *"Boy!"*

If Coscarelli liked an actor, he'd want to keep working with them. Reggie Bannister became part of Don's filmmaking family when he saw the actor performing in a play.

Bannister has played music most of his adult life, and Coscarelli was able to incorporate Reggie playing guitar with Bill Thornbury in the film, a fun little bit where they play a classic rock tune they improvised on camera.

"We can put these two guys together, and that will be part of their characters," Coscarelli said. "They're musical friends, they went on the road together, now they're kinda settlin' down in their small town together, but they still played together because it was fun."

Bannister also had a lounge gig at the West Coast Bodega in Belmont Shore. One night he was needed after the club closed at two in the morning, and Scrimm also recalled a three in the morning call from *Phantasm*'s producer, Paul Pepperman, asking, "Okay, we're ready for you now, can you drive out to Long Beach?" Bannister says, "*Phantasm* was always, 'Grab your shit, we gotta go film this before the weekend is up.'"

Bannister also drove a bitchin' car that became another beloved feature in *Phantasm,* a Plymouth Barracuda. Coscarelli remembered a kid in his high school had a Barracuda, green with a white interior, and Don would drool over the car. "It was really hot with the pistol-grip shifter," he said. "He'd roar out of that parking lot." Then it hit Coscarelli: "Oh, the brothers will drive one of those 'Cudas! It will give me a chance to get my hands on one."

Don got lucky because the prices on Barracudas were going down due to the energy crisis, and because insurance costs for Barracudas were going up as well. "We bought it off a kid who wanted to get rid of it." Unfortunately, any collector who wants to buy it is out of luck. It was sold after the shoot, and was subsequently junked.

Coscarelli recalled that *Phantasm* was "probably a full year of production, probably another six to eight months of postproduction." Coscarelli couldn't recall exactly what *Phantasm* cost, they didn't have accountants keeping track of everything, but it was believed to be about $300,000.

Bannister believes a lot of the budget went to film, because Don loved to shoot in 35 mm, a much more expensive proposition than shooting in 16 and blowing it up. "If you want to do a 35 mm film today, you're gonna have to have two to three hundred thousand dollars for the camera rental, lenses, film processing," Bannister says. "It's a lot of money to shoot in 35 mm, and that's why we took so long."

Phantasm was released through Avco Embassy in March 1979, and the company went on to become a horror powerhouse in the early eighties. When United Artists was bought by TransAmerica, and Paramount was bought by Gulf+Western, Embassy was also bought by Avco Corp, which stood for Aviation Corporation, an industrial company that made wings and engines for jets.

Yet throughout the seventies, Avco Embassy went for years losing money until Bob Rehme, who was previously vice president of New World Pictures, came aboard at the end of the decade. "Then we started to make some horror films," he says.

Bill Condon, who went on to direct *Gods and Monsters* and *Dreamgirls*, also worked at Avco Embassy in the publicity department for a year, where he made about a hundred a week, while he also wrote for film magazines. "In fact, I was a major champion of Don Coscarelli's *Phantasm*, which the executives there, except for Bob Rehme, just didn't get."

The art for the *Phantasm* poster was illustrated by Joseph Smith, who also did the poster art for *It Came from Outer Space*, *The Mole People*, *Blood of the Vampire*, *Horror of Dracula*, the 1959 Hammer version of *The Mummy*, *Brides of Dracula*, *Curse of the Werewolf*, *Gorgo*, *Day of the Triffids*, *King Kong vs. Godzilla*, *Kiss of the Vampire*, *Silent Running*, *Lady Frankenstein*, *Earthquake*, and *The Dark*. "Don was blessed, I have to say," says Bannister. "He was blessed with the ability to draw supertalented people to him."

Coscarelli was twenty-three at the time of *Phantasm*'s release. At

Filmex, which was the premier film festival in Los Angeles, he appeared at the festival's mystery and suspense marathon. The marathon's moderator told the audience, "The movie you are about to see won't get terrific reviews, but it's one of the most entertaining movies you'll see this year."

Yet the reviews for *Phantasm* were actually quite good. In the *L.A. Times*, Charles Champlin called it "a thoroughly scary horror film . . . Simply as an act of film-making, *Phantasm* is a smooth and terrifically impressive technical achievement . . . The suspense, all the way to a smashing and quite unexpected finish, is very craftily engineered and sustained." *Variety* noted, "*Phantasm* is a fine example of what can be done with a little cinematic ingenuity and a lot of red and yellow blood. . . . Strong point of the feature is that it's played for both horror and laughs." *Variety* also called Angus Scrimm "delightfully frightening" and said that Coscarelli "directs all with ease and excels as cinematographer, avoiding the cheap, Grade B quality."

"I think I knew our last day of shooting *Phantasm* was going to do something, and it really did do something," says Bannister.

Phantasm opened on March 28, 1979, first going out with thirty-six prints. Don and the cast made five or six trips around the country for local releases in the States, like they did back in the days of low-budget B movies where the stars would go around the country, making personal appearances at the screenings, meeting the fans.

Predicting the movie's prospects, *Variety* wrote, "pic seems a natural for fine drive-in play, and judging from popularity of recent horror items like *Halloween*, could have some hardtop potential too."

And indeed, *Phantasm* did well in the drive-ins, which were still hanging in there, and theaters. "The drive-ins were still very healthy around the country," Rehme says. "They still had a few years left."

Phantasm also had perfect timing getting released in late March.

"The time of the year we would look forward to would be the middle of March on, particularly because of the weather in California," Rehme continues. "It usually stops raining there in the middle of March, so I would always try to release [horror] pictures from the middle of March on. With those kinds of budgets, the drive-ins in California could pay for a movie. Middle of March to April also coincided with fairly nice weather back east as well, so that was the period we looked for."

It would soon get a lot tougher for the true indie companies to survive, but for now a low-budget horror film could compete in the marketplace and do well. As Roger Corman recalled, "If you were to open a Friday issue when the big ads are in for the weekend for the *L.A. Times,* and you were to open one in the fifties, sixties, seventies or eighties, you would have seen a full amount of independent low- and medium-budget films competing against the majors."

Phantasm made $12 million, a big return investment for a film that cost about $300,000. Everyone worked on deferment on *Phantasm,* and the film made so much money, everyone actually got paid.

Thankfully, there's no *Phantasm* remake for right now. "Out of respect to the fans, it's off the table," Coscarelli said. "I get a phone call every week it seems from somebody who wants to do it. It's something I've been resisting for a while." Bannister also said, "We don't need no stinkin' remake. That movie stands."

And on the thirtieth anniversary of *Phantasm,* the film played at the Hollywood Forever cemetery. "It was like a *Phantasm* Woodstock," says Bannister. "There were probably like six thousand people there as far as the eye could see. To see *Phantasm* on the side of a mausoleum wall was priceless."

The year 1979 was pivotal for horror not just for the movies, but for what became one of horror's great institutions: *Fangoria* magazine. When the first issue debuted in the summer of 1979, it was the new generation's horror magazine that showed gore in full color, and would cover the genre's ups and downs for more than three decades.

When everything was first coming together, the magazine that became *Fangoria* was going to deal with the realm of fantasy films. *Starlog*, which came out through the same publisher, was already going like gangbusters with their coverage of *Star Wars*, and this would be the fantasy counterpart.

The idea originated with publisher Norm Jacobs. In the late seventies Universal announced *Conan* was going to become a film, and Jacobs felt it would launch a number of fantasy films and crossover to mainstream audiences much like *Star Wars* did with science fiction. The magazine was originally going to be named *Fantastica*, but then had to change its name because of a lawsuit threat from a magazine called *Fantastic Films*.

So Bob Martin sat down with *Starlog* editor Howard Zimmerman, and jotted down possible names for the magazine. Martin came up with *Fantasmagoria*, a title inspired by the work of fantasy artist Richard Corben, who did illustrations for *Heavy Metal* magazine, and who also had his own graphic novel, *Fantagor*.

"Nah, it's too long," Zimmerman said, and shortened it to *Fangoria*.

"Howard, whatever you do, don't show that name *Fangoria* to Norman Jacobs, because he'll go for that, and tomorrow I'll be editor of a magazine called *Fangoria*." As Martin wandered in to the offices the next day around noon, he was told he was indeed the editor of *Fangoria* magazine.

"And that was just horrible news to me," Martin says. "I hated that name! I was also very aware of the fact that I had to deal with publicists, and I'd have to tell them I'm from *Fangoria*. The trepidation I had turned out to be true, because they would say, 'How do you spell that?' I was constantly spelling the name to publicists with their noses in the air and up their asses. It's painful dealing with publicists because of the type of people they are, but I'll tell ya, dealing with a publicist in 1984 when you're from *Fangoria* was a whole lot easier than dealing with a publicist when you're from *Fangoria* in 1979 and no one's heard of it."

Before *Fangoria* came out in 1979, *Famous Monsters* was still going strong, and there was also *Castle of Frankenstein* and *The Monster Times*. As wonderful as Ackerman's contribution was to the world of fandom, Martin wanted the magazine to be more in the vein of *Castle of Frankenstein* than *Famous Monsters*.

"I thought it would be great if I could re-create *Castle of Frankenstein*," Martin says. "Both *Castle of Frankenstein* and *The Monster Times* were way more intelligent than *Famous Monsters*. *Famous Monsters* always seemed to talk down to the ten-year-old readers, and I didn't want to do that. All due respect to Forry, I would never say a word against Forry Ackerman. He wasn't talking down because he was ten years old his whole fuckin' life!" Martin wanted a magazine that spoke to the editorial staff as well as to the fans. "I was never gonna make it more kiddie than it would allow itself to be."

Even back when print magazines were thriving, starting a new magazine from scratch was never easy. "It's a killer now, then it was just daunting," says Martin. "Paper, ink, distribution, those are the bears. We spent a huge amount of money on paper, huge amount of money on ink."

At first, like any start-up company, *Fangoria* had a rough time establishing itself, although it had several things going for it from the get-go. The first issue of *Fangoria* had a story on Tom Savini, right as he was becoming a superstar in horror makeup, and when

Fango was preparing the second issue, Martin saw an ad in *Variety*, one of those phone book–sized special issues put together for a major film market. The ad had the *Friday the 13th* logo smashing through glass with the address and phone number of the outfit shopping the rights. Bob thought, "This is something I've got to cover," so he called the number and got in touch with Sean Cunningham.

"*Friday the 13th* put us on the map for sales," Martin says. "That was our *Star Wars,* like how *Star Wars* put *Starlog* on the map. The success of *Friday the 13th* and the success of *Fangoria* were so in parallel. Not only did we cover it, we covered all the sequels to death, and they aided our growth the first couple of years. Absolutely a crappy bunch of movies, not one of 'em worth a plugged nickel as far as cinema is concerned, but still fun to watch late at night. The guys who made those movies always loved *Fangoria,* and we always treated the guys who made those movies very well."

The first issue of *Fangoria* that finally made a profit was issue number seven, which featured a crazed Jack Nicholson from *The Shining* on the cover. The issue was two weeks late to the newsstands, but it was definitely worth the wait.

"It was that iconic shot of Jack Nicholson, an exceptional cover," Martin says. "I think it's the best we ever did. Kubrick had the photos on his desk for weeks while we were trying to get him to approve them and pass them on. That's why we had to delay the printer for the cover. Stanley was a real tight-ass, he wanted to approve everything, so we got that stuff at the last minute."

At first, getting a major Hollywood publicist to help out a new magazine named *Fangoria* wasn't easy, but once the publication was firmly established as the first name in the genre, things changed for the better. "In 1979, there was a big wall up," Martin says. "After 1982 or so, all the publicists who were gonna handle a horror film knew they had to bring a strategy to *Fangoria*. They wanted their movie in *Fangoria*, and they weren't gonna put up a wall when you called 'em."

Growing into the eighties, *Fangoria* also got a big help from the VCR boom. "During the years that *Fangoria* became established and something of an institution, what really happened was the video age," Martin continues. "An R didn't mean you couldn't see a movie because you were sixteen anymore. When video came in, that's what opened it way up, and it created a larger audience for *Fangoria,* because kids would actually be able to see the movies we wrote about."

When Dan O'Bannon and John Carpenter were attending USC and working on *Dark Star*, the spaceship needed an alien mascot. "We had to pull that off on no budget," O'Bannon recalls. "And I was just stymied to come up with a space monster that looked halfway decent." This clearly wasn't going to be easy on a film student budget.

At first they rented a rubber suit from a movie house, but it looked so terrible on film they scrapped the footage and decided to start all over again. When O'Bannon realized they couldn't get a credible-looking monster, he decided to give whatever creature they were going to use a lot of personality and have as much fun with it as they could. Then one day director Jonathan Kaplan (*The Accused*) came walking onto the set carrying a beach ball with a toilet plunger attached on each side. Everyone on the soundstage broke into hysterical laughter at the sight of this thing, but O'Bannon had a brainstorm.

"That's it!" he said. "Get me a great big beach ball, and get me some of those rubber *Creature from the Black Lagoon* hands from Hollywood Magic Shop. Paint the hands like chicken feet, paint the beach ball up in some silly organic pattern, and we'll make it a real pest, jumping and squeaking. It'll immediately make you look past its deficiencies to watch what's fun about it."

Although it solved a major problem on the film, O'Bannon later said, "I was never *thrilled* with it," and the experience left him wanting to create a frighteningly real alien one day. "It was that beach ball that made me want to do *Alien* so badly."

Before O'Bannon had his big career breakthrough, he was broke and living with Ron Shusett. (Shusett would also contribute to the *Alien* screenplay.) "I knew I had to write something to get off of Ronnie's sofa," O'Bannon says. "I had gotten good responses the previous year from another sci-fi-horror script I had written called *Omnivore*. The studios liked it, but they didn't know how to do the special effects. So I thought on *Alien* I could do something with a similar feel and quality to it, but make it very clear that the special effects were very manageable by seventies standards, which were, of course, pretty primitive at the time."

Writing *Omnivore* proved very valuable to the development of *Alien*, and trying to keep the story within budget limitations helped shape the screenplay. "I wanted it to be really obvious to studio executives in 1976 that the monster was not going to be cripplingly difficult to pull off," he continues. "I wanted to write it so most of it was clearly a man in a suit, I described it as a tall humanoid, and I limited it to one because *Omnivore* had dozens of these complex creatures. But it had different parts to its life cycles. I modeled it after microscopic parasites that move from one animal to the next and have complex life cycles. I just enlarged a parasite. I was interested in the biology of aliens, so I wasn't interested in streamlining the thing below interest level just for the sake of economy."

O'Bannon also had an ace in the hole by already having über-frightening Swiss artist H. R. Giger aboard to design the monster before the project sold. They were going to work together on an adaptation of *Dune* with Alejandro Jodoworsky (*El Topo*) directing that never got out of development. "I was struck by the originality of Giger's paintings," O'Bannon said. "Not only were they frightening works, but they were absolutely, utterly original and beautifully executed. Looking at them I thought, 'If somebody could get this guy to design a monster for a movie, it would be something no one's ever seen before.' So I went in knowing that I had the cherry on top with the visualization of the thing."

The hideous beauty of H. R. Giger's art was part of the *Alien* package O'Bannon pitched to everyone. When O'Bannon showed Ridley Scott the Giger art, the director was blown away, and immediately got what O'Bannon was going for with his sleek, cold, airbrush designs. The Giger designs also helped sell the film to Harry Dean Stanton and Sigourney Weaver, who thought the illustrations "were so startling. I realized I'd never seen anything like this in a movie."

O'Bannon recalled, "When I first took Giger's work into the air-cooled arenas of power, the producers said, 'That's disgusting, this man's sick.' And I said, 'Yes, yes, yes—can't you see he's the one!' But they just sort of turned green. I'm used to having all my weirdest ideas edited out, but when Ridley Scott was hired he recognized immediately that Giger should design the alien. Ridley's vision was parallel to mine. The producers fucked around with a lot of things—story elements, visual designs, and script details. But thanks to Ridley, they didn't touch the weirdest stuff." (In addition, Scott was also looking at the graphic comic magazine *Heavy Metal,* and it was another influence on the look of *Alien*.)

An influence Scott took from *Star Wars* was how the spaceships and equipment didn't look shiny and brand-new, but dirty, smashed-up, and broken-down, like everything's been out in space for a long time. Scott personally hired Roger Christian because of the look he gave the interiors and weapons on *Star Wars*.

"I had to invent an entirely new cinema technique for set decorating *Star Wars,* using scrap from stripped-down airplanes and junkyards," Christian says. "I didn't just do this because I felt that was the way things should look, but we also didn't have the budget to build anything from scratch."

On *Alien,* Christian again used scrap, "and we took the look much further. I grew up with a vision of space as oily, used, and practical. *Alien* was the used army look, the military ship like a submarine in *Das Boot.*"

The production design and environments of *Alien* were indeed frightening, "But also in a beautiful way," says the late Fox executive Gareth Wigan. "It was Ridley's second movie, but it was an astonishing visual feast. Think back to those images of the spaceship's interior. Think back to when they wake up in the spaceship, when the pods open. There was an exquisite beauty in that. Even the alien itself was a horrific, but beautiful creation. A beautiful monster, or a monstrous beauty."

Also impressed with the look and feel of *Alien* was director David Fincher: "When I saw *Alien* I said, 'That's what movies should look like.' That was the first time I was aware of a visceral response to art direction, the first time I was aware that I was being told things about the people and the story through their surroundings, and not through exposition."

O'Bannon says that *Alien* got the green light from Fox because of the success of *Star Wars.* "They found themselves off balance because they hadn't expected it to be a humongous success, and suddenly they wanted to follow through very rapidly [with another movie]. The only thing that resembled that was my script. It was a spaceship movie and it was lying on Laddie's desk."

Like the horror genre, the major studios didn't get science fiction until the enormous success of *Star Wars*, and later that same year, *Close Encounters of the Third Kind*. "*Star Wars* was the very first science fiction film to really find that big audience," says Roger Christian, who worked as a production designer on *Alien*. "Before that it was stigmatized as a genre, and despite its huge success, that stigma still remained. Certainly Fox, being cash rich from *Star Wars,* were able to take a gamble on *Alien*."

Ridley Scott made commercials for ten years before making his first feature, *The Duelists,* which was based on the Joseph Campbell story, and was released in 1977 through Paramount.

"My training in commercials was really my film school," Scott said. "It helped build my awareness of how to present suspense and—manipulate is a bad word—fascinate the audience and hold it in a kind of dramatic suspension. I learned how to communicate visual and aural devices to work on the senses and grab the viewer's attention for a particular time span."

Scott was thinking of making *Tristan and Isolde* as his next film, but like millions of theatergoers that year, he fell under the spell of *Star Wars* when he saw it at the Egyptian Theater on Hollywood Boulevard.

"I'd never seen or felt such anticipation," he recalled. "The air was excited. I'd never seen so many crowds outside a theater. To me this was what cinema at its best should be."

Except for a few films like *2001, The Day the Earth Stood Still,* and *Dark Star,* Scott wasn't a science fiction fan, but he loved *Star Wars* so much he saw it three days in a row. "I'd done my little film, which I was happy about, but this film was massive. It actually changed my mind about what I would do next."

Scott felt *Star Wars* was a milestone in the genre, and that sci-fi films would be great from there on out. Little did he know he'd be directing the next milestone in the genre himself, and it would make a great counterpoint to *Star Wars*. "*Alien* is to *Star Wars* what the Rolling Stones were to the Beatles," said David Giler, who rewrote the screenplay with Walter Hill. "It's a nasty *Star Wars*."

When Scott read the *Alien* screenplay, he finished it in an hour and twenty minutes. "It was just *bang! Whoompf!* straight through . . . I accepted *Alien* almost immediately."

Alien was also one of the first examples, along with *Jaws,* of a B movie done the A way. Ridley Scott said that *Alien* "could easily have turned out as a bad B movie. What elevated it was me."

"*Alien* was meant to be low budget, but it was not meant to be a toss-off or something amateurish-looking by any means," O'Bannon says. "The intent was always obsessively serious on my part to make an outstanding movie. As far as I was concerned the distinctions between A and B movies had collapsed long before I was thinking about *Alien*, they had been crumbling for some time. The fact that it was technically a B picture didn't worry me at all, as long as it got an A execution." O'Bannon also added, "Ridley took it to a stage which I'm sure they never believed it would go."

Two B movies that film buffs point to that contain remarkable similarities to *Alien* are Mario Bava's *Planet of the Vampires*, and the late fifties drive-in monster flick, *It! The Terror from Beyond Space*. "I was aware of *Planet of the Vampires*, I don't think I had seen it all the way through," O'Bannon says. "I had seen clips from it and it struck me as evocative. It had the curious mixture that you get in these Italian films of spectacularly good production design with an aggressively low-budget mentality," which in spirit you could say *Alien* followed as well.

"As soon as anybody finds a single source that they recognize, they immediately assume that the picture is a variant of that source," O'Bannon continues. "They have found the source of *Alien*! I thought about *Forbidden Planet* a lot more than I thought about *It! The Terror from Beyond Space*. My mind was a big basket full of every science fiction story and movie that had been written in the last forty years, so the imagery was simply there for selecting, I didn't have to limit myself to plagiarizing a single source."

O'Bannon also grew up with the great classics *Invasion of the Body Snatchers* and *The Thing*, which were also clearly influences on *Alien*. "That type of grim tone of a few people trapped in a small, technological space while this really scary something is coming after them."

Alien's pacing, which many would consider too slow by today's standards, also worked to the film's advantage. O'Bannon says, "That's where you get all your mileage, is out of the slow scenes where nothing is happening, but what some filmmakers don't seem to grasp is that you have to earn the emotional state before you drag the audience through those lulls.

"I didn't write 'play it slow,' which is what Ridley did! He played it slow and he was damn lucky that slow worked so well for that kind of material. It could be deadly, but in this case it worked fine. I had imagined it unfolding more rapidly, but I also believed in taking your first act to set up your situation and not firing off all of your guns in it, because that doesn't leave you anywhere to go in the second half. The condition we have today is those kind of attention spans don't exist anymore. Films today are actually seen as fragments, intermixed with pieces of video games and God knows what else. People just hit the button and go to the next channel."

"The whole thing was an exercise in seeing how far back you could cock the pistol before you had to release the trigger," said Scott. "Now, of course, things are frantic from the word go but with *Alien* it was a big waiting game."

One of the legends of *Alien* is that the character of Ripley was originally written as a man, and was changed to a woman, but everyone's gender in the screenplay was deliberately left up in the air, and O'Bannon figured the gender of each character would be determined in casting. O'Bannon and Shusett only used last names in the script, and a note at the end of the screenplay read: To broaden the appeal, any two characters can be female.

Making Ripley a woman was another factor that worked in the story's favor, a nice bit of misdirection. An audience wouldn't know she would be the lone survivor against the monster, or expect her to be, adding another element of surprise to the film. Alan Ladd Jr. told *The Wall Street Journal,* "If a man like Clint Eastwood is playing the lead, you know he's going to escape the alien. You're more terrified if there's a woman in peril."

"My surprise with *Alien* was afterwards when the reaction was the importance of the leading character being female was tremendous," said Scott. "I thought, 'Wow, okay.'"

"I didn't see it as that revolutionary to cast a female as the lead in an action picture," O'Bannon says. "It didn't boggle me then, and it doesn't boggle me now. My conception from scratch was that this would be a coed crew. I thought there was no reason you had to adhere to the convention of the all-male crew anymore. Plus it was in 1976 that I was writing the thing, and it just seemed like an obvious thing to do. I mean *Star Trek* had women on for years."

Alan Ladd Jr. said making Ripley a woman was his idea. "I was kind of in my woman movie phase with *Julia, The Turning Point, An Unmarried Woman*, and I figured why wouldn't it work in this?"

When the idea was run by Scott to make Ripley a woman, he thought, "What a good idea. Yeah, let's do that. If I make this lead character female, it will be really powerful." Scott also thought, "Why not make the person who's least likely to survive be the survivor, and in the process of survival become a leader?"

"We thought it was a bold stroke," says Wigan. "In that period in the seventies, there were very few movies done for women."

Like Scott, Sigourney Weaver only had one movie to her credit, but everyone was impressed with her audition, and convinced she could take care of herself against the beast. "Sigourney exudes authority," Scott said. "She's six feet tall, and with that slightly intimidating height comes a strong personality. She is also a very smart and good actress. Sigourney hadn't had a major role before, and the studio wanted someone better known. The problem was, the females I'd met didn't have the physicality. It was an act of faith."

At least with *Jaws* you know what a shark looks like, but *Alien* kept you in a state of confusion about what the complete monster looked like until late in the game. "We wanted to show he was big, but we didn't want the audience to know *how* big," Scott said. "You're not quite sure where he stands, hangs, or what."

The alien itself was seven feet tall in a suit, and Scott didn't want to go stop-motion or use an optical approach where you add the monster in postproduction. "I preferred to take the chance of putting the creature in with them even though I knew it would be a bloody hard thing to try and do."

O'Bannon kept the monster hidden in the screenplay for budgetary reasons. "There are many good reasons for doing that, just as a simple dramatic principle of writing something scary, the unknown is the most frightening thing, and you want to make the audience squint, stare, and try and catch glimpses of the thing in the shadows. So underexposure is always more effective than overexposure when you're trying to scare people. And on top of that, the less you saw of the damn thing, the less trouble it was to do!"

The acidic fluid spewing out of the alien's mouth was K-Y Jelly, which is often used for horror movie goo. "I can remember our production secretary on the phone at nine o'clock at night, calling every hospital, every overnight chemist, getting all the K-Y Jelly she could," said Nick Allder, the FX supervisor on the film. "She sounded like a sex maniac on the telephone. We had unit drivers over the whole of London and that part of England trying to get as much K-Y Jelly as they could."

O'Bannon knew the monster had to get on the ship "in an interesting way," but he couldn't figure out how. It couldn't just sneak aboard. "If we could solve that, then I think the whole movie would unfold right into place."

Shusett came up with the idea in his sleep that the alien "screws someone. It jumps on his face and plants his seed in." As soon as O'Bannon heard it, he said, "That's it!" and later added, "That was one of the ideas that made it possible to making the thing worth doing at all."

The infamous chest bursting scene happens close to an hour into the film, and it took the audience completely by surprise. But after that horrifying moment, there's still another hour of the film to go, leaving the audience helpless, wondering what could jump out of nowhere next.

"I thought, well, we ought to do something in here, something fairly early that is excessive," O'Bannon continues. "Something over the line. Something so awful that you just shouldn't do it. I'll just do it once, and I'll do it early enough that most of the picture still has yet to play. Then after that all you have to do is make sure there's a lot of dark shadows in the corridors as you're walking around so you can't see anything. You can stretch those scenes out until the audience's teeth will shatter into nothing waiting for the unpredictable moment where the next dreadful, unacceptable thing is hurled at you."

Yet surprisingly O'Bannon didn't think the chest bursting scene was going to be *the* pivotal shock moment in the film. "I lucked out on that," he says. "I had a lot of shock scenes, not all of them made it to the screen. But when I started handing the script around and people's reactions began to come back, their attention seemed to focus in on that scene. Before the picture was even made, people started to tell me, 'That's your *Psycho* shower scene.'"

"We wanted to do something so outrageous that no one would know it was coming," Scott said. "It's not a door being wrenched open with the monster behind it or the monster coming roaring through some metal sheering or grabbing somebody from behind."

Scott shot the chest bursting scene in one take with five cameras. He had no problem with reshooting the actor's reactions twice, but wasn't going to shoot the blood spraying again. (The alien that bursts out of John Hurt was pretty much a hand puppet that was pushed through by designer Roger Dicken.)

"From a technical point of view I think we were more worried about it than any other effect in the film," Scott continued. "If we hadn't gotten it right, we might as well have forgotten the whole thing."

Scott added, "When you're making certain movies, you start to feel you've got a shot at a big one. Everything was falling into place. The sets were remarkable. The ensemble was great. We probably had the best beast since Nosferatu, and that's your driving force."

Which certainly didn't mean *Alien* was an easy shoot. Like *The Omen* and *Star Wars, Alien* was shot in England to save money. "It was made really inexpensively," Christian says. "Below the budget it should have been, at half of what it would have cost in the United States at the time. About $600,000 was slashed from the budget late during prep, so it shows that the studio wasn't exactly throwing money at it."

Scott also famously didn't give the actors direction, and they were left up to their own devices to develop their own characters and figure things out. Weaver wondered, "Where's the stroking? Where's the diplomacy? And there just wasn't any." Although Weaver initially resented this, she would later say, "There was something about Ridley's honesty and lack of bullshit that gave [*Alien*] so much authenticity."

"Sometimes what [actors] do forget about my job is that I'm carrying millions of chapters of minutiae in my head," Scott said. "Usually when I'm being attacked I'm thinking about the fabric of their suit, or their shoes, or some other part of the story, and suddenly having to address in great detail about a specific part of the narrative, I'm not necessarily going to be on my toes."

As a newcomer making his second film, Scott was micromanaged during the *Alien* production. On the fourth day of the shoot, nine Fox executives came to the set, complaining that he wasn't moving fast enough, although Roger Christian recalled that all things considered, he was moving pretty quickly. Scott said, "I was repeatedly called on to justify my every move whereas my natural inclination is to say, 'I know what I'm doing. Just let me get on with it, all right?' So the tension on the *Alien* set, I think, was partly due to my own insecurity and partly because I was being asked what, in my opinion, were so many stupid questions." One day, Scott stood on the set of the ship's bridge, and got so angry at being second-guessed he punched a hole in the ceiling.

In spite of the hardships in making the film, Christian says, "I loved every single minute working on *Alien*. We worked seven days a week, and every night I fell asleep while trying to eat supper I was so tired, but I could not wait to drive back into the studios early the next day."

Alien's immortal tagline, "In Space, No One Can Hear You

Scream," was created by Barbara Gips, who was a copywriter for Frankfurt Communications, and it popped into her mind while she was washing the dishes.

There were a number of people trying to write potential taglines for the film, and Steve Frankfurt went through pages and pages of taglines when "In Space, No One Can Hear You Scream" leaped out at him. Frankfurt said, "I was just lucky enough, or wise enough to find that among pages and pages of dissertation of what the movie was about. It was the only line to me that made any sense with the picture."

"The concern was how the hell do we sell it?" says Gareth Wigan. "We had what was for then a very expensive movie that had absolutely nobody in it that anyone had ever heard of, and on top of that, the lead was played by a woman, and a woman that no one had ever heard of. It was a real problem: how do you get exhibitors to book this movie? It was daring because you had nothing else to sell."

Still, Wigan felt the huge success of *Star Wars* fortified the studio to take chances. "We all felt a great creative confidence," he recalled. "We had a really good run, and we approached it with overweening self-confidence. The sheer chutzpah of it pulls it off. The period of 1977 to 1979 the sun was shining very brightly on Fox, and the majority of credit for that goes to Alan Ladd, Jr. We were full of confidence, we felt we took a lot of gambles that have came off. We've done all these pictures with women that have come off, we've done *The Omen, Star Wars,* we're winning, so let's go."

"For sure the surprise for the audience was a large factor in *Alien*'s initial success," says Christian. "The poster forewarned danger, that's all we really had to go on. I think the endless trailers and predocumentaries on how films are made, and the showing of so much of a movie in advance these days is a shame. I understand it's for the studios and marketing departments trying to insure their risks, but the element of surprise is really exciting for audiences."

When *Alien* had a preview in Dallas, Scott was nervous, eating popcorn like crazy to work off his nerves. He was talking to a Fox executive in the lobby when an usher passed out. "There was this incredible crash!" Scott recalled, and the manager ran in saying, "This is too much, man!"

"I was standing right next to the usher," Alan Ladd Jr. recalls. "He was standing right next to me and dropped. I tried to help him, the manager came in and started screaming at him. I said, 'What the hell are you screamin' at him for? He didn't do anything wrong.'"

"There was this moment, should we stop the movie?" recalled Gareth Wigan. "And there was a palpable sense in the audience, *Don't stop this movie*. Not a word was spoken, but you could feel it in the theater. People could have been dying all around you, but you have to see the end of the movie. I think we knew then we had a hit movie."

For superstitious reasons, Fox released *Alien* on the same month and day as *Star Wars*, May 25, now a sacred tent-pole date studios fight for years in advance, and it was a superstition that paid off in spades. It made $78 million on an $11 million budget, and the critics were also very impressed.

In the *L.A. Times*, Charles Champlin wrote, "With only his second feature, Ridley Scott has emerged as a major filmmaker. What he has to say is still not clear, but he certainly knows how to say it effectively." Gene Shalit called *Alien* "a corker, a walloper, a rouser, a screecher, and a ton of fun . . . if all movies were as thrilling I would happily spend all of my time in the movies."

Jack Kroll wrote in *Newsweek*, "*Alien* will scare the peanuts right out of your M&M's. It was about time someone made a science-fiction thriller that thrills, that has no truck with metaphysics, eschatology, religiosity, philosophy or theosophy and just boils everything down to the pure, ravishingly vulgar essence of fright."

Kroll also wrote "newcomer Sigourney Weaver, a strong young

actress with a touch of Jane Fonda, takes the classic B-movie woman's role—all the heavings and hysterics of noble women like Fay Wray, Faith Domergue, and Julie Adams—and raises it to a kind of abstract energy and ambushed grace that's like watching a ballet of pure terror."

When Scott revisited *Alien* twenty years later, he recalled thinking, "Boy, we got everything right." "The sets are as good as it gets," Scott continues. "The cameraman, Derek Vanlint, was one of the best I've ever worked with. It was a masterful job by everybody. Sometimes when you look back on a film you've made, the seams stick out like crazy, but here they just don't show."

TEN

DID YOU CHECK ON THE CHILDREN?

How Tobe Hooper returned with *Salem's Lot*, creating the modern horror miniseries, while *When a Stranger Calls* redefined the phone as an instrument of terror

The era of American miniseries was launched in 1976 with the adaptation of Irwin Shaw's *Rich Man, Poor Man*, and *Roots* in 1977, which became the biggest television event of its time. The first attempt at a horror miniseries adaptation was *The Dark Secret of Harvest Home* in 1978, based on the Thomas Tryon novel about a supernatural cult masquerading as a rural Amish-style society, but it was a ratings bust.

The following year, *Salem's Lot* was the first breakthrough TV horror miniseries, a perfect format for Stephen King's longer novels. TV didn't do horror miniseries much before the success of *Salem's Lot*, because as producer Richard Kobritz says, "They weren't considered prestigious. In the opinion of the networks, they would be appealing to the lowest common denominator."

By the late seventies, Stephen King was on his way to becoming one of the million-selling "mega-authors" of all time, and the rights to his novels were rapidly getting snapped up by the studios. But because of their length, several King books wound up getting stuck in development hell.

The Stand was especially unwieldly. Even after the success of *The Lord of the Rings* trilogy, it would still take another decade before *The Stand* and King's *The Dark Tower* would be looked at as potential multipart film series. (And even after the enormous success of *The Lord of the Rings*, Universal passed on *Tower* because of the budget.)

Back in the late seventies, there was no way a horror novel would be done in multiple parts like a cliff-hanger, it all had to be crammed into one film of a reasonable length. (Except for *Dawn of the Dead* with a two-hour-and-twenty minute American cut, horror, like comedy, usually doesn't go the epic distance.)

Salem's Lot was first bought by the features division of Warner Bros., and it was originally going to be a theatrical feature. Stirling Silliphant (*In the Heat of the Night*), Robert Getchell (*Alice Doesn't Live Here Anymore*), and Larry Cohen (*It's Alive*) all attempted scripts, but Warners didn't think they worked, and the rights languished.

Dario Argento also said that Stephen King wanted him to direct *Salem's Lot* and *The Stand*. "I feel guilty about turning King down as he has always written positive critiques of my movies," Argento said. "There's affection between us like an international brotherhood. That mutual esteem is also felt between Clive Barker and I although he has never asked me to direct one of his stories."

Richard Kobritz was executive vice president for Warner Brothers Television, and he had previously produced John Carpenter's TV movie *Someone's Watching Me*. Kobritz went on to be the president of the TV division and said, "Get *Salem's Lot* because I think we can do it as a miniseries."

"It was a big effort to get the feature department to give up the book because they had a medium-sized bestseller at the time," Kobritz says. "My feeling all along was, 'Let's keep it long and do it as kind of a prestigious but eerie miniseries.'"

Kobritz agreed with Stephen King that *Salem's Lot* was pretty much vampires in Peyton Place "because everybody has a dirty little secret in the picture," he says. "I thought it was more fun to play that up and that's really how we did the picture."

This was also why it couldn't be done as a two-hour theatrical feature. "There's just too many little stories going," Kobritz says. But the story could work in a three-hour format with commercials spread over two nights. Kobritz also figured taking *Salem's Lot* to TV could solve the script problems, giving the story a longer format to work with.

Paul Monash, who produced *Carrie* and *Butch Cassidy and the Sundance Kid*, and also wrote for television, was now the head of Movies of the Week for CBS. As it turned out, Monash was tired of the pressure of being a TV executive, wanted to go back to being a screenwriter, and wrote the teleplay for *Salem's Lot*.

Once it was pitched as a miniseries, *Salem's Lot* got set up fairly quickly at CBS, with Bill Self, who was then in charge of the network. "It was as quick of a deal as I've ever experienced," Kobritz says.

Kobritz watched a bunch of horror films, and was most impressed with *The Texas Chain Saw Massacre*. He wanted a director with a strong visual style who knew how to move the camera, could follow a script, and stick with a tight schedule. Part of the reason Hooper was hired as director was that Kobritz also didn't want *Salem's Lot* to have a "TV look."

"I wanted somebody who hadn't done television," Kobritz says. "I wanted somebody from the outside, just like John Carpenter had done *Someone's Watching Me*, I wanted somebody who didn't know the rules, so to speak, who didn't know the clichés of television. I loved *Texas Chain Saw*, I thought it was a fabulous picture, so we hired Tobe."

After *The Texas Chain Saw Massacre*, Hooper's career hadn't gone well, with a lackluster follow-up, *Eaten Alive* in 1976, and he'd also been fired from the low-budget feature *The Dark*, which came out in 1979. Hooper called *Salem's Lot* "a quantum leap for me," and Kobritz adds, "He needed that respectability."

Hiring Hooper was a battle, but Kobritz eventually won. "You can't show *Texas Chain Saw Massacre* to the network, it's too grainy, too hand-held, but in a sense that's what we wanted. We were able to convince them, it wasn't an easy battle, but we won."

Hooper was thrilled to get the assignment. "I do not have to cheat the audience to bring it to television," he said. "Television is a good format for it. It's a long story, it's fragmented, and you acquire the information that makes you respond cumulatively. And making it longer enables you to get most of the punches in."

Oddly enough, although he was hot from *Starsky and Hutch*, hiring David Soul to play the lead, novelist Ben Mears, was also somewhat of a left-of-center choice. "They originally wanted Jim Garner or David Janssen for the male lead," Kobritz says. "They were in their fifties and I was determined to get somebody in their thirties, ergo David Soul. We tried to break as many rules as possible in a very conservative medium."

Lance Kerwin, who played Mark Petrie, the young boy who teams with Soul to defeat the vampires, recently had had a short-lived TV show, *James at 15* (later retitled *James at 16*), created by Dan Wakefield, and also starred in TV movies like *The Boy Who Drank Too Much* with Scott Baio. Kerwin had the haunted quality Kobritz was looking for. "The depth of this kid," Kobritz says. "You didn't need to look further. He had all the nightmarish quality the boy should have, that lost look. Lance was a terrific actor, I thought he would have had a much better career."

There were changes made to the book, but Stephen King stayed hands-off throughout the production. "Let's make the book into whatever we want it to be," Kobritz said. "I want to be true to the story, but I don't want to be prisoner to it."

Kobritz didn't even meet King until after the production wrapped, and Stephen was pleased with the end result. He wrote a letter to Kobritz saying it was the best horror miniseries he'd seen, and that it was a big breakthrough for them. "The reason I got *Christine* as well as some other manuscripts of his was because he liked *Salem's Lot*," says Kobritz.

The miniseries took the dialogue away from the vampire Barlow, played by Reggie Nalder, who was a smooth talker in the novel. Now he was a frightening monster incapable of speech, and the dialogue was given to Richard Straker, the vampire's keeper. Barlow's makeup was Nosferatu style, bald head, sharp ears and fingernails, and Barlow is still one of the ugliest and frightening vampires in history.

"This was the era of *Dracula* with Frank Langella and *Love at First Bite*, the comedic Dracula [with George Hamilton]," Kobritz says. "I didn't want this kind of swarthy, good-looking, romantic English villain. There was always something extremely seductive about him in a sexual way, but I never wanted a romantic Dracula, I wanted a monster. We went back to Nosferatu and we made sure he didn't say a word. That's why the James Mason role was so important to the picture. We gave him all of Barlow's lines and he became the human go-between between Barlow and the town of *Salem's Lot*."

Kobritz wanted a dignified actor to play Straker, and he wanted the best cast he could get for *Salem's Lot* because "we wanted complete credibility, complete believability." Kobritz couldn't come up with anyone until the president of Warner Bros. television called one day from London: "I'm staying at the same hotel as James Mason. What do you think?" "Oh, my god, let's go for it!"

Mason did a terrific job as a cultured, dignified villain, and as Hooper said of his performance, "You can almost see the tail feathers of the canary sticking out of his mouth."

Barlow and Straker's home was also changed from a Victorian gothic mansion in the book to a rotting dump in the miniseries. There were pockmarks and craters in the walls that were oozing epoxy, "as if it were an open wound," art director Mort Rabinowitz said. "We wanted a rotting, sick appearance."

Salem's Lot was shot on an eight-week schedule on an estimated budget of about $4 million. A miniseries gives you more time to tell the story, but not as much time to make the story as you would a film because TV schedules are usually very tight and require more setups per day than in a feature film schedule.

Hooper did thirty-five to forty setups a day, and got by on three hours of sleep a night for the duration of the shoot. "It was murder," Hooper recalled. "We were tying up two stages, and we'd jump from one to another."

Kobritz felt it was important to structure the film with good cliff-hangers in the commercial breaks to keep audiences tuned in. "You can't say, 'Well, they're gonna stay tuned,'" he says. "You gotta do a cliff-hanger, you gotta put people at the edge of a precipice every time there's a commercial break or they're gonna go away. I think one of the keys to *Salem's Lot* is every commercial break we had a cliff-hanger."

Yet Kobritz wasn't happy the film was divided into two parts, which was a network decision he had no control over. "You never did two Saturdays in a row, people have short memories," he says. Still, by breaking *Salem's Lot* into two parts, Kobritz was able to make the weeklong cliff-hanger work to the story's advantage. "We knew part two would be better than part one, because you're laying the ground-work for part two with the first one," Kobritz continues.

Salem's Lot hit a generation of kids who were too young to be watching it on television, and segments of it were absolutely terrify-ing to watch without parental guidance. One of the scariest scenes that burned its way into many people's brains was when Mark Pet-rie's friend, Danny Glick, who is now a vampire, floats up to his room, raps on the glass, and whispers, "Open the window . . . He commands it . . ."

"From what many people have told me, the floating kid outside the window is consistently the moment that people cite as the one that invades their sleep," says Jules Brenner, the director of photogra-phy on *Salem's Lot*. "Those who have shared their reactions with me, almost to a person, told me they have never gotten the image of the boy floating in the window out of their minds." And similar to the dinner table scene in *Texas Chain Saw*, the scene where David Soul drives a stake through Barlow's heart while a gang of vampires are crawling out of the dark to get Lance Kerwin, does a great job of keeping you on the edge of your seat for what feels like an eternity.

Salem's Lot was also left open-ended, but not for a potential se-quel. "It was my theory that evil is smited for the moment, but it will come back somehow, some day, some way," Kobritz says.

Salem's Lot aired on CBS, 9:00 P.M. EST on November 17 and 24, 1979. CBS wanted *Salem's Lot* to be a two-parter so they could blunt the competition, which was then *The Love Boat* and *Fantasy Island*.

Although it didn't destroy the competition, *Salem's Lot* did well in the ratings. "You're talking *Grey's Anatomy* and *Desperate Housewives*, that kind of duo by today's standards," Kobritz says. "But it was able to keep ABC out of the sweeps that November, and put CBS into it. I think it worked out okay, it certainly worked out for the benefit of CBS."

Mick Garris, who directed the miniseries adaptation of *The Stand,* says, "*Salem's Lot* was really something game-changing. Television had tackled horror before, particularly in series, but *Salem's Lot* was the first time they got a real horror filmmaker, somebody who knew the genre, to do it long form. Rod Serling, *Outer Limits,* things like that had happened before, but never had there been someone associated with a classic horror movie that had done television. *Salem's Lot* was stylized in a way that only a fan of the genre could have done it. Tobe brought something fresh and wonderful to a medium that was not known for fresh and wonderful in the world of fear."

If you want to learn a great lesson in suspense and how to scare the hell out of an audience, watch the first twenty minutes of the original *When a Stranger Calls.* Still effectively constructed, and still effectively scary, *Stranger,* along with *Halloween,* established babysitters in jeopardy as an effective horror theme, and *Stranger* also very effectively used the phone as an instrument of terror.

The team that put together *When a Stranger Calls* was cowriter and director Fred Walton, cowriter Steve Feke, and producer Doug Chapin. Feke told Walton a story he was sure he'd read about somewhere, an incident that happened in Santa Monica, Pacific Palisades, or Brentwood, somewhere like that, of a babysitter being terrorized by someone over the phone. "He told me this story in 1977," Walton recalls. "It was basically the first act, about the babysitter, the house, the phone calls, and it immediately struck me as a great story."

Some remembered the story as an urban legend, like writer Jack Bond, who was shown a preview of the first twenty minutes by Columbia. "Okay . . . now I'm scared . . . ," he wrote in his report for *Marquee* magazine. "I remember this story. It used to scare me to death every time I was alone in a strange house. Now it's scaring me to death in a screening room in the middle of the afternoon."

The story also appealed to Walton because "it was cheap to do! You only needed one actress! I didn't think, 'Oh boy, babysitter, everyone can relate to that, certainly all the girls in our audience will be able to relate to that.' I didn't think those thoughts. There was nothing more analytical going on other than it was a good story, and it was commercial, scary and cheap to do.

"Even before you pick up the phone, I would assume most people have had the experience of having the phone ring in the middle of the night," Walton continues. "And it's just unsettling because you don't know who it is, and if you've ever had someone close to you die and the news comes to you from a phone call at 3 in the morning, then that puts an extra burden on you whenever you hear the phone ringing late, late, late at night. You know it's a bad sign, it's a really unpleasant experience."

The phone had also been used effectively as an instrument of terror before in *Black Christmas*. It's amusing to watch the film now in the age of *69 and caller ID, and it's also funny to see how long it took the police to run down corridors of intertangled wires trying to trace the call.

Bob Clark, the late writer and director of *Black Christmas*, said, "I don't know where it was used [before], I'm sure it has been used, not quite to this extent. It's something about being able to project horror in a way you can't deal with. On a phone they try to catch him with the wiretapping they had at the time, but it invades you. And where is he? There's a mystery to a phone, he could be anywhere. That guy uses the house. I'm sure we weren't the first to do that, but I think the first to be famous for it."

When a Stranger Calls first started out as a short called *The Sitter*, and it was what became the first twenty minutes of *Stranger*. Walton and Feke were trying to break into the business somehow and Walton thought if they made a short film out of the story, they could get work from it. They shot *The Sitter* on 35 mm with a professional cameraman and tried to make it look as slick as possible, so no one would think it was a student film.

The short turned out well, but Feke and Walton didn't have many connections to show it to, and the executives who saw it weren't impressed. There wasn't much of a market for short films, although they were still being played before features mixed in with the coming attractions. They thought, "Well, if we can get nominated for an Academy Award, *that* might get us some attention." In order for them to get Academy consideration, the short had to play for a week theatrically in either L.A. or New York.

Feke knew someone who could get the short played in Mann's Village Theater, where it was shown before *Looking for Mr. Goodbar* from a Friday to the next Thursday. "We went for the first showing Friday night to see how it really played for a real live audience, not just for a couple of friends or snotty studio people who weren't impressed by anything."

Walton recalled, "All during the short, which was a little over twenty minutes, people are coming down the aisle with their popcorn, looking for seats, and they're sort of glancing at the screen, going, 'Is that Diane Keaton?' and we were just dying. Then at a certain point, the theater got really still, and at that moment when she tries to get out of the house, the door opens and the detective is there, there was this really big scream. We realized no matter what else happens with this thing, at least it works. We pulled it off."

Feke and Walton realized they'd never get anywhere trying to sell the short. They figured they'd expand the story, pitch it to a low-budget company, tell them the first twenty minutes were already shot, they'd only need a few hundred grand to finish it, and they'd have a really scary, wonderful little picture. Producer Melvyn Simon liked the idea, and put up the money to turn it into a feature. "It turned out to be a nice showcase, and we got lucky," said Feke.

When a Stranger Calls, which starred Carol Kane, Charles Durning, and Colleen Dewhurst, cost $1.5 million. "Without as professional a cast and crew as we had for our first time we could never have done it," said Walton.

Once the film was completed, Columbia picked it up for distribution. Opening on September 28, 1979, *When a Stranger Calls* opened at number one at the box office, and made $20 million domestic.

Again, you can learn a lot about building suspense from watching the first twenty minutes of *Stranger*, and based on how he constructed the introduction, Fred Walton advised, "Don't be afraid to slow down and get into the details of what's happening each moment. The clock is ticking, the wind is blowing outside, the ice cream bar is melting, all these little things flesh out the environment that the protagonist is struggling in." The geography of where everything is happening is important as well.

"You have to give the audience a clear sense of geography of the locations. Where is the door, where is the window, where is the hallway, how does it all play into each other. A lot of filmmakers don't bother with that, and I think the suspense suffers as a result."

The first act of *Stranger* also builds scares with simple ideas. "The things that scare me are the most realistic things," Walton says. "And for most people, the realistic things tend to be really small—like the phone ringing, a knock at the door—it doesn't involve supernatural things, or aliens, or any of that stuff."

Taking time to set it up is essential, and Walton feels the audience will give you leeway provided the payoff is worth the wait. "No one in the theater is going to walk out in the first thirty minutes, they just aren't," Walton says. "So you've got 'em for at least thirty minutes. Now you better deliver at the end of thirty minutes, but you've got all this time that you can build, build, build."

ELEVEN

BE AFRAID, BE VERY AFRAID

How John Carpenter had trouble following up *Halloween* with *The Fog*, while Stanley Kubrick tried his hand at horror with *The Shining*, creating a flawed masterpiece in spite of Stephen King's displeasure, and David Cronenberg brought an intellectual and scientific approach to scares

Following up on the phenomenon of *Halloween*, *The Fog* was a switch in gears for John Carpenter, a traditional ghost story. "It was something I wanted to try my hand at, and I got kicked in the butt for it," Carpenter says. "But I did want to change it up."

The Fog was Carpenter's first movie on his deal with Avco Embassy. Mick Garris, who was then in charge of special marketing and publicity at Avco, says, "People had high expectations with *The Fog*, which John had originally set out to make more like the Val Lewton movies of the forties, something more subtle and not nearly as overt as *Halloween*. When they tested it, it was a little quieter than audiences expected. To me it was exciting that John was taking a different direction."

The scene in the beginning with John Houseman telling the ghost story around a campfire wasn't added later as some have suspected, but was part of the movie from the beginning. Tommy Lee Wallace says, "John and Debra felt strongly they needed to frame the movie with the sense of an old-fashioned story told round the campfire to capture the difference, to tell people in no uncertain terms, 'This isn't *Halloween*, this is something different, so sit back, kiddies, and we're gonna tell you a little story.'"

Halloween was "doing something artful with a genre film," says Dean Cundey, and the same approach "was really evident in his choice of his next film. *The Fog* was a genre film, a ghost story. It was not a surprise when he said the next film would be a ghost story, and not a conventional horror film. Nothing John did was ever the formula of the previous success. I think that's the mark of a good director. It's always about the material and the film as opposed to how can we make the sequel to my last film so I can make a lot more money."

The Fog had many of the same people from *Halloween*, including Jamie Lee Curtis, who also got to act with her mother Janet Leigh. "John couldn't believe that I didn't get any jobs after *Halloween*," Curtis said. "I got no jobs. The only job I got after *Halloween* was an episode of *Charlie's Angels* where I played a lesbian golfer, and I did a *Love Boat* episode with my mother. The coupling of *Halloween* and *The Fog* then led to other horror films going, 'Ooo, we should put her in the movie because she's sort of that girl now,' and then that's how that really took off. It was really the second movie that made that happen."

Since making *Halloween*, Carpenter's life had gotten complicated. His relationship with Debra Hill ended when he fell for Adrienne Barbeau, who he cast in *Someone's Watching Me*, and they married on New Year's Day in 1979. It was a tough breakup for Hill, and a hard transition for Barbeau as well. "I was freaking out because I'd 'lost my freedom' and he was disappointed because our courtship had ended," she recalled.

Their careers were also going in different directions. With the success of *Halloween*, Carpenter was now one of the hottest young directors in Hollywood, and Barbeau was now done with *Maude* and turning down TV work in the hope she'd have a feature film career.

Barbeau also began starring in horror films at Carpenter's urging, and even though she didn't like the genre she loved working with Romero and Craven on *Creepshow* and *Swamp Thing*. Barbeau saw *Halloween* "under duress—I was engaged to the director. I watched the entire movie screaming and grabbing onto John, praying for it to be over. I love doing them, I don't like watching them." Barbeau loved *Dark Star* though, and the ending always brought her to tears.

Principal photography on *The Fog* started in March 1979. Carpenter found the lighthouse in Inverness, California, and he loved the location. The path down to the beach was 365 steps, which was hard to travel because there were thirty mile an hour winds. Nearby was Point Reyes Station, with a population of three hundred people, and Carpenter got them to turn off all the lights for the scene where the fog causes a blackout. Nearby was the Western Tavern and the Two Ball Inn.

"Virtually all the credits were the same on *Halloween* and *The Fog*," says Wallace. "We had three times the budget, and it should have been fine, but it was very, very difficult. I think the heart of the matter was it was a much more ambitious story. *Halloween* is a knife movie, *The Fog* is a ghost story, and that's a whole other matter. It's about tradition, it's about special effects, it's about controlling this completely uncontrollable substance, which was the fog, and it just about made us all crazy."

Once the film was first put together, Carpenter and Wallace watched it, and it just didn't work. "There was something about that movie that didn't want to cut together that smoothly," Wallace continues. "We were sitting there watching it, it just sat there like a big glob of mud. So John displayed a great deal of courage and said, 'We've gotta tear this thing down and start over.' And we did."

Three months before the release date, Carpenter told Avco Embassy, "I need to restructure this film and save it." Carpenter was willing to pay for the reshoots himself, but Avco agreed to pay for it, and was glad he was willing to put his own money on the line to make a better movie. Carpenter confessed to Barbeau he felt he failed and wanted to quit directing.

Carpenter said, "It was very shocking to go from a movie that was as easy to make as *Halloween* to a movie that seemed to be simple on the surface when you read it and that was in the end a much more difficult film to pull off. It was quite a humbling experience." Wallace said, "It was the anti-*Halloween* final payback for our smooth ride with Jamie Lee and the Shape."

"One of the surprises of the preview was the fact that it was so minimal, the audience didn't quite get it at first," Cundey continues. "We went back and shot some additional footage of meat hooks and things, because while it was a stylish ghost story, when people disappeared into the fog there wasn't that fear of the threat to someone's life. So we had to go back and explain to the audience this terrible fate of the victims that disappeared into the fog, and at that point the audience got the theme of the movie."

When things felt the lowest, Carpenter and the gang were moping at one of John's favorite hangouts, the Formosa Café. Then Carpenter pointed to a group of workers on top of the Goldwyn Studio, tarring the roof on a hot summer day. Putting things in perspective, Carpenter said, "Just remember, that could be us up there."

Released in February 1980, *The Fog* grossed $15 million, and was one of Avco's biggest hits. "*The Fog* was very, very successful for us," says former Avco Embassy president and CEO Bob Rehme. "It was one of the biggest openings Embassy Pictures ever had, and we were very happy with it."

Avco just had a big success the month before with David Cronenberg's *Scanners,* and it would also have big hits in the near future with *Prom Night* and *The Howling.* "Avco Embassy became the horror studio where they had all the good guys," says Garris. "It was an unbelievably great and exciting time to be there, working with people like Joe Dante, John Carpenter, and David Cronenberg. It was exciting to be a part of it and to be in the middle of an incredible boom."

Looking back on it now, *The Fog* is not a perfect film—it feels uneven and doesn't pack the visceral punch of *Halloween*—but in spite of this, it's still a fun and enjoyable campfire story. And considering how little it cost, John did a lot with a little (Carpenter would joke the film was done with a million dollars and two or three fog machines). "If you watch it now, you'd be way more impressed," says Cooper Layne, who wrote the remake of *The Fog.* "I know I was. I was watching it going, 'Wow, they had little models built for the ghost ship,' they did a bunch of stuff we didn't have to because we had a decent budget, and they made a pretty scary movie. It's really a pretty cool, classic telling of a ghost story."

The Shining was the next major Stephen King adaptation before they started flooding movies and TV en masse, and it was not a straightforward adaptation of the novel. How could it be with Stanley Kubrick making it? *The Shining* also wasn't a perfect film, but like with Kubrick's best, there are scenes, segments, and shots you'll never forget, even if you only see it once.

King himself would never be happy with the film, most of the reviewers didn't like it at the time either, but Hitchcock saw reviews on his films turn around, which happened with both *Psycho* and *Vertigo,* and it didn't take long for people to give *The Shining* a second look either.

Knowing that Stanley Kubrick was interested in making a genre film, and was also interested in ESP and the paranormal, John Calley brought Stephen King's novel, *The Shining,* to his attention when it was in galleys.

"When I finished *Barry Lyndon* I spent most of my time reading," Kubrick recalled. "Months went by and I hadn't found anything very exciting. It's intimidating, especially at a time like this, to think of how many books you should read and never will. Because of this, I try to avoid any systematic approach to reading, pursuing instead a random method, one which depends as much on luck and accident as on design. I find this is also the only way to deal with the newspapers and magazines which proliferate in great piles around the house—some of the most interesting articles turn up on the reverse side of pages I've torn out for something else."

Kubrick locked himself in his office and began to read. Outside his office, Stanley's secretary heard book after book hit the wall and fall into a reject pile. Once Kubrick got to *The Shining,* the books stopped thunking against the wall.

Kubrick felt the King novel was "one of the most ingenious and exciting stories of the genre I had read. The novel is by no means a serious literary work, but the plot is for the most part extremely well worked out, and for a film that is often all that really matters."

Kubrick also thought the idea of ghosts was an optimistic one, meaning there was an afterlife, and saw the "closed loop" of the story where Jack Torrance was always the caretaker at the Overlook as a happy ending. "I think the unconscious appeal of a ghost story lies in its promise of immortality," Kubrick said. "If you can be frightened by a ghost story, then you must accept the possibility that supernatural beings exist. If they do, then there is more than just oblivion waiting beyond the grave."

Diane Johnson, who wrote the screenplay for *The Shining* with Kubrick, recalled that Stanley was "also interested, almost abstractly, in the idea of making a horror film, trying to understand what frightened audiences and why they enjoyed being frightened. It was a kind of inquiry that continues within the film itself."

Another part of Kubrick's motivation in making a horror film was he wanted a hit. "He was very vulnerable to criticism as to whether a movie was a success or not," said John Milius, who had a "phone relationship" with Kubrick since the early eighties. "He wasn't completely comfortable with *Barry Lyndon*. He just felt that people didn't understand it. People were bored by it. I think after that picture he felt no one was going to let him make a film again. Apparently the only thing that really bothered him a great deal was that *Barry Lyndon* failed commercially. He made *The Shining* after that."

King had written a screenplay for *The Shining*, but Kubrick wanted to start from scratch. Like the relationship he had with Anthony Burgess on *A Clockwork Orange*, Kubrick didn't want King to adapt his own novels, but did want him available by phone to answer questions about the story.

To write his own screenplay for *The Shining*, Kubrick brought on Diane Johnson, a novelist who had never written a script before. Kubrick liked a novel Johnson wrote, *The Shadow Knows*, and at the time he enlisted her, she was teaching a class on gothic novels at UC Berkley.

"I was interested in several of her books and in talking to her about them," Kubrick recalled. "With *The Shining*, the problem was to extract the essential plot and to reinvent the sections of the story that were weak. The characters needed to be developed a bit different than they were in the novel. It is in the pruning down phase that the undoing of great novels usually occurs because so much of what is good about them has to do with the finesse of the writing, the insight of the author, and often the density of the story. But *The Shining* was a different matter. Its virtues lay almost entirely in the plot, and it didn't prove to be very much of a problem to adapt it into the screenplay form."

Kubrick felt it was better to adapt a book instead of writing something original from scratch, and he felt you should choose a book that wasn't a masterpiece, so you could build on it, and improve it.

As they worked on the script together, Kubrick and Johnson talked about H. P. Lovecraft, Bruno Bettelheim's analysis of fairy tales, how Freud theorized parapsychologial experiences, as well as the work of Kafka.

"It seemed to me that the perfect guide for this approach could be found in Kafka's writing style," Johnson said. "His stories are fantastic and allegorical, but his writing is simple and straightforward, almost journalistic. In fantasy you want things to have the appearance of being as realistic as possible." Kubrick instructed Johnson: "It must be plausible, use no cheap tricks, have no holes in the plot, no failures of motivation . . . it must be *completely* scary.'"

Danny's visions, as often cited in ESP, had to be fragmented, and they had to be short. "If Danny had perfect ESP, there could be no story," Kubrick said. "He would anticipate everything, warn everybody, and solve every problem. . . . One of the ironies in the story is that you have people who can see the past and the future and have telepathic contact, but the telephone and the shortwave radio don't work, and the snowbound mountain roads are impassable. Failure of communication is a theme that runs through a number of my films."

In casting Jack Torrance, Kubrick and Jack Nicholson wanted to work together since Nicholson broke through in *Easy Rider*. "I hadn't read the book, but it wouldn't have mattered," Nicholson recalled. "I would have done whatever Stanley wanted." Once Kubrick sent Jack a copy of the novel, Nicholson thought it was marvelous, and that it would be a great opportunity to work under "Kubrick's orchestration."

Shelley Duvall was the first and only actress Kubrick considered to play Wendy. "You certainly couldn't have Jane Fonda play the part," Kubrick said. "You need someone who is mousey and vulnerable . . . I had seen all of her films and greatly admired her work. I think she brought an instantly believable characterization to her part. The novel pictures her as a much more self-reliant and attractive woman, but these qualities make you wonder why she has put up with Jack for so long. Shelley seemed to be exactly the kind of woman that would marry Jack and be stuck with him."

Johnson recalled Wendy was more developed in the script, "and therefore, the psychological situation was richer. I felt that Kubrick didn't get along too well with Shelley Duvall and that he eventually cut part of her dialogue and shortened her scenes. In the end, it was okay, but her character could have been more interesting if her comments had been more sensible and clever."

Danny Lloyd, who played Danny Torrance, was picked out of about five thousand kids who auditioned in the States over six months, and the finalists were narrowed down to five. Joe Turkel, who played Lloyd the bartender at the Overlook Hotel, had previously worked with Kubrick on *Paths of Glory*. Turkel and Kubrick both grew up in the Bronx. "He was twelve and he was hustling chess," Turkel recalled. " 'Fifteen cents? Sure, I'll play you.' He'd win all the money and in the end he'd go to the movies. He went to movies all the time. Every Saturday and Sunday you could find him on Times Square. Forty-second Street had seventeen theaters, one right next to the other. They were open twenty-four/seven and they were always busy."

Kubrick also saw *The Shining* as a great vehicle for the Steadicam, which Garrett Brown, who created the device, operated himself for the film. In 1974, Kubrick saw a demo shot with the first Steadicam prototype, and he was hooked, calling it "a magic carpet." (Kubrick would also mention that the scenes in the hedge maze couldn't have been done without it.)

Brown showed Kubrick a prototype of a new Steadicam model he was working on that could shoot at a lens height from eighteen inches to waist-high, and Stanley was thrilled because much of the film would revolve around a little kid's height and point of view.

Shooting with the Steadicam, everything had to be right on the mark to be in focus, and accuracy was crucial. Brown worked hard on this before coming aboard *The Shining* in December 1978, but he soon realized with Kubrick it was a whole new ball game.

"I would have been happy to be on any of his movies," Brown says. "Stanley moved the camera well in general and purposely, and I would have been happy to debut on *Barry Lyndon* or *A Clockwork Orange*, so I was happy that it was a Kubrick film."

The Shining shoot went from May 1978 to April 1979 at Elstree Studios in England, and was Kubrick's first picture there since *2001: A Space Odyssey*. The shoot was initially only going to be sixteen weeks, but when it obviously went considerably longer, Elstree had to juggle their schedules to accommodate the filming of *Flash Gordon* and *The Empire Strikes Back*.

As always with Kubrick, everything on the film was top secret. A spokesperson for the film told the press, "As befitting of any hotel, Mr. Kubrick has just hung up the 'Do Not Disturb' sign."

Terror often needs isolation, and the beginning of *The Shining* very effectively drops the audience in the middle of nowhere. Kubrick may also have been able to relate to the story being a recluse himself. "I'm certain the subject had a certain resonance for Kubrick, given the way he had chosen to live his own life," Nicholson said.

"But, of course, the difference was that he was a father and husband capable of loving within that isolation."

As he always did, Kubrick shot a lot of takes, and the first day he did thirty takes of a traveling shot in the lobby. Even though he invented the Steadicam, working on *The Shining* taught Brown all new moves in steering and controlling it. "It was an opportunity to bear down on technique that you wouldn't find anywhere else," Brown said. After shooting several takes, Brown would concentrate on the finer points of using the Steadicam. "That's where I really learned to control the damn thing."

The Steadicam was a great device to take the audience through a very large, complex hotel and hedge maze, and it gave the audience a sense of scope with everything. "Your sense of the geography in *The Shining* was so much larger in scale than in most horror films," Brown says. "Most horror films you're learning the ins and outs of claustrophobic spaces, with *The Shining* it felt much bigger, like you were learning your way around the whole place for a purpose that was not in view at all in the tour that took place in the beginning."

For the Overlook design, production designer Roy Walker went around America taking pictures of hotels. The main hotels that inspired the film were the Awanee in Yosemite Park for the interiors, and the Timberline Lodge, where Diane Johnson went on ski trips with her family as a little girl, for the exteriors. "I wanted the hotel to look authentic rather than like the traditionally spooky movie hotel," Kubrick said. "The hotel's labyrinthine layout and huge rooms, I believed, would alone provide an eerie enough atmosphere."

"Stanley brought you into spaces in a really interesting way," says Brown. "His storytelling shots walked you in, and moved you into places that were memorably beautiful, memorably beautifully lit, or strikingly presented in some way or another. But there are no ordinary spaces in his films."

Real lighting was used for the Overlook, as if they were shooting in a real hotel, and the entire set was wired up four months before principal photography. The interior lighting of the chandeliers and lamps were adjusted from a central control board by John Alcott, Kubrick's longtime director of photography, who controlled the lighting via a walkie-talkie to the control room. Because there were so many Steadicam shots, no floor or overhead lights that could create shadows were used.

When Danny was on the Big Wheel, Brown was following him in a wheelchair that was built for *A Clockwork Orange*. The wheelchair was designed to have a platform on it, and you could lie on it or stand up on it while it was moving. Brown used the wheelchair a lot because "in a number of instances it was the only way to get the lens right down to floor level."

Brown originally tried to follow Danny on foot, got tired after three minutes, and he couldn't get the low shots at that speed without the wheelchair. "I never even tried running after the kid, that would've been just a joke," Brown says. "A kid on a Big Wheel can go about seventy miles an hour."

A wonderful element of the Steadicam shots was the sound of Danny's Big Wheel ricketing across the floor, then quietly coasting over the carpet. "None of us had any idea how great the carpet and floor sounds would be until the dailies," Brown says. "You couldn't hear it when you were a few feet away from the actors. As soon as we heard it, we knew that the sound was essential to that scene, because it was so bizarre." (Because the wheelchair had rubber wheels, you couldn't hear it running across the floor behind Danny.)

Brown called his work "the Steadicam Olympics," and he added, "it's like playing a piano while you're simultaneously moving the piano. It's fine motor skills working in conjunction with very big muscle exertion."

It was probably on *The Shining* that Kubrick first became known for wearing the same outfit every day. He had a dozen pairs of the same shirts and pants, a bluish colored jacket, and well-worn sneakers. "It was so he didn't have to devote any part of his attention to selecting what to wear," Brown says. "It was just intriguing because it was like time was moving on for all of us, but Stanley was like an optical effect. He was there looking the same every day."

"It soon became clear that he didn't care what he wore," said his widow Christine Kubrick. "Later, the children tried to dress him up a bit better but it was hopeless." He did, however, buy a suit for his daughter's wedding.

As many know per Kubrick's legend, he was very demanding, and well known for asking for endless takes of a scene, which the cast respected, even if it could be a tiring process. The scene where Nicholson comes out of nowhere and chops Scatman Crothers with an ax was forty takes. Then when Crothers worked with Clint Eastwood on *Bronco Billy* and only had to do a scene in one take, he nearly burst into tears of relief.

Still, Crothers, who hadn't heard of Kubrick before working with him, later marveled, "He had Shelley, Jack, and the kid walk across the street. Eighty-seven takes, man, he always wants something new, and he doesn't stop until he gets it."

Nicholson himself didn't mind it. "You felt a lot less pressure because he didn't stop until he got exactly what he wanted," he said. "I didn't care how many takes we did. What bothered me was not reaching the level of perfection he was accustomed to. This was okay with me, because I can be a very technical actor, which was often what he wanted."

For the "Here's Johnny" scene, Nicholson chopped through ten doors. "There were cumulatively hundreds of ax strokes, and we were examining whether the splinters were better in this one than in that one," says Brown. Brown was crammed in the corner filming, and he also recalled it "took a lot of fortitude on my part when that blade kept coming through."

Both Nicholson and Duvall respected Kubrick, but it was a rough shoot for them both, Duvall especially. She felt she wasn't getting the attention or consideration Nicholson got from Kubrick, and it took its toll. "From May until October I was really in and out of ill health because the stress of the role was so great," she recalled.

Kubrick was also abusive to her during the shoot, once yelling at her when she screwed up a take: "There's no desperation! We're fucking killing ourselves out here and you've got to be ready! When you do it, you've got to look desperate, Shelley, you're just wasting everyone's time now."

"He knew he was getting more out of me by doing that," Duvall continued. "So it was sort of like a game. I resented Stanley at times because he pushed me and it hurt. . . . We had the same end in mind, it was just that sometimes we were different in our means, and by the end the means met."

Duvall was a favorite actress of Robert Altman, and when they worked together again on *Popeye,* Altman could clearly see *The Shining* had changed her as an actress. "Stanley pushed me and prodded me further than I've ever been pushed before," she continued. "It's the most difficult role I've ever had to play. . . . If Stanley hadn't pushed me as hard as he did, I would never have produced the performances I did."

When John Boorman saw the film, he remarked, "I could see what Kubrick had been up to. He was trying to get performances that came out of extremity, exhaustion."

A year after the film's release, Duvall said Kubrick was like Altman in that he was "very witty, but also sardonic. He made life miserable for me, but he expanded my scope as an actress. It's much easier for me to go from one extreme to another, and now I can play extroverted characters . . . I have no regrets about my experience working on *The Shining*. Kubrick took a second-rate book and transformed it into a first-rate psychological thriller. It was a fantastic success. And as Stanley said to me, 'Nothing great was ever accomplished without suffering.' "

Kubrick also said that making a film "can be like trying to write *War and Peace* in a bumper car in an amusement park," but added, "when you finally get it right, there are not many joys in life that can equal the feeling."

The ending of the film, a long shot that goes through the Overlook lobby to the photo of Jack on the wall, took days to finish. Kubrick kept seeing camera bumps so they first put the dolly on a different cart. When that didn't work, they put it on a track. When that didn't cut it, they changed the wheels. Then they figured weighing down the cart would keep it still. "People were hanging on to this cart trying to keep it still so they could get this shot," recalled Tony Burton, who had a small role in the film as Larry Durkin, the owner of an auto repair shop.

It had been more than twenty years since Kubrick and Joe Turkel had worked together, and at the end of the shoot, Stanley told Joe, "Your scenes in *The Shining* are some of the finest in the picture. I want to thank you very much." Turkel remembered that Kubrick didn't like to hug people, so they shook hands and tapped each other on the shoulder. "No more twenty years between pictures," Turkel said. Kubrick laughed and said, "We'll see what we can do." "And I never saw him again," Turkel recalled.

Kubrick had control over every aspect of his films well beyond final cut. Poring over the newspaper ads for *The Shining*, he was upset that the 1 A.M. show wasn't listed for one theater. At a theater that played *A Clockwork Orange*, the ceiling was reflecting too much light from the screen, so Kubrick had the ceiling repainted twice until it finally stopped the glare.

The initial reviews for *The Shining* were largely negative. *Variety* wrote, "With everything to work with, director Stanley Kubrick has teamed with jumpy Jack Nicholson to destroy all that was so terrifying about Stephen King's bestseller. The truly amazing question is why a director of Kubrick's stature would spend his time and effort on a novel that he changes so much it's barely recognizable. . . . The answer, presumably, is that Kubrick was looking for a commercial 'property' he could impose his own vision on and Warner Bros., not having learned its lesson with *Barry Lyndon*, was silly enough to let him do it."

Variety was also harsh on Nicholson's performance, and couldn't believe his scenes were the result of fifty or so takes. "If Nicholson's performance is what the director wants after fifty takes, it's no wonder he demands final cut—it's impossible to imagine what the forty-nine he threw away could look like." Not to mention he considered Duvall "a simpering, semi-retarded hysteric."

Stephen King was famously unhappy with the movie. "There's a lot to like about it," he said. "But it's a great big beautiful Cadillac with no motor inside. You can sit in it and you can enjoy the smell of the leather upholstery—the only thing you can't do is drive it anywhere. The real problem is that Kubrick set out to make a horror film with no apparent understanding of the genre. Everything about it screams that from the beginning to the end, from plot decision to that final scene—which has been used before on *The Twilight Zone*."

The passing of the years didn't change his opinion. "I don't like movies that are cold," King told the *L.A. Times* in 2007. "I don't like movies that approach it like an exercise. A movie for instance, where, say, Jack Nicholson and his wife are trapped in a hotel and you don't feel any love between them, you don't feel any caring, it just becomes sort of an exercise. And that bothers me. . . . I want to go to a movie and root for them to live."

The horror community wasn't happy with it at the time either. As David Cronenberg told *Cinefantastique* magazine, "[Kubrick] said he wanted to make an epic horror film. Since he didn't trust the genre, he felt like he had to turn it inside out. But he didn't really understand the power of the genre. He didn't know how to scare people, probably because he doesn't understand them."

Brian De Palma also said, "In *The Shining* you're dealing with a director who is working for the first time in this genre and who seems to have a bit of contempt for it. He is obviously not interested in the conventions of the genre he's chosen; in fact he seems to feel there would be something cheapening or demeaning in drawing from the conventions. Instead you sense that he wants to revolutionize it and make it something profound or significant. But the result is inevitably heavy-handed because what he has actually done is failed to realize the intrinsic beauty of the basic form per se."

"I was disappointed in the initial reviews," Brown says. "The reviews were cruel. It's said that Stanley wept. And I think there was something a bit off-putting about calling it 'A Masterpiece of Modern Horror,' because you're preempting the reviewer's job by saying that. I don't think it was marketed very well at all. I didn't like the posters and the initial logos. It got better when they used the 'Here's Johnny' picture."

A few critics at the time got it, like Jack Kroll of *Newsweek* who called *The Shining*, "The first epic horror film. *The Shining* is to other horror movies what *2001: A Space Odyssey* was to other space movies."

Janet Maslin of *The New York Times* also called it "spellbinding. . . . Everything in the Overlook signals trouble that unfolds at a leisurely pace almost as playful as it is hair-raising. Meticulously detailed and never less than fascinating, *The Shining* may be the first movie that ever made its audience jump with a title that simply says 'Tuesday.' "

Yes, Duvall was an odd match for Nicholson, who Maslin called "furiously alive in every frame," but she felt Shelley's "early banality" makes the terror that follows "all the more extreme." She also called the script "shrewd and economical."

Nicholson biographer Patrick McGilligan wrote that Kubrick and Johnson's script "cannily streamlined the book, subtly enriched the horror, and invented many of the scenes people tend to remember," like the scene when Duvall discovers the manuscript that reads "ALL WORK AND NO PLAY MAKES JACK A DULL BOY" over and over for hundreds of pages. (Those pages were written by Kubrick's secretary, Margaret Adams, and she typed dozens of pages every day for months in different formats.)

As Andrew Niccol, the screenwriter of *The Truman Show,* and writer-director of the underrated *Gattaca,* once said, the real reviews for a film are written five or ten years later, and in time, the reviews for *The Shining* read much differently.

Michael Weldon was way ahead of the game in 1983 when writing in *The Psychotronic Encyclopedia* that *The Shining* is an "unconventional and chilling horror film destined to be regarded as a classic once the initial criticism is forgotten. See it again."

"If you haven't seen *The Shining* recently, rent the video sometime soon," wrote Vincent Canby in 1993 in *The New York Times.* "In some eerie fashion, it gets better every year."

David Thomson called it, "A masterpiece. How wonderful that this straining, chilly, pretentious, antihuman director should have stumbled into it. This is not quite horror; it's more dread which seldom has climaxes but never goes away."

In 2005, the *L.A. Times* called it "A very disturbing film. . . .

Visually, it's a knockout. Every frame, every tracking shot is a masterpiece of cold, paranoid composition."

"I'm more interested that today's kids think it's really something," says Brown. "I think Stanley would be tickled by it."

It's not clear if it was a direct result of his displeasure with *The Shining*, but with future King adaptations King has to like the film, or you can't use his name for advertising and publicity. *1408* was the first King adaptation in a long time King was happy with, and he let his name be used with the ads and publicity.

With *Misery*, King also wouldn't just give it up to the highest bidder. William Goldman first got a call from Rob Reiner about the book. Reiner's producer, Andy Scheinman, read it on a plane and wondered who had the rights. He figured they were probably bought up already because the book was already in print for a while. It turned out nobody had the rights because they weren't for sale. King didn't want it made into a film because he disliked so many previous adaptations of his work.

Yet Reiner had the ace in the hole because King loved *Stand by Me*, so King agreed to let Reiner have the rights as long as King got a lot of money, and Reiner either produced or directed it. After George Roy Hill (*Butch Cassidy and the Sundance Kid*) and Barry Levinson (*Rainman*) turned it down, Reiner, who initially had no intention of helming the film, just producing, said, "To hell with it, I'll direct it myself." (And King was indeed happy with the film.)

Eventually King became philosophical that not everything adapted from his work would be to his liking. When King was asked how he felt about Hollywood "ruining" his books, he would usually reply, "My books have not been ruined. They're on the shelf right behind me. You can read 'em if you want to."

When David Cronenberg's *Rabid* was picked up by New World Pictures in 1977, Joe Dante, future director of *The Howling,* Jon Davison, future producer of *Airplane!,* and Allan Arkush, director of *Rock and Roll High School,* were all working in New World's trailer department.

New World obviously wasn't just a schlock factory. Roger Corman also released Fellini and Bergman movies through New World, as well as the drive-in fare of the day. There was plenty of room for a filmmaker who approached horror in an intellectual way like Cronenberg. "New World was all over the map," says Arkush. "Between *The Candy Stripe Nurses* and Fellini's *Amarcord,* you're covering a lot of territory there!"

And considering the wide range of films New World distributed, from the brilliant to the abysmal, "When something came in that was as good as Cronenberg, you took notice," Arkush continues. "You knew he was a real filmmaker. Watching it on a Moviola, you're watching it back and forth, you're watching the filmmaking, the cuts, the shots, so right away you get an appreciation for the filmmaker."

Cronenberg very neatly fits into the cliché of the horror director you'd least expect, an intelligent, calm, bookish, thoughtful man, the complete opposite of his work.

Martin Scorsese is a big fan of his films, and once said he was scared to meet Cronenberg because of his movies, which David found amusing. "This is the guy who made *Taxi Driver,* and he's afraid to meet me!" (Scorsese also famously said that Cronenberg resembled a Beverly Hills gynecologist.)

Clive Barker, who cast Cronenberg as "the mass-murdering psychoanalyst" in *Nightbreed,* also recalled, "I'd seen him on the BBC doing an interview about himself, and he was so massively calm, so massively in control of himself. I thought if this guy was dangerous, I'd be scared! I'm just glad he's a good guy."

Coming from an intellectual point of view, Cronenberg didn't dumb down his work, and often the concepts of his films were hard to get your head around, like 1983's *Videodrome*, which gained a big following years later. "*Videodrome* was not an easy sell," says Mick Garris, who was then a publicist at Universal. "Marketing wants to go for the simplest line that tells you what you're in for, and there's not a simple line about *Videodrome*."

One critic defined Cronenberg's brand of fear "body horror, where one's darkest fears have a way of expressing themselves biogically," and he often used gory, slimy parasites and disease as symbolism. With *The Brood*, rage manifested itself as murderous demon children. "I'm talking about the transmission of destructive neurosis from generation to generation, and I'm making it physical," Cronenberg said.

"Cronenberg has a very sophisticated sense of biology and the body in his movies," Arkush says. "Even watching *History of Violence*, people's bruises, where they're shot and things like that have a very strong biological content to it, which makes it more real and more horrible."

Cronenberg never felt limited working in the horror genre. "Just because you're making a horror film doesn't mean you can't make an artful film," he said. "Emotions, imagery, your own sense of self—all of this can be included in a horror film."

Like Romero, Cronenberg never left his home base for Hollywood. Pierre David, who produced *The Brood, Scanners,* and *Videodrome* with Cronenberg, says, "David felt he could remain in Toronto with the people he liked, making the movies he wanted, and that Hollywood would come to him, which happened."

It's not easy to try to figure out where Cronenberg's unique brand of horror comes from. He grew up in a loving and supporting environment. "If I decided I wanted to go into science, my father would immediately present me with twenty books on biochemistry, and be enthusiastic," Cronenberg said. "And if a year later I decided to drop out of science—which I did—and went into English, then we would talk about literary criticism, and I'd get twenty books on literary criticism."

Cronenberg's father was a writer, and at first David was following in his footsteps. David started writing when he was nine, and had his first story published when he was sixteen in *The Magazine of Fantasy and Science Fiction*.

Cronenberg's father suffered a terrible unexplainable disease that started as colitis, and progressed to where his body couldn't process calcium, and his bones would break easily. Many tried to draw connections between his father's illness and Cronenberg's films, where the body and disease are the source of horror, but Cronenberg always said it didn't inform his work.

"It isn't that simple," he said. "The death of my parents has sort of confirmed all the bad things that I thought about the world. It wasn't induced by that. They could still be alive and I'd be making exactly the same movies." He also mentioned he had "an ironic distance" from the characters in his films. "So many people identify you with your main character, it's scary."

Cronenberg didn't look at the horror genre as an escape from terrible realities. "I think of them as films that make you confront aspects of your own life that are difficult to face," he said, adding, "If you admit to the possibilities of the most horrific things, then maybe they won't happen. It's what I do when I make movies. You're hoping it's going to stay on the screen and not come into your life."

Cronenberg went to the University of Toronto in 1961, where he studied biochemistry and biology. He was fascinated with science but couldn't relate to scientists. "I felt quite alone among them," he recalled. "I realized that if I were going to have to live my professional life among scientists, I just wouldn't be happy. I guess I prefer the metaphor of science to the reality of science."

Cronenberg made his first films in college. He didn't even realize he could make a movie until he saw a student film, which was a revelation. Someone he knew actually made a movie, and he could get his hands on the equipment and do the same. He taught himself, reading *American Cinematographer* magazine, and looking up the terminology in the encyclopedia. "When I felt I knew enough about the technology, I went out and shot my own film," he said.

"I think being self-taught has a lot to do with the uniqueness of Cronenberg's films," says Uncle Bob Martin. "The fact that Cronenberg was a self-educated filmmaker and didn't go to film school particularly made me like him. Cronenberg makes Cronenberg films, and I think he's done a lot to make film itself different."

John Board, who worked as an assistant director and second unit director on many Cronenberg films, including *Videodrome, The Dead Zone,* and *The Fly,* remembered talking to David one time about why he became a filmmaker, and David told him he initially wanted to be a writer, but when he did it was similar to his heroes like William Burroughs. Cronenberg wasn't finding himself until he made films because he had no gods in cinema.

Cronenberg's first film was *Transfer,* a seven-minute short shot in color on 16 mm in 1966, followed by *From the Drain,* and he moved up to 35 mm three years later with *Stereo* and *Crimes of the Future* in 1970. A small Canadian company called Cinepix took notice. They mostly made soft-core sex films, and wanted Cronenberg to direct a movie called *Loving and Laughing.* Cronenberg had his own script called *Orgy of the Blood Parasites,* which was later retitled *They Came from Within.*

Cinepix wanted to break into markets all over the world, and saw

Cronenberg as their way to do it. It took two years to raise the money for *They Came from Within,* and when it went over well at the 1975 Cannes Film Festival, it sold to thirty-five countries, reportedly making more than $5 million on a $185,000 budget.

Cronenberg's 1977 follow-up, *Rabid,* starred porn star Marilyn Chambers (*Behind the Green Door*), who headlined the film at the suggestion of his friend producer Ivan Reitman (*Ghostbusters*). *Rabid* was also a big seller at Cannes, where New World picked up it for the States.

Arkush remembered there were problems with the ratings board with *Rabid,* and Cronenberg came down to the editing room to make the cuts with Davison. "I don't think he was too happy about it, but we tried to make them as invisible as possible," Arkush says. "We were outraged over what they were putting him through at the MPAA, because the movie wasn't worse than anything else out there. It was the combination of it being a low-budget exploitation movie, and you add in the fact that Marilyn Chambers was the star, right away it was, 'Oh, that's the movie with *her* in it.'"

In Canada, it was debated at the House of Commons over whether the Canadian Film Development Corporation, funded by Canadian taxpayers, should finance his films. One Canadian publication headlined its review of *They Came from Within*: YOU SHOULD KNOW HOW BAD THIS FILM IS. AFTER ALL, YOU PAID FOR IT. In the hallways of the State Department, people would mumble, "What are we going to do about Cronenberg?" (Many years later, when Cronenberg's 1997 film *Crash* caused a flurry of outrage, *The Daily Mail* of London said the film was "the point at which even a liberal society should draw the line.")

"It wasn't easier here in the States, trust me," says Pierre David. "You should have seen what the MPAA put us through with *Scanners,* I mean, my god. And *Videodrome,* it was like nonstop."

Cronenberg actually toned down *Scanners* when Jennifer O'Neil objected to some of the gore, telling the director, "I won't do the film if there's more than one exploding head." As much as Cronenberg's films are a product of his singular vision, he's also a very fair and open-minded filmmaker who will listen to your arguments and consider them.

"I have a strong personality and strong opinions," says Pierre David. "David does too, but David doesn't come from an emotional level. If we disagreed on any part of a project, we would generally go out for dinner and discuss it, and the most logical argument won the day. I never had to put my foot down and say, 'This is my money, I'm the producer,' because he never let it go there."

"I'm very balanced," Cronenberg said. "I immediately see all sides to the story. And they are all equal. That can be a curse, maybe it's very Canadian too." Yet with *Scanners,* Pierre David laments, "I wish we still had kept a few more exploding heads."

Once *Scanners* became a hit in early 1980, mainstream Hollywood took notice, and Cronenberg wasn't averse to working in the Hollywood system. "I want to use the machine," he said. "But if you can slip through the cracks, and you feel you can manipulate the machine without being manipulated back, it's a dangerous game, but you can try it . . . how close can you come to the flame without being burned.

"*Scanners* was a breakthrough film for me, because it was number one on the *Variety* chart when it came out," Cronenberg continued. "That was a big deal for a low-budget Canadian horror film, which was basically the way it was perceived. True, it was a slow week, but that doesn't ever count. If you're number one, you're number one. A lot of people in Hollywood started to notice me then."

When *A History of Violence* played at the 2005 Cannes Film Festival, Cronenberg joked, "I've been waiting for years to sell out. It's just that nobody offered me anything before now." Actually Cronenberg was offered to sell out many times, but he turned down *Flashdance, Top Gun, Witness, The Juror,* and *The Truman Show.*

Cronenberg was also attached to *Total Recall,* but was off the project after writing twelve drafts of the screenplay that were all rejected. Cronenberg was broke and needed a gig, and Reitman tried to come to the rescue, offering him *The Hitchhiker's Guide to the Galaxy,* because he felt David could make a comedy. A week later, Mel Brooks offered Cronenberg the remake of *The Fly.*

Brooks is a horror fan, and he told *Rolling Stone,* "I think when people go to a horror film, they see a coalescence of their darkest fears in the form of a monster, and it's very, very cathartic. It's a pleasure, no matter how horrible it is, to fucking *define* it, instead of having that amorphous anxiety swirl around you."

And as proven with *The Elephant Man,* directed by David Lynch, and *The Fly,* Brooks also liked directors that were a little left of center. Brooks said when he pursued Cronenberg, "I went after him as I haven't gone after anyone since Anne Bancroft."

From the beginning, *The Fly* was not going to be an exact remake where the doctor would come out of the teleporter with a giant fly head, but in the classic Cronenberg mold, it would be "very body-oriented, very body-conscious," where the transformation happens gradually. *The Fly* also had the classic line that's still in the pop culture vernacular: "Be afraid, be very afraid."

The Fly turned out to be the perfect crossover vehicle for Cronenberg, and John Board said, "I think *The Fly* was a great coming together of David's thoughts, the idea of transportation and the parasite within. There was that welding that seemed so natural."

The Fly was a big hit in the summer of 1986 on the heels of *Aliens,* both released by Fox. Head of domestic distribution Tom Sherak knew with Cronenberg and Brooks *The Fly* would be a quality movie.

Said Sherak, "We just didn't know it would be as broad as it was. Fox was struggling terribly, and we needed some infusion of success. We believed there was enough room in the marketplace for two (sci-fi/ horror) movies as long as they were separated by a couple of weeks. And I think those two movies actually started a string of things happening at Fox that was good for the studio."

Thankfully Hollywood success never ruined Cronenberg, and he transcended the horror genre with his sensibilities and singular style intact. "*A History of Violence* is a great movie," Arkush says. "There's no wasted motion in that movie. It covers an enormous amount of territory, and it doesn't feel like a movie that's ninety-five minutes. It feels like you've learned an enormous amount, and it covered a lot of ground."

TWELVE

LONG NIGHT AT CAMP BLOOD

**How Sean Cunningham started a major studio feeding frenzy with
Friday the 13th, which launched a big franchise for Paramount,
sequel mania, and outrage from critics and parental groups**

After *The Last House on the Left*, Wes Craven and Sean Cunningham realized they'd made a hideous movie that was painfully difficult to watch, and neither wanted to go back there, although they also went in different directions with their horror. "I was more interested in psychological underpinnings and irony," Craven said. "And I think Sean discovered after *Last House* that he was more interested in being entertaining than assaultive. *Last House* didn't allow you to have any fun at all."

Instead of making an endurance test of a film like *Last House*, Cunningham now wanted to make a roller-coaster ride, and wanted audiences to enjoy being scared instead of being repulsed and disturbed.

Cunningham next made family comedies. Hallmark wanted a rip-off of *The Bad News Bears,* the 1976 comedy hit about an obnoxious, foul-mouthed Little League team coached by Walter Matthau.

With three weeks of screenwriting and prep, *Here Come the Tigers* was ready to go. Then came *Manny's Orphans* retitled *Kick*, about a soccer team, and United Artists also optioned it as a TV pilot, which never came through.

Manny's Orphans had to go through a title change because distributors told Cunningham the name "Manny" was too ethnic and the word "orphan" was too sad. In frustration, Cunningham thought, Christ, if I had a picture called *Friday the 13th* I could sell that! It won't work for this movie, but that's a title that will sell.

Once the title popped into Cunningham's head, it wouldn't go away. He saw the opening credit sequence in his mind, a tiny white dot growing bigger and bigger until you saw the title, then it crashed through a window. "Just as it reaches the final position, smack! It hits a kind of mirror and everything breaks. And this deep and menacing voice says: '*Friday the 13th*. The most terrifying film ever made.'"

"I had no idea what the movie would be, but with that title I thought at least I'd be off to a good start," Cunningham said.

Cunningham probably could have gotten a horror film made any time he wanted to in the seventies, but he didn't want to get trapped in the genre. Still, after thinking about it for about thirty seconds, Cunningham told himself, What are you going to do? You've got a family, you've got a house . . . so you make a potboiler. What, you're afraid to get your hands dirty? Don't be ridiculous.

"I was trying to figure out what the heck we could do to keep the lights on, to support my wife and kids," Cunningham recalled. "I loved this notion of doing a warm, fuzzy children's series, but that wasn't gonna pay the bills. I didn't want to go back to horror, but we were broke.

"I've always approached filmmaking from a business sense, not an artistic sense," he added. "The bottom line is, can you sell the movie for more than it cost to make? That's a job. After the two family movies, I said, 'Okay, what kind of movie can I get money for? The answer was a scary movie."

Cunningham went to *Last House* alumni Steve Miner, and wanted to take out an ad announcing the production of *Friday the 13th.* "We both knew it was crazy since we didn't have a script, no production funds, and we weren't sure we could get the rights to use the title," Cunningham said. "First, let's see if we can use the title, and we'll work out the rest from there. If the ad runs and no one sues us, I say we have the rights."

They put together just enough money and got a full-page ad in the Fourth of July issue of *Variety*: "*Friday the 13th*—The Most Terrifying Film Ever Made! Available December 1979." No legal threats came in, so for Cunningham and company, *Friday the 13th* was theirs. Now they needed a script.

Victor Miller, who cowrote *Manny's Orphans,* was a Yale-educated writer and playwright who lived twenty minutes away from Cunningham in Connecticut. "We bought into the lie that was current in the late seventies that what America really wanted was a good G picture," Miller says. "So we did two really good G pictures, but judging by the profit and loss statements, America was being lied to. It didn't want good G pictures; it wanted *Halloween,* which is what it got.

"Obviously, from a financial standpoint, which was the most important factor at the time of making *Friday,* the success of *Halloween* was the main inspiration." He also felt *Halloween* was a great title that, even if the movie wasn't good, would still bring people to the theaters, and was obviously hoping the same for *Friday the 13th.*

One day, Miller got a call from Cunningham: "*Halloween* is making a lot of money at the box office. Why don't we rip it off?"

The premise they decided on was taking a remote location and putting a lot of young people in jeopardy. Miller came up with about fifty different location ideas, anywhere kids could get together. Cunningham kept turning them down until Miller recalled how scared he was going away to summer camp when he was young, and that's finally where *Friday the 13th* settled.

Miller had no background in horror movies, and Cunningham made him go see *Halloween* as his crash course. "I'd never written or read a horror film screenplay, so I went to school on *Halloween*," Miller says. "And I saw the most important things with *Halloween* were you had to have a prior evil that happens before the movie begins, you had to have a location or a set of circumstances that prohibited the adult world from coming to the rescue of the sexually active adolescents. I needed a group of absolutely wonderful Pepsi Generation kids to come in, about to have the most wonderful time of their lives, as long as it included getting laid, and there's a force working behind the scenes you couldn't see until the very end. Then it was a question of establishing them, taking them out one by one, and justifying why nobody knows what's going on. You don't notice that David and Victor are missing, and nobody looks for them. The other hard thing is justifying going in there, as in, *don't go in there!*" And, of course, after seeing *Halloween* so many times, the you-have-sex-you-die edict also became part of the road map. (For the names of Mrs. Voorhees and Jason, Miller went to school with a girl named Van Voorhees, and Jason was a combination of his son's names, Ian and Josh.)

Unlike the stylistic approach Carpenter took where he made a few hundred grand look like a major studio production, Cunningham wanted the look and feel of *Last House,* primitive and crude: "I've always felt that a big part of the attraction of these films is that the people watching them probably think they could direct them themselves."

Miller added, "*Halloween* is more of an artistic effort; *Friday* is more meat-and-potatoes and dark." Cunningham also concluded, "The person who calls *Friday the 13th* a film is pretentious."

Cunningham and Miller figured that if *Friday the 13th* could make a profit at the drive-ins, they would be happy. "I was hoping that it would at least not embarrass us," Miller says. "I was hoping it would make a profit and it would allow us to make another movie. I had been freelancing for ten years, my wife was working as a legal secretary, and we were only false pride away from food stamps, so I was primed to be the victim of this."

Hallmark, the company that released *Last House,* soon called Cunningham, and wanted a piece of the action. At first they offered $125,000, then upped their bid to $500,000 once they read the script. Cunningham felt he was moving backward going back to Hallmark, but gave in after thinking it over. "It's not the deal you want, but it's not the movie you want either," he told himself. "You're just trying to put it together, and all these people are counting on you. Fuck, what's the big deal?"

The next day at six forty-five in the morning as Cunningham's children were getting up for school, Cunningham called Hallmark's Phil Scuderi and agreed to the terms, before Scuderi was going to take the money and invest it in a shopping center (*Friday the 13th* was basically a Hallmark production under a different name, George-town Productions).

Auditions for *Friday the 13th* went on the whole summer. The characters in the script weren't terribly deep, and were obviously teen stereotypes of the time, including the good girl, the girl that's a little looser or more sexually experienced, the jock, the class clown, the potential boyfriend, and the last survivor, who was clearly in the Laurie Strode mold.

The most well-known actor to come from the original *Friday* was,

LONG NIGHT AT CAMP BLOOD

of course, Kevin Bacon, who already had a role in *Animal House,* but was back waiting tables six months later. At the time of his *Friday the 13th* audition, he also went up for *Grease* on Broadway.

Bacon used to think there were only two categories of actor—star and out-of-work—but he later realized there were a lot of actors in between, still working day jobs, and he took as many acting gigs as he could, whether it be extra work, soap operas, or commercials. *Friday the 13th* wasn't exactly a movie he connected to, "But I tried to take the size of the budget and the size of the part and the size of the paycheck out of the equation," he said. "And then a huge variety of things open up to you."

Scuderi also added a character to the film, Officer Dorf, the local cop that harasses the kids. Miller was against this addition because he wanted the kids in an environment where no one from the outside world could potentially save them.

"I was livid about it because the point was to keep those kids away from any adult supervision whatsoever," Miller says. "So if you show that in the middle of their horror a motorcycle cop can wander in from god knows where, you can call in the National Guard, the cavalry, or someone else. It went against what I was trying to do, but you know, 'That's Chinatown.'"

Betsy Palmer, who played Mrs. Voorhees, was in *Mister Roberts,* did a lot of television, and said she had "an eight-month fling" with James Dean. She was doing *Same Time, Next Year* on Broadway at the time she was approached for *Friday the 13th*. Driving home from the show one night, her Mercedes broke down and she pleaded to the sky, "I need a new car."

That Friday, Palmer's agent called with the offer to do a movie. It was $10,000 for ten days work, $1,000 a day, but her agent finally said, "Now I have to tell you that it's . . . a horror film." "A horror film?" she wondered. "What do they want me for?" Palmer read the script, thought it was "a piece of shit . . . then I thought about the car again."

Palmer figured nobody would see it, it would come and go, and she really wanted another car. With her eye on a VW, she said yes. It was definitely "reverse casting," as Cunningham put it, and "a little self-conscious" for such a meat-and-potatoes horror film. (Palmer still gets a $15 residual check from *Friday the 13th* every year.)

Despite the fact that she didn't like the script, Betsy was easy to work with, didn't treat the movie as beneath her, and didn't pull any prima donna act. "I think she came from a different era," said Richard Feury, the unit photographer. "There are actors who will just go to their dressing room for lunch and it has to be brought to them by a production assistant. Then there are actors who will stand in line with everyone else. That was Betsy."

The *Friday the 13th* shoot began on September 4, 1979, at a Boy Scout camp in Blairstown, New Jersey, Camp No-Be-Bo-Sco, and the experience of making the film was a lot like going to camp. Actors Jeannine Taylor, Harry Crosby, Mark Nelson, and Bacon were all on the same chartered bus leaving out of New York Port Authority going up to the campsite. The actors introduced themselves to one another on the ride up, enjoyed the scenery, and got to know one another as if they were on their way to camp or the first day of school. Everyone ate together, and although everyone stayed at a motel on the highway, they could sleep in the cabins if they wanted to.

Bill Freda, who edited the film and had previously cut *Here Come the Tigers*, wasn't that impressed with the dailies. "It was like home movies. Everyone was young and overacting." This, of course, wasn't a drawback, because nobody went to horror films for the acting.

As David Cronenberg once said, "I realized that people who love horror films love bad acting. They want the acting to be bad; they want it to be *Plan 9 from Outer Space*. Even by the time I did *The Brood*, where I was working with Oliver Reed and Samantha Eggar, who were very good actors, people would see it as not good when in fact it's not bad."

Miller liked the performances, and felt they were more realistic because the actors were cast out of New York, and weren't typical bleach blond, pneumatic California types. "They looked like just regular kids," says Harry Manfredini, who composed the score for *Friday the 13th*. "We didn't have a cast who looked like they came off a runway."

Cunningham asked the crew if they would take a point in the film in exchange for money, which the crew refused. "We all thought this was going to go absolutely nowhere," said Feury. Still, Feury worked on a number of low-budget films where the checks would bounce, which thankfully never happened on *Friday the 13th*. "I would mail the check home, and after the first one or two cleared I stopped worrying about it."

"There immediately was a great bonding energy because there was no money," said Adrienne King, who played Alice Hardy, the sole survivor of the camp massacre. "When there's nothing, you just have to hang in there. For all of us, it was everyone's first big possibility. Everybody was so psyched and hopeful."

During the shoot, King had to wear a pair of tight, uncomfortable boots that didn't fit. The wardrobe people walked around in the boots wearing three pairs of socks, hoping the leather would expand. Finally Cunningham told King to get her own pair in New York, "Just make sure they're on sale."

In plotting the murders, Miller recalled the killings didn't have to be gory, but inventive, more personal. "One of Sean's rules that I immediately adopted was 'guns are no fun,' because they're impersonal," Miller says. "They don't give you any of the intensity, the passion or the sheer visual delight . . . I don't care how many bullets come out of a pistol and how fast they come out of a pistol, they do not give you the same kind of emotional effect as someone getting right in your face and eviscerating you."

Where *Halloween* was restrained, scaring the audience without blood, *Friday the 13th* delighted in letting the blood and heads fly. "The effectiveness of the film did not come from subtlety," said Cunningham. It was important to get the right makeup artist, because as Miner said, "the effects were, in a large part, going to make or break the film." Cunningham added, "I've always said that Tom [Savini] was, in many ways, the real star of the film."

When Savini arrived from Pittsburgh, he had just made a big name for himself doing the special makeup effects for *Dawn of the Dead* and Cunningham told him, "I want you to do that for our movie." Although *Dawn* was a huge showcase for his talents, Savini would later say it was *Friday the 13th* that made him famous, and he created all the gore effects in the film on a $17,000 budget.

It wasn't specified in the script that Jason would be deformed, and Savini went to town on Jason's look. "Jason was nothing but a dramatic device, and a dead one at that, to justify his mother's continuing murderous outrage," Miller says. Jason was always intended to be "a slow child, perhaps retarded, but I was surprised when Tom Savini tried to make him really gross-looking. I had no problem with it, it just had not been my original vision, but I guess when you have someone as talented as Tom Savini, let him go ahead."

For the end of the film, Cunningham wanted "a chair jumper." "You mean as in *Carrie?*" said Miller. "That's easy enough." Miller adds that the ending, where Jason jumps out of the water and grabs Adrienne King, was "as close as I could steal from *Carrie* without being arrested."

Several others involved in the film, including Savini and writer Ron Kurz, who did some work on the script and wrote the second *Friday,* claimed the ending was their idea, "And I don't know why they're in such a rush to say they ripped off *Carrie* instead of me," Miller continues. "But no, that's mine. I can certainly see where people thought of it at the same time, but that was the conversation I had with Sean, and those were the pages I delivered to him."

For the film's score, Cunningham went to another alumni from his family film days, Harry Manfredini, who composed the soundtrack for *Here Come the Tigers.* One night Harry was sitting in Cunningham's kitchen in Connecticut, and Sean told him, "I'm gonna make the scariest movie ever made. It's gonna be called *Friday the 13th,* and you're gonna do the music."

"Then I finally got to see the first rough cut, and I was . . . I gotta tell you, I was just blown away," Manfredini says. "'Oh my Lord, this is gonna be in the movies?' *Friday the 13th* scared the hell put of me, so maybe that's why I'm good at this, because I really do get scared by some of these things."

The first thing Manfredini worked on was creating a musical presence for the killer, who is in the movie from the beginning, but isn't completely revealed until reel ten. Manfredini also decided the movie would only have music over the killer, and Cunningham was all for it.

One day Cunningham asked Manfredini, "Hey, do you have a chorus? That would be great." Manfredini said, "I don't think we have that kind of budget," but he now adds, "Sometimes a [low] budget is an asset. Poverty was the necessity of invention."

Manfredini was studying a composer named Krzysztof Penderecki, and he was listening to one of his pieces that had a huge chorus. The chorus would pronounce the consonants of the words in very dramatic ways. If they sang the word "salt," they would add a hard T at the end.

"Holy crap, that is so dramatic," Manfredini remarked. "I wish I could get that into the score, it just grabs at you."

In the film, Jason lives on in the madness of Mrs. Voorhees's head, and when chasing after Adrienne King, she says, "Kill her, Mommy, kill her." Inspired by the Penderecki piece, Manfredini picked up a microphone and shouted the consonants K and H. Then he ran it through an Echoplex, which repeated the sounds until they faded away. "Now the killer had a voice and the music became a character," Manfredini says.

The ki ki ki, ma ma ma sound effects became a major trademark of all the *Friday the 13th* films, and Manfredini gets royalties every time they're used.

Friday the 13th could have easily wound up with a tiny, low-budget distributor, but thanks to the success of *Halloween*, it was picked up by Paramount. The film was acquired by Frank Mancuso, Sr., who was then vice president of distribution and marketing at Paramount, and eventually moved up to chairman and CEO.

Mancuso was given the mission of acquiring low-budget "negative pickup" films, or films that were already completed that needed a distributor, to go with the movies Paramount was making in house. (The 1979 comedy *Meatballs,* starring Bill Murray, was reportedly the biggest "pickup" of its time, costing $1.6 million and grossing $43 million.)

When Mancuso screened the film, half the audience jumped at the end. "If we could get this for the right price, it will have a market," he said. "I know exactly who will want to see this, and we have many slots coming up in the year where we could use a movie like this."

"Frank Mancuso, Sr., grew up in theaters, he used to run them, and he loved to see the *Friday the 13th* movies with audiences," says Peter Bracke, author of the *Friday the 13th* book *Crystal Lake Memories*. "He saw them having fun, and I think because he understood the appeal of the *Friday the 13th* movies, he may have been the biggest buffer at Paramount."

It was a big thrill for the filmmakers as well. Cunningham and Manfredini would go to a showing, sit in the front row, then peek over the backs of their chairs to watch the audience jump. Savini was very happy with the audience reaction. He would go to a movie he did the effects for, and pick one person in the audience he'd watch for "the evolution of their heart attack."

"The fourth wall gets broken by the audience," says Miller. "You do want them to participate. It is totally cathartic in a way that you can't get in a chick flick. There's just something engaging at a gut level." As Mick Garris says, "Horror and comedy are best shared experiences. The audience influences you when you share fear and laughs."

"You want to next bring your buddy and your friends to go see it, not so much to see the movie again, but to watch your friends react to the movie," says Manfredini. "The day *Psycho* came out I saw it three times that day, 'cause I brought people I knew and said, 'You gotta see this.'"

Paramount bought *Friday the 13th* for $1.5 million, and Warner Bros., which would distribute the film overseas, put up a million against foreign. "Two and a half million dollars and the picture hasn't even opened!" Cunningham marveled. "This little piece of shit from New Jersey!" He turned forty right before the big sale. Paramount would also spend an additional $500,000 on ads and publicity, and an additional million on marketing when the movie was already doing good business.

"Sean told me what the print order was, and it was astronomical for that era, the number of houses Paramount was going to open the movie in for what it was," Miller says. "That's when I said, 'Well, I think we've left the drive-in circuit.' During the *Friday the 13th* shoot, I'd read that there was a lab in Bridgeport, Connecticut, that was looking for blood with specific kinds of antibodies for thirty-five dollars. I went there to try and get thirty-five dollars and they said I didn't have enough antibodies! That's where I was at! I was not filled with confidence or faith that this movie would make us all famous, and I'd never have to think again."

Friday the 13th was released on May 9, 1980, on more than a thousand screens. The film came in at number one on the box-office charts that Monday with $5.8 million, which would be about $30 million today. Ultimately, *Friday the 13th* came very close to what *Halloween* made, with a $39.7 million gross.

There were no advance screenings for the critics, who to no one's surprise were appalled. Many of the arguments against the slasher films were similar to the ones made against "torture porn" in the new millennium, that they were just showing kids lining up to be slaughtered, and it was sick that people would make these movies, or pay money to watch them.

Siskel and Ebert were especially offended by *Friday the 13th,* and the parade of mad slasher films that followed in its wake. Gene Siskel hated *Friday the 13th* so much he revealed the killer's identity in his review, called Cunningham "one of the most despicable creatures to infest the movie business," and urged people to write Paramount and Betsy Palmer in protest.

Siskel and Ebert certainly weren't antihorror, they gave thumbs-up to some of the best of the genre during this period including *Halloween, The Howling, Scanners,* and *Dawn of the Dead,* but felt the mad slasher films had gone too far, and they even did an entire episode of *Sneak Previews* to denounce what Ebert had personally coined "dead teenager movies."

The charge that kept sticking to the mad slasher films is they were antiwoman, Siskel believing they were part of an antifeminist backlash, to which Cunningham countered, "*Friday the 13th* wasn't meant to be misogynistic. It certainly wasn't trying to demean women. We killed democratically."

"God knows we were forbidden, and we were helped by some of the really awful reviews," says Victor Miller. "One critic said Sean and I should be arrested and put in jail, and I'm sure it greatly helped our box office."

"We couldn't worry about what the critics were going to say," Miner said. "If we made a movie to please the critics, we probably wouldn't have been doing justice to our audience."

Gordon Weaver, a former Paramount executive, says, "We knew pretty well that our largely young audience was getting their information via word of mouth and TV advertising, not reviews. To be fairly crass about it, I think the general feeling at Paramount, as well as in Hollywood in general, was that 'good' movies made money and 'bad' movies didn't. We were a highly professional and highly motivated marketing machine that sold the movie that the studio made or acquired with equal proficiency. Our business wasn't to review or critique movies, it was to move as many asses into seats as possible."

Weaver also didn't recall anyone at Paramount being bothered by the critical controversy either. "While I don't recall the specifics of Gene Siskel's letter-writing campaign, I suspect our reaction was 'Gene, what took you so long?'"

Mancuso said, "While I suppose it is possible there were concerns about *Friday the 13th* at the upper level of Paramount, there certainly weren't at the senior level. At the time, Michael Eisner was president of Paramount, and Barry Diller was chairman. I reported directly to Barry. And I never heard anything negative about *Friday the 13th* from him. Quite simply, there were films that were moneymakers, and they helped our year-end bottom line, they helped our bonuses."

Frank Mancuso, Jr., who went on to produce five *Friday the 13th* movies, added, "If there was any resentment toward the movies, it was simply the fact that they were exercises in commerce."

After the first *Friday* went through with only nine seconds cut for an R, a lot of *Friday* imitators pushed the envelope with gore and violence, and when they submitted their films to the MPAA, they'd complain, "You let *Friday the 13th* get by, and now you're tellin' us we can't do this." Subsequently a lot of horror films had to pay for *Friday the 13th*'s sins.

"Our film became held up as an example," Cunningham said. "After *Friday the 13th,* the ratings board really cracked down, and it had a chilling effect. I think the MPAA may have thought it had thrown a softball with *Friday the 13th,* and then lived to regret it."

But Cunningham wasn't anti-MPAA like a lot of filmmakers who've gone to battle with the organization. "The truth is that the MPAA is, as far as censorship goes, a political committee. And it's meant to evolve, to ride along with public opinion." He also felt "nobody tells you that you can't do something" in a movie "except the marketplace. Anybody who goes out and makes a film bathed in blood is trying to make an exploitation film. You don't have to be a rocket scientist to know what you're allowed to do. I think the people complaining about it are the ones who are getting caught."

Cunningham said he had no clue there would be a sequel to *Friday the 13th,* but right as the first one hit, word came down to Paramount: "People are comin' to this and you killed eight people. Maybe next year, you should kill twelve people."

Mancuso, Jr., said, "The first film was such an immediate success that we looked to establish it on a long-term basis almost immediately." Paramount wanted the worldwide rights "because it was a no-brainer. When you make an acquisition like *Friday the 13th* at that kind of price, the profit margin is built in. And it became such a natural thing to open another one the next year, on Friday the 13th. We wanted it to be an event, where teenagers would just flock to the theaters on that Friday night to see the latest episode. That was the concept almost from the beginning."

Cunningham wanted to keep the title and have each movie be a different horror story, which *Halloween III* tried with disastrous results. Scuderi wanted to bring Jason back, which Cunningham thought was the worst idea he'd ever heard. He just didn't get the idea of Jason coming back from the dead. He didn't see how Michael Myers couldn't die because he was evil incarnate. Savini didn't want to come back either. How could Jason still be alive? Living off crawfish on the side of the lake?

Steve Miner, who was associate producer of the first *Friday*, and who went back with Cunningham to *The Last House on the Left*, then took over. "We had always made a conscious decision to make the same movie over again, only each one would be slightly different," he said. *Friday the 13th Part 2* went into production in September 1980, and made it to the screen on April 30, 1981.

Cunningham said, "Ultimately, I felt I had done it already and I had other films to make. I didn't want to keep making the same movie over again. I thought it would be fine if other people wanted to do it and I could help."

Cunningham certainly hoped that *Friday the 13th* would lead to bigger, better things. At first, when *Friday the 13th* was the surprise hit of the summer of 1980, Cunningham told the *L.A. Times,* "Now I'm inside the club, and I love it." He would soon get a rude awakening.

"I was just like the new girl in the whorehouse and everyone wanted to screw me. After *Friday the 13th* they just wanted me to repeat that film over and over again. I thought the studios would look at this and say, 'Oh, let him direct the new Al Pacino movie.' Here was my sample reel, I was ready to go. But I guess I became trapped too."

After the success of *Friday the 13th,* Savini was bombarded with offers to do slasher films, and he turned many down. "I was getting scripts where the murder weapon was a Cuisinart! A Swiss Army knife! I turned those down."

Jason finally found his mask with part three. 3-D was briefly back in 1982, and the third *Friday the 13th* had the widest release of a 3-D film up to that time. There's several versions of how Jason finally got his mask. Before filming, Miner wanted to do a makeup test to see how Jason looked in 3-D. Marty Brecker, who was head of FX, said, "Well, we don't have anything, so let's put a goalie mask on him." Martin Jay Sadoff had a hockey mask they tried out. It was supposed to be a test, never what Jason was actually going to wear, but it obviously looked great, and it stuck.

Other versions of the story go that a lot of the crew was Canadian and loved hockey, which is where the mask may have come from, and yet another story goes that the technical advisor on the film, Terry Ballard, said he brought a hockey mask to play around with, and when Miner saw it, he loved it.

Fifteen million was spent on the 3-D technology and refitting the theaters with the right equipment so they could play the film. "We had to basically go around and rebuild about 2,500 movie screens," said Sadoff.

Friday the 13th Part 3 opened on 1,079 screens, with an opening weekend take of $9.4 million, a record for the series, and it grossed $36.7 million. *Part 3* was supposed to be the last in the series, then they tried to make it stick with the fourth episode. "Paramount wanted Jason dead," said Barney Cohen, who wrote *Part Four*. "Paramount really wanted to end the series."

Mancuso, Jr., said, "There was a moment in time where I sort of hated the *Friday the 13th* movies because everywhere I went, that's all everybody affixed me to. With the fourth one—which I entitled *The Final Chapter* for a reason—I really wanted it to be done and walk away."

With the success of *Halloween* and *Friday the 13th*, the majors jumped in with *Death Valley*, *Halloween II*, and Tobe Hooper's *The Funhouse* at Universal, *Terror Train* and *Visiting Hours* at Fox, *April Fool's Day* and *My Bloody Valentine* at Paramount, and *Happy Birthday to Me* at Columbia. Not to mention there were tons of low-budget, indie knockoffs like *The Burning* (one of the first Miramax in-house productions), *Graduation Day*, *The Prowler*, *New Year's Evil*, and more.

With all this oversaturation, the mad slasher films were pretty much done by 1984, and it was a good time to try and kill off Jason for good. Tom Savini came back to finish the job, and Jason got wacked in the head with the same machete Tom used in *Dawn of the Dead*. The fourth *Friday* wrapped in January 1984, and Mancuso was impressed with the footage. He had a window open for April, and *Part Four* had to be rushed to meet the April release date, six months earlier than planned.

Friday the 13th Part Four: The Final Chapter, opened on April 13, 1984, to an $11.2 million opening weekend, a record for Paramount, and it made $32.9 million. Still, when it all came to an end on the set months before, it was actually a sad moment. "Jason's gone," said director Joseph Zito once the film wrapped. "He's dead." A long silence was broken by Mancuso, Jr., who finally said, "Yeah . . . it feels kinda odd to know he's really gone."

364 ☠ REEL TERROR

"It was a very emotional scene to watch because we all thought that was the end," Mancuso, Jr., continued. "We couldn't believe it was over."

Of course once *Part Four* made big bucks, Paramount wanted to keep giving the public, and the shareholders, what they wanted, and the sequels kept coming. It wasn't long before there was indeed a *Part Five*, but Wes Craven would soon bring in some heavy competition with a new monster on the block.

Sequel mania first got rolling in the late seventies with *Jaws 2* and *Rocky 2*, and it really started kicking into gear in the early eighties. And it goes without saying that with the *Friday the 13th, Halloween, A Nightmare on Elm Street*, and *Saw* franchises, sequels went up into ridiculous numbers. (*Jaws* screenwriter Carl Gottlieb jokes that the rule in Hollywood is only the last sequel loses money.)

Today, of course, franchises are planned from the beginning, and actors have to sign up for the sequels from the get-go, which wasn't how the sequels of the seventies and eighties came together. Friedkin, Carpenter, and Spielberg were all resistant to the sequels for *The Exorcist, Halloween,* and *Jaws*. "Not for any price would I do a sequel to *The Exorcist*," Friedkin said. "Not for one hundred percent of the profits." All felt their films were complete exercises, and there was no further story left to tell. Even though it was left open-ended, Carpenter said *Halloween* "was over when I finished with the first one. There's nothing left to say."

One of the reasons Spielberg resisted directing *Jaws 2* was because he felt he'd made the ultimate shark movie, and it clearly still is. Before Jeannot Szwarc won the director gig for *Jaws 2,* twenty directors turned it down because they didn't want to compete with the original. Yet *Jaws* producer David Brown felt if they didn't make a second *Jaws* film, someone else would, which is also what happened with *Halloween II*.

Tommy Lee Wallace says, "When somebody suggested to us, 'Let's do a sequel to *Halloween*,' we all kind of laughed. 'Oh, come on . . . please. What possible reason could we have for wanting to do a sequel to that movie. It was a classic, just let it be.' It finally sank in with John that this train was on the tracks and it was roaring along, he was going to have to be on board in some fashion, it would be something out there with his name on it that he'd have no control over. So suddenly he was on board."

Carpenter offered Tommy Lee Wallace the opportunity to direct *Halloween II,* and to be offered such a big movie for his first feature was clearly a huge opportunity, but Wallace had to turn it down. "Some time had gone by since *Halloween,* and in that time a whole big slew of horror movies had come along that had steadily gotten more graphic, violent and gory. I had an idea for a script that sort of resembled what they did with *H20.* Years had gone by, Laurie was off in graduate school or something, but John was very strong on the idea that this was a five minutes later kind of sequel. When he showed me what he came up with, it was like hypodermic needles in eyeballs and stuff. I was just so thoroughly turned off that I held my breath and said, 'No, thank you.' "

Wallace knew he was turning down a big break as a filmmaker, and adds, "I was terrified I'd never get another opportunity, and this was the most foolish career self-destruction I could ever commit, but I was simply not the right guy for that movie. I just hated it, I hated the very thought of everything it stood for. So I felt if I tried to fake it, I would be doing a disservice to the movie, and possibly making a mess of the whole thing myself because my heart wasn't in it, so I withdrew."

Halloween II was an unpleasant experience for all involved, but it certainly made money, grossing $25 million on its 1981 release, making a little more than half the original's gross. It's doubtful the studios felt sequels would equal or surpass the originals at the box office, but even making 40 to 50 percent of what *Jaws* or *Halloween* made would still be a lot of money. (*Jaws 2* made about 40 percent of what *Jaws* grossed, and was the highest-grossing sequel until *The Empire Strikes Back*.)

Like Cunningham had suggested with *Friday the 13th,* at one point the *Halloween* films were going to be a different story every year, and they tried to launch the idea with *Halloween III*, released in 1982. Wallace directed *Halloween III,* and he recalls, "I don't remember who convinced us it would be an okay idea to put out a movie called *Halloween* on a completely different topic with different characters, but somehow we got lulled into the idea that this would be the beginning of an anthology series, and we'd release a new story each year. That's actually a marketable idea, it just shouldn't have been called *Halloween*. My God, the brutality with which we were rejected! It was a serious backlash against the idea that this wasn't Jamie Lee, it wasn't the Shape, it wasn't Donald Pleasance, and yet they called it *Halloween III*, so screw them!"

Wallace feels without question the movie would have been better received if it was released as its own movie instead of as a *Halloween* sequel. "If we had marketed it as just *Season of the Witch* (the movie's subtitle), I think it would have gone out and honestly found its audience," he continues. "It's actually found a cult audience of its own at long last, and it's come to be appreciated in its own right." From then on, the *Halloween* sequels stuck with the original formula. "They wanted the Shape back," says Carpenter.

Jaws 2 and *Halloween II* took the same approach in the sense that they both had more shark and more blood respectively, thinking that's what audiences wanted to see. In Leonard Maltin's review of *Jaws 2,* he felt the shark scenes delivered, but Hooper and Quint were sorely missing on land. And in Roger Ebert's review of *Halloween II,* he said he'd been waiting a long time for the scene where a character slips and falls in a big puddle of blood, obviously an appropriate metaphor for the mad slasher movies of the eighties.

Straying too far from what made the first film popular was the same deadly mistake *Exorcist II* made. John Boorman (*Deliverance*) turned down the opportunity to direct the first *Exorcist,* but for the second one he was lured by a big director's fee and a big budget to play with.

Boorman wanted to take a completely different approach with *Exorcist II,* making "an experimental metaphysical thriller," but Stanley Kubrick warned him that the only way to do an *Exorcist* sequel was to give the audience more blood and horror than the first one. (Reportedly part of Warners motivation in making *Exorcist II* was getting shown up by another satanic film that slipped through their hands, *The Omen.*)

Anticipation for *Exorcist II* was huge, but audiences were appalled by what they saw. When the film took a nosedive, Boorman told *Variety,* "We're victims of audience expectation. The sin I committed was not giving them what they wanted in terms of horror. There's this wild beast out there, the audience. I created this arena, and just didn't throw enough Christians to it. It all comes down to audience expectations," Boorman continued. "The film that I made, I saw as a kind of riposte to the ugliness and darkness of *The Exorcist*—I wanted a film about journeys that was positive, about good essentially. And I think the audiences, in hindsight, were right. I denied them what they wanted, and they were pissed off about it."

Thankfully, *Jaws* has such a strong fan base today, the geeks would revolt en masse if there was ever a *Jaws* remake, and the last *Jaws* film was so bad it killed off the potential for any more sequels. The late comedian Richard Jeni included a routine about *Jaws: The Revenge* in his act, and the crowd laughed hysterically just from Jeni recalling the film's plot.

THIRTEEN

A DIFFERENT KIND OF ANIMAL

**How Joe Dante and John Landis gave moviegoers dueling were-
wolves with *An American Werewolf in London* and *The Howling*,
showed the world what makeup masters Rick Baker and Rob Bottin
could do, while Stephen King and George Romero joined forces
with *Creepshow***

Two werewolf movies would find themselves going head to head with
each other in 1981: *An American Werewolf in London* and *The Howling.* One would come out through the home of the original movie
monsters, Universal, the other through Avco Embassy, the hot new
horror powerhouse with John Carpenter and David Cronenberg making movies under its roof.

With two filmmakers shooting werewolf movies so close to each
other, you would think they would have more similarities, but they
were different in many key ways, especially in their creature transformations, and their approaches to blending horror and humor.
And both movies reinvented the wolfman in fresh ways that still
hold up nearly thirty years later.

If there's one similarity they share, it's that both films featured
groundbreaking special effects for their time, created by makeup

masters Rick Baker and Rob Bottin. Baker earned his first Academy Award for his incredible work on *An American Werewolf,* but the film is also celebrated today for the ground it broke in a lot of other areas as well.

John Landis's epiphany with film happened when he was eight years old. He went to see *The Seventh Voyage of Sinbad,* which featured the incredible special effects of Ray Harryhausen. Harryhausen was the master of stop-motion, where he animated miniature models one frame at a time, and blended them together with live action. (This technology went back to the original 1933 *King Kong,* which was the state-of-the-art FX movie of its time.)

Landis came home and asked his mother, "Who makes a movie?" "The director," she answered, and from that point forward, Landis knew what he wanted to do with his life.

Landis became obsessed with film. He bought every book on cinema he could find, and watched the *Million Dollar Movie* on Channel 9 religiously. He paid attention to the names that kept popping up in the credits, and would follow their work.

Although Landis would go on to primarily make comedies, he liked all kinds of films, and one of his favorite directors was Michael Curtiz who directed *Yankee Doodle Dandy, The Adventures of Robin Hood, Captain Blood,* and *Casablanca.* "I admired the fact that one man could work in so many genres," he said. Landis also followed the work of Hitchcock, Cecil B. De Mille, Frank Capra, William Wyler, Howard Hawks, and George Stevens, just to name a few.

Landis dropped out of school in the tenth grade, and when he was seventeen, he got a job in the mailroom of 20th Century-Fox. The old Fox lot was sold off when the big-budget debacle *Cleopatra* was eating up a lot of the studio's money, and Landis worked at the studio when Century City was being built on the land.

The head of the mailroom, William Paparhistos, who worked at the studio for fifty years, would let Landis ditch and watch movies being made on the lot. While Landis was there, Fox was making *Hello Dolly!, Tora! Tora! Tora!, Beneath the Planet of the Apes*, and Robert Altman's *M*A*S*H*, and the TV division was making *Batman, Lost in Space,* and *The Green Hornet.* (Bruce Lee taught a martial arts class on the lot, and Steve McQueen and James Coburn were two of his students.)

Landis met George Stevens, the legendary director of *Giant* and *The Diary of Anne Frank,* on the Fox lot. People didn't recognize or approach directors on the street, let alone a seventeen-year-old kid, but Stevens bought Landis lunch when he was able to prove he was really a fan by naming five of Stevens's films.

Information on movies wasn't everywhere like it is today. There was no Internet Movie Database, no DVD commentaries, information wasn't accessible to the point where practically everybody knows a little bit of trivia about their favorite movies. (The term "film buff" wasn't even created until the sixties.)

"When I was a kid, I was very, very passionate about movies and movie people," Landis says, "and it was considered odd. Now it's considered so chic to be a filmmaker, but as I've said many times, Spielberg, Lucas, Coppola, these guys did revenge of the nerds because the guys who were interested in movies were people like me. We were the audiovisual guys, the guys who brought the 16 mm projector in class to show films. It was considered a geeky thing, but it changed in the seventies."

On the Fox lot, Landis also got to know Andrew "Bandi" Marton, the second unit director who helmed the famous chariot race in

Ben Hur. Bandi got a gig on the World War II comedy *Kelly's He-roes,* which was shooting in Yugoslavia, and he told Landis, "If you can get yourself to Yugoslavia, maybe I can get you a job."

Landis took the money he made in the year and a half he worked in the mailroom, about $800, and flew to London one-way when he was eighteen years old. "When I got to London, I found out just how far away Belgrade was!" Landis recalled. "I hitchhiked and rode the rails and had all kinds of adventures on the way there." Once Landis made it to the *Kelly's Heroes* set, he was given a gofer job, "which nowadays is called a production assistant."

After the *Heroes* shoot, Landis drove to Spain where a lot of films were in production at the time. Landis mostly worked on Westerns for about a year, then returned to L.A. in 1971. Landis tried to get into the DGA's assistant director's program, but the guild wouldn't take him because he didn't have a college degree. So Landis figured, "Fuck 'em. If I can't be an assistant director, I'll be a director." Landis took the money he made working in Europe, about $30,000, and raised another $30 gs from friends and relatives to make his directing debut, *Schlock.*

Schlock was, as Landis put it, a "low-budget parody of low-budget monster movies." Landis also wrote the screenplay for *Schlock* and starred as the Schlockthropus, a pseudo-prehistoric term for a shaggy gorilla. The gorilla suit was created by Rick Baker.

Where John Landis wanted to know who made movies when he was a kid, Rick Baker wanted to know where monsters came from. Baker grew up seeing the Universal classics on TV as part of the *Shock Theater* package. Watching Dr. Frankenstein bringing his mad creation to life, Baker thought making monsters would be a pretty cool job.

Baker started off working on the *Gumby* children's show, and his first feature was the low-budget stinker *Octaman,* where he built the eight-limbed octopus monster of the title. Because *Schlock* was a spoof of movies where it's obviously a guy in a suit, it would have been fine if the costume looked schlumpy or silly, but Baker's suit was so well made, the Schlockthropus became believable as a character.

One day during the *Schlock* shoot, Landis showed Baker a screenplay he'd written while he was over in Yugoslavia working on *Kelly's Heroes.* "This is going to be my next movie," Landis said, and it was *An American Werewolf in London.* "It's basically the script we shot many years later," Baker says. "It was very ahead of its time in so many ways, and the fact that John had written it ten years before he made it, it seems that much more amazing."

Landis told Baker he wanted the transformation from man into werewolf to be like no transformation before it. In the 1941 classic *The Wolf Man*, the transformation would concentrate on Lon Chaney Jr.'s face, and each stage of the transformation would dissolve into the next every five to ten frames. Even if you knew nothing about special effects, it was obvious somebody was progressively applying more and more hair on Chaney's face until he became a full-blown monster, and all the shots were blended together.

The original *The Wolf Man* makeup and transformation were still revered as classic monster effects, but *An American Werewolf* would be a whole new ball game. Landis wanted the audience to see the transformation happening clearly, with no dissolves. He wanted to show the pain of someone's body contorting into a monster, the nails, hair, and fangs pushing through.

The werewolf would also be a four-legged beast. In the original *Wolf Man,* Chaney wore clothes, so you only had to apply the fur to his head, hands, and feet. Landis didn't want "a guy running around in pants," this would be a full-blown werewolf from head to toe that would provide some terrific comic relief when he wakes up the next day with no clothes on.

To create the Schlockthropus suit, Baker recalls, "I had three weeks to prepare for it and five hundred bucks or something." He dreamed of having six months of prep time and a healthy budget to create something amazing.

"What would it take to pull this off?" Landis asked.

"Time and money," Baker said.

As it turned out, Baker had a lot of time to think things through, because *An American Werewolf* didn't get made until 1981.

Schlock was released by Jack H. Harris in 1973, the same distributor that released Carpenter's *Dark Star*. "I never realized it was distributed as widely as it was," Landis recalled. "It was kind of successful in France. It won all these prizes I didn't know about. I didn't know any of this stuff because Harris is a crook. He stole a lot of money from us."

Landis also appeared on *The Tonight Show* practically as a novelty guest as a twenty-one-year-old kid who made a feature film, which was unheard of in those days. "I was actually twenty-two when I went on Johnny Carson," Landis says, "but I was told, 'No, no, say you're twenty-one.'" Carson also gave a favorable quote for *Schlock*'s ad campaign, the only time he ever gave a quote to a film: "Really wild, really funny."—Johnny Carson.

After *Schlock* came and went, the major studios weren't beating down Landis's door, and he had to endure several hard years before he finally got to direct another movie. Landis was especially frustrated Hollywood was picking up film students in college, while he had years of real practical experience working on movies, and he still couldn't break through.

Then Landis hooked up with the Zucker brothers, David and

Jerry, who along with Jim Abrahams formed a live comedy troupe called Kentucky Fried Theater. The trio desperately wanted to turn their comedy skits into a movie, and when they saw Landis on *The Tonight Show,* they figured if this young guy could get a movie made, so could they.

Landis and the Kentucky Fried trio all ganged together and filmed a ten-minute reel of skits they shot for $30,000, which they raised by putting together all the money they had, along with some help from their families.

Every studio that saw the reel passed, but they knew a theater owner named Kim Jorgensen who loved it, and he decided to run it as a short subject that would play before the features in his theaters. Audiences loved it, and Jorgensen raised a $650,000 budget for Landis and company to make a full-length feature film. Financially he felt he couldn't lose, because if he couldn't get a distributor, he could make his money back playing it at his own theaters. Released in 1975, *Kentucky Fried Movie* was a big indie hit, making more than $20 million at the box office.

But even greater success was just around the corner for Landis. It was the moment filmmakers dream of, when after years of struggle the planets finally align, and you're finally in the right place and time with the right movie.

After seeing *Kentucky Fried Movie,* Universal approved Landis to direct *National Lampoon's Animal House.* Released on July 28, 1978, *Animal House* was one of those phenomenon films that seemingly come out of nowhere. Almost no one at Universal believed in it, but it hit the youth generation of the late seventies right between the eyes and exploded at the box office. Budgeted at $2.5 million, *Animal House* grossed more than $100 million, making it the biggest moneymaking comedy of the time.

It was in *Animal House* where Landis started incorporating tone shifts you didn't see in traditional comedies. Executives at Universal thought Landis had lost his cookies when he hired Elmer Bernstein to compose the *Animal House* score, and hired serious actors like John Vernon to play roles like Dean Wormer, but instead of killing the laughs, it made the movie even funnier.

"It was serious to heighten the comedy, to make it more real," says Landis. "The Zucker brothers and Jim Abrahams took it further in *Airplane!* where they hired all these old straight actors. Leslie Nielsen had a fifty-year career as a leading man, now he's considered Mr. Comedy."

With the huge success of *Animal House*, Landis got that ticket to make any movie he wanted, but *An American Werewolf in London* was still a tough sell. "The reason it took so long was because literally everyone who read the script had one of two reactions: 'This is much too scary to be funny' or 'This is much too funny to be scary,'" Landis says. "They could never see that it was meant to be both."

Landis also had issues with Ned Tanen, who was then Universal's head of motion pictures. Tanen, who passed away in 2009, loved movies (an increasing rarity in today's Hollywood), and was a sharp, intelligent executive, but he was also manic-depressive and suffered the terrible mood swings and rages that come with the illness.

"I liked Ned, I have to say," Landis says. "You look at the movies he made, and they're extraordinary. *Jaws, The Sting, Fast Times at Ridgemont High, Animal House, Missing, Coal Miner's Daughter,* the John Hughes movies. . . . He made a lot of great films, and he was a very smart guy, but kinda crazy."

Landis's follow-up to *Animal House, The Blues Brothers,* went overbudget and overschedule, and Universal took a lot of crap for it in the press. At the same time, a number of big Hollywood productions were careening out of control, like *Apocalypse Now,* Steven Spielberg's expensive flop *1941,* and the infamous debacle *Heaven's Gate,* which helped put United Artists out of business. These films were prime examples of what the press called "Hollywood out of control," and the major studios were called to task for letting directors like Coppola, Landis, and Spielberg run amok.

Landis didn't bear the brunt of Tanen's explosions during *The Blues Brothers* production (Sean Daniel, a production executive beneath Ned, did), but Landis still wanted to go to another studio.

Tanen wasn't nuts about *An American Werewolf* anyway. Landis gave Tanen a copy of the script, and told him, "Ned, I want this to be my next picture."

"I hate that movie, John."

"Well, don't you have to make it?"

"No, I don't."

Landis was free to shop *An American Werewolf* around, and he took it to Paramount next where the president of worldwide production Don Simpson told him, "Absolutely we have a deal." The next day Landis was called in to meet with Barry Diller, then Paramount's CEO, who bluntly told John, "We don't make monster movies here."

Then Landis and his producing partner George Folsey, Jr., went to the PolyGram offices on Sunset Plaza. PolyGram's film division was run by Jon Peters and Peter Guber, who later went on to run the Japanese conglomerate Sony, and run up billions of dollars in losses. PolyGram was a Dutch corporation, and as Landis says about Guber and Peters, "Before they raped the Japanese, they raped the Dutch."

When Landis and Folsey met with Guber and Peters, "they clearly hadn't read the script, but I was a hot director at the moment and we were talking. They asked me if I could get certain actors in it, and I didn't want them, I wanted unknowns. It went back and forth, and finally Peter Guber said, 'Do you have room in your $10 million negative pickup for a $250,000 producer fee?' I said, 'Well, who would that be?' He said, 'Us.' I immediately said, 'Yes. Deal.'

"We get out on the sidewalk, and George says, 'Wow, that was great, what great guys.' I said, 'George, do you have your wallet? Do you have your watch?' I mean, it was outrageous. They're the heads of the company, and by green-lighting my picture they just made a quarter of a million dollars, but you know, that's Hollywood."

An American Werewolf was made as a negative pickup deal, which gave Landis complete artistic control over the movie. "It's a way of financing that puts all the risk on the filmmaker, but it also gives all the power to the filmmaker as well," Landis explains. "What you do is PolyGram says, 'We will give you $10 million when you give us a finished feature film on 35 mm film in color.' Often they specify, 'No longer than this many minutes, no shorter than this many minutes, no more than an R rating based on this screenplay with you directing. When you hand us this movie, we'll hand you ten million bucks.' So you have that piece of paper, then you go to the bank and borrow the money." (Landis was not happy about being blamed for *The Blues Brothers* overruns in the press, so his negative pickup deal on *An American Werewolf* also gave him complete financial control over the film as well.)

Ironically, *An American Werewolf* wound up at Universal anyway. It was bought by the distribution branch of the company, who didn't have to go through the head of production. Landis found out during the shoot that the film had landed at Universal, but says, "It was fine, it all worked out well."

Coproducing the film through PolyGram also hedged Universal's bets on what they knew was a risky film. As former president of Universal Thom Mount recalls, "That was one of the ways I was able to get edgy pictures like that made at Universal, just share the risk with other companies. We did that on *The Deer Hunter* (cofinanced by EMI), we did that on a handful of other pictures with other companies, which is very status quo today. You can't find a movie studio that fully finances their pictures today, but back in those days it was unheard of."

Like Landis and Baker, director Joe Dante was a "monster kid" who grew up with the classic horror films on TV, read *Famous Monsters* magazine cover to cover, and took his love of the genre into his own films.

Where Landis already had his big commercial breakthrough when he directed *An American Werewolf in London*, Dante was still in the low-budget B-movie world when he directed *The Howling*. Of the two werewolf films, *The Howling* went into production first in 1980, and was made on a much faster, cheaper schedule.

Dante first broke into Hollywood with the best hands-on training he could get: working for Roger Corman. Dante first edited coming attractions for Corman's New World Pictures, then moved up to direct his first feature film, *Hollywood Boulevard,* which New World released in 1976.

Dante directed his second picture, *Piranha,* for New World as well. Dante got paid $8,000 to direct. You knew going in you'd get paid bubkes working for Corman, but he'd give you your crucial first break, and everyone knew his rep for giving Jack Nicholson, Robert De Niro, Francis Ford Coppola, and Martin Scorsese their first breaks as well. As Corman would often tell up-and-coming filmmakers working for him, "I'm getting the money, you're getting a career."

Piranha was written by John Sayles, the acclaimed screenwriter and director of the indie classics *The Return of the Secaucus Seven* and

Eight Men Out. Corman's assistant at the time, Francis Dole, had her finger on the pulse of new writers, and recommended Sayles for the *Piranha* gig.

Dante gave Sayles an acting job in the film so he could rewrite on location, just as Carl Gottlieb was hired to act and do a major rewrite on *Jaws.* "I think John looked at *Piranha* for what it was, which was the opportunity to experience the making of a movie," Dante says. "There was already a script written by somebody else we inherited which was not especially great. John reworked it, gave it a bit of political overtone, although essentially it was a *Jaws* rip-off. Everybody knew that, and we frankly figured we ought to acknowledge it right away so people could sit back and not grumble through the movie that it was a *Jaws* rip-off!"

Piranha was released in the summer of 1978 so it would go head-to-head with *Jaws 2,* and it opened to surprisingly good reviews and box office. *Piranha* was also Steven Spielberg's favorite *Jaws* knockoff, and when Universal considered suing Corman for imitating their beloved shark, Spielberg told the studio, "No, you guys don't get it, it's a spoof, it's okay," and they backed down.

After *Piranha,* Dante primarily got offers for a lot of big fish stories. "I had just done my underwater movie and they figured, 'Well, this guy does underwater.' If you do something that does well, then they assume that's your specialty. I got a lot of offers for giant turtle movies and stuff."

Two of the underwater monster movies Dante was up for were *Orca II,* the sequel to producer Dino De Laurentiis's notoriously tasteless *Jaws* rip-off where a killer whale seeks revenge on the fisherman who harpooned his mate—De Laurentiis pitched the film by saying, "We make-a the shark the hero"—and what was going to be the third *Jaws* movie, a spoof produced by *National Lampoon* called *Jaws 3, People 0.* (The script was written by the late John Hughes, who later went on to hit it big with his eighties teen films like *The Breakfast Club* and *Ferris Bueller's Day Off*.)

But soon Dante got cold feet. The script was constantly being re-written, and Dante and the studio could never agree on what kind of movie they wanted to make. "I was more interested in wandering around the Universal lot and looking at where they shot the *Frankenstein* movies than I was looking for locations for this thing," Dante says.

Then Dante got an offer to do *The Howling*. Dante would take over for a director who wasn't working out, and he needed to come up with a workable script. Dante always wanted to make a werewolf film, and he figured, "Maybe I should get off this sinking *Jaws* boat." Dante left, and *Jaws 3, People 0* fell apart.

Where *An American Werewolf* was a completely original idea, *The Howling* was originally based on a novel by Gary Brandner. Terry Winkless was the first screenwriter on *The Howling*, but Sayles gave the script a major overhaul, changing the characters' names, rewriting all the dialogue, and making the setting a group therapy retreat. "Terry did a lot of good work on the script, but I don't think much of it ended up in the movie," Dante says. "It's definitely a Sayles script. He reimagined the whole picture where the werewolves are into group therapy and it made all the difference."

The Howling was released by Avco Embassy, and the time was right to strike gold with the horror genre. In 1979, according to the MPAA, 90 percent of ticket buyers were between the ages of twelve and thirty-nine, and a whole new generation of fans who couldn't wait to be scared. "Kids get to be a certain age, they get to go to R-rated movies, and they want to go see the forbidden," Dante says. "*Halloween* sparked a lot of it because it was such a phenomenon."

"The morbid interest in things having to do with death is a very adolescent thing," says Bob Martin. "That's certainly why *Fangoria*

had a lot of readers in that age group. You go through preadoles-
cence, your body doesn't change that much from when you're two
years old to when you're twelve. When your body changes, that's a
big honking reminder from Mr. Death that you're going to die. Life's
a journey, and you're kick-started on it now. Teen age is a time when
death becomes a fascinating mystery because it's real, it's not just a
story they told you when you were ten and you couldn't compre-
hend it at the time. You see changes happening in your body, and
you know the body's mortal."

Bob Rehme previously worked for Corman's New World Pictures. When making a movie for Corman, he'd tell you how many
murders, car chases, nude scenes he wanted, and as long as you gave
him the exploitable elements he wanted, and the movie was in focus,
he was happy.

"Rehme stayed hands-off with directors," Dante says. "He would
check in to see how things were going, but if it seemed like you knew
what you were doing, he would leave you alone. There was very little
interference on the movie. One of the things I don't think I understood about studio filmmaking until I actually had to do it was how
many people try to interfere with the making of the picture. I didn't
find that in the independent world, but when you got to the studios,
there was a lot of micromanaging going on, which was a lot more
difficult to deal with."

The drive-ins, where a lot of low-budget horror films played
throughout the fifties, sixties, and seventies, were on the way out by
this point, but Avco booked *The Howling* in what was left of the drive-
ins, as well as in the hardtops (regular theaters). "It opened in New
York at the hardtops and it did very well, but it was also a big drive-in
movie," Dante says.

Dante hired Rick Baker to do the makeup effects for *The Howling,* but when Landis found out, he went crazy, and held Baker to

his promise to do his werewolf movie, a promise he made back in 1971. Dante feels that when he got his werewolf movie up and running, "it galvanized John into action. I don't know if he would have done *An American Werewolf* if he didn't have this other movie competing."

Baker hooked Dante up with his protégé, Rob Bottin, who went on to become a makeup effects star in his own right with his groundbreaking work for *The Howling* and John Carpenter's remake of *The Thing.*

Bottin had sent Baker some of his sketches when he was a fourteen-year-old freshman in high school. Baker liked what he saw, and decided to take Bottin under his wing. Bottin suggested he and Baker could make monster masks you'd buy for Halloween so they could make some money. "I became his one-man mass-production crew," Bottin continued. "Molding, pouring latex, trimming, painting and finishing . . . I worked like a dog, but I was making monsters! I wouldn't take a dime—learning the basics was fair trade."

Then Bottin became Baker's paid assistant on the 1976 remake of *King Kong, The Incredible Melting Man,* and Brian De Palma's *The Fury.* Next they got a job on a little picture called *Star Wars,* creating creatures for the cantina bar sequence. Lucas wouldn't let anyone working on *Star Wars* see the entire screenplay, just whatever parts they were working on. One day Bottin asked Baker what the movie was about, and Baker figured it was about a bunch of aliens getting drunk at a bar.

Bottin was twenty-one when he worked on *The Howling,* his first big solo gig. "He was wonderful," Dante said, "although the makeup took like two days to apply. We were woefully behind schedule all the time."

The transformations in *The Howling* were done in long takes to really show off the marvels of the special effects makeup, and Bottin was able to make actors twist and contort into werewolves with the help of bulbs and air bladders bubbling and expanding underneath rubber latex skin. Bottin also built several full-size werewolves, and they were shot out of air cannons to make it look like they were leaping through the air. The crew called these creatures "rocket wolves," and one night when a werewolf was blasted into the air, the condensation hilariously caused a jet stream of smoke to trail out of its ass.

The Howling was supposed to come out in October 1980, but the release was delayed when Dante decided to add more effects to the movie. *The Howling* shoot took twenty-eight days, and Bottin had a $50,000 budget for special effects. Dante showed the movie to Avco and told the studio, "If you could give us a couple of more bucks, we can do better." Avco brought in another partner on the movie, and Dante did a week of reshoots with a full werewolf suit.

"We went back and replaced a lot of things in the movie with this new stuff, and it made all the difference," Dante says. The film exhibitors flipped when they saw the werewolf footage, and felt the transformations were the selling point of the picture. "It's great!" they screamed. "We're gonna book it! Don't change anything in that scene!" *The Howling* was finally released in March 1981.

The Howling did werewolf transformations the more traditional way—in the dark, with a lot of shadows. "We kept it in shadow, because it's scarier," Dante says. "It's also to hide the flaws. When you're dealing with latex and rubber, it's better not to see that it's latex and rubber."

When Landis wrote the *An American Werewolf in London* script at nineteen years old, mixing comedy and horror made sense. Landis felt your first reaction to a monster would be laughter because they don't exist. He often gave a hypothetical example: You're coming out of the movies with your date on a Saturday night when you hear a man say, "Good evening." You turn around and see a tall man with his hair slicked back in a pompadour, wearing a purple velour cape, white greasepaint all over his face, black lipstick and eyeliner. Next he tells you, "I'm going to suck your blood."

"Seriously, what would you do?" asks Landis. "You'd laugh at him. You'd look at your date and make a crazy face. Even if you were scared, you'd still laugh. Then let's say the guy leaps on top of you, drags you to the ground, and rips out your throat with his teeth. You're terrified, you're in pain, you're fighting, you're panicked. But from the time you were on the ground bleeding to death, not once did you even think that he's a vampire, or that vampires are real, because they don't exist. The first reaction is always laughter. When something is profound like a werewolf or a ghost, most people scoff, certainly most educated people."

That said, Landis still wanted to treat the movie as realistically as possible, "and that's why Rick Baker was so essential." In both *An American Werewolf* and *The Howling,* the makeup effects were the feature attraction, and neither film had big name actors, although a year after she starred in *The Howling,* the world would know Dee Wallace as Elliott's mom in *E.T.*

Landis was pretty adamant on casting unknowns, and for *An American Werewolf,* he picked David Naughton to play the lead role of David Kessler. Naughton was best known for starring in the upbeat Dr Pepper commercials where he sang the memorable theme song, "I'm a Pepper, you're a Pepper, he's a Pepper, she's a Pepper, wouldn't you like to be a Pepper too?" Landis thought, "If you have that much empathy for someone who's singing and dancing about a fucking soft drink, you know, he might be able to make it work." Griffin Dunne, son of author Dominick Dunne, was cast as David's friend, Jack Goodman. It was important to believe the boys were old friends, and Landis thought Dunne and Naughton would have good chemistry together.

An American Werewolf in London begins with Naughton and Dunne, two regular American college kids hitchhiking through Europe for the summer, coming off a truckload of sheep. After wandering the countryside for a while, they wind up at a pub called the Slaughtered Lamb (it's obviously not subtle, these guys are gonna get it).

The Slaughtered Lamb is full of ruddy-cheeked Englishmen drinking, throwing darts, and playing chess, but when the two outsiders come and go, the mood is grim. Naughton and Dunne are warned to stay away from the moors, but they stray off the roads when it starts raining. Soon they hear a howling beast, and realize it's circling them.

Then Dunne is jumped by a werewolf, a vicious attack he won't survive, and Naughton is wounded before a shot rings out, and the beast is killed. The werewolf was killed by one the patrons of the Slaughtered Lamb, who knew the boys would be in trouble once they left the pub.

Naughton wakes up in the hospital, and will soon learn his fate from Dunne, who visits as a ghost. When Dunne first appears to Naughton, his face is torn to shreds from the wolf attack, and he looks pretty revolting. "I realize I don't look so hot, David, but I thought you'd be glad to see me," Dunne says.

One horror tradition *An American Werewolf* sticks to is the tragedy of the wolfman legend. Once bitten by a werewolf, you become one during the next full moon, and you commit wild, animalistic murders you can't recall the next day. There is no cure for being a werewolf, and the only way to stop the killings and carnage is a silver bullet through the heart.

"The wolf's bloodline must be severed," Dunne explains. "The last remaining werewolf must be destroyed." It's no fun being a ghost in limbo, Dunne explains. "The undead surround me. You ever talk to a corpse? It's boring!"

Dunne had a hard time the first time he was made up as a decomposed spirit. As Baker was applying Dunne's makeup, Dunne was growing increasingly depressed.

"What's the matter, Griffin?"

"Look at me."

"Yeah?"

"Look at what I look like."

"Well, didn't you read the script? Doesn't it say your throat's torn out and half your face is gone?"

"Well, yeah, but somehow I just didn't imagine it looking like this."

"Griffin was devastated," Landis says. "He sat there during the process, watching himself becoming more and more grotesque, mauled, and dead, and he was profoundly distressed on many levels. He was upset because it was his first movie and he was gonna look like that, and he was upset because he really looked dead. It looked very realistic, and no one wanted to look at him, people would avert their eyes."

Baker now says, "I've had that happen where you make somebody up, especially something gory, and it has a real visceral effect to see yourself mangled like that. In the end, he accepted it, and I thought he gave a really good performance."

Before Naughton's first transformation into a werewolf, Landis has a funny segment in the movie where he shows David trying to kill time before the full moon. Naughton paces his loft, searches the fridge for a snack, tries to get into a book, and looks out the door to see if it's dark yet, with Creedence Clearwater Revival's "Bad Moon Rising" on the soundtrack.

CGI has been so overused in recent years, it's become a cliché that anyone can spot a computer-animated effect. Many of the most believable horror films, such as *Alien* and *The Exorcist,* did the effects on the set, "in camera," with no optical effects added in later. *An American Werewolf* did the transformation scene in camera on the set and it also featured the first transformation done in a brightly lit room instead of a dark, shadowy environment.

As the werewolf transformation proved, it's much harder to do horror in a well-lit environment because scares are often dependent on darkness, shadow, and the fear of the unknown.

"You'll notice the next time I had the opportunity to do a metamorphosis, which was in Michael Jackson's 'Thriller' video, I did every trick in the book," Landis says. "It's in the dark, you keep cutting away from [the monster] to the girl screaming, there's big music pounding, I did every cinematic trick you would [usually] do. The sequence in *An American Werewolf,* my intention was no tricks. In the whole sequence, there's only one cutaway. That was all in the script, and it was all designed to make it as visceral and realistic as possible, to take something patently absurd and make it realistic."

At the time, Baker wasn't happy to learn that Landis wanted to do the transformation in a well-lit room, because it's a makeup artist's nightmare. "It's always nice to have a few shadows keeping it a little dark and mysterious," he says. "But John was absolutely right. He wanted this to be happening to this real guy. This apartment we'd been in couldn't have spooky lighting all of the sudden. It would be like, 'Where'd that come from?' John thought it would just seem more real if it was lit the way it was normally lit for the scenes that took place there, and he's right in that respect, but it made it that much harder to do what we do."

Still, Baker learned a valuable lesson from having to pull off a transformation in the light. "I try to make my stuff so it works under any circumstances."

At first, the transformation scene was going to be done in one take, but Landis decided against it after some consideration. Landis told Baker, "Even if you could do it all in one take, I don't want it that way. I want to point out the parts, I want to see the feet and hands changing."

Joe Dante also thought about shooting the transformation in *The Howling* in a single take as well, "but we ultimately decided that was a pretty limiting way to go," he says. "Later when stuff like morphing came along, I was really glad we didn't do it that way, because you got used to it so quick, and it became such a cliché. Even though the effects in *The Howling* are over thirty years old, the scenes still work."

"Another thing John did that was really smart was he basically shot the transformation postproduction," Baker says. "They filmed everything but the transformation, then they kept the apartment set up the way it was gonna be lit. We had the wrap party, then the next day we started the transformation with a smaller crew. Knowing the makeups were gonna take a while to put on, we could only do one or two variations in a day, so it was a lot more cost-effective to do it like that."

Landis shot the scenes with Naughton at his hairiest first, then shot the transformation in backward order, with Baker trimming off more and more hair as they went. Naughton's back looked like a carpet, and he wanted to keep the hair on for a while, and walk around in public wearing a tank top to see how people would react.

At first, Baker wasn't sure if Landis's blending of horror and comedy would work. When Landis said he wanted to use the song "Blue Moon" over the transformation scene, Baker thought, Don't you want to use something scary?

Before the film's last transformation, Naughton and Dunne meet in a porno theater in Piccadilly Circus, where the horror and humor shift rapidly. In the theater are the undead spirits of the people David killed when he was a werewolf. One victim, a fresh kill that's still pretty bloody and torn up, delivers his lines completely straight: "You left my wife a widow, and my children fatherless." But then a couple David murdered, also drenched in their own blood, greet Naughton with a cheeky, "Hello!"

Making this scene even more absurd, Naughton's undead victims, six in all, try to offer suggestions on how he could kill himself.

"Sleeping pills?"

"Not sure enough."

"A gun would be good."

"I know where you can get a gun . . ."

While this scene was being shot, Baker thought to himself, Is this really funny? I hope he knows what he's doing. Today Baker says, "I think John made a unique movie that makes people still talk about it today. If it was a straightforward horror movie with horror movie lighting and horror music, I don't think it would be remembered as well."

The ad campaign for *An American Werewolf in London* was smartly understated, and revealed little of what audiences could expect from the film. It was a picture of Dunne and Naughton hiking, looking over their shoulders at a full moon in the sky with weary looks on their faces. Because Landis had primarily done comedies, and because *An American Werewolf* was not a typical horror film, the tagline for the poster was: From the Director of *Animal House*, A Different Kind of Animal.

Landis liked the campaign, but Richard Pryor told him, "John, that picture's not gonna sell a ticket. That just looks like two honkies in an alley scared of a [brother] with a baseball bat."

When *An American Werewolf in London* opened on August 14,

1981, the reviews were predictably mixed. *Variety* called it "a clever mixture of comedy and horror which succeeds in being both funny and scary . . . special-effects freaks will get more than their money's worth."

The New York Times's Janet Maslin, like a number of the film's critics, liked the first reel of *An American Werewolf,* but also felt, "when the movie backfires, which it finally does, it's because too much grisly footage has been used too lightly."

The *L.A. Times* was much more favorable, and headlined their review, GRISLY BUT FUN. Reviewer Kevin Thomas wrote, "Leave it to John Landis, of *Animal House* et al., to juxtapose humor and gore in so thoroughly outrageously a way that from one moment to the next you can't tell whether you're going to laugh or cringe . . . *American Werewolf* is the work of a confident filmmaker who knows exactly what he's doing, who goes right smack up to the edge but never falls off. Between the laughs and the scares he lets us discover that, after all, we care about Naughton, a sweet person who surely doesn't deserve his ghoulish fate."

Years later, Griffin Dunne recalled, "It really hit below the belt. It must have been perplexing to audiences . . . here you just have this brutal murder by a wolf, and then you have slapstick just a few minutes later . . . this was always a major complaint of critics, that the movie couldn't decide what it was. And then later, of course, it became kind of standard in horror."

Reviewing the movie almost twenty years after its initial release, *The New York Times* called *An American Werewolf* "Landis' most accomplished work." Wes Craven picked *An American Werewolf in London* as the perfect werewolf movie. "[Landis] introduced a state-of-the-art transformation, which had never been seen before," Craven said. "The other great thing is that he introduced this weird combination of terror and humor. And the humor made it incredibly human. . . . If you look at what came for the next twenty years, there was nothing really like it."

The humor in *The Howling* was more subtle, but it also received similar criticism, although much less than *An American Werewolf* did at the time. "Things that are funny in one place are not funny in another," Dante said. "As Lon Chaney used to say, a clown is funny in the circus right, but he's not funny at your door at midnight."

"I felt we were blazing difficult and dangerous territory with *An American Werewolf* but I felt we should," says Thom Mount. "I love *An American Werewolf,* but it was a difficult sell. It was difficult to find a very broad audience for, although we made a lot of money on that one. When Landis showed us the script, I was thrilled with the idea that we could press the genre buttons.

"With *An American Werewolf,* John had this wacky vision," Mount continues. "It was very much his vision, that he could make comedy and horror coexist in the same film with a little sexiness. I think he executed it as well as it could be executed, and that genre-shifting approach opened up a lot of filmmaking for a lot of people. Spielberg quickly adapted it, he was a huge Landis fan in the beginning, and I think he was very influenced by John's willingness to change gears."

Landis and Dante, who are friends and mutual fans of each other's work, didn't know what the other was doing on their werewolf, and they worked far away from each other, Dante in California and Landis in Europe. "I had no idea what the story of *An American Werewolf* was until I saw it," Dante says. "We never talked about it until many years later." Baker and Bottin were in touch during *The Howling* shoot, making sure they weren't creating effects that looked too similar.

"It really wasn't a competition," Dante continues. "Very frequently you'll find in Hollywood two people making movies about the end of the world, two mermaid pictures, two witch pictures . . . there's always two of something, and it's almost never because one guy knew about the other's project. It's always because it's in the zeitgeist."

"At the time we made *Animal House* there were four fraternity movies being made at the same time," says Mount. "We thought ours was singular, so we went ahead and made it, even though we were worried about the competition from the other movies. I defy you to think of those other movies today. People have forgotten them in the wake of *Animal House*'s success.

"Studio filmmaking is dependent almost entirely on the ebb and flow of the culture," Mount continues. "The extent that you're able to tap into the culture to see where it's going, what people think is cool and why, that gives you some edge. When something is in the zeitgeist, more than one person will pursue it."

And as far as Dante and Landis could tell, neither movie hurt the other at the box office. During its initial release, *An American Werewolf* was "a modest success in the States," Landis recalls, "but it was the number two picture after the James Bond movie, *For Your Eyes Only*, in England, and the number one picture in Australia that year, I think because both Americans and Brits die in it. But it was a huge success around the world."

The seed for John Carpenter remaking *The Thing* was first planted back in his film school days. Producer Stuart Cohen went to USC with Carpenter, and he recalled talking with John about redoing *The Thing* way back in the day. Carpenter was definitely interested, but terrified at the same time. He was a big Hawks fan, loved the original, and felt, "The whole stylistic approach . . . you just can't touch that, and I was afraid to try."

Years later, Carpenter reconsidered. "I realized then the original's vibe is very dated, very cold war, early fifties' movies," he says. "I thought, 'Let's not do that, let's do the original short story,' which Hawks didn't do. So rather than a big old monster running around, we did it where it could imitate anything." Carpenter added, "I realized there wasn't much that I could do to improve on the original, so I had to go my own way."

You couldn't blame Carpenter for treading cautiously. In addition to his love of Hawks, the original *Thing* was a major influence on many horror films and filmmakers. "*The Thing* was the movie that knocked me down," said George Romero. "That's the one horror film . . . everyone says, 'What attracts you to the genre?' Probably *The Thing*. I was at the right age, at exactly the right time, and it had exactly the right effect on me. I've never forgotten it."

Several years later, Cohen had a TV deal at Universal, and met up with producer David Foster (*McCabe and Mrs. Miller, The Getaway*), who also had a deal with the studio. Cohen asked Foster if he was familiar with *The Thing*.

"Oh God yes, Jim Arness with a stocking over his head."

"I think it would be a great remake."

"Let me look at it."

Foster set up a screening, and thought, "Wow, yeah, that could be a hell of a movie."

Former Universal president Thom Mount says, "If we found a classic picture like *The Thing* that we thought we could remake and in some way upgrade, we were all over that. Generally I hate remaking films, but in that case I thought we did a great job. It didn't bother me to remake *The Thing* because I thought the original was kind of clumsy, and there was a way to remake it that was much more vital and edgy and interesting. I think the remake's much better than the original, I loved what everybody did with it. The direction was terrific, the effects at the time were cutting edge, and it's a damn scary movie."

Right before his remake of *The Thing,* Carpenter had dipped into the Hawks well again with *Escape from New York,* the second film he made for Avco Embassy from a script he and Nick Castle wrote together in 1974. "Hawks used to make movies within confined times and confined spaces," Carpenter said. "I was always very impressed by those kind of films, and the countdown is a great suspense tool."

Bill Lancaster, Burt Lancaster's son, wrote *The Thing* screenplay, and had previously written Paramount's comedy hit *The Bad News Bears.* Both Carpenter and Foster were impressed with the script, and Foster says Lancaster went from a raucous comedy to a horror film because "he just didn't want to type himself. Bill was a big fan of the original movie, and it was a chance he had to spread his wings, and be more than just a kids' comedy writer."

The Thing was a major tour de force for makeup artist Rob Bottin, who'd learned the tricks of the trade being Rick Baker's protégé, but was now becoming a major effects artist in his own right. Carpenter was blown away by Bottin's work on *The Howling,* and threw down the gauntlet: "Rob, I just saw *The Howling,* that's the scariest stuff I've seen in my entire life. How is anyone ever going to top that? Can you top that? Can you?"

Carpenter loved Bottin's set pieces in *The Howling,* and Carpenter wanted six segments like that in *The Thing* where Rob could really show off his abilities. Bottin later recalled that Carpenter "entrusted his entire movie to me, so I had to live up to his never-ending enthusiasm and support for me as an artist. I will always be extremely thankful to John Carpenter—he changed my life."

Of course there were effects that Carpenter wondered about—whether they could be done—but Bottin said, "I don't think of ideas in the sense of can I do them because I think it restricts me."

Bottin liked Lancaster's screenplay, but the creature in it looked too much like the one in *Alien.* Bottin then came up with the idea

396 ☻ REEL TERROR

that the Thing could assimilate and duplicate anything it captures and invades. It tied into the paranoia of the original story, which was really about the Red Scare, and put the audience in an environment where you don't know who or what the enemy is. When working on the film, Bottin tried to think like the Thing, and tried to think what it would do in certain situations, how it would grow, attack, and so on.

The Thing began principal photography in late August at Universal, and like *An American Werewolf in London*, the effects were shot postproduction. "I don't think anyone should ever do the effects while they're shooting live action," Bottin said. "It's disruptive, and there's a lot of actors on pay standing around waiting for you to get your gooey boogers right."

Out of *The Thing*'s $15 million budget, $1.5 million went to effects. Bottin had a forty-person FX crew, and the chicken-dog creature was created by Stan Winston, whose own star would explode with *The Terminator* two years later. Winston very graciously stayed out of the spotlight and wouldn't take a credit on the film because *The Thing* was Rob's baby. In return, Bottin gave Winston complete freedom to design the creature however he wanted.

"I think that's one of the things I really appreciate about what we were doing at the time," says Dean Cundey, who once again was Carpenter's director of photography. "It was all leading edge stuff. There was no CG morphing of creatures and all the stuff anybody can do in their garage now with a Macintosh. It was absolutely, completely unthinkable as far as technique. You couldn't even imagine that somebody would be able to do that, so we had to find new but conventional ways to do it."

On *The Thing*, Carpenter said "evil hides in the light," and like Landis in *An American Werewolf*, Carpenter wanted the transformations in well-lit environments, where Bottin wanted the effects in a darker light so you couldn't see how they were done.

Cundey says, "Rob was really insistent that it be in the dark, and if Rob had his way it would have been pitch-black except for a silhouette or a couple of little highlights on the Thing. He was completely paranoid about showing the rubber, the cables, the seams. He was always covering it with goo to make it mucusy and hide the textures. I kept saying, 'Rob, they're never gonna see that. The audience better feel the whole thing. So I was constantly struggling to show more. I would light something, I'd look at it and say it looks pretty good and Rob would say, 'Oh no, can you take some light off of that part over there? I hate the way I painted this, can you put that in a shadow?'"

To pull off the groundbreaking effects in *The Thing,* Bottin had to reinvent the wheel to make everything come to life. Bottin recalled, "I couldn't call anybody and go, 'How did you make someone's neck stretch to the floor, then make their head sprout spider legs and run away?' It was basically me sitting there trying to figure out how to make this stuff happen, and it damn near drove me crazy!

"I worked without a day off for a year and five weeks," Bottin continued. "I literally had no life outside of working in that compound. Nobody knew how to do any of this stuff, so I had to get it done."

Like the shark in *Jaws,* there were also creature malfunction problems, and sometimes you just had to wait until the effects were working. Carpenter recalled, "One night we waited so long we decided to take a little nap, woke up the next morning and it still wasn't ready."

The incredible spider head effect, where a head snaps off, grows legs, and scurries across the floor, actually wasn't too difficult to pull off. The head was on a remote control car, the aluminum legs that went up and down were attached to the side of the car, and the remote controls were made out of hobby store electronics.

When Bill Lancaster was told about Bottin's idea for the spider head scene, the screenwriter said, "You've gotta be fuckin' kidding," and they used the line in the film when a member of the Antarctica crew sees it creeping along the floor.

Carpenter also insisted the real spider head, not the stunt one, go up in flames when it's torched in the film. "I was sad to see the little guy go," Bottin said, "but it was fun seeing Carpenter's eyes fill with sadistic glee as we watched it burn, baby, burn!"

Running up against a mid-May deadline for the effects, sculptors had to work double shifts and Bottin was working eighteen-hour days. One crew member quit from mental and physical exhaustion, and Bottin had to take a trip to the hospital, reportedly from a variety of stress-related illnesses including ulcers, pneumonia, allergies, and nervous exhaustion.

Still, Bottin wouldn't complain about the toll everything took on him. "Frankly, I thrive on this stuff," he said. "I love being under pressure. That's the way movies are made, and it's never going to change. I love being tortured."

Bottin also didn't see *The Thing* as doing splatter effects. When the head breaks off and grows spider legs, "that's not splatter. That's a Walt Disney imagination; it's not gross, it's fun!"

At the end of *The Thing*, when Kurt Russell and Keith David are alone in the snow, many assume they're going to freeze to death, which Carpenter felt "was the ultimate heroic act, but audiences didn't see it that way."

Some audiences wanted a more definite ending. At the end of one screening, a young woman asked, "What happened in the end? Who was the Thing? What happened up there?" Carpenter replied, "Well, that's the whole point. You never find out. You have to use your imagination." The woman said, "Oh, God! I hate that!"

The poster for *The Thing* was illustrated by legendary poster artist Drew Struzan, who also created the campaigns for the *Star Wars* and *Harry Potter* films, among many others. He got the call at the eleventh hour: "We have this movie coming out, we don't have a poster for it, and we need something we can print tomorrow. Have you seen *The Thing from Another World*? Well, this is pretty much the same."

"This was the sum total of advance information I got," Struzan recalled years later. At the time, Struzan lived up in Arrowhead, and he used himself as the model for the ad campaign, a figure in winter clothes with a blinding beam of white light in place of the face. Struzan put on a winter coat, jeans, and gloves, his wife took a Polaroid of him, then he drew the basic concept, and sent it off by an early version of a fax. "Great—paint it. We want it in the morning."

Struzan worked all night on the poster. A delivery guy came by to pick up the painting at six in the morning, yet Struzan didn't finish up until nine. The paint was still wet, and Struzan figured it would dry by the time it got back to Los Angeles, which was a hundred miles away. "Acrylic paint dries really fast, but the snow splashes I had added were really thick," Struzan said. "So when they went to put it under the glass to photograph it, the paint stuck to the glass because it was still wet."

In spite of the intense creature effects and gore, and as tough as the MPAA was getting on horror films, *The Thing* got an R rating without any cuts. "We just went right through," Carpenter says. "Never had a problem with it, which was sort of shocking to me at the time."

By all accounts, Universal was behind *The Thing,* and the studio thought they had a hit. Because Carpenter was a shy, inhibited person and wasn't big on hyping himself, Foster did a promotional tour for the film, something he was comfortable doing being a former publicist. "We put together a twenty-minute highlight reel of scenes from the movie, and went on the road with it," Foster says. "I went to Phoenix, Dallas, Houston, New Orleans, Miami, where we showed it to theater chains and press people. Sumner Redstone came in Boston."

The sneak previews were also strong. Foster recalled a preview on a Sunday in Century City on Avenue of the Stars where the line snaked around the block. Foster said, "Jesus, am I gonna get rich here!" and Carpenter thought he hadn't had as good a reaction since *Halloween*.

"I was already counting on my second home in the South of France," Foster says. "It was disappointing at the box office for sure. I could never figure out why. I thought it was a well-made movie, a really good monster movie, that's what we thought we were making."

The Thing was released on June 25, 1982. The summer of 1982 was reportedly the biggest in cinema history up to that point, led by the box-office juggernaut of *E.T.*, which was released two weeks earlier on June 11, 1982. Yet in a summer of big blockbusters, including *Star Trek II, Rocky III*, and *The Road Warrior, The Thing* flopped at the box office, and it was hammered by the critics.

David Denby wrote, "This movie is more disgusting than frightening, and most of it is just boring." Kenneth Turan wrote, "*The Thing* is a film with the worst intentions: it wants only to bludgeon you into submission." And Vincent Canby called it "a foolish, depressing, overproduced movie . . . aspiring to be the quintessential moron movie of the '80s."

"Universal was excited by *The Thing*," says Mick Garris, who was now working at the studio as a publicist. "They thought it was going to be a big movie. But when it became clear that *E.T.* was what audiences were looking for . . . I think they gave *The Thing* a good push, but when it didn't initially resonate with an audience, I think they gave up real quick. *E.T.* really reached out and touched people's hearts in a special way, where a more subversive movie like *The Thing* takes a while to gather its momentum. Hindsight is something that's been kind to *The Thing*."

Like another groundbreaking film that also flopped in the summer of 1982, *Tron*, *The Thing* threw a lot of new special effects art at the viewer, and it may have been too much to take in. *Cinefantastique* magazine noted, "the sum experience for a viewer can be a bit draining," and "the film's makeup effects—by most standards its strongest selling point—proved to be its biggest liability."

"For all of its innovation it was definitely much more graphic than anybody had ever seen before," Cundey says. "Now commercials and kid shows can do the same kind of graphic morphing, but at the time when that first dog splits open, that's a pretty shocking thing. It wasn't an awful alien creature to start with that morphed into some other awful alien creature, it was a warm, fuzzy, friendly dog."

"I think people weren't ready yet in some way," says Thom Mount. "The first *Alien* was an extreme movie and it worked. We didn't do *Alien* kind of business with *The Thing*. Nevertheless, Carpenter did a great job, and we were immensely proud of the picture."

With the enormous success of *E.T.*, Carpenter felt audiences wanted "an uplifting cry." Clearly they weren't in the mood to puke. "I think the social climate in the country at that time had a whole lot to do with it," Carpenter said. "There was a recession under way and people rejected its downbeat, depressing view of things." Carpenter would also later say he'd never made a film as savage or bleak as *The Thing*, and probably never will again. "I don't think the audience, and especially the audience out there now, wants to see that."

Carpenter took *The Thing*'s failure hard. "I can't think of a way it didn't change my career," he recalled. "Nobody wanted to hire me for a job after that because of the reputation of *The Thing*. I was treated like slime." He added, "Look, I was just a skinny kid from Kentucky who came to Hollywood, and I got real lucky in my life. If you want to play in the big leagues you've got to be ready for the hits. So that was my first big one."

Still, Carpenter was very proud of *The Thing*, and he'll always have a special place in his heart for it as a filmmaker. "I thought at the time—and I still think today—that I had made a very powerful, very scary, very strong monster movie unlike any other . . . I love the movie a great deal. I never stopped loving *The Thing*. It's my favorite film of my own."

Not long after it came and went from theaters, *The Thing* started developing a following through cable and video, and it enjoys a big fan base today. "People appreciate what John did more today," David Foster says. "It's actually better now to my eyes. It's a lot more tense. I think John was at the top of his game. He really knew how to scare the shit out of you. He knew how to get the most out of a moment."

Years after they made *The Thing* together, David Foster and John Carpenter ran into each other on a studio lot. Foster had lost much of his hair and was keeping his head chrome dome, while John's hair had now turned wispy and ghostly white. They spotted each other, and Foster joked, "So it's come to this!"

For the horror fans that loved it from the beginning, *The Thing* was the pivotal movie that launched a new generation of makeup artists and special effects technicians. Rick Baker was especially proud to see how far his protégé had come.

"When I saw *The Thing*, I was just as blown away as anyone else was," Baker says. "In the old days Rob Bottin and I would sit around and go, 'Wouldn't it be cool if we did *this*? Wouldn't it be cool if we did *that*? We talked about things that would be cool to do, then he did 'em all in that movie!"

With the innovations of *An American Werewolf in London*, *Dawn of the Dead*, *The Howling*, and *The Thing*, the golden age of makeup effects was now in full swing, and it would soon turn into a virtual industry.

"*The Exorcist* was such good box office, now there were so many films big and low budget that had special effects," says Dick Smith. "It grew so fantastic you had these shops spring up like Rick Baker's and Stan Winston's. Here I did *The Exorcist* with one assistant in my little basement, and wham, twenty years later Rick Baker has a factory-sized shop, and they joked when they opened it up that he should get a golf cart so he could get down to the other end of the hall quicker! That was truly a revolution, and *The Exorcist* was the birth, it was the seed."

On one of the first movies Miramax produced, 1981's *The Burning*, a *Friday the 13th* knockoff, the Weinstein brothers sent Tom Savini out on the promotional tour as the star of the film. "It was kind of unique that they sent the makeup artist on the publicity tour and not the director," Savini says. "I think with *Dawn of the Dead*, *An American Werewolf*, the fans, the public who were aware of what goes into making a movie, they were going to see the next exhibit from their favorite artist."

Baker says, "I know I was doin' that when I was a kid. I'd go see a movie if I knew Dick Smith did the makeup, or I'd go see a Ray Harryhausen movie. Most of the time you'd suffer through movies that were not very good for a thirty-second shot of the Cyclops!"

Many filmmakers were now shooting for the sky, hoping Baker, Bottin, and Savini could pull it off. "After *An American Werewolf* came out, I started getting these scripts that had things in them I had no idea how the hell I was gonna do them, and some things we couldn't do," Baker recalled. "David Cronenberg's *Videodrome* was one of them. When I got that script, I didn't think I could do half of what was in it. Cronenberg writes these scripts, *then* they get turned into something that's shootable."

Savini would be the reigning king of gore, while Baker stayed with creatures. But even with movies hitting new levels of gore and violence, there were some places even Savini wouldn't go.

"I would turn stuff down if it was too much in the script description," he says. "I'll never do anything that happens to kids, although Romero reminded me that we shot two kids in *Dawn of the Dead,* but they were my niece and nephew so it didn't matter! When Joe Spinell and I were sitting around talking about effects on *Maniac,* he wanted to do incredibly hideous things to women and I wouldn't do it."

"I don't mind gore in a zombie movie or an all-out monster movie," Baker says. "But I don't like the whole concept of these human killer guys murdering teenagers in the most horrifying way they can, gore for gore's sake. It's just too real for me, it hits home too much. That stuff really happens. It's scary to me to be in a movie theater and see people cheering when some teenager gets a spear showed through his eye or whatever. You should be repulsed by the violence [in movies]. I think it's bad to be desensitized to all those kinds of images, those aren't things we should want to look at."

Baker had certainly done gore in *An American Werewolf* and *Videodrome,* but he also says, "Part of it is also I need to work. In that time of my life, I especially couldn't be real selective about this stuff. This is how I paid my bills, and if I got on too high of a horse and said, 'Oh, I'm not gonna do that,' I wouldn't have a job. But I tried to refrain from those kind of things."

As the makeup masters of the period tried to point out, the violence they were re-creating on-screen was supposed to be horrible and rattle the audience, not something that looks fun or painless. Says Savini, "If I can blow my horn a bit here, I think my reputation came from the realism I was creating. Don't forget, I saw the real stuff in Vietnam. My job was to photograph damage to bodies. I saw horrible stuff over there, but I felt safe behind the camera lens because I thought of this as effects. Then when I was doing effects in movies, if it didn't give me the feeling I got when I saw the real stuff, then the fake stuff wasn't real enough to me."

Yet by the time of *Creepshow*, even Savini was glad to move away from the films *Friday the 13th* had spawned. "Now I'm more pleased to be getting away from the gore," he said. "When I first started, with *Dawn of the Dead* and *Friday the 13th*, there weren't many films like that around. They were blockbusters; they were different; they showed everything. And pretty soon every movie that came out was just another excuse to butcher people . . . I'm more than happy that's on its way out and the *monsters* are making a comeback."

Stephen King and George Romero had both wanted to do a project together for a while. Both were mutual fans of each other's work, and as King said, "We both like a funky, flat-out, unapologetic approach to horror. A plain old steak on the coals, maybe a little salt and pepper. No A-1, no Worcestershire, and, heaven forbid, no bean sprouts or avocado. Occasionally a cob o' corn is nice with the meal. And a beer."

Warner Brothers liked *Martin*, and approached Romero about

directing *Salem's Lot*, but Romero and producing partner Richard Rubinstein bowed out, afraid that TV would water it down too much.

King wanted Romero to direct *The Stand*, which originally was going to be a theatrical feature. The book was so huge that Romero liked to joke no one wanted to take it on "because they were looking at it sideways," meaning at how tall the pile of script pages was.

King wanted to write the screenplay himself because he was very close to the book, and insisted on as much creative control as possible. "If it's gonna get bitched up, I want to do the bitching up," he said. "I don't want to let someone else do it."

The Stand was going to be an expensive project for the time, somewhere in the neighborhood of $20 million, and although King was becoming a big, bestselling author, he had to prove himself as a screenwriter to the studios (many authors have tried to write their own scripts, and are often washouts as screenwriters because it is a completely different medium of writing). And, of course, getting the story down to a reasonable length was a big concern.

Romero, Rubinstein, and King then regrouped at King's house, throwing out ideas while they had a few brews. They decided to do what King called a "tune-up" project, a smaller, low-budget film that could make some money, and show the powers that be they could pull off *The Stand*.

King and Romero wanted to do a series of horror vignettes, like *Lights Out*, and the EC comics, which they decided would be the perfect format for it. And like the EC comics, they wanted to do horror with a moral: If you're a bad person, some kind of horrific karma's gonna bite you in the ass in a hurry.

Two of the stories were based on King short stories, "The Lonely Death of Jordy Verrill," which was originally called "Weeds," and "The Crate." "Weeds" was first published in the men's magazine *Cav-*

alier in May 1976. King wrote it circa 1970–71 and it was going to be the first chapter of a novel. "The Crate" was first published in *Gallery* magazine in the July 1979 issue. For "The Crate," King took an ordinary, real event, when a hundred-year-old crate was found beneath the stairs of his alma matter, the University of Maine, and turned it into horror. (The monster inside was inspired by the Tasmanian devil.)

King set aside the evening for fun projects, and he wrote the *Creepshow* screenplay at night. Two months after the first meeting at King's home, he had a first draft screenplay ready to go in October 1979. Romero loved the script, and pretty much stuck with the first draft.

Romero took the script around with a poster designed by EC artist Jack Kamen, who lived next door to Rubinstein when he was growing up, but they couldn't get the deal they wanted. At one meeting, they suggested Romero turn it into a *Twilight Zone* movie. They ended up staying with UFD, who put up a budget of $7.2 million, and preproduction began around the time of the release of *Knightriders*.

Unlike his experience with *The Shining*, King was absolutely welcome on the set, and he and Romero enjoyed working together because there was mutual admiration and respect. "Neither one of us is trying to outmaneuver or outpower the other," Romero said. "We're trying to get a job done." King would later call *Creepshow* "the most satisfying movie experience I ever had," as well as having the most camaraderie he ever experienced on a film.

Romero hadn't worked with name actors before, but he and Rubinstein decided it was important for *Creepshow* because it would be the opposite of actors bringing their famous baggage to a movie, and that known actors would help build up the reality of the stories in the short time they had.

Creepshow starred Ed Harris, Ted Danson, Leslie Nielsen, King himself as Jordy Verrill, and, at John Carpenter's urging, Adrienne Barbeau.

Barbeau loved working with Carpenter and Craven, but her favorite role was playing Billie, the loudmouth bitch wife fed to the monster in "The Crate" episode. She liked the cast, a good group of classy actors, but when she read the script she thought, "Oh, I can't do this. This is too gruesome, too gross, too vile."

Actor Tom Atkins was a close friend and told her it's a comic book, it's clearly not going to be real. Reading the script again, she recalled, "I still wasn't sure about it but I figured I just didn't know the genre, so I'd better take a chance." Turns out she had a great time, and became close friends with George, and his then wife Christine. "I would go anywhere, anytime to work with George again," she said.

The last episode of *Creepshow*, "They're Creeping Up on You," where a rich, reclusive, germphobic man, played by E. G. Marshall, is overrun with cockroaches, really hit a nerve. "Everybody had a bug phobia by the end of the show," King recalled. "Everybody had their pants wired shut."

There were 25,000 real cockroaches used for the segment. The big Trinidadian South American roaches moved slowly, and fittingly the New York roaches moved fast. A lot of actors would have balked at having roaches crawl all over them, but E. G. Marshall was a real trooper. "Just put 'em on me," he'd say.

In bringing a fictional, *Tales from the Crypt*–style comic book to life, Romero and his director of photography Michael Gornick did a lot of experimentation with *Creepshow*'s look.

At one point, they thought of giving each segment a different look, one in color, one in black and white, one in 3-D, but then decided against it, thinking it would be too radical of an experiment for the audience to take in. A number of scenes had strong red lighting that made it harder to see the blood, and the red lighting was so vivid, they had to tell the lab to stop trying to color-correct the print.

In addition to being Romero's assistant director on *Creepshow*, John Harrison also wrote the score, which sounded like demonic children's music. "*Creepshow* had it built in because it was about a kid reading a comic book, it had that kind of 'nah-nah-nah-nah-nah' kind of attitude, so it was easy to go that way," Harrison says.

Again, Romero stayed in his home base of Pittsburgh, refusing to go Hollywood. Fritz Weaver recalled studio executives asking him, "What's the matter with [Romero]? Why does he stay out there? We tried to get him and he said no!'"

"They want to lure him out there and make him like themselves," Weaver continued. "But he won't go. He's very bright that way." Savini says, "George has been up to direct a bunch of major studio films. He sits down and has meetings with these suits, and as soon as they say something stupid, he just gets up and leaves. He can't tolerate or put up with that, and that's not how he makes movies."

"A couple of people have made the observation that it's like working in a foreign country working in Pittsburgh," Romero said with a laugh. "There's issues of freedom. It gives you a different perspective. You're not so much a victim of trends, popular thinking."

Creepshow was screened at the Cannes Film Festival, and picked up by Warner Bros., the first Romero film distributed by a major studio. *Creepshow* was released in November 1982 in 1,140 theaters, opening at number one, and it made more than $25 million domestic. In spite of *Creepshow*'s success, Romero wouldn't make another film for a major studio until 1988's *Monkey Shines* for Orion.

John Amplas, who played Dead Nate in the "Father's Day" segment of *Creepshow*, says, "As it turned out, the Hollywood elite still didn't let George in. George has never been able to crack that wall, and I think he would have liked to have been able to do more mainstream work. He certainly has the creative energy to do things other than zombie flicks, I just don't know if he can get the backing for it.

"At least for the most part the critics understood George's work," Amplas continues. "It was this kind of elitism on the part of more mainstream producers that didn't want to take the risk, which doesn't make any sense because if somebody has critically acclaimed work, why wouldn't you back them?"

FOURTEEN

A THUNDERSTORM IN A BOTTLE

How Sam Raimi launched his career with the shoestring master-piece *The Evil Dead*, while Wes Craven reinvented himself with *A Nightmare on Elm Street*

At the end of the seventies, Sam Raimi and his friends, Bruce Campbell and Rob Tapert, were thinking about making a horror film, and to research them they went to the drive-ins, where you could catch two movies for two bucks a night. A lot of the movies they had to sit through left a lot to be desired.

Whenever the audience didn't like the movie, they'd honk their horns, or white out the screen with their headlights. Sitting through a lackluster, low-budget horror flick, Tapert would think, "God, we can make something better than this, there's absolutely no doubt about it."

"They always had thirty minutes of slow stuff," Raimi said. "Then they had a good scare. Then there was another fifteen minutes of slow stuff. Then there was a good suspense sequence. Then there was more slow stuff. Then a good ending. So after about twenty of these,

Rob and Bruce and I said, 'Why don't we just make one that has all the good stuff and skip the slow stuff?'"

"The message was loud and clear," said Campbell. "Keep the pace fast and furious, and once the horror starts, never let up. We determined, whether our movie was good or bad, to go all-out, nonstop. If we were going to make a horror film, we were terribly concerned to make a horror film with a capital H."

Growing up in Michigan, Sam Raimi watched in awe his father shooting home movies on 8 mm. With film you could capture time, manipulate it, slow it down, speed it up, and run it in any order you wanted. Raimi recalled, "It was incredible to me that my father could capture reality and then replay it for us. I thought that this magic was something I had to be involved with, that I had to consume myself with. It is so fantastic, so boggling that anything else on earth pales in comparison with it."

Sam met Bruce Campbell in 1975 in drama class, Scott Spiegel in biology class, and they all made 8 mm movies. Sam and Scott became friends when Spiegel told a joke, and Raimi knew it was from the Three Stooges. Spiegel was also making little movies on 8 mm. Spiegel used to take soundtracks to Three Stooges shorts shoot his own visuals to them, and he made his own Stooges-inspired comedies like *Three Pests in a Mess* and *Half-Wits Holiday*. Among the films Campbell directed were *Supa Bad* and *Son of Hitler,* where the "chip off the ol' Adolf" has to be driven around everywhere by his mother in her station wagon because he's too young to drive.

Much of the humor in the *Evil Dead* films came from the slapstick of the Stooges, and the inspiration for the blood filling up the lightbulb and coming out of the wall sockets came from the Stooges short *A Plumbing We Will Go.* They also brought in sound effects from the Stooges for *The Evil Dead*, recorded off TV low-tech style, then cleaned it up for sound quality. Naturally the Stooges effects were "particularly effective for eye gouges and body falls," said Campbell.

When Campbell, Raimi, and Spiegel joined forces, everyone pitched in acting and directing, but Campbell was clearly the movie star of the group. He had the jaw, the face, "so we found out that girls liked watching him," said Spiegel. "He became the actor and I ended up behind the camera, but we just kind of fell into those roles."

Raimi and company kept making 8 mm movies in their college years, and the budgets started to climb. *The Happy Valley Kid* cost $700, which Campbell joked was "something like $2.5 million in 1978 dollars." They showed the film on campus, charged $1.50 admission, and the movie made $250 a night for a total gross of $5,000. The print got beat to hell after forty-four screenings, and they decided to put it away before it fell apart.

They next made a comedy on Super 8 called *It's Murder!* that was a disaster, "the *Heaven's Gate* of Super 8," as Campbell put it. It cost $2,000 and the first night the only people who saw it were the cast and crew. The next night only one person showed up, and he walked out, telling Raimi and company, "This sucks, I don't even want my money back." Even Raimi didn't want to sit through the rest of it. Dejected, he started rewinding the film, and sat in the balcony thinking, "I gotta somehow figure out a way not to be in this position again."

Spiegel got Raimi into horror movies. "At the time, horror films scared me, and I didn't like being scared," Raimi said. "It was an unpleasant experience for me. But since making my first horror film, I've come to appreciate them, and to appreciate the great artistry of the classics."

Watching horror films, Raimi realized there was an art to building suspense and scaring people, and he began learning how to manipulate the audience through film. "I began to understand that making a horror film was like writing a piece of music," he said. "It's like watching the work of a composer."

Raimi also looked at making movies like being a magician. If the audience forgets you're doing a trick, you're succeeding, and you have to blow yourself away as well as the audience. If you think what you're doing is cool, chances are everyone else will too.

When Sam and his brother, Ivan, went to Michigan State, they met the next crucial member of *The Evil Dead* team, Rob Tapert, who was studying humanities and economics. Tapert did sound on *It's Murder!* when he and Ivan were roommates at Michigan State.

Tapert was gung ho about trying to make a real movie that would play in theaters, but Raimi and Campbell weren't sure. Tapert started thinking, "Well, I know a few guys who have money, maybe I could get the money together," while Raimi thought, "Poor Rob will learn it's impossible, but we'll humor him."

Campbell, Raimi, and Spiegel all loved comedy, but horror seemed the way to go. They didn't want to make a comedy because "a failed comedy will make less money than a failed horror movie," as Campbell reasoned. They made plenty of comedies, but "horror is the entry level that most people use."

Bob Clark, who started out in horror with *Black Christmas* and *Deathdream* before moving on to *Porky's* and *A Christmas Story*, said, "It was smart to go into horror films to get yourself started if you wanted to build a career. You could get together with your college buddies, make a movie, and have a market for that genre, whereas anything else is a tough sell."

Then Raimi saw *Halloween* with his girlfriend, and the women in the audience were screaming their heads off the whole film. Could they make something that good? The *Evil Dead* boys were more than willing to try. "*Halloween* was something to aspire to, but we never thought we could make anything that would have the same mass appeal," Tapert says.

Tapert started calling distributors, learned how to raise money from investors, and began working out what the movie could potentially cost.

To have something to show potential investors, they made *Within the Woods* in the spring of 1978. The thirty-two-minute demo film cost $1,600, and was shot on Super 8 in eight days on the Tapert family farm in Marshall, Michigan.

Raimi and company were still experimenting with sound speeds, slowing recordings down a third to make it sound like monsters, and also shooting film at eighteen frames and twenty-four frames a second.

"Sam has never been one to stick to the industry standard of filming at twenty-four frames per second," Campbell said. "Twenty-four frames to Sam is slow motion." Once during dailies Raimi yelled, "That's the worst reverse-motion acting I've ever seen!" which Campbell said was "something you would only hear on a Sam Raimi film."

Within the Woods was also the beginnings of the famous Shakey-cam. Instead of the Steadicam, which they couldn't afford, the camera would be bolted to a two-by-four. Shooting at eighteen frames a second, two people held on to each end, and ran through the woods with it. When it came time to run through the house with it, one guy would creep to the center, and the other guy would let go and let the main guy with the camera run with it.

Tapert recalls, "We did a lot of tests with it, and we were actually very pleased with how it turned out. We never considered the shakiness a problem, we thought it showed the energy of the force behind it."

Other clever *Evil Dead* camera tricks would include the "ram-o-cam" where a T-bar would smash the glass before the camera would go through it, and for the swamp scenes, Raimi would be pushed along in a raft with a camera strapped to his arm, lifting it in the air whenever anything got in his path.

Within the Woods was then shown at a local theater called the Punch and Judy on Detroit's east side in August 1979, running before *The Rocky Horror Picture Show*'s Saturday midnight show. "There was our crappy little Super 8 projector taking up about a quarter of the screen, with the sound system hissing and humming," said Campbell, "but it worked, and audience members actually reacted."

It also got a good review in *The Detroit News* on August 24, 1979. Seeing Raimi's potential, Michael McWilliams wrote that the young filmmaker "has looked at *Night of the Living Dead* and knows the terror of the grave. He has looked at *Carrie* and knows the effect of the bloody arm out of the blue. He has looked at *Psycho* and knows our fear of knives and cellars. He has looked at *Texas Chain Saw Massacre* and knows our primal fascination with blood. . . . Raimi displays a wealth of learning in *Within the Woods*. Perhaps he will be able to make a more extended work, a feature film, in which he can clean up some of his technical deficiencies and prove that he has the personal depth to provide a context—a thematic meaning—for all his gore."

Still learning how to put a movie deal together, Tapert's family lawyer helped the gang work out a partnership agreement, a limited production entity, calling it Renaissance Pictures Ltd. "It never oc-curred to us to go to California, because it was three thousand miles away," Campbell said. "We felt we'd have as good a chance raising money independently, and it finally worked."

It was a perfect time for everyone to take off and make this crazy movie in the woods in that they were beholden to no one. "Not even to a family," Tapert says. "The movie was all-encompassing. It's very hard within the normal system that we work in to make something really unique and original because everything goes through a development process. The financial commitments to getting something made is so large that it will get watered-down from the original intent of punishing the audience. And probably now in hindsight, looking back on *Evil Dead*, the best thing I can say is we made exactly what we wanted to. It was pretty much the same on *Evil Dead II*, and probably less so on other films. Money comes with other people's opinions, so that's the trade-off, even to this day."

"We had complete control over our very first movie and your very first movie is the one you're not supposed to have control over," Campbell said. "You make a movie and it makes $100 million and the filmmakers never get anything back. Guess what? We got something back because we own the movie, we own the negative."

The idea of *The Book of the Dead* invoking the spirits in the woods came from Raimi's ancient history class. Raimi's teacher had mentioned the Sumerian *Book of the Dead,* the series of scrolls that were a guidebook to entering the next world with burial prayers, incantations, and so on. Raimi thought, "What if someone found the book by accident and released the spirits from the spirit world?"

With Campbell playing the lead, it was also decided that instead of having a helpless woman, it would make the movie even scarier if the strong, square-jawed hero was the helpless, terrified one, reduced to a bowl of Jell-O in the face of evil.

With *The Evil Dead*, everyone had to step up their game. At first, Raimi thought they could shoot in Super 8 and blow it up to 35 mm, but once they tested the blow-up process, it looked horrendous, and they realized they had to do it in 16 mm.

The first investor was Campbell's father. They also got a dentist uncle to invest, and the person who developed their 8 mm movies at

Kmart also chipped in. Raimi was hoping for $150,000, but they managed to raise $85,000. The money was put in escrow, and the investors gave permission to let them open the account and make the movie short of the amount they were hoping to raise.

Locations were scouted in Tennessee, with the hope the weather would be warmer, but it turned out to be Tennessee's coldest winter in decades. Everyone left in a U-Haul in November 1979, going south on Interstate 75 to Tennessee, a twelve-hour trip. The U-Haul could only go fifty-five miles per hour, thirty-five uphill.

In the Tennessee woods, they found the perfect cabin to wreck, with low ceilings, cow dung all over the floor, no power, and supposedly it was also haunted. The locals believed this legend and no one went near the cabin for forty years. Although there was also no running water, there was a coffeemaker, so they had to wash the blood off with coffee, and they also added coffee to the usual stage blood formula of clear Karo Syrup and food coloring.

Shooting began on November 16. Once everything was up and running, Raimi took charge and was really in his element as director. "Never doubt Sam Raimi," says Josh Becker, who worked second unit on *Evil Dead*. "He had everything in his head. There was barely a script, no shot list, and only a couple of storyboards he did under duress. Every movie Sam has made since then he's storyboarded." (The *Evil Dead* script was only sixty-six pages long.)

"Every single shot was a problem-solving puzzle," Tapert recalled. "'We want to do *this*. Sam has this great idea, there's no question it would be cool, how do we do it with a quarter and a piece of wire?' That problem-solving, then seeing it on-screen and ultimately seeing it work and get a reaction from the audience, was a great accomplishment. It certainly satisfied your ego that you were able to solve a problem, realize something, and have it all come to a satisfactory conclusion. It was a great experience. And the truth is, you seldom get that feeling again because you've never been so involved doing everything."

Becker was amazed the film was coming out so well considering how much everyone was flying by the seat of their pants. "You could tell even in the rushes that it was exciting footage," he says. "I'm still amazed it all cut together. I thought it was going to have the worst continuity of any movie ever made. Every day we'd start having no idea where we'd left off, nor where any of the broken dishes or furniture went, nor what color blood or bile Bruce had on his face. It was all pure guesswork. But the film is so compelling it doesn't matter. If people are scared shitless and on the edge of their seats, they're not paying attention to continuity."

It was freezing in the Tennessee woods, even with two space heaters and a roaring fire going, and near the end of the shoot whatever furniture that wasn't needed was burned for heat. One night the synch cable on a dolly froze and they had to bring it into the cabin and let it thaw.

The *Evil Dead* gang also got drunk on local moonshine, and learned the difference between drinkable moonshine and bad moonshine by lighting it on fire. Blue flame it was okay to drink, orange flame was bad because that meant it was distilled in a car radiator. The moonshine was kept in Styrofoam cups, which disintegrated from the toxicity of the booze.

As with many low-budget horror shoots, there was little money and time to spare. At one point during the production, the *Evil Dead* gang reportedly shot for sixty-two hours straight. Everyone was so exhausted, the cast and crew would fall asleep during the dailies, and would be awakened by the flapping of the film at the end of the reel. Becker recalled that Raimi "pretty much tested all of us on just what the limits of our own stamina were. Every day was eighteen, twenty hours on that film. He just loved to keep going and keep going; Sam has more energy than anyone else."

The original *Evil Dead* schedule was six weeks, but it ended up going twelve. Campbell called the *Evil Dead* shoot "a borderline Vietnam experience," which also was how the *Jaws* and *The Texas Chain Saw Massacre* shoots have been described by the survivors. "We didn't even know we were going to finish the damn movie," Campbell recalled. "That was the hardest part. It took us four years just to finish it."

Raimi recalled, "It really went on forever. It never stopped, honestly, until we didn't have the money to buy more film." Josh Becker says, "Quite frankly, I thought Sam had lost his mind. I can't believe I went through that. As Bruce and I have discussed on many occasions, there's nothing like having your most difficult shoot first up. Every shoot since then has been easier. As tough as any of the movies I've made have been, nothing was as tough as *Evil Dead*."

Becker adds, "I didn't go to film school, but I doubt they have a class in loading Arriflex mags with frozen fingers, or what it's like to shoot for thirty-six hours straight, or working while injured. I saw Sam stick his hand into the electrical box and get about twenty amps in his finger, enough to throw him about five feet, but he just kept on working. I saw Rob Tapert collapse in a frozen mud puddle and fall asleep, but he just kept on working too."

The shoot in Tennessee finally ended on January 23, 1980 (the last third of the film was completed in fits and starts in Michigan during the spring). A time capsule was buried below the floor of the main room in the cabin, and it contained a used shotgun shell, a sample of fake blood, and a handwritten "visual code" for the movie. Campbell and Tapert also blasted the props with a shotgun. Long after everyone got out of Dodge, the cabin burned down. It was either struck by lightning or a bunch of drunks accidentally set it on fire.

Raimi and Tapert went to New York to edit it the film, driving up to the big city with the print in the trunk of their car. It was Raimi's first time driving to New York, and he recalled the feeling as being "unbelievable. It's visceral . . . the buildings that well up around you; it's *overwhelming*."

Evil Dead was edited by Edna Paul, and her assistant Joel Coen of the Coen brothers. Paul would tell the *Evil Dead* guys, "You've gotta read the Coen boys' scripts—they're such good writers."

When they needed a break from the cutting room, Raimi and company would go to a nearby arcade called Fascination, and play Asteroids and Berserk. One day at the arcade they saw Brian De Palma playing video games, taking a break from the sound mix of *Blow Out*, which he was doing at the same facility. Raimi challenged De Palma to a game of Berserk, and whooped his ass.

The Evil Dead was first shown publicly October 15, 1981, at the Redford Theatre in Detroit, Michigan, and it was done like a real Hollywood premiere with limos and searchlights. The Redford was the same theater where Campbell had seen *Ben-Hur, The Sound of Music,* and *Bridge on the River Kwai* when he was a kid.

A Wurlitzer organ in the theater played Bach's Tocata and Fugue in D Minor, which most people recognize as the *The Phantom of the Opera*'s theme. They planned the premiere with specially made tickets, programs, a wind soundtrack playing in the lobby, and in the time-honored horror tradition they also had an ambulance outside the theater.

They went around to booking agents, exhibitors, lawyers, everyone they could show *The Evil Dead* to, and everyone passed. "We began to get the impression we'd be lucky to get any deal at all," Campbell recalled. Tapert said, "We totally tied up and invested our life in that movie, and no one would handle it or distribute it."

Then they showed it to Irvin Shapiro, a producer who imported and distributed films who went way back. Shapiro got *The Cabinet of Dr. Caligari* and *The Battleship Potemkin* distributed in the United States. He also brought Renoir's *The Grand Illusion* and Godard's *Breathless* to the States, not to mention that he was a publicist for RKO, was one of the founders of the Cannes Film Festival, and was also one of the first people to buy TV rights for films.

The *Evil Dead* gang wanted to meet with Shapiro because he worked with George Romero, handling foreign distribution for Laurel. Other films Shapiro handled included Scorsese's *Mean Streets*, Neil Young's *Rust Never Sleeps, Dona Flor and Her Two Husbands,* and *Eating Raoul.*

The Evil Dead was screened for Shapiro on December 10, 1981, and Irv told them, "It's your lucky day, boys. It ain't *Gone with the Wind*, but I think we can make some money with it."

The film was then titled *Book of the Dead*, and Shapiro suggested they change the title. "If you call it *Book of the Dead,* people are gonna think they have to read for ninety minutes," he said. "I think we can do better." Some of the titles they came up with were *101% Dead, Blood Flood, Death of the Dead, These Bitches are Witches, The Evil Dead Men and the Evil Dead Women,* and finally, *The Evil Dead,* which was "the *least worst*" of the group.

Raimi and company were fond of Shapiro and Sam called him "a rare breed of honest man." The film went to the Cannes Film Festival in May 1982, and Sam went by himself because they couldn't afford to send everyone over.

It got a great response overseas, but more important, Stephen King loved it. Reviewing the film for *Twilight Zone* magazine, King called

The Evil Dead "the most ferociously original horror film of the year. *The Evil Dead* has the simple power of a good campfire story—but it's simplicity is not a side effect. It is something carefully crafted by Raimi, who is anything but stupid . . . the camera has the kind of nightmarish fluidity that we associate with the early John Carpenter. The camera dips and slides and then zooms in so fast you want to plaster your hands over your eyes." King also called the film "a thunderstorm in a bottle, just relentless."

"That was our version of Pauline Kael," Tapert says. "The ultimate validation. We had been huge Stephen King fans, so that was one of those once-in-a-lifetime thrills." The King review "validated all of the work we had done on that project," Tapert continues. "It legitimized the movie, and it gave us something that differentiated the movie."

"You can't buy that kind of promotion," Campbell said. "A plug from one of horror's legends sent up a protective force field around our little film. Eventually, with the invaluable assistance of Mr. King, our film began to sell, territory by territory, around the globe."

New Line Cinema would distribute it in the States. The company wanted world rights, but with Shapiro watching their back, New Line got North American theatrical, with shared TV and home markets, while Renaissance kept foreign rights.

They got their first domestic check on January 6, 1983, for $125,000, and they went to their accountants the same day, trying to figure out who got paid where and when. It took six years for *The Evil Dead* to break even, and it finally went into profit when they got money for the sequel rights.

Raimi put a great deal of importance on paying the investors back because they put up the money to make the movie happen in the first place, and he and the *Evil Dead* gang intended to keep their promise of paying them back. "It's a different way than most people come into Hollywood," Tapert said, "because we sat at those damned kitchen tables with doctors and their wives saying, 'We promise we'll get your money back out of this.' We always saw their faces looming up in the background."

The Evil Dead opened in L.A. and New York in April 1983, and everyone loved to watch people in regular paying audiences react to the movie. One couple was peeking through the sleeve of a jacket like a tunnel and when the movie got too scary they closed up the sleeve. Coming late in the horror cycle, *The Evil Dead* was also a fresh breath of air from the same old slasher shtick.

The reviews were very positive, pointing to Raimi's brilliance on a budget, and his clear potential for bigger and better. Kevin Thomas in the *L.A. Times* wrote, "*The Evil Dead* is wholly a product of the vivid imagination of Samuel M. Raimi, for whom this film is clearly just the beginning."

The Los Angeles Herald-Examiner called *The Evil Dead,* "A shoe-string tour de force," and compared it to *Night of the Living Dead*. "It achieves a similar claustrophobic intensity on a microscopic budget. In horror movies, recklessness is often a virtue. When high-tech directors such as Stanley Kubrick (*The Shining*) or Tony Scott (*The Hunger*) set out to 'redeem' the horror genre by pumping it full of art, they end up killing it. They're too fastidious to deliver the grisly goods."

Becker felt the film's low-tech quality, "certainly makes it more raw. By the time you get to *Evil Dead II*, which had a lot more money and a real DP, it's a much better-looking movie, just not as scary." Says Tapert, "The heart and soul of the movie is not tied up in the technological. It touches the audience that likes these type of movies, and that will always supersede any technical accomplishments."

Like Carpenter with *Halloween, The Evil Dead* was created in an innocent time, and the hard realities of moviemaking were just around the corner. "At the time, we had no idea how good of an experience *Evil Dead* was," Campbell recalled. "Sure, we burned off four years of our lives and didn't pocket a cent, but we had total creative control." Now they had to deal with "the excruciatingly specific and alternatively vague demands of a studio."

Raimi's next film was the 1985 comedy *Crimewave*, and it was a thoroughly miserable experience for everyone. Raimi made the film for Embassy, who second-guessed him at every turn. They made Campbell do a screen test, then said he couldn't star in the film. Embassy also wanted name actors so they could sell the film overseas, despite the fact they just sold *The Evil Dead* overseas without stars.

Refusing to let Raimi edit the film in Michigan, Embassy yanked *Crimewave* to L.A., where it bogged down in postproduction reshoots and reediting, all of which didn't matter because Embassy had no idea what to do with the movie in the first place.

With the disaster of *Crimewave*, Hollywood wasn't beating down Raimi's door, but *The Evil Dead* was always something he could come back to. "My responsibility was to the investors of *Evil Dead*, who still hadn't made any of their money back," Raimi said. "Three years later, when I still hadn't broken even, I figured the thing to do was write a sequel, put a big rights fee into the package for whoever made it, and that way we could break the investors even and make them a small profit." Also making another *Evil Dead* movie "was my only job opportunity at the time."

Raimi took *Evil Dead II* to the overseas branch of Embassy, and they wanted the film, but they were also going out of business. The video division of Embassy agreed to put up the financing, but they strung Raimi along for five months, and eventually stopped returning his calls.

Again Stephen King came to the rescue. King was working with legendary producer Dino De Laurentiis on his 1986 directing debut, *Maximum Overdrive,* and Stephen put in a good word for Raimi.

Once Raimi finally met with De Laurentiis in his office, Dino asked, "How much you need to make *Evil Dead II*?" Raimi replied, "3.25 million." Dino started rubbing his hands together, and told Raimi, "I'll give you the money, now go make the picture."

Raimi then finally, happily, cut his ties with Embassy, who collapsed soon after the *Crimewave* disaster. "God later dismantled Embassy Pictures for their cruelty to filmmakers," Raimi said.

Evil Dead II was shot in Wadesboro, North Carolina, and Raimi set up shop at a local high school. They built sets in the gym, ran dailies in the auditorium, made food in the cafeteria, and set up the production offices in the library. A gym was also set up in one of the classrooms so Campbell could bulk up. From the first *Evil Dead* to the second, he was going to transform from wuss into a brawny, he-man superhero. Campbell worked out with Mr. North Carolina two hours a day, six days a week for three months.

Now *Evil Dead* also had professional special effects makeup, with Mark Shostrom, who created the Henrietta suit for the film, and Savini protégés Greg Nicotero, Robert Kurtzman, and Howard Berger, who formed KNB.

Shostrom got the gig thanks to Irv Shapiro, who forwarded photos of his work to Raimi. "It changed my entire career," Shostrom says. "It consistently got me work over the years on any number of different kinds of films because I was the guy that did *Evil Dead II*. These days it's so easy to blow people off and not even answer e-mails. He didn't have to answer my letter and call me back, but he was really helpful."

Shostrom didn't have much prep time. He had just finished working on Stuart Gordon's *From Beyond* on a Friday, and started *Evil*

Dead II that Monday. He also wouldn't have a day off for the next six months.

Still, he loved working on the film. "Sam could tell me exactly what lens he would use, film stock, what camera speed," Shostrom says. "He was like an encyclopedia of camera work. That made it wonderful to work with him as a director. There was no question of what you had to do because he knew exactly what would be on the screen, what the results should be.

"On *Evil Dead II* there was a sufficient budget, sufficient equipment for the art department, a really great set, but I think at the end of the day if Sam didn't have the equipment for something, he was very inventive and creative, and he'd figure out a way to do it," Shostrom continues.

Shostrom would show his sketches to Sam, and Raimi would offer suggestions, like he'd want something "50 percent scarier." "He was good at talking percentages. 'Give me 25 percent more humor, and 50 percent more scariness.' Raimi would point to a creature's forehead and say, 'I love the forehead but make it 25 percent more lean and mean.'"

Sam's brother, Ted Raimi, got his SAG card from being in the film, and he definitely earned it. Sam loved to torture Ted when they were kids, and he really had something special lined up putting his brother in the Henrietta suit, which was a real piece of work.

The design for the hideous monster Henrietta was a whole bodysuit, which also had an undersuit with beanbags in it for weight. It also had a wig, twelve appliances for the face, dentures, and a fake tongue. Ted would sweat away five pounds a day in the suit. When he'd take off the monster feet, his sweat would fill Dixie cups. After two weeks in the suit, Ted recalled losing fifteen pounds.

"They had to bring an oxygen mask for me to breathe because otherwise I would pass out," Ted recalled. "It was unbelievably difficult but I was twenty when I did that. If I did it today I would die. I wouldn't last twenty minutes, but when you're twenty years old, you know . . ."

They wouldn't do the Henrietta scenes two days in a row because of the physical demands of acting in the suit, and the muggy, North Carolina heat. "We would have to have a day off for Ted in between," says Shostrom. "It was too demanding."

The idea of Ash losing his hand and it crawling back to haunt him came from a short Sam was in called *Attack of the Helping Hand!* where the cute, animated white chef's glove from Hamburger Helper goes on a rampage against a housewife. A robot-controlled hand was used as well as stop-motion, and Nicotero's hand was also used in some shots.

Evil Dead II was comically overloaded with gore, which flew through tubes and insecticide sprayers. Sam tried to make the blood look more like bile to try and get it past the ratings board. Raimi was hoping for an R rating and said, "We had to cut our blood flow from five hundred gallons to five gallons."

"During the blood flood Bruce almost got hurt," Scott Spiegel recalls. "The force of the water almost broke Bruce's back. You can see it in the film, it's like whoah, *bam*! I think it gave him a bloody nose. The blood was so cold, he said, 'Something warm's running out of my nose and it's not snot!'" Campbell recalled, "I lived to tell the tale, but every time I blew my nose for the next two weeks, the snot was bright red."

Kaye Davis, the editor of *Evil Dead II,* recalled she was quickly trying to put together a scene to show Sam and the gang when she accidentally cut her finger on the piece of film as it ran through the moviola. Her blood shot through the air, and some got on the film.

As Davis was taping up her finger, she noticed Raimi had turned a slight shade of green at the sight of real blood.

As a producer, Dino was hands-off during the making of *Evil Dead II*. They had to deliver an R movie, but even with the prospect of an X, Dino liked it as it was, and was willing to release it unrated.

Raimi recalled, "When we delivered a picture that was potentially X-rated [DEG] said, 'Okay, we realize that the strength of the picture lies in its current form. We won't go for an R rating. We'll just release it as is.' So we were able to preserve the integrity of the picture."

DEG put out *Evil Dead II* through Rosebud Releasing Corporation, a separate arm of the company. Studios that are signatories of the MPAA can't release unrated movies, so they'll often put them out through other companies they form, and can bypass the MPAA. (Miramax did this with the 1995 film *Kids*, and AIP did it on several films that were sleazier than their usual fare.) *Evil Dead II* wasn't submitted to the MPAA because they knew it would get an X, but ironically it later played on the Syfy channel uncut.

Evil Dead II was released in March 1987 and again, the reviews were enthusiastic. *The Hollywood Reporter* thought it blew away the original and that Raimi "exults in joyously demonstrating the mastery of his craft. Deftly combining shocks and yuks . . . Raimi seems poised on the verge of a major genre career."

The second *Evil Dead* was infinitely more humorous than the first, and it clearly was a big influence on Peter Jackson's slapstick splatter films. Again it sparked debate among fans about how much humor should be in horror. Tapert says, "*The Evil Dead* sells more DVDs on a year-in, year-out basis than *Evil Dead II* nowadays. I think the people who like horror really like horror, and they found *Evil Dead II* too tonally challenging because it had too much humor. I think the really hard-core horror fans only want *The Evil*

Dead. As I've come across more and more horror fans, that seems to be a consensus. They want the horror, they want the unrelenting grueling horror, and they don't want the filmmaker to tell them when to laugh. If something's too gruesome, they want to decide to laugh on their own. They don't need a joke there."

Raimi was clearly headed for bigger things, but it would still take some time. He again went back to *The Evil Dead* when *Darkman,* starring Liam Neeson, took time to get set up at Universal. Irv Shapiro came up with the title *Army of Darkness,* and the third *Evil Dead* would be more of a fantasy film with Ray Harryhausen–style creatures and magic. As Campbell put it, "We all decided, 'Get him out of the cabin.'"

The *Army of Darkness* production was a lot of fun because it brought the gang back together, and at least during the shoot they had the freedom to make the movie they wanted. That was the easy part. Once it was completed, *Army of Darkness* was held up for six months. Dino De Laurentiis was again producing, but he was now caught up in a lawsuit with Universal, and Raimi also butted heads with the MPAA over the film's rating.

Raimi and Universal wanted a PG-13 for *Darkness,* but the MPAA wouldn't budge on giving it the R because, Raimi believed, the first two *Evil Dead* films were unrated. Raimi went to the MPAA to plead his case, and at the end of his speech, a member of the board stood up and said, "Mr. Raimi, twice in the past you've thrown our ratings back in our faces." Later Raimi reflected, "I realized they *do* have a memory and they *do* hold grudges."

Universal gave the film to another editor, again to no avail in getting the PG-13, so everyone settled for the R, even though a lot of cool scenes were cut from the film, and Raimi had to shoot a happy ending as well.

Campbell got tired of the big studio politics, and recalled, "It was frustrating because the lines of communication were not clearly drawn, and things got lost in the shuffle like crazy." In his autobiography, *If Chins Could Kill,* Campbell had an illustration of a grinder, the Hollywood homogenizer, and in its jaws went "well-crafted dialogue, shoestring budgets, emphasis on story, thought-provoking drama, appropriate casting." Out the other end came "absurd casting, snappy one-liners, mean-spirited violence, emphasis on effects . . ."

It was clear there was a better movie that didn't make the screen, and *Boxoffice Magazine* wrote the film was like "watching a Sam Peckinpah western that had been edited for television: you recognize the tone of voice, and there are flashes of inspired lunacy marbled throughout, but the overall feeling is that something critical is being withheld." (With the advent of the director's cut, we can now thankfully see the original *Army of Darkness* before it got wrecked by Universal.)

Raimi clearly had a tough time with his unique vision in mainstream Hollywood, but in 2002 he finally moved up to the blockbuster big time with the *Spider-Man* trilogy. When it was announced Raimi would take the reins of the long-awaited superhero epic, Scott Spiegel said, "It's about time. Sam's such a visualist and that's a perfect marriage to come up with cool and innovative stuff."

Yet Raimi's low-tech past is never far behind. Watching Raimi's *Spider-Man* films, Tapert laughs when he sees the same shots and sequences from the movies they made back in the day on 8 mm.

"Sam has an incredible style, an incredible touch, and a wonderful visual sense unlike any director I'd seen," Shostrom says. "The *Spider-Man* films would not be the same with any other director. If I saw a *Spider-Man* movie and didn't watch the credits first, I'd say, 'Jesus Christ, Sam Raimi must've directed this,' 'cause his visual style is unique among directors, hands down."

The fans would love to see Raimi and company make one more

entry in the series, and while no one's said no, no one's exactly jumped at the prospect either. Even though the *Evil Dead* gang has come a long way from their 8 mm beginnings, the freedom they enjoyed when they didn't have a dime would be tough to give up today. "I'll do another one when we get money from doctors and lawyers to do our own version," Campbell said. "Then I'm interested again. I'm not interested in making a $60 million studio film with a bunch of twenty-four-year-olds telling me what to do."

After *The Last House on the Left*, Sean Cunningham tried to make his return to horror more of an exhilarating experience, and Wes Craven tried the same with 1977's *The Hills Have Eyes*.

Craven had gone through most of the money he had made on *Last House* and had two kids to support when he was approached by producer Gary Locke about doing another film similar to it. Craven was glad to make *The Hills Have Eyes*, but knew even then he'd be labeled a "violence-horror director."

As he did in *Last House*, Craven would return to the family theme, and again a gang of scum are trying to kill off a suburban family, this time in the desert. "I try to stay close to the family in my films, because I find that's where some of our most powerful, primitive emotions are buried," Craven said.

Hills certainly has its down and dirty moments, but it's nowhere near as grueling to watch as *Last House*, and at the end when the suburbanites defeat the bad guys, it's exhilarating and fun. *Hills* was shot in Victorville, California, basically the middle of nowhere, and on the DVD commentary Craven joked that today the area's probably overrun with meth labs.

After *The Hills Have Eyes*, Craven had several projects that didn't work out. He did a rewrite on 1981's *Deadly Blessing* when he was working as a script doctor. "It was the first of my films that I really did as just a job," Craven recalled. "Following *Hills,* I didn't have Hollywood pounding on my door, and I was staying alive doing rewrites." What happened with the *Deadly Blessing* script is what often happens in Hollywood: it got pulled in all directions by different producers, everyone wanted input, and it turned the story into mush.

Then Craven did an adaptation of the DC comic *Swamp Thing,* which was a hard shoot because of the locations and the extensive makeup. Craven started rushing through the film, shooting only master shots, no coverage, trying to finish up before the completion bond company could take over. Craven liked the end result, which was released in 1982, and it was a fun movie to make. He also liked the fact that kids could see it, and felt it had a positive message about inner beauty. There was also a lot of merchandise, *Swamp Thing* toys, games, bubble gum cards, books and albums for kids, which didn't sell because the movie didn't take off.

The first *The Hills Have Eyes* did good business in England on video, and the British tape distributors wanted a sequel. Craven wrote a script quickly while he was in the middle of another project, and *The Hills Have Eyes Part II* was shot on a twenty-four-day, $1 million schedule. Craven did *Hills II, A Nightmare on Elm Street,* and a TV movie, *Invitation to Hell,* all back-to-back. "It was nice to be working steadily, because there was a period after *Swamp Thing* when I didn't get the go-ahead on a project for almost three years," he said.

During that period, Craven went through his savings, and wondered if he'd ever direct again. "It's a strange business, because once you finish a film, there's this deafening silence," he said. "You say, 'I'm not working,' and the phone doesn't ring. You utterly panic."

Craven started keeping a record of his dreams when he was in college, and the seed for *A Nightmare on Elm Street* was planted with the nightmare sequence in *Last House on the Left*. Many fans would tell the director how strongly they remembered Weasel's nightmare in the film, and Craven said, "I felt I was on to something there, so I did a whole film about dreams."

If his memory served correct, Craven first put the idea on paper in 1979. In the *L.A. Times*, Craven read about three people unrelated to each other who had nightmares so dreadful they were too terrified to go back to sleep. When they did finally did go back to sleep, they died, and the cause of death couldn't be determined with an autopsy.

Craven said, "I just turned these occurrences around and asked, 'What if the death was a result of the dream? What if the dreams were actually killing these men? And what if they were all sharing a common frightening dream?' So I started constructing a villain that existed *only* in dreams."

Like the Frankenstein Monster, Craven constructed Freddy Krueger from a number of disparate parts. There was a kid named Krueger who beat Craven up when he was a kid. Krueger sounded Teutonic and German, and it was also an extension of Krug from *Last House on the Left*. There was also a scary derelict guy in the neighborhood who once stared at Craven from across the street, then wound up on his doorstep. The hat the derelict wore wound up being Freddy's chapeau. As for the rest of Freddy's wardrobe, Krueger's sweater meshed together two ugly colors that Craven read in *Scientific American* were the most difficult shades for the human eye to put together side by side.

As for Freddy's famous steel claw, "I think that came after *Halloween* and *Friday the 13th*, which both had the mask and specialized weapons like the machete," Craven says. "I started thinking, 'Masks really work,' so I was devising Freddy's mask and I wanted a mask that somehow had expressions, and at one point I thought a scarred face would be perfect. With the weapon, I knew I wanted it to be an edged weapon—a cutting, stabbing weapon—and once I started thinking about that primal idea, I thought, 'What are nature's knives and daggers? It's fangs, talons and claws, like the claw of a bear or a saber-toothed tiger.'"

Craven is a very articulate storyteller, and he knew he was on to something describing *A Nightmare on Elm Street* out loud to people. Craven says, "I usually try to think of how to describe the movie I'd like to make in about one minute, and I try that out on friends because I've found that a good script, especially a genre script, has to be able to be told almost like a good joke. It has a beginning, a middle, and an end. It's self-contained and can be boiled down into something quite simple and succinct. When I thought of the idea of making a movie about people that were being killed in their dreams, it was a very bare bones beginning of *A Nightmare on Elm Street*. Eventually I was able to describe it as a story of a group of kids that all killed a man who is now coming back in the nightmares of their children. Then one girl succeeds in staying awake during the time he was assaulting all her friends until she was able to devise a way to go into her dreams, capture him, and bring him out, because everybody else thought she was either going crazy, or told her she was going crazy because they were in denial and hiding their crime. As soon as I could bring it down to that, everybody said, 'Wow, I'd love to see that movie.'"

Robert Shaye, founder of New Line Cinema, agreed as well. New Line Cinema was started in a fifth-floor walk-up apartment in Greenwich Village on Fourteenth Street and Second Avenue by Bob Shaye, the chairman and CEO. Shaye founded the company in 1967 with $1,500.

The Shaye family business was wholesale groceries in Detroit. Bob graduated from the University of Michigan with a business administration degree, and went to Columbia Law School in New York. At twenty-seven, Shaye became head of the stills department at the Museum of Modern Art's film division, where he was told he could make money distributing movies.

"I knew that distribution was something I kind of understood," Shaye recalled. "I put together little packages with four feature films and two shorts to be distributed on college campuses."

As a lawyer, Shaye also knew what public domain was, and took movies in the public domain on the road for college audiences, like *Reefer Madness,* which became a big cult hit. Shaye said, "We probably made $150,000 profit—until the rest of the world figured out what public domain was, and then we moved on. I paid for my law school education with *Reefer Madness.*"

In the early days, Shaye wanted New Line to be another New World, a company that could make money doing genre films, while also releasing art films as well. New Line did acquisitions, showed 16 mm movies on the college circuit, and distributed foreign films. They won for best foreign film at the Academy Awards with *Get Out Your Handkerchiefs* (1978), and also distributed kung fu flicks like *The Street Fighter* and *Crippled Masters* series.

New Line was also the home of John Waters back in the day when many found his films, like 1972's *Pink Flamingos,* reprehensible. (This was long before he became more family-friendly with *Hairspray.*)

"When we had a picture that worked, it was like oxygen," Shaye said. "And then we'd have to start all over again. I spent so much time trying to raise money it was not a good situation."

New Line Cinema gradually moved into making their own movies and their first in-house production was *Stunts* in 1977, an action murder mystery where someone's bumping off stuntmen, and they also made a high school comedy called *The First Time*. "We had been surviving for about ten years before we made *A Nightmare on Elm Street*," says Sara Risher, who was president of production at New Line.

In an article about New Line, Shaye was described by those who knew him as "fiercely loyal," "charismatic," "prickly," "mercurial," "moody," "emotional," "driven," and in a business terminally full of shit, "a straight shooter." Robert Englund, the man who would be Freddy, found Shaye "far from your typical suit," and when he met a good-looking, charismatic guy with long hair wearing blue jeans, he thought, "This is a producer I can relate to."

"Bob is a very smart businessman," says Risher. "Very cautious, very careful, but he also works a lot of times by the seat of his pants. He's intuitive. A lot of times he'll bet on things because he thinks something is gonna be good without any proof because he just knows he likes it, and he thinks other people will [too]. He'll gamble if his gut tells him, that's what he did on *Lord of the Rings*. "And Bob had a lot of cool ideas. He was in touch with the zeitgeist maybe more than any studio type."

New Line first tried to get into the horror game with *Alone in the Dark* in 1982, which starred Jack Palance, Donald Pleasence, and Martin Landau, and was directed by Jack Sholder, who edited New Line's trailers. "We hired him to do a horror film because we thought that's where we could make some money," Risher says.

Alone in the Dark made its money back, but it wasn't a hit. As Sholder once told Uncle Bob Martin, "To me, the whole idea of a horror film is it's maybe a little harder to scare people than it is to give them a hard-on."

Then Shaye met up with Wes Craven. "To Bob Shaye's credit, he saw it immediately," says Craven. "I met him at a club in New York where somebody had taken me to lunch, one of these big uptown places that I would normally never be taken to. He said, 'I think you're really talented. If you ever get an idea, send it to me.'"

Shaye first read the script in the winter of 1981, and by page twenty he was hooked. "*A Nightmare on Elm Street* was not read that night," he recalled. "It was consumed. And it became my personal passion to make, no matter what."

At the time, Craven wasn't thrilled about potentially setting something up at New Line, which was then a small company. New Line offered Craven $700,000 to make *Nightmare,* but Craven didn't think he could make it that cheaply. He tried elsewhere, but when *Nightmare* made the rounds in mainstream Hollywood, everyone passed on it, and the project languished for three years.

In the three years *A Nightmare on Elm Street* sat collecting dust, Craven went completely broke. "In three years I went from making a series of films in a row and having money in the bank to being unable to pay my last debts," he recalls. "I remember borrowing five grand from Sean Cunningham to pay my taxes. If you look at my filmography, there's a three-year chunk after *Swamp Thing* where everything kind of died and I thought I was done as a filmmaker, that I'd had my run and I was looking for teaching jobs."

Executives who read *Nightmare* dismissed it as "too bloody," and "not scary at all." Craven was also told "the horror genre's dead," and even his old friend Sean Cunningham said, "It's just not scary. People will know it's a dream so they won't be scared. I don't get it."

"I was really concerned about the script for *Nightmare,*" Cunningham said. "I just didn't know if anybody would believe that dreams could interact with real life. I was like, 'That doesn't happen! How are you going to sell that?' I was so happy to be wrong."

Craven liked that the story took place in a dreamworld, which meant you didn't have to follow linear logic. "That's what I like about horror," he said. "It's an area much less hampered by rules and conventions. And in this, which is about dreams, there's very little limitation on what I can do."

Bob Shaye stayed in touch with Craven the whole time, and they finally struck a deal. "In the end, Bob Shaye might have been the only studio boss who could've brought the *Nightmare* franchise to fruition," said Robert Englund.

Robert Englund was a working actor for a number of years, and had small roles in *Hustle,* starring Burt Reynolds, *A Star Is Born, Stay Hungry,* Tobe Hooper's *Eaten Alive,* and TV shows of the day like *Alice, Soap, The Hardy Boys/Nancy Drew Mysteries, Charlie's Angels, CHiPS,* and more.

Englund finally broke through with the miniseries *V* in 1983, and he had already developed a following from the show. He was recommended for *Nightmare* by casting director Annette Benson, who tried to get Englund into *National Lampoon's Class Reunion,* a lame spoof of the slasher genre that was written by John Hughes.

Englund didn't know what to expect from Wes before meeting him, and like many was amazed to find "a tall, slender gentleman with an articulate, charming demeanor." As many others did, Englund loved hearing Craven tell the concept of *Nightmare* out loud. Englund found Craven "a hypnotic storyteller, a mesmerizing raconteur with a wonderful sense of humor, and I was spellbound."

Unlike other horror stars who hated being typecast, Englund has never regretted or resented the fact that he's best known as Freddy Krueger. Like fans chanting "Hannibal!" when they see Anthony Hopkins, Robert Englund also has fans who spot him on the street, honk their horns, yell "Yo, Krueger!" and claw their hands in respect.

"Freddy has allowed me to travel all around the world, probably ten times now," he said. "He bought my little dream cottage for my wife and I down on Laguna Beach. He has made me very comfortable."

The *Nightmare* shoot went about thirty-two days, and the film cost $1.8 million. Craven wanted *Nightmare* to be a step above the usual horror fare, and you couldn't use the term "splatter" on the set.

Other than Freddy's makeup, *Nightmare* was fairly bare-bones effects wise. "I think there was one special effect, where he walks through the bars, and that was a simple optical," says Craven. "Everything else was shot at the time it went onto film. The only real weapon was the cutting edge of his steel, and that's like a ten-dollar item."

As Englund discovered, as much as he relished playing Freddy Krueger, doing full-blown, extensive makeup wasn't fun. "Getting my head cast was just as much fun as getting whacked in the nuts with a pool cue," he recalled. "After about the second movie I got something in my contract where they treat me to a good facial. If they don't, you treat yourself to one. Back when I started, it was kind of a girly thing to do. Now I love it. They cleanse you and get all that gunk out."

Englund saw Freddy as someone killing the future. "You can imagine what it is like to be seventeen or eighteen today and enter a world with a drug culture and hardly any jobs on the horizon, and AIDS and racial unrest," he said. "It is very disheartening . . . Freddy represents all of these things that are out of kilter in the world, all the sins of the parents that are being passed on." Because evil doesn't die, you can only vanquish Freddy temporarily and "keep this horrible future they are about to inherit at bay."

During the shoot, Craven was confident he had something good. "I really feel this will be a landmark film for me, my watershed film," he told the *UCLA Daily Bruin*. "It's not an ordinary, run-of-the-mill little film. There's really something quite extraordinary about it. It's going to be a nice piece of work."

New Line was on the hook for a lot of money, and the company almost went under several times trying to keep *Nightmare* alive. Shaye was putting the money together for *Nightmare,* and New Line decided to go ahead once they thought they had all the cash they needed.

"As we were in preproduction, we lost a big piece of the money," Risher says. "I'd say maybe even half of it. So it was a huge thing for us if we couldn't finish this film. I came out to L.A. and had to tell everybody that we couldn't pay them for a week, please stay on with us and trust us, and everybody did."

Much like he would years later on the *The Lord of the Rings* series, Shaye gambled the company on *Nightmare*. They didn't realize at first the company was riding on the film, but once *Nightmare* started rolling, everyone realized what a precipitous position they were in.

"If we had to stop in the middle because we couldn't pay our bills, the company definitely would have gone under," Risher continues. "Once we finished it, it didn't have to be a hit because we had presold foreign territories, and once we finished and delivered it, we were okay. If Bob hadn't kept things going, or if Bob hadn't found the money, we could have lost everything."

New Line had already endured one financial crisis during the shoot, then another one came right before the film's release when the company didn't have the money to pay the film lab. Risher had just given birth to her son when word came in that DuArt Labs wouldn't deliver the prints for release the next day because they hadn't been paid yet.

With her newborn baby in her hands, Risher broke down and cried. After all they went through, now the lab said they wouldn't deliver the prints to the theaters. New Line then gave DuArt a convincing song and dance, and finally it was able to get the film into theaters. Risher says, "We gave them all kinds of reassurances and pledged a lot of other stuff to them, and they finally agreed, so we got the film into the theaters."

Craven also had to do battle with the censors over the scene where an enormous fountain of blood comes out of the bed and another scene when the character Tina dies. Craven tried to compare the scene to the elevators full of blood on *The Shining,* but the MPAA wouldn't listen. He had to cut about twenty feet of footage out of the blood fountain scene, and made some trims in Tina's death before finally winning the R.

Because New Line didn't have a lot of money, they did a lot of guerilla advertising on the streets and through radio ads, which they had many years of experience from working the college circuit.

"We had our hands into all the college and university towns across the country because we were very successful selling films and lecture series there, so we knew how to tap into that," Risher says.

The week before *A Nightmare on Elm Street* opened wide, Englund did his first sci-fi and horror convention, which was at the Roosevelt Hotel on Madison and Forty-fifth Street in New York. The line to meet Englund went out the door and around the block, and Englund figured they were there because he was on *V.* Bob Shaye saw the line and smiled.

"Shit, the movie hasn't even opened wide."

"I think they're here for *V,* Bob."

"Nah. *Nightmare.*"

A week later, Englund saw Penn and Teller, and they made a Freddy Krueger joke in their routine, which showed Englund that *Nightmare* was now in the pop culture zeitgeist. For Risher, it was seeing a newspaper headline after a stock market crash: NIGHTMARE ON WALL STREET, and then President Ronald Reagan also made a joke in one of his speeches: "The truth is when you take a walk down our opposition's memory lane, it starts to look like *Nightmare on Elm Street.*"

"It took a while to know that we had a big success because we rolled it out across the country," Risher says. "But for us at the time, the New York opening was very big." The Monday after the movie opened, "we could breathe more easily because it seemed to recoup its adverting costs at least."

"It was a totally grass roots phenomenon," Englund said. "You have to remember the original two *Nightmare* movies were not forced down people's throats. They were not oversold and the public was not browbeaten into appreciating them. Like *Phantasm,* they were discovered by an audience."

Yet as Risher also adds New Line really didn't turn around until they got a deal with RCA/Columbia to put out their movies on video, a deal they sealed with two horror flicks, *Nightmare 2* and *Critters.* "Then the company started having a cushion." New Line also made money on the Freddy dolls, Halloween masks, and claw gloves. (Shaye kept two Freddy dolls in his office.)

It was obvious opening weekend that *Nightmare* was a franchise, and they started working on a sequel right away. They immediately recruited David Chaskin to write the screenplay, and Chaskin was the one who brought humor to Freddy, which Craven wasn't nuts about: "Freddy's like Shecky Green with claws now." Craven walked away from the series, although he did return to finish the series off with the seventh one, *Wes Craven's New Nightmare.*

The third *Nightmare, The Dream Warriors,* written by Frank Darabont of *Shawshank Redemption* fame, was the best reviewed of the series, and was also the first *Nightmare on Elm Street* movie to get a wide release. "We were making money and were able to book theaters and hold them," says Risher. The highest-grossing film in the series was part four, *The Dream Master,* which made $49 million at the box office.

All told, the *Nightmare* series reportedly grossed more than $500 million in box office, home, and TV revenue, and New Line would become known as the house that Freddy Krueger built. "It took New Line about ten years to be called creditworthy," Shaye said. "It wasn't until *A Nightmare on Elm Street* opened and made something like $20 million that we realized we might have a franchise that would allow us to make a sequel or two. After the second *A Nightmare on Elm Street*, we got Drexel Burnham interested. Things started getting more like a business."

FIFTEEN

TO STAY SANE YOU HAVE TO LAUGH

How Stuart Gordon brought H. P. Lovecraft to the big screen with *Re-Animator*, while the road led back to zombies for George Romero, and Clive Barker brought British horror back with *Hellraiser*

Before Stuart Gordon adapted H. P. Lovecraft's work for the big screen, there were the Edgar Allen Poe films. The Poe adaptations of the sixties were an ambitious step up for American International Pictures, because they worked with much bigger budgets and schedules than the company was used to.

The first Poe adaptation, *House of Usher*, cost $300,000, AIP's biggest budget feature for the time. *Usher* was shot in color and Cinema-Scope, and it was shot in fifteen days, a longer schedule than the usual AIP quickie.

AIP believed in its Edgar Allan Poe movies so much it even screened them for the critics. Usually low-budget B companies didn't screen movies for critics or do advance press for them, because the movies were often so bad, any advance word would have killed them. AIP went all-out courting the press with a preview party for *House of Usher* in Palm Springs with red carpets and klieg lights, and the critics liked what they saw.

House of Usher made more than a million in rentals, and the next AIP Poe film, *The Pit and the Pendulum*, made close to two million on the same budget. AIP didn't mean to launch a franchise with Poe's work, but as AIP founder Sam Arkoff recalled, "They were doing so well, we just didn't want to stop."

Martin Scorsese has said that the AIP Poe films were an "important stimulus to would-be filmmakers of my generation. *House of Usher* had a beautiful atmosphere in its use of color and Cinema-Scope. We loved this blend of English gothic and French Grand Guignol mixed together in an American film."

Where the Poe films did big business in the sixties, H. P. Lovecraft hadn't been done as successfully. AIP put out two Lovecraft adaptations, *The Haunted Palace* in 1963 and *The Dunwich Horror* in 1970. Because Poe was better known, AIP did a misleading ad campaign for *Haunted Palace* with a Poe quote in the ad campaign to fool audiences into thinking it was one of his stories instead.

"In those early days, Lovecraft wasn't really known to audiences," says Stuart Gordon. "When Lovecraft was done, they essentially trashed the stories, although *The Haunted Palace* was particularly well done. They appreciated Lovecraft when they made it. I think over time the appreciation for Lovecraft has grown, and he's become a name almost as much as Poe."

H. P. Lovecraft truly didn't get his due in films until Stuart Gordon took him on with *Re-Animator* and *From Beyond*. Gordon had been reading Lovecraft since he was a teenager. "His work is really terrifying," he says. "His stories really hold up and they really scare the crap out of you."

When Hollywood was making a number of vampire films at the end of the seventies, Gordon wondered to a friend why there wasn't a new Frankenstein movie in the works. "Have you ever read Lovecraft's 'Herbert West—Re-Animator'?" the friend asked him. Gordon had never heard of it, and he read *a lot* of Lovecraft. "That piqued my curiosity." The story was long out of print, and Gordon finally found a copy of it at the Chicago Public Library in the special collections department.

Re-Animator was a story Lovecraft had disparaged in his career because he wrote it for a magazine serialization, and part of the reason he disowned it was he wrote it for money. "Lovecraft would usually write his own things, then try to sell them after he'd written them," Gordon explains. "Lovecraft always felt that anything for money was nowhere near as good as the art you created on your own. For this they had come to him, asked him to write a serial. It appeared every month. He'd dashed this off, and didn't consider it one of his best pieces of work."

Whatever Lovecraft's feelings about his work, Gordon loved it. *Re-Animator* was an action-packed story, where Lovecraft's story was usually more moody and internal with little dialogue. Like AIP had done with Poe, Gordon was hoping to do adaptations of Lovecraft's work with the author's name above the title to reestablish him in a big way in popular culture.

Gordon and his producing partner Brian Yuzna both wanted to go over the top with *Re-Animator*. "Brian's take, and I have to say I agree with him, was the only way you can make your mark in horror is to go beyond whatever's been done before." Lovecraft was prudish and tried to avoid sexual subtext as much as he could, but Gordon and his screenwriting partner went where even a master of terror such as Lovecraft would fear to tread. "I was thinking that one of the most horrifying taboos is still necrophilia," Gordon says. "The idea of reversing it, instead of making love to a dead person, having a dead person make love to you, seemed like a pretty interesting approach."

Gordon originally thought *Re-Animator* could be a miniseries that could run on HBO at midnight, and saw it in six parts, just as the story was serialized. Gordon got no takers, he was told no one wanted to do horror on television (this was several years before *Tales from the Crypt*), and H. P. Lovecraft wasn't a name like Poe was then, so Gordon decided to make it as a movie. "That story is so outrageous, you probably wouldn't be able to do half of it on TV anyway," Gordon said.

Friends asked Gordon, why a horror film? Don't you want to make a *serious* film? Don't you want to make a bigger statement? But Gordon didn't feel limited by the genre at all. "Working within the horror genre is like writing a sonnet . . . there are rules you have to follow, but once you follow those rules, you can say whatever you want to say."

You would think it would be hard to make necrophilia funny, but *Re-Animator* did a very good job of it. "I've always felt you can never find an audience that wants to laugh more than a horror movie audience," Gordon explains. "You can laugh at something, you're not afraid. I always think it's a good thing to give the audience something to laugh at without hurting the movie."

In researching the film, Gordon went to a lot of morgues, talking to pathologists, and discovered, "You'll never find people with more sick senses of humor than people who work with dead bodies. In order to stay sane I think you have to be able to laugh."

Re-Animator was made in twenty-two days on an $800,000 budget. "*Re-Animator* had a very small cast, it's got very few locations," Gordon recalls. "I don't think there's a single exterior scene in the whole movie. There's several exterior establishing shots, but those were done after the fact."

Gordon definitely wanted *Re-Animator* to be R-rated, which past a certain point he realized would be impossible. "We actually submitted the film, just to see what they would say, and they told us that we would have to cut everything after the second reel." Empire released it unrated, and Gordon says, "It took a lot of guts on the part of the distributor. I think it actually helped the movie, made it forbidden fruit."

But it came back to bite Gordon on the ass when he followed up *Re-Animator* with *From Beyond* in 1986, which he called "a real wrestling match" to get the R. The MPAA wasn't happy *Re-Animator* was released unrated, "and I think they came down extra hard on us for that."

He purposely used less blood than in *Re-Animator,* not that the MPAA noticed. "When you ask them what you should change, and they say, 'Everything,' it's kind of rough." Gordon also adds, "There are no real rules, so it's completely arbitrary, and it depends on how they feel that day when they're watching the movie."

He doesn't recall how many times he took *From Beyond* to the MPAA, but he took it to the board as many times as he was allowed to, and he had to go to New York to appeal the decision. "I ended up requesting a meeting with the MPAA, which is something they never do."

One woman on the ratings board scolded Gordon for making *From Beyond.* "I felt like I'd been called into the principal's office." She shook her finger in his face and said, "What did you think we would say when you show us things like this?"

As Gordon and many other horror filmmakers have discovered, you couldn't bring up other movies with similar scenes as an argument for the R. "You couldn't say, 'You let *Friday the 13th* do this,'" Gordon says. "'Well, if we had to do it over again we wouldn't let *Friday the 13th* do it either.'"

As Romero recalled, there was a scene in *Martin* the MPAA objected to that was twenty-eight frames, and they told Romero, "Make it seventeen frames." Romero said, "Is that going to protect anyone's innocence? Either take it out or leave it in."

Wes Craven loves to joke about the old saying where a film is made three times, first in the screenplay phase, second on the set, third in the editing room, "then the censors make their own fourth film," he said, laughing. A company that reprints horror posters on T-shirts came up with a design that replicated the MPAA logo, except here it stood for "must punish all artists."

After the Lovecraft films, Gordon would cross over into writing for family films with the *Honey, I Shrunk the Kids* series. "I think *Honey, I Shrunk the Kids* is a horror film!" Gordon says. "I think it's a horror film for kids. Mad scientists, giant bugs, it's got all the elements of a horror movie, it's just the tone is a little bit different."

Director Jeremy Kagan's kids went to the same school as Brian Yuzna's kids, and the class was invited to a screening of Kagan's 1985 film *The Journey of Natty Gann*. When Yuzna's kids came back, they asked, "Dad, how come we never get to see any of your movies?" which led to, "Why don't we come up with an idea for a movie our kids could see?"

When the idea of *Honey, I Shrunk the Kids,* which was then called *The Teenie-Weenies,* was pitched to Disney, Michael Eisner and Jeffrey Katzenberg were "the new guys" at the company.

Gordon is a big Disney fan, and *Honey, I Shrunk the Kids* was the first live action film the company had made in years. "At the time *Honey, I Shrunk the Kids* was made, calling something a family film was the kiss of death," Gordon says. "The guys who made *Re-Animator* got Disney back into family films!"

If Disney had any reservations about working with a horror film director, it was because they wanted the movie to be more *The Nutty Professor* and less David Cronenberg's *The Fly.* They also wanted the giant ants to have blue eyes so they'd look more like *E.T.* and wouldn't be as scary to kids, but Gordon was trying to teach kids that sometimes when something looks scary, it's not necessarily evil or bad.

"It bothers me in movies that good people are always beautiful, and bad people are always ugly, and in real life it's often the opposite," Gordon says. Gordon had to take the Disney executives to the creature lab, and once one of the giant ants came over and gave Stuart a hug with his antenna, they got it.

The same year *Re-Animator* was released, Gordon also had undead competition with Romero's *Day of the Dead* and the horror comedy *The Return of the Living Dead*. Laurel had a three-picture deal with UFD, and *Day of the Dead* was going to be a bigger, more ambitious movie than *Dawn of the Dead*. The initial script as written was going to have a $6.5 million budget, which UFD weren't going to put up unless the movie could get an R rating. With *Dawn of the Dead* costing $1.5 million it wasn't a big financial risk for an unrated movie, but $6.5 million plus advertising and everything else was a considerably bigger risk.

Where *Dawn of the Dead* was a fun, exhilarating experience for Savini, he recalled *Day of the Dead* was "strictly business. You had to go through six people just to get a message to George. I didn't enjoy it, personally."

Day of the Dead marked the end of an era for Romero and the gang. Romero would leave Laurel Entertainment on June 19, 1985, right before *Day*'s release, and he lost the rights to *Dawn of the Dead* in the split, which is why it was remade without his say in 2004 by Zack Synder.

It was also one of Savini's last hurrahs as a makeup artist, and he passed the gore effects torch to his assistant on *Day of the Dead*, Greg Nicotero, who later formed KNB. "I believe *Day of the Dead* was Tom's pinnacle in a way," says Harrison. "He did some very innovative stuff in *Day of the Dead,* and it was really state of the art for the time. And it spawned a whole generation of guys who worked for him to come up after him."

Savini turned to consulting and teaching at his own school in Pennsylvania, and he doesn't miss his time as an effects artist. "I had my day as the magician," Savini says. "I don't need to be involved in effects any more than being a consultant, solving problems and letting [the effects team] do the physical stuff."

Released on July 3, 1985, *Day of the Dead* came in third behind *Back to the Future* and *Cocoon,* a good debut for an unrated horror film in a regional release, but the ultimate box-office take was disappointing.

Reviews for *Day of the Dead* were mixed, and some reviewers wanted more out of the film, wishing it had the subtext and satire that worked great in *Dawn of the Dead.* Gene Siskel felt Romero had "run out of ideas of what to do with his zombies . . . I think he should stop now. I think he's sort of trapped commercially, thinking 'I've gotta do another ghouly one.' I think George Romero probably has enough talent to make a wholly different kind of film, and I'd like to see him do it."

Day also went up against Orion's *The Return of the Living Dead,* which back in 1972 was going to be a sequel to *Night of the Living Dead,* again written by John Russo. To make a long story short, by the time the rights wound up with another producer, and the project was rewritten and directed by Dan O'Bannon, it was very far removed from Romero's brand of undead. *The Return of the Living Dead* was a much funnier take on zombies, and reportedly the humor in the film was added after the first preview. (The theme song, "Partytime," from the punk band 45 Grave, was also added on after the movie was finished.)

An American Werewolf in London and *The Howling* proved rival horror films could have healthy competition, but *Day of the Dead* took a hit at the box office in *The Return of the Living Dead*'s wake. *Return* had a bigger ad campaign and release pattern behind it, and Romero wasn't happy with the audience thinking it was one of his films. "It was all dirty pool," Romero said, and the confusion continued many years later when Romero was interviewed for *Vanity Fair,* and contributor Eric Spitznagel asked Romero about zombies eating brains, which referred to *Return*, not one of Romero's films (the article was even titled "Who Says Zombies Eat Brains?").

Day of the Dead enjoys a healthy cult following today, and John Harrison, who composed the music, said, "I think we all felt *Day of the Dead* was kind of underrated." Asked why it wasn't well received in its time, Harrison replied, "It's a very grim picture, what can I tell ya? It's not a feel good movie, and it doesn't have the same level of humor that *Dawn* did."

When Clive Barker broke through in America in 1987, he was a welcome breath of fresh air, a new voice in the genre who wrote intelligently and didn't scrimp on the extremity. "The whole point is actually going beyond the limits—pushing yourself into territories which others would think of as taboo or forbidden," he said. "If you're not doing that, you're not using the *strength* from the fiction."

The ads for his directing debut, *Hellraiser,* featured a sole endorsement, but when it comes from Stephen King, who else did you need? "I have seen the future of horror, and its name is Clive Barker," King exclaimed.

The Liverpool native knew an endorsement from King was a heavy anointing. "It comes from a master of the genre, and somebody who has made the genre 'box office,'" Barker said in 1988. "In literary terms he has made it an acceptable 'read.'"

Many can't help but notice that those who create horror aren't the kind of people you expect. For many years Barker maintained his youthful, boyish look, and he had a regular childhood. "I had a perfectly normal upbringing," he said. "I wish I could say rats were put down my trousers, but I'm afraid there's nothing like that."

"Everyone I've met who's worked in horror has really been a nice guy," says Wes Craven. "When you're in that inner circle, you realize that you've dealt with a lot of inner demons, and therefore you come to terms with a lot, or at least you devise tools for dealing with the kind of general base level of terror that is part of human existence."

Barker also didn't grow up with EC Comics, *The Twilight Zone,* or any of the usual influences his peers had in their formative years, which made him push his imagination much harder to come up with his own stories. "My childhood imaginings fed upon themselves," he said. "My formative years were spent with my own imagination. At the time it was deeply frustrating, but now I see it as a blessing in disguise."

Barker loved to draw and paint, and the character of Pinhead came to him in his sleep. Barker usually discarded 98 percent of the sketches that came to him in his dreams, but his drawing of Pinhead was very close to what wound up in the movie. At first the character was billed as the Lead Cenobite, and he was called Pinhead on the set as a goof, but eventually the name stuck.

Doug Bradley, an old school friend of Barker's, was surprised and delighted he became a famous horror icon playing Pinhead. Considering his character initially had no name, was unrecognizable under heavy makeup, and was in the movie less than ten minutes, he never could have predicted it. Bradley never cursed being best known as a monster, and even wrote a book, *Behind the Mask of the Horror Actor,* comparing other classic monsters and discussing Pinhead's place in their pantheon.

H. R. Giger said he never censored himself in his art, and similarly

Barker said, "I will never apologize for being gross. When people say 'stop' to me, when people say 'don't do that,' I begin to suspect them. I think they're scared or repressed."

He also wanted to give his creatures the power of speech and intellect. "Generally the monsters don't talk about their condition," Barker said, but he wanted them to in *Hellraiser* because "I think what the monsters in movies have to say for themselves is every bit as interesting as what the human beings have to say. That's why in stalk and slash films I think half the story is missing. These creatures simply become, in a very boring way, abstractions of evil. . . . I like the idea that a point of view can be made by the dark side."

Barker had two previous screenplays made, *Transmutations* and *Rawhead Rex*, which he said were both "massacred . . . I think there are about seven of my lines left in the first one." For *Hellraiser,* an adaptation of his novella *The Hellbound Heart,* he held the screenplay hostage by pitching himself as a package deal. If you wanted the screenplay, he had to direct it.

Barker had only directed two short films before, and he panicked when he went to the library, and found the two books it had on filmmaking were both checked out. "Oh, I'm so fucked," he said. "I don't even have a book!"

With Barker directing for the first time, "I always knew it was going to be raw," he recalled. "There were things which, if we'd had more time, money, and experience, I would have done differently." He added with a laugh, "It's a slightly misshapen baby, but it's mine."

Barker also knew his first time out he wouldn't have unlimited resources. He recalled that New World, who produced and distributed *Hellraiser,* "would only give novices enough money for one haunted house and not sets and it turned out to be true." Yet once New World saw the rushes, they did give Clive Barker more time to make the movie and more money for special effects.

Barker ultimately found directing "a great ego fix, you feel like a cross between Napoleon and God," although it was much more work intensive and exhausting than he realized. He was up at six every morning, worked until eight at night, watched the rushes and prepared for the next day, was in bed at one, and then started all over again.

Hellraiser was considered a comeback for British horror, which had remained moribund since the demise of Hammer, and it was also marketed as a thinking person's horror film that eschewed the sexism and clichés of the mad slasher era. "I think we've made a horror picture with intelligence and style," Barker said. "What we have is an adult horror film . . . one that is going to be made with the maximum amount of intelligence and class we can muster."

For Barker, horror also had to be hard-core, without comedy, although one Pinhead line got a good laugh in theaters: "Oh, no tears, please. It's a waste of good suffering."

"I like my horror *dark*," Barker said. "It's not tongue-in-cheek like *Re-Animator* . . . I have fun with those kinds of pictures but I much prefer to believe that people are intending to really scare me.

"I want to be able to say to the audience, 'Look, you're in the hands of a dangerous man,'" he continued. "You should always show things a little stronger than people think they can take. I like to come out of horror pictures thinking, 'Boy, that was tough.' It has to be a little grueling."

Like Cronenberg, Barker found horror in the body. He was terrified of "the general condition of being flesh and blood. Of minds to madness and flesh to wounding." He was also terrified of boredom, which is what drives the main characters in *Hellraiser* to seek out perverse, supernatural pleasures. "My characters are constantly escaping from banality," he said.

Also like Cronenberg, Barker felt horror was a vehicle for confrontation. "I don't believe that there are worlds which take us away from our own," he said. "I think there are finally worlds which help us confront our own. I think good fantasy and good horror fiction is finally a way of offering metaphorical solutions to the world in which we live. I think bad fantasy is merely escapism."

Hellraiser, made on a budget of about a million dollars, made $20 million back, launched a franchise, and cemented Barker's name in the States as a horror force to be reckoned with. On welfare until he was thirty, Barker became a "mega-author" who commands huge advances for his books (he owns three homes in Beverly Hills).

In the new millennium, Barker felt the need to branch out, and crossed over to children's entertainment with the *Arabat* series. Barker wanted to write fantasy stories for kids since he first read *The Chronicles of Narnia,* and perhaps sensing another *Harry Potter,* Disney paid $8 million for the *Arabat* rights and had big franchise plans for it, but the movie never got off the ground.

It was initially hard to imagine Barker at Disney, but of course they also took in Stuart Gordon post *Re-Animator* and *From Beyond,* and as Barker explained, "*Arabat* could not have sprung from an earlier Clive Barker. It springs from a Clive Barker who is happier in his spirit than he's ever been, and who wants to express that.

"One of my great idols, Noël Coward, was asked, 'How did you manage to maintain your popularity through the years?' His answer, 'Darling, it's very simple. You always pop out of another hole.' Whenever they think they've got the hole you'll pop out of, you find a new one. If you think you're a horror novelist, you go write profanity. If they think you're writing a thousand words of profanity, you go write a kid's book."

SIXTEEN

HAVING A FRIEND FOR DINNER

How Jonathan Demme directed the only horror film to ever sweep the Oscars, *The Silence of the Lambs*, Peter Jackson outsoaked Sam Raimi in gore with *Dead Alive*, and David Fincher made the feel-bad movie of the year with *Se7en*

The Silence of the Lambs certainly wasn't the first horror film to be nominated for best picture, but it was the only horror film that's swept the Academy Awards in cinema history. Perhaps some day another horror film will win, never say never, but *Silence*'s combination of cast, screenplay, source material, and director would be a tough act to repeat.

"Everything with this picture was against the rules, but this is the business with no rules," says Eric Pleskow, then president of Orion. "You don't do this, you don't do that. One person told me, 'You don't make movies about boxing! Women won't go!' We had *Rocky* and *Raging Bull*. *Dances With Wolves*. 'You don't do Westerns, you don't do anything about Indians. Don't even bother to read it. It's about Indians, it's got subtitles, and it's too long.' An Oscar picture that was released in February? And a horror film? And then a

Western? We had best picture back-to-back with *Silence* and *Dances With Wolves.*"

In a funny bit of serendipity, screenwriter Ted Tally and Thomas Harris had crossed paths several times before Tally became the screenwriter of *The Silence of the Lambs*. Harris was frequenting an art gallery in New York where Tally's wife was the director. Tally had met Harris several times, had dinner with him, and was a fan of his previous books *Red Dragon* and *Black Sunday*, which was adapted into a 1977 Paramount film directed by John Frankenheimer.

One night Tally asked him what he was working on, and Harris was just about finished with his third novel. Before long, an advance copy of *The Silence of the Lambs* showed up in Tally's mail. "I'm not even sure he knew I was a screenwriter; maybe vaguely aware," Tally recalled. "Clearly, he had no ulterior motive in sending it to me. It's just that he was a friend of my wfie's and knew I liked his work."

Tally found it a "great yarn" once he read it, the kind of book that comes along every ten years, and thought it would make a phenomenonal movie. He also had the feeling William Goldman was already adapting it, but Tally's wife kept telling him to look into it, and see if it was available. Finally Tally's wife called Orion, found out they were negotiating for the rights, and there wasn't a screenwriter attached yet.

Tally also found out many studios had already passed on it, thinking it was just a slasher film. Some were also willing to buy the project if a big director wanted to do it, but when said director would pass, so would the studio.

Meanwhile, Gene Hackman read the novel and got Orion to option it for him. Eric Pleskow called the New York offices and said, "Let's go ahead. If Gene Hackman doesn't know how to direct a movie by now, nobody ever will." And indeed, Orion also gave first directing gigs to Kevin Costner with *Dances with Wolves*, Danny De

Vito with *Throw Mama from the Train,* and Ron Shelton with *Bull Durham.* Hackman was going to direct and star as Lecter, and he also had the fallback position of playing the role of FBI agent Crawford if he decided against playing Hannibal. (Crawford was ultimately played by Scott Glenn in the film.)

Tally was working on a project for Orion, which brought him to the attention of Mike Medavoy, who cofounded the company. Tally first worked with Lindsay Anderson, the British director of *If...* and *O Lucky Man!* on a script called *Empire* for Orion, which was going to be "*Gone with the Wind* Goes to India," but it never got made because it was too expensive. Tally went on to write other screenplays that went unproduced until Griffin Dunne, who acted in two of Tally's plays, offered him the adaptation of *White Palace,* which Dunne was producing.

Medavoy knew Tally's *Empire* screenplay, as well as *White Palace,* which hadn't been made yet, but was getting Tally a lot of notice as a writing sample. Based on the quality of Tally's work, Medavoy approved him to work on the script, and it was clearly a big step up for an unproven and unproduced screenwriter. (*White Palace,* which starred James Spader and Susan Sarandon, didn't do well at the box office, but it was very well received by the critics.)

Tally met with Hackman in Santa Fe, and Tally recalled the actor was "very shrewd about the book. He'd done his homework; really knew the novel." Hackman liked the treatment Tally wrote, and gave him the go-ahead to write the screenplay. Tally flew back to New York and went to work, then didn't hear anything from Hackman for weeks until he got the call from his agent that the actor was quitting the project. After starring in *Mississippi Burning,* Hackman decided he didn't want to make violent films anymore and backed out.

"He was very honorable, and wanted to stay in and go fifty-fifty with him buying the rights," Pleskow says. "We paid him out because

I didn't want a partner. Even if it's a dollar you have to be honorable about it and consult with him. I wanted to be free in the decision making."

Tally also ran the risk of not getting paid for all his hard work, because Orion still hadn't officially bought the book, but Medavoy assured him it would be okay, and to keep working on it. As Tally was finishing his first draft, Medavoy called and asked, "Do you know Jonathan Demme's work? I'm thinking of offering this to him. What do you think?"

At first, Tally thought Demme was a *horrible* choice, but instead told Medavoy, "*That's* an interesting idea."

"I think maybe he needs this project, and it needs him," Medavoy explained.

"I loved him as a director," Tally said later. "I loved his comedies, but I couldn't picture him doing something this scary."

And indeed, Demme's work was wonderfully odd, sensitive, and human, not the first qualities that come to mind for something like *The Silence of the Lambs*. "Most people thought I was really being foolish to go with Jonathan on a picture like this," said Medavoy. "But I knew Jonathan's work and so I felt that he could do a really good, tight thriller, and that's what this was."

Choosing Demme to direct *The Silence of the Lambs* wasn't a complete shock to Ron Bozman, who came a long way from working on *The Texas Chain Saw Massacre* to producing a number of films for Jonathan, including *Something Wild, Married to the Mob,* and *Philadelphia*. "Demme has such a wide range," Bozman says. "Jonathan has such an amazing mind, he can encompass a whole range of things. Jonathan was never just gonna do a romantic comedy or a simple film. He just has too many layers with which he perceives the world."

Demme's *Something Wild* took a darker turn, a gear change he handled very smoothly, and the heart Demme brought to his movies would give much-needed humanity to the proceedings as well. "That was Medavoy's genius," Tally said years later. "Because I don't think that one executive out of ten in Hollywood would have thought of Jonathan Demme for this expensive and by now bestselling thriller."

Although he'd never made a horror film before, Demme was absolutely a fan of the genre, and felt that every director wanted to make a movie that scared the audience. Yet Bozman adds, "I never thought of *The Silence of the Lambs* as a horror film. It's too intricate."

Medavoy wanted Demme because he wasn't a genre director, and *Silence* was character-driven, much like Demme's other films. Also as a preemptive strike, Demme was a critics' darling, and Medavoy wanted good reviews as well.

"He was a multifaceted director who had an affinity for odd people and places, and he was a master at delivering the unexpected," Medavoy said. "Though he was clearly smart and talented, he was too original and idiosyncratic to be on any studio's A list for thrillers."

"I have a tendency towards the offbeat," Demme once told an interviewer. "I would pick being perceived as unpredictable. 'Cause for *me* I'm unpredictable: I haven't the foggiest idea what's going to speak to me as something that I want to make. I haven't got a clue what the subject matter is going to be, as proved by *The Silence of the Lambs.*"

Moving away from his smaller, more personal films, *Silence* now gave Demme a chance to flex his muscles technique-wise. "The filmmaker and the moviegoer in me loved making *Silence of the Lambs*," he said. He had seen *Manhunter*, Michael Mann's 1986 adaptation of Harris's *Red Dragon*, and liked it, finding it very effective and disturbing, but he didn't watch it over and over when making *Silence*, and was clearly going to make his own movie.

Demme also had a close relationship with Orion, having made *Something Wild* and *Married to the Mob* for the studio, and initially he wanted to make an adaptation of the Russell Banks novel *Continental Drift* with the company. It was a very depressing book, but Jonathan tried to pitch it in his own unique way: "I know it looks like a bummer, but it's not a bummer. He's going through doors, every time he's going through doors." Writer Jesse Kornbluth, who helped get Jodie Foster the role of Clarice, remembered thinking, "Man, what a great pitch . . . no fuckin' way, but a great pitch!"

Then Medavoy told him, "I'm going to send you a book. See what you think of it." Demme first read the studio's synopsis of *Silence,* and the one-line description, "Young female FBI agent hunts down serial killer with help of demented psychiatrist," didn't interest him. "I was repelled by the idea of doing a film about a serial killer," he recalled. Then he started reading the book while the screenplay was still being written and from the first sentence of the book, "I knew this was something fresh," he said, adding, "I leapt at the chance to get involved with characters of such dimensions and a story with so many complicated and interesting themes."

From the get-go, Demme and Tally both saw *Silence* as Clarice's movie. "It had to live or die with her," Tally said. "She's our guide through the movie. We should experience these events emotionally and physically through her. She interested me more than Lecter."

Just as Demme saw *Continental Drift* as a guy going through doors, he saw *The Silence of the Lambs* as a women's picture, just as his directing debut, 1974's *Caged Heat*, wasn't just a chicks-in-prison exploitation flick.

"Ever since my days of working with Roger Corman, and perhaps before that, I've been a sucker for a woman's picture," Demme said.

464 ☻ REEL TERROR

"A film with a woman protagonist at the forefront. A woman in jeopardy. A woman on a mission. These are themes that have tremendous appeal to me as a moviegoer, and also as a director."

"Jonathan says he's a heavy estrogen director," said Tally. "He loves women's roles, loves to work with actresses. I think what attracted each of us was the idea of a strong central female character who was nobody's girlfriend and nobody's sidekick, who really would carry this story by herself."

In reviewing the film in *The Village Voice*, Amy Taubin also called *Silence*, "Deliberately, unabashedly, and uncompromisingly a feminist movie," and Demme said, "I'd much rather see a strong story with a lead character as a woman than the lead as a man, because the odds are stacked higher against the woman."

When Demme and Tally finally met, they hit it off immediately. Demme promised Tally he'd be the only writer working on the film, would never ask him to live with anything in the movie he didn't like, and Demme was as good as his word. Unlike many directors who suffer from the auteur disease and treat writers horribly, Demme treated Tally like a collaborator, actively listened, and wanted his advice and opinions. "This guy is so cool," Tally thought.

There's a joke in Hollywood that directors don't want writers around once a movie's under way, comparing them to hookers that won't leave after they've been paid, but Demme kept Tally around for just about everything. He was very welcome on the set as well as in the editing room, which is a rarity. The only part of the process Demme didn't want Tally there for was the first two or three weeks of production. "I have to establish my authority over the actors and find my working methods with them," he explained. "I don't want them going around my back to ask you for shortcuts. They'll come to the writer and ask, 'What did you mean by this? How do you think I should do this?' I want them to figure it out for themselves."

"They wouldn't admit it, but I think directors feel threatened by writers," Tally said. "Writers are the only other people who have the entire movie in their head." But Demme is "very confident within himself. His ego is not fragile. He can hear ideas from anybody and take them seriously and really process them."

Bringing Demme aboard also made sure *Silence* wouldn't totally slip up in gore. "Even in a movie like this, there are questions of taste," Demme said. "We were both very conscious in the writing and in the filming of trying to minimize the on-screen violence, because a tiny bit goes so far." Tally said, "People think of this movie as a very violent movie. But there's probably less than sixty seconds of on-screen violence in that two-hour movie. You think you've seen things that you haven't actually seen." (One of the most graphic scenes shown in the film, when prison guard Charles Napier is disemboweled and strung up by Lecter, is described as a "snapshot from Hell" in the script, and it was inspired by the work of Francis Bacon.)

Another reason Demme was a great choice to direct *Silence* was that he is wonderful with actors. Much like Hal Ashby, Demme would step back and let the actors discover the roles themselves, and let them take full responsibility for their characters. "I still don't want to talk to the actors very much," he said. "I'm afraid I'll say too much or say the wrong thing." Method acting? Forget it. "I can't work with actors who look to the director each morning for guidance, actors who ask historical questions—you know, 'Where did my guy go to college?' I'm like, 'Uh-oh.'"

The casting of Clarice and Hannibal was crucial, and as Bozman puts it, "Casting is everything. It's all you have." Jodie Foster had a guardian angel that helped her get the role of Clarice, the aforementioned Jesse Kornbluth, a former contributor for *Vanity Fair* who did a number of cover stories for the magazine.

Kornbluth had previously profiled Foster for *Vanity Fair*, and says, "One of the many conclusions that I drew was that she was the only authentic and credible blue-collar American actress, largely from seeing her in *The Accused*. Thirty-year-old actresses who could really be gritty at that time, I never got beyond Jodie on that short list."

Kornbluth can't recall if he read *Silence* in galleys, or right as it came out in stores, but he did read the book on an airplane coming back from Paris, and loved it. "It's not so much that it's a great horror story, it's really a great book," Kornbluth says. "George Orwell talked about prose like a windowpane, and Harris's writing is very clear writing. It's unadorned. It's all plot, and in my view it's the most daring and naked kind of writing, much more interesting than more stylized writing. You see the movie in your head when you read the book, which is to say it's taut, visual writing, as opposed to adjective- and adverb-rich poetic writing."

He then contacted Foster and told her, "You should read this book, you should go after this part. It's tailor-made for you." Demme had his heart set on Michelle Pfeiffer, but Kornbluth told him, "I don't think Michelle's as credible as Jodie. Give her a shot." Years later, Kornbluth adds, "Not to denigrate Michelle, but it wouldn't have been the same." (Pfeiffer reportedly found the story revolting and turned it down.)

Foster was advised against the film. She had just won the Academy Award for *The Accused* and was told, "Why are you going to do that movie? It's a total second fiddle. Anthony Hopkins got the good part and you are just quiet and don't speak in contradictions." Foster replied, "That's who she is, and that's how I'm going to play her. I'm not going to try and compete with him."

With the role of Hannibal Lecter, Anthony Hopkins also finally got the big break he always deserved as an actor. Demme loved Hopkins's performance in David Lynch's *The Elephant Man,* and Tally also said, "I was obsessed with having an actor who was great but not that well known. If Hoffman plays him you say, 'Yeah, he's brilliant but that's Dustin doing a star turn.' I just thought that for Lecter, the audience has to believe he's this genius-cannibal-lunatic. How are they going to believe that unless he's played by an actor they're not all that familiar with?"

"I just got a bee in my bonnet early on about him in this part," said Demme. "I think he has the ability to project an extremely heightened intelligence, which was key to Lecter as a lover of words—words just roll off Tony's tongue." Tally agreed, "I couldn't think of a single American actor with whom I'd have been comfortable speaking that language."

Without Hopkins, "it wouldn't have soared as gracefully," Bozman says. "Anthony's a particularly elegant actor and he brought such refinement and elegance to Hannibal. It wouldn't have been the same with an American actor. It wouldn't have soared as gracefully, and it would have been hard to achieve that kind of special sophistication. Hannibal is such a refined individual with such taste, he's so erudite. I think any American actor would have had trouble pulling that off."

"Lecter has sort of a weird charm in the book and we were very conscious of that," said Tally. "He had a smiling face and was very witty and bright. We found in Anthony an actor who can play any role, like Hitler, and we knew he could do the craziness needed for Lecter. We also knew he could handle language better than most actors can. Lecter speaks in such a classical and grammatical way that the American actors would be stumbling over the dialogue. To write that dialogue to fit an American actor would have been very difficult.

I assumed that Anthony Hopkins, being a classically trained British actor, would bring in himself the style needed for that dialogue."

In adapting Lecter for the screen, Tally had great source material with the novel, and he stayed close to it. "It is very difficult to make up lines for him [Lecter]," he said. "Fortunately, Thomas Harris writes brilliant dialogue . . . a lot of Lecter's dialogue is intact [from the book]. Where I had to make up dialogue for Lecter it was difficult, because he has to surprise you all the time, and he never just says what he means. He has to be obscure and yet the audience has to get it."

Hopkins saw Lecter as a cross between a panther and a lizard, feline and reptilian, and also compared him to a tarantula. "It's stationary for hours, and then suddenly it goes, tsst . . . tsst . . . tsst. That's the most terrifying moment. The movement is real terror. For Lecter, he just stares and watches, and then he moves."

Other ideas Hopkins brought to the role were slicking back his hair so it looked like a steel lid, "like he's bursting to get out of his skull," and changing Lecter's uniform from an orange boiler suit to an all-white ensemble because when he went to the dentist as a child, the overwhelmingly white and sterile environment terrified him.

"Everything Anthony does is very conscious," Bozman says. "He doesn't like last-minute script changes because he works hard on the lines and the character. He has it just down and he doesn't like last-minute changes because it throws him off."

Hopkins's first turn as Lecter was indeed a remarkable performance, so much so you don't realize he's only in the film a whopping twenty-seven minutes. "Is that all I'm in for?" the actor asked incredulously. "That's amazing." Because Hopkins was in the film less than half an hour, there was some debate at Orion whether to go for Best Actor or Best Supporting at the Oscars, but because his performance was so strong, Orion went for Best Actor.

Demme was a big fan of Hitchcock, and per Hitchcock, Demme wanted *Silence* to have a lot of subjective camera work. With the lenses Demme used, 100 millimeter, the actors were very close in low light, and he had the actors look right into the barrel of the lens instead of looking off axis.

"I love putting the audience in my characters' shoes," Demme said. "If you choose your moments well, it's powerful." Demme added, "You always had to see what Clarice was seeing. So as the scenes between her and Lecter intensify, inevitably we work our way into the subjective positions. And maybe that brings that heightened sense of intimacy we associate with confessionals or with the psychiatrist's couch."

Another interesting technique Demme used was walking into the frame after calling action and whispering to the actors while the camera was rolling because he'd either have a last-minute idea or to shake them up. Demme didn't want the actors to rely on their usual bag of tricks, and wanted them to work outside their usual thinking.

The Silence of the Lambs was shot by longtime Demme director of photography Tak Fujimoto. Tak got his big break working as a camera operator on *Badlands*, and when the original cinematographer had to be replaced, he was moved up to director of photography, thanks to production manager Lou Stroller. Demme first worked with Fujimoto on *Caged Heat*, and Tak went on to shoot *Melvin and Howard, Something Wild, Married to the Mob,* and *Philadelphia* for him. (Other Fujimoto credits include *Ferris Bueller's Day Off, The Sixth Sense,* and *Signs*.)

Like many directors who grow creatively with their crew members, Demme and Tak had an unspoken shorthand, and Jonathan gave him great leeway to shoot the movie how he wanted.

"One of the reasons I work so consistently with Tak Fujimoto is that Tak comes up with a brand-new look for every movie," Demme said. "I've almost stopped talking to him about lighting going into films, because his conception of a look for the film is inevitably going to be a lot more interesting [and] appropriate than what I might have dreamed up. Because that's not really one of my strong points—conceiving the kind of lights and shades of a look for a movie."

With *Silence,* they specifically wanted to avoid genre clichés from the get-go, and were inspired by a classic, groundbreaking horror film that also had an atypical look for the genre. "My only thing was, I didn't want the film to look like another modish, stylish, moody broody, long shadow catch the killer movie," Demme said. "And because of the incredible heaviness of the subject matter, it was important to aspire to a certain brightness whenever possible. To that end, Tak and I looked at *Rosemary's Baby* together a couple of times. A very bright picture most of the time. Tak then spun off from there."

Probably the biggest challenge in the film was keeping the long talks between Clarice and Lecter visually interesting. "It was a challenge to keep it fresh and varied so you didn't have the same coverage," Bozman recalls.

There was a similar problem with the adaptation of *Misery,* because 75 percent of it takes place in one room. Rob Reiner later recalled that when James Caan finally made it into the hallway of Annie Wilkes's home, "We were all like, 'He's in the hallway!' Literally, we moved two feet, but it was like being led out on the playground at recess: 'Yay! We're out of the room!'" Being laid up in bed for months also drove James Caan stir-crazy, and as William Goldman recalled, "That pent-up energy you saw on the screen was very real. And it was one of the main reasons, at least for me, the movie worked."

"I was very conscious of the fact that I've got two people just sitting there, pretty static, for seven or eight minutes," Demme said. "But I knew there was such a weird, powerful dynamic going on in those scenes. They were menacing and sexual and had a twisted kind of father-daughter thing going on, and they were unexpectedly funny and surprising in places. I knew that they worked on many, many levels . . . I also saw those scenes as the heart of the movie."

"They were the most original part of the movie," Tally said, "That this woman is having her demons exorcised by a person who is a demon himself. And this sort of strange, half-playful, half-terrifying, very sexual exchange which goes on between them, in which each of them has to give some gift to the other. It's an amazing creation by Thomas Harris. When you have something like that as an adapting screenwriter, you just try to not get in the way."

"Those scenes are so critical, and yet the Big Book of Screenwriting says that you don't just put people nose-to-nose in a room and let them talk to each other for minutes at a time," Tally continued. As it turns out, it wasn't the first time Demme broke the rules like this, as shown in Bo Goldman's screenplay for Demme's underrated classic, *Melvin and Howard*.

"To open a movie with an eighteen-page dialogue scene, two people riding along in a truck at night? Outrageous idea!" Demme said. "It breaks every rule known to man, and yet the emotion he poured into that scene makes it wonderful."

The decision to separate Clarice and Hannibal with Plexiglas was inspired by the heavy, bulletproof glass you'd see in a bank or a liquor store. "I didn't want people to feel, for a second, they were seeing anything remotely like a prison movie," said Demme. "We aspired to create a setting for these encounters that would not evoke any other films, that would have a freshness and a scariness all their own."

And when Foster explains the story behind the title, her performance was so strong, Demme decided not to potentially ruin it with a flashback. "It would be impossible to intrude on this performance with cutaways to a little girl doing something," Demme recalled. "Nothing we could film would equal the power of Jodie's telling of the experience. That it saved us several hundred thousand dollars in the bargain was a delightful conceit for me—it's the kind of thing I think Roger Corman would be proud of." Demme would also tell Tally if he cut away from her performance, he'd be drummed out of the Director's Guild. "She could win an Academy Award because of that scene," Demme remarked. "We can't cut from that."

Anthony Hopkins was similarly impressed. "The close-up on her face. She works with such economy. She doesn't do a thing, and yet you can see all the thoughts going through her eyes."

Considering Hannibal Lecter was the male lead, one of the big rules *Silence* broke is when Hannibal's suddenly out of the film in the third act after escaping from jail. "I always wondered if the story was going to feel too diminished after he left," Tally recalled. "I was worried that it was going to be such a letdown for the audience, so once Lecter was out of the movie I was superconscious of racing the movie along."

Of course somebody would try to keep Lecter in the movie more, just like people would want more shark in *Jaws*, but Tally said, "It just wasn't possible. We knew we'd have the great moment at the end, after the audience felt that they wouldn't see him again, so we thought that would save any disappointment that he wasn't in the third act."

The Silence of the Lambs shoot went for sixty-five days in a desolate part of Pittsburgh. The weather was dreary, the subject matter of serial killers was ugly for Demme's team to research, and Kristi Zea, Demme's longtime production designer, jokingly hoped Jonathan's next film would be a comedy set in the south of France. Still, as Tally recalled, "It sounds odd, considering how dark the subject matter was, but this was a fun film to make. People would say they'd never had so much fun. It came from Jonathan."

Once *Silence* was completed, the sneak previews went very well. Pleskow doesn't remember the scores, which many studios take as gospel, but as he recalls, "The audience reaction was important to me, not when they become critics and write." The only suggestion Pleskow had for Demme was to trim the night goggles scene a little. Pleskow couldn't recall clearly if it was cut shorter or not, Demme likely had final cut on the film, but Pleskow always hoped there was enough mutual respect between the filmmakers and the executives that they would try suggestions, even if they couldn't be enforced.

Released on Valentine's Day, 1991, *Silence* was met with rave reviews, and was a huge hit at the box office, earning $130 million domestic, $142 million foreign—a huge recoup on a $19 million budget.

When Medavoy decided that *The Silence of the Lambs* was what Demme's career needed, he was dead right. The director had built a wonderful body of work throughout his career, but had never had a genuine hit film until *Silence*. "At certain points, I was afraid there was something—a missing chink of skill—that was going to prevent me from having a movie that was financially successful," Demme said. "That frightened me. So when *Silence of the Lambs* became an unqualified success, I took a huge sigh of relief." (Demme also laughed when, after making so many uniquely offbeat movies, he was suddenly flooded with offers to make serial killer films.)

Silence was also the only time a horror film swept the Academy Awards with seven nominations, and five wins, winning Best Picture over *Beauty and the Beast*, *Bugsy*, *JFK*, and *The Prince of Tides*. *Silence* was also the third film in Oscar history to win the five major Academy Award categories, the others being *It Happened One Night* and *One Flew Over the Cuckoo's Nest*.

On awards night, March 30, 1992, at the Dorothy Chandler Pavilion, the show opened with host Billy Crystal being wheeled on-stage wearing the Hannibal mask. Crystal then walked right up to Hopkins, put his hand on his shoulder, and said, "I'm having some of the Academy over for dinner. Care to join me?"

When Jodie Foster won for Best Actress, she thanked Jesse Kornbluth for recommending her for the role. Kornbluth recalls he was "half asleep in bed drooling when I suddenly hear my name in Jodie Foster's thank-you in front of billions of people, which was an extremely nice and typical Jodie thing to do."

When Demme won for Best Director, he was so nervous and overwhelmed, it was reported he said "Uh" ninety-four times during the course of his speech. Hopkins was also similarly stunned at his Best Actor win: "After I got home and got to bed, I woke up at four in the morning and went down to the parlor to take a look at it—just to make sure it was real."

Among horror fans in the States, Peter Jackson's work first came over from New Zealand to America on video with his feature debut *Bad Taste*. Then his underground legend grew with *Meet the Feebles*, which took years to come over for a brief theatrical release (although bootleg copies had circulated for a while), and *Dead Alive* in 1992. Jackson had a similar journey to the Hollywood A-list as Sam Raimi, and his early work is clearly influenced by Raimi, but neither were overnight successes.

Jackson took the same path as many geeks turned pro. He was part of the TV generation growing up in front of the tube, and loved the *Thunderbirds* sci-fi puppet show. He also loved a lot of the film geek common denominators like Ray Harryhausen and *Famous Monsters of Filmland*.

The Jackson family got a Super 8 camera from a neighbor, figuring they would want to document Peter growing up. Peter eventually took over the camera, and as he recalled, "I was marshalling my friends and filmmaking the Second World War in the back garden." Being from New Zealand, with its sweeping landscapes, cliffs, and oceans, he had a wonderful backyard to film in. Ambitious even then, Jackson put a CinemaScope lens on his 8mm camera to make his movies look bigger.

The movie that made Jackson want to be a filmmaker was *King Kong*, which he saw on TV in 1971. "I remember being totally swept away on this great adventure," Jackson recalled. "The ingredients of this film were everything that I loved."

The Jackson family also watched *Monty Python's Flying Circus* on Sunday nights, a major influence for Jackson's irreverent and gory humor. "Because I saw the *Flying Circus* at just the right age—I was 11 or 12 years old and just starting to form adult sensibilities—it had a profound influence on the way my sense of humor developed," Jackson continued. "*Monty Python* taught me to love the ludicrous and love the extreme."

Jackson loved the scene in *Monty Python and the Holy Grail* where the knight is dismembered piece by piece, as well as *Monty Python's* Sam Peckinpah sketch, which turned into a bloodbath. "I remember watching that episode on TV and being absolutely gobsmacked," he recalled. "Quite simply, it was the most extraordinarily funny thing that I'd ever seen. That sketch did more to steer my sense of humor towards over-the-top bloodletting than any horror film ever did. My splatter movies owe as much to *Monty Python* as they do to any other genre. It is about pushing humor to the limit of ludicrousness, the furthest and most absurd extreme imaginable—so extreme that the only possible response to it is to laugh because there's nothing else to do."

Where Raimi and company took their love of slapstick from the Stooges, Jackson recalled his slapstick fave growing up was Buster Keaton. His early horror films were often labeled "goremedies," and Jackson called his approach "splatstick."

Like Raimi when he was making *The Evil Dead,* Jackson knew he had to step up from 8mm if he was going to step up as a filmmaker. His parents loaned him $2,500 to buy a used Bolex 16mm camera, and Jackson quickly learned one of the toughest lessons of making movies: that it's damn expensive. He realized it cost twenty times more to shoot three minutes of film on 16mm instead of Super 8, and he had to be more disciplined because of budget limitations. "I couldn't just muck around with this camera, popping off shots without thinking," Jackson said. "From the get-go I really had to have a plan."

As he was teaching himself how to use his Bolex, he decided to make a ten-minute short, originally called *Roast of the Day,* which eventually grew into his first feature film, *Bad Taste.* Jackson shot with friends on the weekends. "I would save up several hundred dollars in order to buy four or five rolls of film, we'd shoot for a day, and use them all up. Then I'd realize that I couldn't afford to process the film, so I'd have to put them in the fridge until I'd get my next wage check." When Jackson had to pay the lab bill, he couldn't afford any more film, and would lose a weekend until he got his next check.

Like Raimi, Jackson was also very inventive on a budget. He built his own Steadicam for twenty dollars, and also built his own camera crane out of aluminum for the swooping cliff shots. For the alien masks in *Bad Taste,* Jackson baked the latex in the family oven, but the ceiling was a little too low, which is why the creatures have slightly flat heads. Also like Raimi, Jackson liked a lot of shots and fast cutting. It's been pointed out that the average movie has 800 to 1,200 shots, where *Bad Taste* has about 2,500.

Roast of the Day cost $8,500, and with fifty-five minutes of usable footage, Jackson realized it could be expanded into a feature, which took four years to finish. "It just became a weekend thing," said lead actor Craig Smith. "We thought we could knock it off in six weeks or something. We were incredibly naïve, thought, 'Oh, yeah, let's do it for a laugh,' and it would all be done by the end of the year."

Once *Bad Taste* was completed, Jackson finally launched his career at the age of twenty-six. It went to the Cannes Film Festival in 1988, selling in thirty countries, except theatrically in America oddly enough. Lindsay Shelton, marketing director for the New Zealand Film Commission, recalled, "All the horror film companies I targeted found it too extreme."

Reviews for *Bad Taste* were similar to the notices Raimi got when he first broke through with *The Evil Dead*. The critics agreed that *Bad Taste* obviously wasn't meant to be taken very seriously, but the guy who made it clearly had talent, and what limitations the budget didn't cover, he more than made up for with enthusiasm. One review noted, "Peter Jackson is a filmmaker with more than a hint of inspiration and fearsome dedication," and another reviewer wrote that *Bad Taste* was the arrival of "a new and considerable talent."

From early on, Jackson had fans in the States that were trying to help him break through. Mark Ordesky, an executive from New Line Cinema, was an early champion of Jackson's work, but *Meet the Feebles* didn't open doors for Jackson. When Ordesky wanted to buy *Meet the Feebles* for the States, he was told, "Are you out of your mind? You want to buy a pornographic puppet film? No way!"

Ordesky's enthusiasm for *Meet the Feebles* did get Jackson a gig writing a Freddy movie, which briefly kept him afloat until he had *Dead Alive* set up (Jackson got paid $20,000, the Writer's Guild scale at the time). New Line was developing Jackson's script, as well as a script by New Line president of production Mike De Luca, and they'd make the script they liked best.

Jackson's idea for a *A Nightmare on Elm Street* film was to have a group of thugs going into a drug-induced sleep so they can beat the shit out of Freddy, whose power is waning. When Freddy kills one of the thugs, it brings him back to power. Then a cop winds up in a coma, and is trapped in a dreamworld where he has to battle a newly recharged Freddy.

New Line ultimately picked De Luca's draft for *Freddy's Dead*. Jackson quickly ran out of money and ended up crashing on Ordesky's couch before the financing finally came through for *Dead Alive* and he went back to New Zealand to make it.

Jackson said, "There was this great feeling of trying to top the previous zombie film—to go as far as possible beyond what they had done—and without any concern about what censorship or ratings were going to do to you."

In addition to letting enough gore fly that he made *The Shining* elevators of blood look like a rain puddle, Jackson also paid tribute to Ray Harryhausen with the stop-motion rat monkey that carries the undead disease over to New Zealand. A precursor to the motion capture techniques Jackson used years later with Golum and Kong, Peter acted out on video how he wanted the rat monkey to move, then the animators would watch the video, and re-create the movements frame by frame in stop-motion.

Jackson also shot a cameo with Forry Ackerman in the zoo. Low-budget films usually would shoot without permits, and Jackson didn't have one for Forry's scene. A zoo official saw Jackson filming, and started giving Peter crap for filming something without the zoo's permission. Jackson tried to bullshit his way out of it and say it was for a home movie, but the official wasn't buying it. Jackson couldn't recall if they got kicked out or just left, but they got the shot and got the hell out of there. (An avid *Famous Monsters* fan since he was twelve, Jackson bought Forry's original *King Kong* stop-motion models when Forry had to sell off some of his collections.)

Jackson's formula for film blood was maple syrup and red food coloring, and he had pumps that shot out five gallons of gore a second. When the set got covered in blood, Jackson wouldn't clean it up for continuity. The layers got thicker and thicker, and it smelled like burned maple syrup under the lights.

As with the Romero films, Jackson would ring up friends, ask "Would you like to be a zombie?" and many of them, including Jackson's wife Fran, really enjoyed playing dead. At the end of *Dead Alive*, when the zombies are literally mowed down, Jackson said, "it's a kiwi icon, actually; the rotary lawn mower was invented in Australia and spread to New Zealand before it went anywhere else, so we can claim it as our very own zombie-killing device."

Dead Alive was screened for distributors in mid-June 1992, and it was shown to Universal, Warner Bros., Fox, New Line, Miramax, and Trimark. Trimark won the film, and the advance for U.S. and Canadian rights was twice what had ever been paid for a movie from New Zealand.

Mark Amin, the CEO of Trimark, says, "It was a campy horror film, but it had a special style to it. Normally on a low-budget horror movie, we usually just pick it up and do it straight to video, but we knew this one was special, and we decided to release it theatrically." Amin also knew Jackson had a cult following, which is why they did a theatrical release, hoping to target his underground fan base.

Dead Alive was also released in the States unrated. Where the MPAA often asks horror filmmakers to trim seconds from their films, Amin knew an R rating would have cost the film minutes.

"With an R rating, it might have better box-office potential, but it wasn't so huge that we were willing to take a chance," Amin says. "The movie was such a director's vision, that we were better off just not touching it. Peter also didn't want to cut it, he wanted to keep it as is, he made that very clear, and we didn't want to go against the director's vision. Peter was very sure of his movie."

Amin also knew good reviews didn't matter for a straight-ahead horror film, "but for a horror comedy they were essential," he says. "It's much easier to make and market a straight horror film than it is to market a horror comedy. On the other hand, horror comedies tend to be generally auteur driven, they are the vision of a director, and they're harder to pull off, but if you can pull it off, you'll have something exceptional."

And indeed in the States, Jackson's good luck with the critics continued. *Time* called *Dead Alive* "the season's best cannibal movie . . . there is good, broad humor amid the very gross gore effects." "Only a dedicated lunatic could mix hilarity and dismemberment so successfully," wrote *The Village Voice*. *The Hollywood Reporter* called it "one of the bloodiest films in cinematic history. . . . You'll laugh, you'll gag."

Amin remembers that *Dead Alive* did modestly in the States, the box office was about $7 to 8,000,000. In the home market it went into the millions, and Amin says, "As these movies do, it did better on video, and it continues to sell to this day."

The year *Dead Alive* made it to the States, Jackson said, "I'm not in a desperate rush to direct in Hollywood. I know some people don't take you seriously until you've made a Hollywood movie, but it doesn't worry me what people over there think. I like to have as much creative control as possible. And working in New Zealand allows that." He also added, "My interest in filmmaking goes deeper than gag-driven 'splatstick' films. I feel I have more to offer than the limited skills needed to keep turning them out."

It made sense for Jackson to move on after making the most over-the-top gore film he could make. He went as far as he could with his unique brand of comedy and horror, and he absolutely left the genre with a bang. "I had just made what I thought was the *ultimate* splatter film. What else could I do, make another one and set it in a different place, a different time?

"The Hollywood machine has pigeonholed a lot of very fine filmmakers—which is frightening," Jackson continued. "It can take a Tobe Hooper, a John Carpenter, or a Wes Craven and force them to stay in that genre because Hollywood is a very unimaginative town and pigeonholing is one of its specialties. It's all too easy to be stifled by the genre you're in and never really be offered anything else."

As Richard Taylor, the head of Jackson's Weta workshop said, "What was wonderful about *Heavenly Creatures* was the realization that the world had now accepted Peter as a George Romero–Sam Raimi goremeister and had assumed that that was to be his future; and yet there he was, planning to turn round and slap them in the face with a beautiful, poignant, incredibly intimate, revealing story."

Jackson said, "What I find curious is that if people like two or three splatter movies that you've made then they somehow can't get their head around the fact that you can make other types of films, and if you do, then it comes as a total shock to them. They say, 'How did you make this? It's just so *different!*' "

Like De Palma and Raimi, Amin knew Peter had the skills to move in and out of the mainstream. "When you see a director do an exceptional piece of work, you know the director's going to go on to

bigger things," he says. "We knew from *Dead Alive* that we were dealing with a very talented director who'd go on to bigger things. I've
worked with enough first-time directors to know whether they're
truly talented and will do other things or not. After that, it's really
up to the choices they make. You see some extremely talented directors that end up choosing smaller, niche, art house films that are
very accomplished artistically, but they don't have the mass box-
office appeal. Peter, on the other hand, decided to go for the big box
office as well as the artistic, which is rare. With *Lord of the Rings,* I
think Peter very smartly chose material that took advantage of his
talents."

Jackson has also always been a shrewd businessman, and has re-
tained final cut his entire career. "Peter's an excellent poker player,"
says Michael Pellerin, who produced Jackson's production diaries
for *The Lord of the Rings* and *King Kong.* "You don't see him shake
under pressure. Peter's a student of military history, and I think he
just knows good strategy.

"Peter has a very calm way of dealing with things," Pellerin continues. "He does have an aura around him that you don't want to
mess up and let him down. Some people just have that weird light
around them like 'We gotta make it good for Peter.' Someone like
that who has integrity, passion, commitment, who doesn't yell, or
treat people badly, you want to go that extra mile for him. I think he
gets people to perform better by having that quiet strength, but it's
also a demanding strength. Peter definitely burns the midnight candle
at both ends, and he expects you to as well. You gotta tow the line,
'cause you're gonna go into some hard, difficult areas, and you gotta
be up for it."

As Wes Craven marveled, "Peter started out making really harum-
scarum horror films, he made one of the goriest, craziest, jokey horror films I've ever seen in my life with *Dead Alive.* Then he goes off

and makes these beautiful fantasy films where we hardly see real blood, everybody has perfectly shampooed hair, and he's hugely rewarded. Fantasy pays much better than the nightmare."

The screenplay for *Se7en,* written by Andrew Kevin Walker, was like *Taxi Driver* in its day. It was a must-read among industry insiders, but no one seemingly had the cojones to make it. Yet against all odds, *Se7en* did get made, and was the surprise hit of 1995. *Se7en* also cemented Brad Pitt's star power, sprung David Fincher from bad-movie jail after the debacle of *Alien³,* and resurrected the unhappy ending. Many imitations followed in the wake of its success, usually with happier endings—no head in the box, we promise— and some, like *Kiss the Girls,* even brought Morgan Freeman along, but they missed the uncompromising vision that made *Se7en* a great film.

Walker, a native of Pennsylvania, knew early on he wanted to work in film, but focused on becoming a writer when he was attending Penn State. "I saw writing as a way to get to directing and that was my intention, but once I actually got out of college and saw how hard directing was, I wasn't that interested!" he says. "But I really got focused on writing in college and was lucky that I was able to work on a feature-length script there rather than just a short film."

After college, Walker moved to New York instead of Los Angeles because he couldn't afford a car, and he unhappily lived there for five years, which played a big hand in inspiring *Se7en.* "I lived in New York City in the mid- to late-eighties, and it was overwhelming to me," Walker recalls. "I'm from suburbia. New York City was an assault on my senses. I was just expressing some thoughts that occurred to me as I wandered hither and thither in New York. It did actually seem like you could just go around and find all the sins everywhere in the people, in stores, on billboards, in Times Square and the subways. *Taxi Driver* and *Midnight Cowboy* really got certain aspects of New York right on the money if you ask me."

While he lived in New York, Walker worked as a production assistant for a very low-budget company called Brisun Entertainment. As he recalls, "The kinds of movies they were making were things like *Blood Rush*, which was murders in a fraternity house, and they had one idea they wanted to do called *Abusement Park* with somebody sabotaging all the rides, putting piano wire in front of the roller coaster and everyone's heads get lobbed off! They never did write that script. And there was something called *Brainscan* that I worked on that actually got made, which was for no pay. So I was in a very exploitational mode, and the idea of the seven deadly sin murders kind of made sense to me. Now as I developed it and worked on the characters, it hopefully became a little more than what *Abusement Park* may have been!"

Walker quit working for Brisun because he needed the structure of a regular job where he wouldn't work long and erratic production hours. He then worked at Tower Records on Sixty-sixth Street and Broadway for the next three years. As for how long it took for *Se7en* to go from idea to a finished draft, Walker says, "I would say probably once I started writing, probably five months or so. It took a long time to write *Se7en* because I was working full time at Tower Records, and all the research had to take place after work, but I think it does go to show you you can carry off a full-time job and still find time to write."

Walker didn't exactly write *Se7en* with commercial considerations. When Walker wrote it, he was "utterly convinced" it wouldn't sell, which was fine because he could use it as a writing sample. "I wasn't stupid enough to sit down to write *Se7en* and say to myself, 'Hollywood's just chompin' at the bit for a movie that ends with a woman's head in a box. What a big spec sale this will be.'"

Walker ended up getting his big break by calling David Koepp, screenwriter of *Jurassic Park, Mission: Impossible, Spider-Man,* and *Panic Room,* out of the phone book, and asking if he'd check out *Se7en.* "With David Koepp, he happened to have a few articles written about him in *Premiere* magazine at the time, and *Bad Influence* had just come out," Walker continues. "He was at a smaller agency that wasn't ICM or CAA, and I really thought that if you went to a smaller agency there would be more of a chance of them taking a chance on somebody who's new, which is true."

Once Koepp checked out the screenplay for *Se7en,* he recommended it to his agent Gavin Polone. It wasn't long before Andrew got the phone call every struggling screenwriter dreams of. "When Gavin called me up in my tiny Astoria, Queens, apartment and said he'd represent the script for *Se7en,* I literally leaped [for] joy. And I'm not using the word 'literally' like so many people do nowadays. I *jumped* in the air! I hope I never forget how impossible it felt to ever get an agent to look at anything, let alone shop it around. I know what desperation is, that feeling of wanting and trying and yearning to work in the film business. I don't ever want to forget that."

Se7en went out to many of the major studios, who all passed on it, then it went to a second round of studios and production companies, who also passed on it. "I knew there would be a problem, because I've gone out with stuff that was too dark before," Polone recalled. "But I actually felt that because of *Silence of the Lambs* we would have a shot. Unfortunately we didn't." (Koepp even offered the script to Universal with himself attached to produce, and they passed).

Se7en was optioned by Penta Films, an Italian company, for

Jeremiah Chechik (*Benny and Joon*), who was interested in directing it. When Penta fell apart, producer Arnold Kopelson (*Platoon, The Fugitive*), knew the partners at the company, and the *Se7en* screenplay was brought to his attention by one of his executives, Sanford Panitch.

Then in January 1994, Ted Turner bought New Line, giving the company an infusion of money to buy new projects. Lynn Harris came over to New Line from working for producer Lynda Obst (*Sleepless in Seattle)*, and Pantich, who had previously interned for New Line, recommended *Se7en* to the company.

"New Line was all about certain financial limitations that forced us to find movie stars and directors," said Mike De Luca. "That mission statement became hardwired into our DNA and was hard to change even after the company got more capitalization. Bob Shaye was great if you met certain benchmarks. [*Se7en*] was made at a price, and Brad Pitt was locked in. *Se7en* made him a global star, but he was already an important element."

CAA agent Kevin Huvane thought it would be good for Brad Pitt, who was hot from *Interview with the Vampire*, and had *Legends of the Fall* coming up, and Kopelson personally delivered a copy of the script to Morgan Freeman on the set of *Outbreak*. It was also CAA that brought David Fincher to the table. Fincher had just gone through the disaster of *Alien³*, and wasn't on anyone's A-list at the time.

Phyllis Carlyle, one of the producers of *Se7en*, recalled, "At that moment, Fincher wasn't anybody's idea, except CAA's, and they were quite committed to resurrecting Fincher's career as a feature director."

Mike De Luca loved Fincher's videos, and he recalled the director "won the job in the room, pitching a vision for *Se7en* that was so detailed and articulate, you just knew what the movie was going to be. He was a harder sell with Arnold Kopelson, who wasn't up late at night watching MTV the way the rest of us were, the way I was."

David Fincher was born in Denver, Colorado, and two years later his family relocated to Marin County, California. Although he recalled hearing about the Zodiac Killer growing up and saw cop cars driving around looking for him, he recalled growing up in a happy, safe environment.

Fincher did all forms of art growing up, drawing, painting, sculptures, matte paintings, photography, and felt a director "needed to know a little bit about everything. I didn't want to be a canvas chair dilettante. I wanted to be able to do it."

When Fincher was ten, George Lucas moved two doors up the street to 52 Park Way, which demystified directing for him. "There were no big gates and a driveway with a Bentley with smoked glass driving in," Fincher said. "He was just the guy next door with a beard. That was very encouraging—it was like, 'you can do it.'" One morning, young Fincher saw Lucas picking up the newspaper in his bathrobe. "I went 'Hi' and he went 'Hi.'" (*American Graffiti* was filmed on Fourth Street in San Rafael, which was five blocks from Fincher's house.)

When Fincher moved to Ashland, Oregon, with his family at the age of fourteen, he worked as a projectionist at a theater called the Varsity. "I wanted to work in the movie theater because I wanted to see 35 mm film, see how it worked, and get comfortable with the machines." Fincher got to see Bob Fosse's *All That Jazz* 175 times, and was also impressed with Fosse's *Star 80*. (Fincher's video for Paula Abdul's "Cold Hearted Snake" was his tribute to *All That Jazz*.)

Fincher didn't want to go to film school, and went to work as a production assistant at Korty Films, an animation studio, instead. He also worked at ILM from 1981 to 1984, when the company was at its peak with FX geniuses Richard Englund, Phil Tippett, and Joe Johnson still working there. Fincher received a credit on *Return of the Jedi* as an assistant cameraman on miniature and optical effects, and he also did matte work on *Indiana Jones and the Temple of Doom* and *The Never Ending Story*.

Fincher wanted to make commercials because it was how Ridley Scott broke into features. In 1984, Fincher directed a well-known commercial for the American Cancer Society that showed a fetus smoking a cigarette that he made for $7,000, and it got him a lot of attention and offers to shoot music videos. Fincher then moved to L.A., got an apartment in Westwood that he said had the "*Miami Vice* hospital" eighties look and was later the archetype for Ed Norton's IKEA apartment paradise in *Fight Club*. When Fincher moved to L.A., he couldn't believe there was hardly any traffic, but he soon found out this was because many were attending the summer Olympics.

Fincher directed commercials for the N. Lee Lacy ad agency, and would later cofound Propaganda Films with directors he worked with at Lacy in 1986. Propaganda became a wildly successful music video company, and some of their best-known videos were directed by Fincher including "The End of the Innocence" by Don Henley, "Express Yourself" and "Vogue" from Madonna, Aerosmith's "Janie's Got a Gun," and all the hits from Paula Abdul's first album. (Fincher also directed commercials for Coke, Budweiser, Heineken, Pepsi, Nike, Levi's, Converse, AT&T, and Chanel.)

At twenty-seven, Fincher was hired to direct *Alien³*, helming a $60 million movie his first time out, and when it tanked, he was blamed for destroying the *Alien* franchise. (Not to defend *Alien³*, but *Alien Resurrection* also did a fine job of that as well.) The studio figured they could push him around because he was a young video director, which clearly wasn't the case. "That was a bad situation," he recalled. "I don't respond well to that." When asked years later if he disowned *Alien³*, Fincher said, "I never owned it."

Fincher then went back to directing commercials and videos, and didn't seriously look at a feature script to direct for a year and a half. "I got sent stupid crap," he recalled. "Commensurate with my station in life—'You're the guy who fucked up what should have been an interesting movie'—and that was true."

Then Fincher got sent the first draft of *Se7en*, complete with the notorious head in the box ending. He called his agent and asked, "This movie, are they going to make this? There's this head in the box in the end, it's just amazing. Are they really going to do this?" "No, you've got the wrong draft."

Se7en went through a number of subsequent drafts that watered down the movie, and once when Fincher read a later draft he said, "This is just crap, the first one is much better."

As it turns out, Walker and Fincher were very much of a like mind, and were both completely in synch on *Se7en*. "I give Fincher full credit for *Se7en*'s success," Walker said. "I couldn't have been happier with how that movie turned out."

Like De Palma, Fincher was a bad boy who wasn't afraid to stir up trouble. He also had sensibilities similar to William Friedkin and worshipped Kubrick. Walker as well is a big fan of Friedkin's work, and the script reminded Fincher of *The Exorcist* in the sense that "You don't have any control over this, you're just along for the ride."

Walker has always enjoyed what he calls "cinema of discomfort," movies that are uncomfortable and disturbing. "I love movies that take me to places I would never want to go to in real life, because from the safety of my cinema seat I'm all for fulfilling my perverse curiosity about what's behind all those closed doors. There is a great appeal in that, I believe, because you are experiencing it from the safety of a theater."

"Movies make a pact with the audience, there's an expectation," Fincher said. "You pay your eight bucks and you're going to be taken *this* far but not *that* far . . . I don't like those sort of movies. I feel most alive at a scary movie when I truly feel like this could go places even I couldn't predict."

And like Walker, Fincher also didn't want to present a bunch of rose-tinted nonsense to moviegoers about life. "Some people go to the movies to be reminded that everything's okay," Fincher continued. "I don't make those kinds of movies. That, to me, is a lie. Everything's not okay."

Se7en wasn't going to be a safe choice for Fincher to make after coming off a major bomb. Richard Francis-Bruce, *Se7en*'s editor, recalled when he read the script, his reaction was, "This is going to be fantastic, or just *horrible*! I didn't think it was going to be anywhere in between. That's why I took it on." (Francis-Bruce also felt that *Se7en* and *The Shawshank Redemption,* which he also edited, were two of the best scripts he'd ever read.)

Se7en never showed as much as you thought, but people swear it's a much bloodier movie than it really is, an approach Fincher called, "I'm *not* going to show you something you absolutely don't want to see and you're going to sit there breathlessly waiting to see it."

In the editing room, Fincher would tell Richard Francis-Bruce, "Just glimpses of things," and when making *Zodiac* years later, Fincher said, "I want to make a movie that has enough impact that it's going to do what it needs to do. But I don't want to make a film that serial killers masturbate to."

Surprisingly, Walker says, "Nowadays they don't show anything which to me is a huge disappointment. I grew up with *Dawn of the*

Dead, which was showing something, there's just certain things that it's appropriate for. Nowadays everything's PG-13, or if it's an R, they're worried about getting an NC-17. To be honest, I can go either way on it. People sometimes talk about *Se7en* like it was restrained, I mean you see a lot of stuff. And yes, you don't see the murders, that's what suited the story. It doesn't mean that was the way it should be done, it just means it worked for that. It would have been ridiculous to show the lust murder. It was better that people imagine it and see the reaction of the characters, that made sense."

When he was first writing *Se7en*, Walker also wanted the audience to know absolutely nothing about John Doe for the entire story. But as he came to realize, "A serial killer story where there's a series of murders and a cat-and-mouse game with the police, you kinda have to tell a little bit about the character towards the end at least. I really wanted to leave it almost all unsaid because the more you describe it, the more you're gonna push it into pure fiction. When you're trying to explain exactly what spanking it was, what age it was inappropriate that his mother gave him one, and that's when his mind snapped."

Even though he wasn't well-known then, Spacey agreed to do *Se7en* on the condition that he would get no billing until the end credits, going by the reasoning, "If I'm sitting in a movie theater knowing that Brad Pitt and Morgan Freeman are chasing a serial killer, and that Kevin Spacey is in the movie and hasn't shown up yet, I know he's got to be the bad guy. It would be much better if nobody knew who was playing the character."

At first Spacey tried to research the role, believing the audience would think of Jeffrey Dahmer because his crimes were closest to John Doe's. "So I watched an interview with Dahmer," he recalled. "Talk about a schlub! I realized that as long as I wasn't in the back-seat drooling, I could portray this guy."

Then Fincher went crazy when *The Usual Suspects,* which Spacey finished right before he went into *Se7en*, came out the month before *Se7en* was released. "Spacey! Why didn't you say something? How many times do you want to be the evil mastermind?"

One of the best scenes in *Se7en* wasn't a graphic or bloody one, but a tender moment between Gwyneth Paltrow and Morgan Freeman where she confesses she's pregnant and is unsure whether she'll keep the baby. Walker said, "I liked that scene because it had Tracy asking Somerset to keep a secret, that she was pregnant, from Mills. And that played a part in the final scene, because Somerset knew even before Mills just all that was lost with Tracy's death. That scene between Somerset and Tracy, along with Mills and Somerset's argument in the bar about whether they can make any difference at all or should even try, these were scenes that some involved in the making of *Se7en* wanted to cut out, I guess because they were slow, maybe even boring, scenes for some. I've come to seriously appreciate a movie that isn't afraid to bore me occasionally. I find that a really daring choice these days, to be applauded and celebrated as a great achievement."

Many adjectives fit the ending of *Se7en*. Shocking and controversial certainly come to mind, but it also seemed the most logical way to end the film. It's hard to think of any other way the movie could convincingly end, but Walker smiled and said, "Well, the studio had all kinds of different ways! The killer had to do the thing that guaranteed that this cop was gonna complete the cycle, so it was only natural that that head should be in a box." In a sense, the ending was there practically from the beginning. When the idea for the movie first popped into his mind, at a certain point Walker thought, "Well, there has to be something where the cop becomes that seventh sin," and that became the conceit of the film.

Of course, not everyone understood this line of reasoning. During one meeting *Se7en* producer Arnold Kopelson reportedly said,

"There's no way that there will be a head in the box at the end of this movie, there is absolutely no way that will ever happen, don't even talk to me about that." He also reportedly scolded Fincher about the finished film, telling him, "You took a perfectly good genre movie and turned it into a foreign film."

Walker was lucky in that he had a tough director who was willing to dig in and fight, and Pitt, Freeman, and Spacey fought for the ending as well. "It's not like I'm saying the only good endings are really depressing, down endings," Walker continues. "The only ending that's good is the ending that's appropriate to it. *Sleepy Hollow* always had a happier ending." (Pitt had it in his contract that the ending couldn't be changed.)

Two months into prep, Fincher went to Kopelseon and said, "Long after we're all gone, fifty, sixty years from now, a bunch of twenty-somethings are gonna be at a cocktail party, talking about a movie they saw on the late show the night before, and someone's gonna go, 'I don't remember the name of the actor, but it's the one where the van pulls up at the end and the guy has the head in the box. The head in the box movie!' This is the head in the box movie. Everybody that I've talked to, every development person in town who knows about *Se7en* knows it as the head in the box movie. You can't take the head in the box out of the head in the box movie." Kopelson finally agreed.

As difficult as it would be for many audiences to swallow, years later Mike De Luca recalled, "Everyone, from David to Bob Shaye on down, felt the ending made it a provocative watercooler movie."

"My argument was always that anybody who sits through this and makes it through the LUST murder, if they're still in the theater, they're ready for whatever!" Walker says. "The LUST murder was the real sweaty palm moment when you watched the test screening. The thing I remember when they were test screening *Se7en* was that you were subjecting this movie to an especially unsuspecting audience, recruited from a mall, for example, and so I was expecting everyone to stand up and leave. But luckily they didn't."

Anyone who's a fan of *Se7en* probably knows the story of the film's disastrous test screening. Unassuming audiences were lured in with the promise of the new film from Brad Pitt, from *Legends of the Fall,* and Morgan Freeman, from *Driving Miss Daisy*, with predictably disastrous results.

"*Se7en* was a hard movie to test screen because it's kind of designed so that the audience walks into the same buzz saw that Somerset and Mills walk into," Walker said. "There were no credits and no music, no period for anyone to catch their breath. So if you were an audience member at one of the test screenings, basically there's the last scene with the head in the box, and all that agony and violence, and then suddenly the lights come up, and someone hands you a scorecard and pencil and says, 'How'd you enjoy *that*? What do ya think?'"

Looking back on it years later, Fincher giggled at the absurdity of it all. "They couldn't have been more offended," he recalled. "You couldn't molest the audience more than to promise *Legends of the Fall* and *Driving Miss Daisy* than to unleash this on them. They'd just been gang-raped." At the end of the screening, a group of three women stormed past Fincher and Bob Shaye, one of them exclaiming, "The people who made that movie should be killed."

"The audience was just . . . it was the worst," says Francis-Bruce. "I don't think I've been to as bad a screening. They were yelling at us as they were walking out. It was a terrible ride back in the plane from the preview. There were a lot of grim faces, no one was talking." Eventually Fincher and Walker told Kopelson, "This is the movie we've all signed on to make. Let's go through with it."

Se7en also had great postproduction touches including the opening credits, which were directed by Kyle Cooper of RGA/LA (it was

Cooper's idea to show John Doe working on his diaries for the opening credits). Also like *The Exorcist, Se7en* had a dense sound mix, with a lot of great little touches and noises deep in the background. "I wanted to exhaust the audience with sound," Fincher said.

Francis-Bruce was also happy with how the segment where Freeman and Pitt chase down John Doe came together, which Fincher did with his own style of Shakycam, inspired by the show *Cops.* "When we saw that scene in dailies, my reaction was it was too shaky," the editor says. "But when you put it together it works. Fincher was totally confident it was going to work. He didn't shoot an alternate with a Steadicam to be safe, he just went for it."

Not surprisingly, reviews for *Se7en* were mixed. Kenneth Turan of the *L.A. Times* wrote, "Noticeable skill has gone into the making of *Se7en*, but it's hard to take much pleasure in that. If movies were rated by how many showers are needed before viewers can feel human again, this picture would go off the chart.

"*Se7en* does not seem like anyone's idea of entertainment, but public executions drew big crowds in their day, and there is little reason to believe that human nature has gotten any more refined and elegant in the interim." The *L.A. Times* ratings guideline for *Se7en* also called it "the equivalent of a forced tour of a morgue."

Variety called it, "dark, grim, and terrific. An intensely claustrophobic, gut-wrenching thriller." "The big surprise of this thriller? It's intelligent," wrote Roger Ebert. "*Se7en* is a dark, grisly, horrifying and intelligent thriller—a film too disturbing for many people, I imagine, although if you can bear to watch it you will see filmmaking of a high order."

Sigourney Weaver didn't want the serial killer film she was starring in with Harry Connick Jr., *Copycat,* coming out at the same time as *Se7en.* "They said, 'Oh, it's just David Fincher and Brad Pitt in a mustache.' 'No, believe me, David made one movie that didn't make money and he's going to be really careful with this one.' And of course, it was a masterpiece, and everyone saw that one and very few people saw *Copycat*. They should have listened to me."

Se7en came in at number one at the box office its opening weekend, and remained in the top spot for several weeks. "It wasn't that it opened huge, but it hung on pretty well week to week," says Walker. "The thing that was hard to grasp regarding *Se7en* being successful financially, which is so important in this town, was it was hard to stop worrying about whether it would do well. The thing is I loved it, and so did all the people who were involved in it and fought for it, so I'd be very, very proud of it regardless. But it took the longest time for it to sink in that the movie did well financially, how lucky I was in that respect, because frankly with the bleak subject matter and ending, it certainly wasn't a given that it would recoup."

Se7en also proved to be a surprise hit in a season of bombs, including the notorious disaster *Showgirls, Jade, Strange Days,* and *The Scarlet Letter,* starring Demi Moore. VIOLENT SE7EN OUTDRAWS SEXY SHOWGIRLS AT BOX OFFICE, read the *L.A. Times* headline. Another box-office report in the *L.A. Times* noted, "Executives bracing for multimillion-dollar losses are trying to figure out why the grisly *Se7en* is the only bright spot in a string of recent disappointments."

Se7en cost a reported $30 million, a big budget for New Line then, and worldwide it made more than $316 million. Brad Pitt's price also went through the roof from the $4 million he made on *Se7en* to $17.5 million.

Mitch Goldman, New Line's president of marketing and distribution, told the *L.A. Times,* "No one in the industry expected the performance of this picture."

"We had *no* idea," agreed Lynn Harris. "There's not a single person in this company, and they'd be *lying* to you if there was anybody in the world who said they knew this movie would make over $300 million worldwide. Nobody knew."

While Fincher went on to a varied career, raising even more hackles with *Fight Club* and coming close to Oscar gold with *The Social Network,* Walker has yet to have another screenplay made to his satisfaction. His original draft of *8mm* was a terrific script that was completely ruined into an unforgivable mess by Joel Schumacher (look up the first draft online, which also been published in book form along with the screenplay of *Se7en* through Faber and Faber).

Sleepy Hollow, an idea he created with Kevin Yagher, the makeup artist who created Chuckie, turned out okay, a decent mix of Hammer gothic horror and Mario Bava, who Tim Burton's a big fan of. (Walker also did some work on *Fight Club* uncredited.)

Recently Universal tried to revive *The Wolf Man* with Walker as the original writer and it became another overbudget, major studio mess. Director Mark Romanek left the project a week before the film was going to start with Joe Johnson coming in at the last moment. Rick Baker was brought in to provide the old-school makeup effects, which were later redone in CGI, a number of expensive script doctors came and went, and Walter Murch tried to save it in the editing room, to no avail. Where you usually have to shoot a werewolf in the heart with a silver bullet, this one shot itself in the foot.

There's still hope Walker and Fincher will work together again, or that another screenplay he's written will turn into a great movie, though Walker knows *Se7en* is a tough act to follow.

"*Se7en* is a movie that I would not [change]," Walker said. "It just exceeded all my expectations. *Se7en* is one of those [movies] where if nothing else gets made that I'll be happy with, at least I have that. There's plenty of people who make a fine living as screenwriters and never get anything made, and there's plenty of people who get a lot of stuff made, but are never really happy with anything that gets made. That's not the case with me because *Se7en* not only saves me from that, but spoils me in a way."

SEVENTEEN

THE LITTLE HORROR FILMS THAT COULD

How Wes Craven reinvented himself again with *Scream*, while two guys with a video camera created *The Blair Witch Project*, and M. Night Shyamalan crafted a clever supernatural thriller with *The Sixth Sense*

For Michael Gingold, managing editor of *Fangoria*, *Scream* is the film that relaunched horror films in the nineties. "I think at one point the studios weren't willing to make them," he says. "I think the whole slasher movie craze in the early eighties had something to do with it. Most of those movies were very low-rent and for ten years it seemed when someone said 'horror films,' all they thought of was slasher films. Which makes it kind of ironic that one of the films that jump-started the whole thing again was *Scream*."

It's funny to think that an ironic take on the eighties slasher films would relaunch the horror genre, but that was the whole point. It was a self-referential time in the movies and pop culture, and Kevin Williamson used it to his advantage. It would also provide Wes Craven's reinvention as a director as well. Since the advent of the VCR boom, a new generation was now discovering horror films from the eighties that Williamson held dear.

"All the kids in the movie are from the VCR generation," Williamson said. "They all grew up next to a Blockbuster, they know their movie lingo. The whole idea that their love of movies, their knowledge of movie conventions, may save them, is sort of interesting."

Halloween was Williamson's all-time favorite horror film, and he knew it backward and forward. He would host *Halloween* nights with his friends where they'd watch the entire series in order, except they skipped #3.

Besides Carpenter, Williamson loved another John, writer-director John Hughes, and with *Scream* he tried to bring together the horror of Carpenter's work and the sharp observations of teen angst in the Hughes films. "I felt teen movies were going to come back," Williamson recalled. "I knew it, I felt it. The timing was right. That's one of the things that *Scream* did; it sort of helped start that."

In 1991, Miramax founders Harvey and Bob Weinstein thought of founding a new division, Dimension, with the idea of genre films that could fund their art films, and again, it showed how often the major studios would think about horror. The drama gets the awards, the genre films bring in the money.

The Weinsteins also reportedly wanted to form the company when New Line formed their own art house division, Fine Line, which Harvey and Bob took as an insult. (Fine Line's Ira Deutchman later facetiously took credit for Dimension, one assumes facetiously. The company's in-house nickname was Dementia.)

In 1992, Dimension released *Hellraiser III* and *Children of the Corn II,* which provided a quarter of Miramax's profits that year, and *The Crow* was the company's big breakthrough release in 1994, grossing $51 million.

Next came the sequel to *The Crow,* another *Hellraiser, From Dusk Till Dawn*, and the Wayans Brothers spoof *Don't Be a Menace to South Central While Drinking Your Juice in the Hood*. Then came a spec script that was first called *Scary Movie*, written by Kevin Williamson.

Williamson was a native of New Bern, North Carolina, and was raised near Dawson's Creek. Williamson came from a poor family, his father was a fisherman, and they lived in a big trailer on a creek. "If you called us white trash, we probably couldn't argue the point too well," Williamson said. "We were like really classy white trash—we were happy about it. We enjoyed the hell out of it. In fact, I still have sort of a poverty consciousness; it's hard for me to spend two hundred dollars on shoes."

Williamson didn't think he would be a writer, as much as he wanted to be one, because he had a teacher who scolded, "You can't spell, your grammar's awful, and you're from the hills of North Carolina—it'll never happen," and he believed it for twenty years.

"I didn't think I could write," Williamson recalled years later. "I didn't believe I had any talent at all as a writer . . . I never wrote because I thought I was from the South, backwoods, inarticulate, and had no command of the English language. Only when I tried to figure out a strategy to direct did I realize that maybe I could write something. If I can write it, then I can hold on to it until someone lets me direct it."

Williamson moved to New York in hopes of becoming an actor, and got some bit parts on TV and on stage. He thought "twenty times a day" success wouldn't happen, and he packed up and moved back home three times. "When I originally left I always thought it was for good," he recalled. "Then I'd get home and realize that there was nothing there for me, and I'd come back."

His lowest point came in 1991, when he was completely broke in New York, and living on the good graces of a friend who was paying his rent. "Man, I was just so emotionally and spiritually bankrupt," he said. "I didn't think I had any future. I just thought I'd be better off dead. It was just a painful existence—in New York City with no job, no money, nothing. Finally, the tables started to turn. I got a job and I started building from there. But that was really the bottom."

Williamson moved to L.A., working as an assistant to a music video director, and was writing whenever he had time. He borrowed money from a friend so he could attend a screenwriting course at UCLA, and was only writing for two years by the time *Scream* got made. The first screenplay Williamson wrote was *Killing Mrs. Tingle*, inspired by the real-life Mrs. Tingle, who told him to give up his dream of being a writer. As often happens in Hollywood, Williamson knew somebody, who knew somebody, who knew somebody, and it paid off. "My best friend walked his dog with a lady who had an agent who owed her a favor—or something like that," Williamson said. An assistant to an agent at Agency for the Performing Arts read *Tingle*, passed it on to his agent, and it was sold as a spec script to Interscope.

Joe Dante, George Huang (*Swimming with Sharks*), and Trey Parker (*South Park*) were all considered to direct, but Interscope went under, and the project languished. Williamson's option on the script was just enough to pay off his college loans, buy a new car, and move, and then he was broke all over again. "The only difference now was that I had a bigger car payment and higher rent!" Williamson said. (*Killing Mrs. Tingle* finally got made in 1999, when Williamson was already a brand name, but it was retitled *Teaching Ms. Tingle*, a knee-jerk reaction to Columbine.)

Williamson was doing temp work for the studios when he came up with a germ of an idea: someone is talking on the phone with somebody who could be a killer and is using her love of horror movies to torment her. At first Williamson thought it could be a one-act play, just the girl and the voice on the phone. In a day or two he wrote an outline, went away for three days to a friend's house in Palm Springs, and wrote *Scream* over the weekend.

"It took me three days altogether," Williamson recalled. "I worked pretty much 'round the clock, sleeping for just a few hours." After he finished the script, he put it away for a couple of days, then wrote outlines for *Scream 2* and *3*. Williamson always intended *Scream* to be a franchise, "unlike a lot of movies that end up having sequels."

Williamson also wrote *Scream* quickly because he was desperate. He gave the screenplay everything he had, because if his agents didn't love it, they weren't going to send it out. "I was starving and I wanted them to love it so much."

The clichés that Williamson played with in *Scream* included a direct take-off of *When a Stranger Calls* for the opening segment, which was also combined with *Psycho* in that the first death was a name actor. There were also the jokes about when you say you'll be right back, that's when you'll get killed, and, of course, the infamous "have sex, you die" rule.

Williamson also wrote the line, "Movies don't create psychos, movies just make psychos more creative," in response to a Bob Dole rant against violent movies, especially in the wake of *Natural Born Killers,* which was a hot button film of the time. "I had to have the killer say it," Williamson said. "It's gotta come from the source."

With films in the mid-nineties becoming increasingly self-referential, and a lot of nineties dialogue referencing other movies

504 ☻ **REEL TERROR**

post-Tarantino, some accused *Scream* of being a gimmick or novelty script. "That may be accurate with regard to the fact that I was trying to draw attention to myself as a writer," Williamson responded. "But that is the way I write—it's the way I talk."

Williamson gave the script to a junior agent at APA, the Agency for the Performing Arts, on Friday so they could read it over the weekend. "I was on pins and needles, saying, 'Please let them like it. Please let them like it!' I couldn't get it out of my head—it was one of those moments when your skin is the only thing that holds your body in." As it turns out, Williamson's agents loved the script and sent it out the day after they gave Kevin the good news.

Williamson was hoping they could sell it to Roger Corman and make a few bucks, but once the script went around the APA offices, they felt it had a good shot at something bigger.

Scream went out on a Tuesday. Williamson was hoping to wind up at New Line, but they were the first to pass, and his heart sunk to his boots. But then Miramax called on Wednesday. "We love it, we want to bring it in, we've just got to let Bob read it."

Once the script made it to Bob's desk, Dimension executives kept poking their heads into Weinstein's office to gauge his reaction. Once Bob got to page seventy-five and found out who the killers were, he said, "Make an offer." Another company had already made a bigger offer than Bob's, so once Weinstein got to page ninety, he said, "Go out with a bigger offer." By the time he got to the end of the script, Weinstein finally said, "Oh, my fucking God, make an offer. Get this movie!"

The final bidding came down to Weinstein and Oliver Stone. Stone offered more money, but Williamson's agent told him they should go with Dimension because they wanted to start production immediately. *Scream* was sold to Miramax for a reported $500,000 plus points.

As Bob recalled, "I asked the agent, 'How much?' The agent told me the price, and I said, 'Yes!' He says, 'Let me call the writer; I'll get back to you.' I said, 'No. I told you *yes*.' They never expect you to say yes. He said, 'Maybe I undersold this.' I said, 'There's no going back. *I just said yes*. You see, that's them not knowing what they've got. I *knew* what it was."

In one fell swoop, Williamson, at thirty years old, went from broke and desperately struggling to having sold a script for six figures, and getting offers to write other screenplays on the strength of *Scream*. (Not to mention *Scream* actually got made a year to the date after the script got sold, instead of languishing in the development hell quagmire so many spec scripts fall into.)

Bob and Kevin bonded over the original *Halloween,* which was a pivotal film in their lives. "You know what? I remember the day when I saw *Halloween*," Weinstein told him. "I remember exactly where I was, how I felt."

Although *Scream* would reinvent Craven's career as well, and introduce him to a new generation of horror fans, he initially turned it down, primarily because he didn't want to make any more horror films. When he first dove in and read the Drew Barrymore segment of the script, Craven thought, "God, it's so dark." "I didn't want to go there again," Craven says. "It's tough to think of going in this space. And to his credit, Bob Weinstein just waited."

Williamson met Craven for lunch at Paramount, where the director was making *Vampire in Brooklyn* with Eddie Murphy. Craven told him, "Don't get pigeonholed. Try not to do any more horror movies," which is where Craven was trying to go himself.

After Craven turned it down, producers Cary Woods and Cathy Konrad took the script around, and a lot of filmmakers saw it as a comedy, which they were trying to avoid. Over and over they kept hearing, "It sounds like you're looking for the new Wes Craven."

And as it turned out, Wes Craven was trying to get a remake of *The Haunting* going, but it was stuck in development going nowhere, and he finally committed.

"Actually the turning point was when a kid came up to me at a film conference or a panel I was on," Craven says. "The kid said, 'You know, you should really do a movie like *The Last House on the Left* again. You really kicked ass back then, and you haven't done it since.' I went home and I thought, 'Am I getting soft?' I've always had this ambivalence about doing violent films, and I've also had this other side that says, 'This is your voice, this is what comes naturally to you. You do it really well, go do it.' So I called Bob and off we went."

In spite of his initial misgivings, Craven ultimately liked the script because it was "a very interesting thriller—a whodunit—as well as a kind of deconstruction of a genre, looking at various levels of reality at the same time, which was very interesting to me.

"I didn't guess who the killer was, I just didn't make the simple leap of saying it's not a killer, it's killers," he continues. "That to me was quite unique. It was also obviously a deconstruction of the genre, although I must say I didn't think in those terms until later. But the fact that it acknowledged that there were horror films out there that these characters would know about. For Kevin, I think his world was so much involved in the actual films. He's a huge John Carpenter fan, he loved *Halloween*, it was natural for him to build it around characters that knew real films and talked about them. I thought that was really fascinating."

Scream was also partly a twist on a film Craven did several years earlier, *Wes Craven's New Nightmare*, where actors from the previous *Nightmare* movies came back playing themselves, instead of the characters they played in the movies, and are caught up in something

supernatural. "With *Scream*, Kevin had kind of flipped it and made his characters people who watch the movies rather than the people who made the movies," Craven says. "I realized it made it much more accessible to the audience because it was talking about them, not the people who made the films."

Many screenplays go through the hell of endless rewrites, and inane notes from studio executives that "improve" scripts into god-awful failures. Williamson was the new kid on the Hollywood block and didn't want to make waves or upset anyone, so he went along with the notes process with Miramax, then the producers, then Craven. Williamson thought Craven would completely rewrite the script because Wes was a writer as well. Williamson went to Craven's house, bracing himself, and must have gone into shock when Craven pulled out three densely packed pages, but it was Craven's list of typos, his professor side coming out.

Once Williamson went through the script with Wes, some bits and pieces here and there were changed, but the shooting script stayed pretty much intact with very little rewriting. "There was very little that needed to be changed," Craven said. "*Scream* was just a beautifully constructed screenplay."

One change that Bob Weinstein wanted was in the second act, forty pages went by where no one gets killed, which was forty pages too long.

"You know, you need to kill someone right in the middle of this movie."

"Who?"

"I don't care—anyone—but somebody has to die." (When *Lord of the Rings* was originally going to be made at Miramax, Harvey Weinstein had also told Peter Jackson that one of the hobbits had to die.)

Bob also didn't like the original title, *Scary Movie,* and like *An American Werewolf in London,* he didn't want a funny movie with scares, but the opposite. Harvey reportedly came up with the new title, *Scream,* which he took from the Michael Jackson song.

The Weinsteins, as they're often known to do, also meddled with the film once it started production. Bob wasn't happy with the rushes, then claimed he never signed off on the killer's mask. (Apparently he didn't get the irony of the *Scream* mask being inspired by the famous painting.) After Craven got a panicked phone call from Bob in the middle of a shot, the director remarked, "What kind of studio head calls a filmmaker in the middle of shooting, kicks him in the balls, and expects him to go to work the rest of the day and do good work?"

The mask was reportedly found by a location scout in a woman's attic, but Bob thought it looked goofy, and wanted Craven to shoot scenes four times with different masks to see which one he liked.

To try and placate Bob, an assemblage was cut together. If he liked it, he couldn't meddle again, if he didn't, they'd walk away and Bob could finish the movie with anyone else they wanted. Bob loved it, and after that, "Wes was God," said B. J. Rack, who produced the film. "He was absolutely golden. When they get their comfort level up, they're fine." (Bob also later admitted he was wrong about the mask.)

Unlike a lot of productions where the writer's the hooker overstaying her welcome, Williamson was very welcome on the set, and was allowed to see the film being cast because he knew he'd direct his own films one day. The big checks and the Hollywood premieres were certainly nice, but Williamson got a big kick out of having his own chair on the set with his name on the back of it.

Despite the usual Weinstein hiccups, *Scream* was pretty much the movie Williamson wrote. Like Fincher and Walker on *Se7en,* Williamson and Craven were in synch as writer and director, and it was a dream shoot for the young scribe. "Really, it hasn't been that easy since," Williamson said.

Once the test screening process began, the Weinsteins were famous for trying to bring up the scores as high as they could, putting in more money in postproduction, intimidating filmmakers into making the changes they wanted. Yet the test scores for *Scream* were a studio's dream. High eighties and nineties for "excellent" and "very good," high eighties for "definitely recommend," and ultimately the film was left alone. "There was nothing to do," Bob recalled. "No notes, no meetings, no anything. We had a monster on our hands."

Scream went to the MPAA eight times before it got the R. It wasn't Craven's first battle with the MPAA, and as he once said in frustration, "You find yourself on day one of production—or page one when you're writing the script—thinking, 'Well, is this going to be offensive to the censors?' We're all being forced to drive at fifty-five miles an hour. There are no more racetracks." The MPAA wanted changes in about six scenes for the R, as well as in the film's ending. "Then it asked for a submission of just our soundtrack," Craven recalled, bewildered. "It's not even visual! It didn't want the music too upsetting. It didn't want the sound effects too explicit."

Bob came up with the idea of releasing *Scream* in December 1996, a counterprogramming move, like opening *The Silence of the Lambs* on Valentine's Day.

"Everybody in the company, everyone outside the company, everyone thought he was crazy," said Jack Lechner, the executive vice president of production and development at Dimension. Cathy Konrad said, "Counterprogramming, niche programming—no one was thinking that way at Christmas."

Bob was repeatedly told he was wrong, Wes's agents called in concerned, but Weinstein wouldn't compromise. Christmas was the season for Oscar bait drama, prestige films, and family movies, but Weinstein's attitude was, "There's nothing for teenagers to see. Great, I'm going against *The Piano*." (Releasing a horror film for Christmas wasn't unprecedented, of course, considering *The Exorcist* was Warners' big movie for that season.)

"Miramax was concerned that if we opened in December we'd be swallowed up by all the Oscar movies, but Bob hung tight," said Williamson. "He felt the potential audience for this film was being ignored, and thought the movie, with some good reviews, would really have legs. It has revived interest in this kind of film, which is great. That was Dimension's aim, and it's really paid off for them."

Scream, which cost about $15 million, grossed more than $100 million domestically, $250 million worldwide, which was a major triumph for all involved, not just for the young kid who grew up poor in North Carolina whose teacher told him he'd never be a writer.

"This is just such a personal experience for everyone involved," Williamson said. "All the way up to Bob Weinstein. Because he was just starting up Dimension Films and *Scream* was his first big hit with the company. I think he put such a personal investment into this, just the way Wes did and reinvented his career. It gave me a career. And it helped a lot of other people, from actors to everyone else involved."

The first three *Scream* movies reportedly made $500 million. In 1992, Dimension contributed 25 percent to Miramax's bottom line, provided 37 percent of Miramax's total gross in 1996, and in 2000, it contributed up to 75 percent. Miramax released thirty-four films in 1997 and made $420 million, with close to half of that money coming from Dimension. Bob would also claim there was a $113 million gross from *Spy Kids* and a nearly $100 million gross from *The Others*.

Also thanks to Dimension, Miramax reportedly made $120 million in profits in 2000, and with the success of *Scary Movie,* which made $157 million, and *Scream 3,* which made $89 million. When Miramax made *Gangs of New York,* Martin Scorsese's risky, personal dream project he'd always wanted to make, Harvey said, "There's no gamble, as long as there's *Halloween* and *Spy Kids* and whatever other shit [Bob] does." Harvey admittedly wasn't the biggest fan of genre movies, and didn't get what Bob was doing with the new company, even when it was bringing in money hand over fist. "He plays in his sandbox, I have mine," he said.

With the success of *Scream,* Craven got the opportunity every filmmaker dreams of where they can make any movie they want, an opportunity some only get once or twice in their career. Craven tried to stretch outside his genre comfort zone with the drama *Music of the Heart,* with Meryl Streep playing real-life music teacher Roberta Guaspari, but when it was released by Miramax in 1999 it didn't succeed at the box office or with critics.

Craven eventually came to terms with being a mainstay in the horror genre, and that it wasn't the worst place to be. He once reasoned he kept doing horror "because it contains more truth than anything else I could do. And I'm good at it; it seems to be where my mind finds its images and works most originally. Maybe it's because I'm basically horrified by the way society works. It's pretty lethal out there."

If you did one right, horror films were "kind of like jazz," he continued. "You really can improvise almost anything out of them.

They're based on standards of human emotions, but what you can do with that is limited only by your own imagination. The genre has a great elasticity to it that I find very exciting."

With the success of *The Blair Witch Project,* young filmmakers realized they didn't need big pimpy equipment to make a movie, and some have said it was like punk rock where you didn't have to be the greatest musician to start a band. Thanks to viral marketing, which was just beginning, the buzz on the film grew from the Internet, and it became the little movie that could in the summer of 1999.

The creators of *The Blair Witch Project,* Eduardo Sánchez and Daniel Myrick, seemed primed for big careers in Hollywood, but several writers looking back on the *Blair Witch* phenomenon couldn't help making the joke that like the filmmakers in the woods, Myrick and Sánchez were never seen again either.

As *The Blair Witch Project* and the diminishing returns of M. Night Shyamalan's career after *The Sixth Sense* have shown, success can be a rare and perishable commodity, and it's easy to take for granted how difficult it is to get a movie made and out into the world, let alone a blockbuster that makes hundreds of millions of dollars.

Eduardo Sánchez and Daniel Myrick met at the University of Central Florida, where they were studying film in the early nineties. They would talk about the movies that scared them growing up like *The Exorcist, Jaws, The Amityville Horror,* and *The Shining,* but they had nowhere near the budget needed to pull something like that off.

They also loved pseudo-documentaries like *Chariots of the Gods,* and the TV show *In Search Of,* which was hosted by Leonard

Nimoy and dealt with unknown phenomena like UFOs and the Loch Ness Monster. "So this idea came out of the whole idea of wondering if you could make a movie that seemed real, that played itself off as a documentary," Sánchez says.

Sánchez and Myrick decided to make a faux documentary about a legend they made up about a group of kids disappearing in the woods, some kind of evil spirit would be the cause of it, and the footage would be found a year later. If they were going to fool people, you couldn't have name actors, the camera work had to be hand-held, and there had to be low-tech light and sound.

"So all the things that were the detriments to normal independent film were the strength of this idea," Sánchez says. "That's where the whole very low-budget, very realistic attitude came about. We made a promise to ourselves to try everything possible not to have anything in the movie that would betray that it wasn't real."

Myrick said audiences "didn't really understand how much work went into making it look like no work went into it. The conceit behind *Blair Witch* was very methodically planned out and we went to great pains to make sure it looked very real and authentic."

The disappearance would happen in 1994, and *Blair Witch* had to be made with what poor film students could afford then. "What would these poor-ass film students be using? At the time there were Hi-8 cameras and DAT recorders, that was probably the most advanced things they had, that's why we shot it with Hi-8," Sánchez said. "People always label *Blair Witch* as the first theatrically distributed digital movie. Well, we didn't really shoot it on digital, Hi-8 is actually a tape format. It's not digital at all, but we came close. It was probably the only film that was ever released to theaters that was shot in Hi-8, which is a pretty inferior consumer format. It's a couple of notches above VHS."

Because they also didn't have a big effects budget, whatever was after them in the woods would remain up to the imagination of the audience. As Sánchez explains, "When you watched *The Legend of Boggy Creek* you'd hear the sound of Bigfoot, and to me, the sound of Bigfoot was much more terrifying than actually seeing it. To me it was like, 'Jeez, there's this boogeyman out there, I don't know what he looks like, but it's obviously out there making this noise. That's not a wolf, that's not a bear, that's a Bigfoot.' So Dan and I said, 'Let's just do audio. It's much scarier to hear footsteps in the woods and not know what the hell was making that noise.'"

It was a simple idea, would be an easy concept to execute, and as Sánchez also recalls, "It was something that came out of desperation. It was our last shot [at success]. Dan and I were like, 'If this doesn't do it for us, we're doomed, because we're never going to come up with anything better than this.'"

Of about two thousand films submitted to Sundance, *The Blair Witch Project* made the cut, and was accepted for competition in October 1998. Ironically, 1999 was the last year you had to make a print of your movie to play at Sundance, which would have saved Myrick and Sánchez the $30,000 they spent duping the film, the biggest expense they had on *Blair Witch* at that point.

"Maybe fifty films usually played Sundance, and the odds are always against you," Sánchez says. "There's no real barometer of what's going to get accepted or not accepted. Sundance was a validation that every filmmaker looks for. We didn't expect to get in, we just thought, 'Well, we'll send it out there, and who the hell knows what will happen.' But once we got in, we realized, maybe we do have something. Maybe at least we'll sell it to somebody and we can make another movie. We never imagined the movie would have the kind of impact it had."

By the time *The Blair Witch Project* was accepted for the Sundance Festival, the Web site www.blairwitch.com was already up and running. *Blair Witch* is now cited as the big breakthrough for Internet viral marketing. "It was totally accidental," Sánchez says. "I happened to know how to build Web sites. I had just broken up with my girlfriend and I had a lot of free time on my hands. In my small way, I was creating the prototype for what was to come afterwards. It was cool that I helped create something that people were emulating."

Sánchez spent a lot of time in the chat rooms and on the discussion boards, tried to put something new up on the site every day, and was building a community for the film. Plus, it proved to be a very inexpensive way to help promote the film. "The Web was just a small percentage of what it is now," Sánchez continues. "For us, the Web was just kinda like where else are we gonna market this movie? How much is a Web site? Fifteen dollars a month? We can afford that."

This, of course, begs the question of how well *The Blair Witch Project* would have done through traditional word of mouth. Sánchez feels the movie would have done well regardless. "I think it would have been successful, I just don't know how successful it would have been," Sánchez says. "Would it have done 75 percent of the business, or 50, or 10? Obviously there's no way to gauge that, but the Internet had a huge impact on the interest level of the film."

The Blair Witch Project premiered on a Saturday night at Sundance, and it was the hot ticket of the festival. All the screenings were sold out by the time Myrick and Sánchez arrived at Sundance, and they had to add a show at their biggest venue. One agent told Sanchez he had to buy a ticket for fifty dollars from a scalper to get into a screening.

There were reports that half the audience walked out at the main screening. Bingham Ray, a founding partner at October Films, was one indie player who left early, and he later remarked, "The only thing scary about *The Blair Witch Project* is how much Artisan paid for it."

Sánchez says, "The whole thing about half the people walking out is bullshit. There was definitely not a mass exodus, that's not true. There was a certain backlash because I don't know what people were expecting. They didn't know what the hell that movie was, they had never seen anything like it, and they were like, 'How the hell do we market this?'"

The Blair Witch Project was sold to Artisan two hours after the first screening for $1.1 million, and it was the first movie at Sundance sold that year. New Line also wanted the film, and people from Miramax told Sánchez, "We were going to make you an offer that morning."

As it turns out, Artisan was the perfect company for *Blair Witch*. "They were hungry, they were willing to take risks, and at the time they had a talented stable of filmmakers," says Sánchez. "They were like the old Miramax when Miramax would do these really strange, esoteric films and somehow make money with them.

"Artisan had released *Pi* the year before," Sánchez continues. "That was a pretty esoteric film, and they got like three million dollars out of it at the box office. So their whole thing was they could put the *Pi* plan in effect here. I think what they saw was if they could do the *Pi* thing on this, they could get six to seven million dollars out of this thing. They got really aggressive with it."

After Sundance, Sánchez began to hear from fans through the site about *Cannibal Holocaust*, the Italian grindhouse film that had the same concept: a documentary crew goes into a jungle, comes in contact with a cannibal tribe, and when the film footage is discovered, it shows how they met their demise.

Like *Blair Witch*, *Cannibal Holocaust* also really fooled people. Not long after its release in Italy, authorities seized the film and the director Ruggero Deodato was charged with making a snuff film. The cast was flown to the trial to prove they weren't actually murdered. *Cannibal Holocaust* also featured real animal cruelty captured on film.

A fan sent a VHS copy to Sánchez and Myrick. "We popped it in and watched an hour of it," Sánchez recalls. "It's not an enjoyable movie. Once they started killing animals, I didn't want to see it anymore. We had never heard of it, and it's probably a good thing we'd never seen it. We're all very sensitive to copying people, and ripping people off, so I don't know if we would have done *Blair Witch* if we had seen *Cannibal Holocaust*. We didn't want to do anything that had already been done. The premise of *Cannibal Holocaust* is exactly the premise of *Blair Witch* if you take all the details out, and we were just shocked by it. We were kinda like, 'Wow, there really are no new ideas.'"

Released in July 1999, *The Blair Witch Project* had a remarkable fifteen minutes of fame, making $248 million worldwide, the most successful film of its time in terms of cost to profit ratio. At one point, it was even reportedly outgrossing *Star Wars: Episode One* per screen.

With *The Matrix, Blair Witch,* and *The Sixth Sense* all coming out that summer, *Entertainment Weekly* announced, "You can stop waiting for the future of movies, it's already here. Someday 1999 will be etched on a microchip as the first year of twenty-first-century filmmaking. The year when all the old, boring rules about cinema started to crumble."

Sean Cunningham said *Blair Witch* "showed that you don't need Hollywood or anything fancy, and audiences supported that spirit. Most people loved the success story behind *Blair Witch* more than the movie itself."

"*The Blair Witch Project* is kind of a unique case," said Joe Dante not long after the film's release. "There aren't going to be a lot of pictures that have the combination of luck and timing that that picture had. People went in expecting a terrifying thrill ride, and what they got was a home movie. Yet everybody had to see it. The Web site thing was unique and brilliantly done."

Sánchez and Myrick themselves realized pretty early on that the *Blair Witch* phenomenon was a once in a lifetime thing. " 'It's absolutely like winning the Lottery," Sánchez says. "Once you see yourself on the cover of *Time* magazine, once you see your actors on the cover of *Newsweek,* you see yourself parodied on MTV and *Saturday Night Live,* you realize 'This is never gonna happen again.'

"We definitely enjoyed it," he adds, "and we enjoyed it as outsiders. None of us moved to L.A. until many years later. We tried to keep our heads screwed on straight. The world that we got a glimpse of was that world. We were huge filmmakers for a little while there, we got to enjoy that, but we also saw the dark side of that too. I don't think any of us pretended at any time that this was going to be the norm."

Myrick and Sánchez, of course, had plans beyond *Blair Witch.* "We're trying to let *Blair* number one do its thing and run its course," Myrick said in 1999. "We really want to do something different, then revisit *Blair* later on and have fresh energy to put into a prequel or sequel."

The pair were going to do a comedy, *Heart of Love,* which they described as a "Farrelly Brothers meets Monty Python," but the project fell apart when the financing fell through. Michael Williams, one of the three actors lost in the woods in *Blair Witch,* went back to moving furniture in New York, "The same job I quit on national television, on Conan O'Brien," he said. He had a family to support, and didn't want to worry "about whether I was going to get the next role on *CSI.*"

Artisan also came apart two years after the *Blair Witch* phenomenon. Artisan was $270 million in debt by 2000, and the company was sold at auction in 2001 to Lionsgate for $160 million. Sánchez laments, "Artisan were a great company during the whole *Blair Witch* thing, then once the movie started making a lot of money, they unfortunately turned into a different company, and just started chasing the buck."

As for their post–*Blair Witch* films, "I can see how people think we're one-hit wonders," Myrick said. "I'll be the first to admit that I've put a lot of pressure on myself to relive the *Blair* days. I can get down on myself sometimes. We've got a lot of movies left in us." With a laugh, he added, "They may all be *Blair* movies, but that's better than nothing."

Today Sánchez says, "I'm proud of the fact that I was involved in *The Blair Witch Project,* but I also realize how lucky I was to have met the guys I met at film school that made the film with me, because it was very collaborative. It's given me a living, and I'll probably be talking about *Blair Witch* for the rest of my life, and I have no problem with that. If I make nothing else even close to the success of *Blair Witch,* I still have *Blair Witch,* and I know I'm extremely lucky."

Sánchez and Myrick had no idea that another big sleeper in the summer of 1999, *The Sixth Sense,* would come hot on the heels of *The Blair Witch Project.* "We weren't that well connected back then," Sánchez says. "We had no idea."

Years after the fact, Sánchez met M. Night Shyamalan at a wrap party for *Lady in the Water* in Philadelphia. Night told him that when he saw *The Blair Witch Project* he freaked out, and said, "Man, I make this movie, I make the first scary horror movie in like ten years, and these guys with video cameras beat me to the punch a month before my film was released!"

"*The Sixth Sense* is a great film, and it marked a new energy in horror films that hadn't been around in a lot of years," Sánchez continues. "It was very strange that those two films came out at the same time. We had the *Blair Witch Project* idea in 1991. If someone had come up to us and said, 'Here's $50,000, go shoot this movie,' we would have made it in the early nineties. It's just weird how the timing came together."

The Sixth Sense was a very clever exercise in misdirection, and you miss a lot of clues the first time watching it, the most obvious ones being that Bruce Willis always wears the same clothes, he's the only one without a video camera at the school recital, he doesn't go to the bathroom, and so on. "An incredible amount of attention was paid to fool you," Willis said.

The Sixth Sense also seemed to come out of nowhere along with *The Blair Witch Project*, and gave the long-awaited *Star Wars* prequel, *Episode One*, a run for the money.

Manoj Shyamalan is a first-generation Indian American who has lived in Philadelphia his entire life. Like Cole in *The Sixth Sense*, he was a very frightened kid. "I was scared of everything," he recalled. "*Everything*. If there was a noise in my room, then I was certain some crazy man had broken in and was sitting on my bed waiting for me. My imagination was just crazy."

He made his first short film at twelve on his father's 8 mm camera, then decided at age thirteen he needed a stage name, and renamed himself M. Night Shyamalan.

Shyamalan grew up in a family of doctors, and he had a number of scholarship offers and connections to the medical world, but he decided to go to the Tisch School of the Arts, which left his family disappointed, but they put up a lot of the $750,000 budget for Shyamalan's first feature, *Praying with Anger*.

Shyamalan then wrote a spec script, *Labor of Love*, which he sold to Fox when he was twenty-three. He wanted to direct, but Fox removed him from the film, and Night later said he cursed it. "That's why they can't get it going," he said with a laugh. His next project, *Wide Awake,* which was made at Miramax, was also a nightmare where he was dressed down and humiliated by Harvey Weinstein, and the film was essentially buried.

Eventually Shyamalan realized doing smaller art house movies wasn't for him, and he wanted to aim much higher. "I wanna have three thousand screens, and make the top, intelligent films that a mass audience can see."

Says Barry Mendel, who produced *The Sixth Sense* along with Frank Marshall, Kathleen Kennedy, and Sam Mercer, "He loved genre films as a movie fan, and by combining the more heavy emotional kind of writing that came naturally to him, those two things would complement each other."

"I know it sounds weird, but I decided I was going to write the greatest script and everything was going to change," Shyamalan said. "It was going to be mine, and they would have to let me direct it because they wouldn't get it any other way."

Shyamalan said he thought of Bruce Willis from the beginning. "Before I wrote the screenplay, I wrote down the title of the movie. I said, '*The Sixth Sense,* that sounds like a great title.' And I put down Bruce Willis's name, and I said, 'You know, that might be somebody to think about.' A little dreamworld."

The first draft of *The Sixth Sense* was a serial killer movie in the vein of *The Silence of the Lambs.* The version that got made was the tenth draft of the script. By the third draft, he realized it was a *Silence of the Lambs* rehash. Bruce Wills became a ghost by the fifth draft.

"It kept changing," Shyamalan said. "Bit by bit, the parts with the ghosts became more and more unique. I've never seen that expressed before, and then the serial killer parts—which were good—I'd seen before, and they started to go away, until I said, 'That's not even part of this movie anymore.'"

The Sixth Sense screenplay sold in two days. Mendel says, "The whole way that script optioning is done is you attempt to get everybody to read it immediately, give them as little time to decide as possible, and in that pressure cooker you hope that they'll make decisions to spend more money, and make bigger commitments because of the fear that if they don't do it in the next hour, somebody else will. The idea is to create competition, just like if you're trying to sell a house, you know?"

David Vogel was an executive at Hollywood Pictures, a flagging studio that had been limping along under the Disney umbrella for years. In September 1997, two weeks after being at Hollywood, *The Sixth Sense* came across his desk, and he was asked to clear some time to read it.

Vogel put aside his lunch hour, and he loved it. He was so caught up in Bruce Willis's attempts to save the kid, he didn't see the twist ending coming on paper. At one thirty that afternoon, he called Jeremy Zimmer, Shyamalan's agent at UTA, and told him, "I want it."

New Line was interested in *The Sixth Sense*, and made an offer for $2 million. But Shyamalan went with Disney because they moved faster, and stepped up to get *The Sixth Sense* made. Shyamalan got $2.5 million up-front against $500,000 deferred, $3 million total to write and direct. The film's start date had to be within six months of the sale, and at the level Hollywood bought *The Sixth Sense*, the movie was very doable.

The Sixth Sense was budgeted at $40 million, and it was originally going to cost even less, but the budget went up with Bruce Willis. Willis was going to star in a movie directed by Lee Grant, *Broadway Brawler*, which fell apart after he and Grant butted heads. Willis agreed to make three films for Disney to make up for the loss, and he had to do them for less than his usual $20 million per film. The first two films he picked were *Armageddon* and *The Sixth Sense*.

Of course the ace in the hole was the kid, Haley Joel Osment. Mendel had also produced *Rushmore* and was rooting for Mason Gamble to play the kid, who did a great audition and would have made a very haunting Cole. Yet Night was "really on the Haley train in the beginning and I kind of came around later."

There were other unpredictable elements that Mendel and Shyamalan were pleasantly surprised by. No one expected Donnie Wahlberg to lose forty pounds and look emaciated. "And I think that added a certain creepiness and weirdness to the opening of the movie, which worked really, really well," Mendel says.

Mendel also recalled, "Nobody thought 'I see dead people' was a big deal until they found it in marketing, and that was a late-breaking discovery if there ever was one. We thought that scene was big, and were superhappy with how it came out, but we didn't see it as a big marketing idea or the hook for the movie at all."

Even though it's under two hours, *The Sixth Sense* took its time building the story, and *Time* wrote that *Sense* "unfolds with a patient intelligence." With audiences wanting movies to move a lot faster these days, both William Friedkin and Ridley Scott have said if they made *The Exorcist* or *Alien* today, they'd have a hard time pacing it the same way, and *The Sixth Sense* was a return to letting a film take its time to scare the audience, making the payoff sweeter.

"Night had a sense of pace that he wanted it to be, and I give him a tremendous amount of credit for having the level of restraint that he had," says Mendel. "There were times I was concerned about it. I remember we were shooting the scene where Cole was talking to his mom about the bumblebee pendent in the kitchen. At the time, Night didn't give himself a tremendous number of options in the editing room. He had an idea of how he wanted to shoot things and he was willing to die with them if they were the wrong thing. The scene kind of had its own rhythm."

Mendel continues, "I remember making a suggestion like, 'Why don't we just have some coverage so when we get to the editing room we'll have the option. If this is going too slow we can speed it up,' because if you're filming in one shot, you can't speed it up. And he just said, 'I'm just totally confident this is going to work, and I want you to back me on this one. There's other situations where absolutely we're gonna need to have choices, and this one I'm confident this is going to work.' I didn't feel confident at all, but I couldn't have been happier with it in the movie. He was 100 percent right."

The Sixth Sense was supposed to open that October, but was moved up to August. Willis' agent Arnold Rifkin claimed he encouraged Hollywood to move the film up to early August, right on the heels of *The Blair Witch Project*.

Mendel says, "You don't have any control in these situations. They told us they were gonna push it." August is not a huge month for a blockbuster, but as Mendel continues, "August 20 is a lot different than August 6. August 6 you have three solid weeks of summer, high school and college kids going during the weekdays, and those days are very important to a movie like this. Plus it was a thrill to be released in the summer at all. We very easily could have been an October or a February movie."

As far as opening the film earlier, to ride the heat of *The Blair Witch Project*, Mendel counters, "You plan a release date nine months in advance when you're releasing it, you book those theaters months and months in advance. So anybody on earth knew that *The Blair Witch Project* was going to be a hit nine months in advance, I would have to give them a lie detector test."

Taking a big leap of faith, there was also no all points bulletin to the public not to spoil the ending or that there was a big twist at the end to potentially spoil. Says Mendel, "There was just a belief that if you sat down and didn't know anything about this movie and were surprised and exhilarated by the ending, then why would you want to take that experience away from another person? So we just believed that people enjoyed having that experience, and they would want to preserve it for other people, and that turned out to be the case."

In Todd McCarthy's review of *The Sixth Sense* for *Variety,* he wrote, "A terrific last-minute story twist goes a fair way toward redeeming *The Sixth Sense,* a mostly ponderous tale of paranormal communication across the River Styx." He also called it "an odd film in that it's borderline dull to sit through but, because of the revelation of its ending, is actually rather interesting to think about."

McCarthy felt the film would be a hit in spite of its flaws, and also predicted repeat viewing because *The Sixth Sense* "could conceivably be more rewarding to watch a second time in light of what one knows after seeing it once. Few pictures have had their effectiveness hinge so completely upon information withheld until the last moment, which is not a particularly recommended way to construct a movie, but undeniably gives people something to chew over after the fact."

The rest of the reviews were mostly good, with critics appreciating that *The Sixth Sense* was done the old-school way without video game pacing, or tons of CGI, and that the twist played fair with the audience. As *Entertainment Weekly*'s Lisa Schwarzbaum remarked, *The Sixth Sense* was "the rare film twist that was genuinely unexpected without being the least dishonest."

But as Sánchez says, it's not just in horror films that you have to play fair. "It's in every movie: you have to set rules and stick to them. The most unsatisfying thing is to get to the third act of a movie or the climax of a movie, and all of the sudden R2-D2 can fly. And I love the *Star Wars* movies, even the prequels, but I mean there's certain things where you're like, 'Well, if he could have flown, then this, and this, and this . . .'"

The Sixth Sense made $26.6 million opening weekend in 2,161 theaters, the largest opening for an August movie since *The Fugitive*. It was the same weekend *The Blair Witch Project* went wide, and it also beat out *Runaway Bride*.

Shyamalan recalled, "I cried on Saturday morning when the call came from Disney to say we were number one and had beat *Blair Witch* by $2 million." Then, thanks to word of mouth, *The Sixth Sense* stayed the number one movie in the country for an additional five weeks.

"I think people cherish shared experiences," says Mendel. "It just becomes something you just gotta see, like everyone's gotta tune in to the last episode of *M*A*S*H* or whatever it is." *The Sixth Sense* made more than $650 million worldwide, and became Disney's most successful live action film.

After *The Sixth Sense,* like a lot of filmmakers after a hit, Shyamalan's ego became insufferable, and some have blamed his post–*Sixth Sense* slide on having too much control over his work. Having a horrible experience with the Weinsteins humiliating you and butchering your movie is enough to make anyone gun-shy, but having total autonomy over his work may have given Shyamalan more rope than he needed to hang himself.

Reviewing *Lady in the Water, Variety* wrote, "There is doubtless an engrossing documentary to be made on the pitfalls of youthful directorial success with M. Night Shyamalan bidding for a place as its focus." *Variety* also mentioned that the last act and climax were "likely to send many opening-weekend filmgoers home head-scratching and grumbling," which they'd been doing with M. Night's movies since *Unbreakable*.

After he took big career missteps with *The Village* and *Lady in the*

Water, Shyamalan was the subject of a short *Newsweek* piece, "Career Intervention," even though he'd been hailed on the cover of the magazine several years earlier as the next Spielberg. One studio executive quoted anonymously asked, "Is there a 12-step program for egos?"

Shyamalan has since continued to be the target of the Razzie awards, and the butt of many film geek jokes, as well as a lot of armchair quarterbacking that says he needs to reinvent himself. As *The Twilight Zone* proved, it's difficult to stretch a story in the Serling style for longer than half an hour, and to pull off an effective twist, a story has to play fair with the audience. As Carpenter learned with *Halloween,* along with the skill of being able to scare the audience in style, being in the right place and time where everything comes together can be very elusive. For a brief shining moment in the summer of 1999, *The Blair Witch Project* and *The Sixth Sense* were both able to pull it off.

EPILOGUE

"THE AUDIENCE IS ALWAYS THERE FOR IT"

How horror fared in the new millennium, and why it's the genre that refuses to die

In the new millennium, horror made a big comeback, although the quality of the movies weren't totally up to snuff. From 2000 on, horror fans saw trends like Japanese-influenced horror and torture porn come and go, a big zombie revival, the birth of a genuine franchise with the *Saw* series, the old classic directors coming to terms with the genre that's defined them, innumerable tired remakes now going under the buzzword "reboots," and the new *Blair Witch* with *Paranormal Activity*.

With both *Paranormal Activity* and *Saw*, horror again showed you could make a lot of money back on a low budget. Like *The Blair Witch Project*, *Paranormal Activity* was another homemade phenomenon that had an insane cost to profit ratio. (Only $15,000 to more than a hundred million at the box office.) *Saw* would cost less than $2 million, and make $53.2 million domestic, $102.9 million worldwide, as well as spawn six sequels, making it the first new original horror franchise in about ten years.

Although the new generation of horror films were often pretty weak, there certainly was a lot of crapola in the genre throughout history, so has it been always been a case of having to dig through a lot of manure to find a gem?

There's been a call to arms that's gone unheeded for better horror films. In the June 2007 issue of *Fangoria*, Tony Timpone wrote in his editorial, "Will we really want to watch the *Texas Chain Saw Massacre* remake (the one that started the craze) ten years from now when the original is still far superior? This reveals a lot about our generation. We've got nothing to say, even living in these extreme times! This could have easily been an era of genre classics, but instead we've released the creative license to fanboys and not artists."

At first with horror's renewed popularity, some felt it was a post-9/11 reaction, and certainly looking back in the past, horror has been very popular in times of trouble. A lot of horror filmmakers blew off any post-9/11 connection, but Stuart Gordon felt the theory had some validity. "After 9/11 horror became even more popular than ever," he says. "I think what that says is about the importance of horror, and how some people need horror as a way of dealing with real-life horror. There's something very healthy about horror movies." And as Romero said, "When people feel threatened, they either go to pure entertainment or to something that might strike a chord with the fears they have in real life."

One of the first horror trends of the new millennium was the Americanized remakes of Japanese horror films like *The Ring* and *The Grudge,* which made a lot of money in the brief time the trend was popular. One cultural change that was made for *The Ring* was the ending. In the original, the curse is ended by the girl's grandfather, who doesn't have much longer to live, and is willing to watch the movie that kills people, and sacrifice himself. Says Ehren Kruger, who wrote the screenplays for the American *Ring* films, "In Japanese culture, it would be perfectly natural for the grandfather to sacrifice his life, of which he didn't have much left, to save that of the youngest generation. Culturally in America, for good or ill, it's more palatable to pass along the cursed videotape to some unknown stranger and kill them, and save Grandpa!"

Romero caught a big break when zombies became a hot monster, and they kept coming back and reinventing themselves with *Shawn of the Dead, 28 Days Later,* books like *World War Z,* and literary spoofs like *Pride and Prejudice and Zombies.* Because of the undead resurgence, Fox and Universal were competing for Romero's *Land of the Dead.* As Savini said in 2006, "We are certainly in zombie times now!"

Romero says, "The only reason *Land of the Dead* got made was based on the fact that the remake of *Dawn, Shawn of the Dead,* and *28 Days Later* have made money. It's all about practical realities. I am cynical. I can sit here and tell you the sun may not come up tomorrow! But I also know I've been very lucky. In the end, you just gotta play the cards. If you have a passion to do something, you have to wait for the market to be there."

Land of the Dead opened on June 24, 2005, competing against *Batman Begins* and *War of the Worlds.* In spite of strong reviews, *Land of the Dead* didn't do well in the United States, but it made a lot of money overseas, and it was also big on DVD. In the new millennium, the windows for theatrical and DVD release have grown increasingly shorter, with audiences often choosing to wait for the home release. Peter Jackson's *King Kong* made $100 million its first week on DVD and *Fight Club* became a huge buy-to-own movie that put the movie in the black when it initially failed at the box office.

With Romero's recent films more overt in terms of message, it's clear to anyone with half a brain who the villain Dennis Hopper played in *Land of the Dead* was. "I got the best reviews I've ever had on *Land of the Dead*, and I owe it to the Bush administration!" Romero says with a laugh. "Because the press swings left, they're looking for things to find in there. Meanwhile, look at the other movies. Look at *Dawn*, look at *Day*, there's shit in there too, it just wasn't so *now*. To any thinking person, the Bush administration is a fucking failure, and anyone in the press is gonna say, 'Oh, man, what a slap in the face.' I got a lucky break that way on the reviews."

Not every master of horror was thrilled with certain trends, such as torture porn, which was launched by horror upstart Eli Roth, or the endless parade of remakes.

Eli Roth was another filmmaker you'd never expect would make horror films. Good-looking, confident, and athletic with a big smile, he doesn't come across like a geek outsider who couldn't get laid in high school. With the success of *Hostel*, Roth became synonymous with what became labeled as torture porn.

Although many found his movies repugnant, the bottom line in Hollywood is money, and Roth's films were highly profitable, reportedly some of the most profitable in recent memory. *Hostel* cost a reported $4.8 million, and had a worldwide gross of $80 million with $47 million domestic.

Like the mad slasher movies of the eighties, Roth's style of horror definitely hit a nerve and disgusted many, including the elder statesemen of terror. Romero called films like *Hostel*, "mean-spirited and Grand Guignol all the way. I don't find any substance underlying it." Craven joked about the torture porn trend, "It's bad, horrible. Disgusting. Those filmmakers should be taken out and shot . . . then we'd have less competition!" Then again, maybe there's something to be said for movies that would disgust the masters of horror themselves, just as they disgusted many themselves back in their day.

Stephen King, however, thought *Hostel* was okay, and told the *L.A. Times*, "I understand 'torture porn.' It's a good phrase. But I would argue with you, there's a fine line there. There's something going on in *Hostel 2* that isn't torture porn, there's really something going on there that's interesting on an artistic basis. Sure, it makes you uncomfortable, but good art should make you uncomfortable."

Those who were disgusted with torture porn didn't have to suffer with it long; it was a trend that came and went quickly. Roth's style of horror was easy to duplicate, and many feeble imitations flooded the direct to DVD and Blu-Ray market, burning the torture porn trend out quickly, although it wasn't going to have that long of a shelf life to begin with.

Once *Hostel: Part II* was perceived as a failure, although considering its cost and profit margin it did very well, like Shyamalan and Tarantino, Roth grew whiny about how he was no longer Hollywood's golden boy. (It's surprising before this happened he never had to listen to any angry ranting from Tarantino about being hoisted and dumped by the public.)

Roth blamed film piracy and critics for *Hostel: Part II*'s box-office performance. A work print of the film was leaked online, some critics reviewed it, and Roth threatened to blacklist them. "I know who they are, as do the studios, and they will no longer have any access to any of my films." (You assume he means access to his films in advance, or maybe he'll have somebody physically blocking them from entering the theater, which surprisingly some directors haven't tried yet.)

As for the remakes, like the very successful remake of *Dawn of the Dead*, Romero said, "It was better than I expected it was going to be, but I thought it was an action film," Romero said. "I didn't think it had soul. I don't like fast-moving zombies, so that wasn't my cup of tea at all," although Romero did find the film "pretty entertaining."

In recent years, *Halloween* was finally, inexplicably remade, and attempts at a new Rob Zombie franchise thankfully collapsed with the second film. The geeks were, of course, thoroughly outraged that one of the *Citizen Kane*s of the genre could be remade, but Carpenter seemed detached about it, and his remake of *The Thing* being remade as well. "It's like everything else in this stupid business," he said. "You can't get attached to shit."

What's especially irritating about a lot of these remakes is how they try to give Michael Myers and Jason backstories, so you see how they became what they are, much like Lucas felt it was important to show the Death Star being built.

"That's totally a Hollywood studio thing, they feel so compelled to give you all the answers," says Eduardo Sánchez. "There it is tied up all in a nice little bow. In a mystery, I understand that, like an Agatha Christie mystery where you're there to see who did it. But in a horror movie, is it really crucial to give you all the details of what happened? Isn't part of the whole idea of what makes UFOs and Bigfoot and the Loch Ness Monster creepy is you don't have all the answers?"

Argento swore he'd try to stop a remake of *Suspiria* at all costs, and Bob Clark also tried to stop a remake of *Black Christmas*. If you wanted to remake one of his earlier horror films, like *Children Shouldn't Play with Dead Things,* that was fine because there was a lot of room for improvement there, but he felt there was nothing to improve with *Black Christmas*. (The remake went forward anyway, to dreadful reviews and a weak box office.)

Romero also felt it would be a better idea to remake his movies that could have been better instead of trying redo one of his classics. He even mentioned he wouldn't mind taking another crack at something like *Season of the Witch* himself. "I really think it would be stronger today, made for a strong woman out in the world being oppressed," Romero said. "Do it with better actors and a bigger budget, with a filmmaker who knows a little more what he's doing than I did then," he suggested, laughing.

Along with Romero, Carpenter and Craven also tried to stay in the game, and Craven told the *L.A. Times,* "My goal is to die in my nineties on the set." Carpenter took a ten-year hiatus from making movies before he went behind a camera again with *The Ward.* "I'd always sworn to myself when it stopped being fun I'd stop, and it stopped. I was really burned out," he said. "I needed to be away from the movie business and rediscover what it was about cinema that I loved."

Several of the elder masters of horror have also come to terms with the genre some of them felt trapped in. "I think I did feel trapped at one time, but not so much anymore," Carpenter says. "It's also a blessing, I got to be John Carpenter, which is a lot of fun. Hey, man, I'm just happy to be here."

Romero finally left Pennsylvania for Toronto, where he continued making zombie films with a new group of investors. "I think George is very happy doing what he's doing today," says John Amplas. "He really enjoys Toronto, he has new partners up there that are backing him, and are happy to do so with no frets, no arguments. I think he's in a great place at the moment, and I'm happy for him."

"I have one little film that I'd really like to make," Romero said. "You know, at my age, I don't know how much energy I have. I certainly don't want to come [to Hollywood] and pitch something for a year and a half, and then have it blow up. I have to pick my shots."

The famous line in *Chinatown* goes that old buildings, politicians, and whores get respect if they stick around long enough, and horror films may still have a ways to go. But the true fans of the genre couldn't care less what the mainstream or the critics think about horror. It never kept them away from the theaters, or held them back from spending millions of dollars at theaters, or piling their DVD collections up to the ceiling.

"Hollywood tends to look askance at genre films, especially horror films," Craven says. "They don't give any awards for them, and they're the first to pronounce: 'The time of those films is gone, we've moved beyond, we're above that.' But the fact is if you look at the history of horror films, it's kind of cyclical. My theory is once one comes along that's original, then it's imitated to death by many other films and the audience is driven underground because they've seen too much bad product. Then somebody comes out with something that's totally original, and the audience comes back. But I think the audience is always there for it."

SOURCES

Introduction: Why We Love Being Scared

Charles Champlin, "A Screamer in Phantasm," *L.A. Times,* March 28, 1979.

Chris Farley, "Beauty of Horror Adds Up for British Writer," *Chicago Tribune,* September 15, 1987.

Laurence F. Knapp, editor, *Brian De Palma: Interviews* (Jackson, Miss.: University Press of Mississippi, 2003).

Maitland McDonagh, *Filmmaking on the Fringe* (New York: Citadel Press, 1995).

Gina McIntrye, "Happy Birthday, Tall Man! Phantasm Turns 30," *L.A. Times,* October 16, 2009.

Robert E. Kapsis, editor, *Jonathan Demme: Interviews* (Jackson, Miss.: University Press of Mississippi, 2009).

Josh Rottenberg, "There's Something About Carrie," *Premiere,* vol. 14, no. 12, August 2001.

Tom Weaver, DVD commentary for *The Wolf Man,* Universal, 2004.

Author interviews with Stanley Mann and Joseph Stefano.

Chapter One: The Foundations of Fear

Forrest Ackerman, *Forrest J. Ackerman Presents Mr. Monster's Movie Gold* (Virginia: The Donning Company, 1981).

Arch Oboler Wikipedia page.

Peter Bogdanovich, *Who the Hell's in It: Potraits and Conversations* (New York: Knopf, 2004).

Richard Bojarski, *Films of Bela Lugosi* (New York: Citadel Press, 1980).

Richard Bojarski and Kenneth Beale, *The Films of Boris Karloff* (New York: Citadel Press, 1974).

Books and Writers. www.kirjasto.sci.fi/ohenry.htm.

Bob Burns and Tom Weaver, *Monster Kid Memories* (New York: Dinoship, 2003).

Christopher Conlon, "Southern California Sorcerers," no. 75–76, *Filmfax*.

Richard Corliss, "The Glory and Horror of EC Comics," *Time*, April 29, 2004.

James Curtis, *A New World of Gods and Monsters* (Boston: Faber and Faber, 1998).

Jason Davis, "The Long Twilight: Carol Serling and the Rod Serling Conference," *From the Trenches, CS Weekly*.

Jason Davis, "Writing in the Fifth Dimension: Marc Scott Zicree on What The Twilight Zone Can Still Teach Us About Great Drama," *From the Trenches, CS Daily*.

Digby Diehl, *Tales from the Crypt: The Official Archives* (New York: St. Martin's Press, 1996).

Alan Doshna, "The King and I: An Interview with Sara Karloff on Her Life with the King of Horror Boris Karloff," no. 123, *Filmfax*.

Dracula vs. Frankenstein press notes.

Anthony C. Ferrante, "Horror Heroes Unite!" *Fangoria,* no. 200, March 2001.

Paul R. Gagne, *The Zombies That Ate Pittsburgh* (New York: Dodd, Mead and Company, 1987).

David Geffner, "Don't Look in the Theater!" *DGA,* vol. 28–5, January 2004.

Elizabeth Gilbert, "My Favorite Martian," *GQ,* March 2001.

Stefan Jaworzyn, *The Texas Chain Saw Massacre Companion* (London: Titan Books, 2003).

Stephen King, *Danse Macabre* (New York: Berkley, 1982).

Stephen King, *On Writing* (New York: Scribner, 2000).

Susan King, "Boris Karloff, A Monster Talent Remembered," *L.A. Times,* August 30, 2010.

Paul Linden, "The Son of Ackermansion: The House in the Twilight Zone," Part One and Two, *Famous Monsters of Filmland,* April 1978/May 1978.

www.lonchaney.com.

Hilary E. MacGregor, "Welcome to His Planet," *L.A. Times,* January 6, 2003.

Gregory William Mank, *It's Alive! The Classic Cinema Saga of Frankenstein* (New York: A. S. Barnes and Company, 1981).

Gregory William Mank, *Karloff and Lugosi: The Expanded Story of a Haunting Collaboration* (Jefferson, N.C.: McFarland and Company, 1990).

Dennis McLellan, "Herman Stein, 91; Composer Scored Horror Film Classics," *L.A. Times,* March 25, 2007.

http://www.radiohorrorhosts.com/lightsout.html.

Roy Milano, *Monsters: A Celebration of the Classics from Universal Studios* (New York: Del Ray, 2006).

Stephen Rebello, *Alfred Hitchcock and the Making of Psycho* (New York: St. Martin's Press, 1990).

Dana M. Reemes, *Directed by Jack Arnold* (Jefferson, N.C.: McFarland, 1988).

John Russo, *Making Movies* (New York: Dellacorte Press, 1989).

Gordon F. Sander, *Serling: The Rise and Twilight of Television's Last Angry Man* (New York: Plume, 1992).

David J. Skal, *Hollywood Gothic* (Boston: Faber and Faber, 1990, 2004).

Submitted for Your Approval, directed by Susan Lacy, "American Masters," Thirteen/WNET Productions, 1995.

Trailers from Hell: Abbott and Costello Meet Frankenstein, commentary by John Landis.

Trailers from Hell: House of Dracula, commentary by Joe Dante.

Kevin Thomas, "A Gift for Camp and Much More," *L.A. Times,* March 24, 2005.

Tom Weaver, "Anatomy of a Merman," *Starlog,* no. 250, May 1998.

Tom Weaver, *Interviews with B Science Fiction and Horror Movie Makers* (Jefferson, N.C.: McFarland, 1988).

Tom Weaver, DVD commentary for *The Wolf Man,* Universal, 2004.

Michael Weldon, *The Psychotronic Encyclopedia of Film* (New York: Ballantine, 1983).

Daniel Zalewski, "Show the Monster," *The New Yorker,* February 7, 2011.

Marc Scott Zicree, "Rod Serling: A Man in Search of the Twilight Zone," *Filmfax Outre,* no. 18.

Marc Scott Zicree, *The Twilight Zone Companion* (New York: Bantam, 1982).

Author interviews with Forrest Ackerman, Rick Baker, Joe Dante, Basil Gogos, Jack Hill, George Clayton Johnson, John Landis, Richard Matheson, Irene Miracle, Thom Mount, Carol Serling, David J. Skal, and Tom Weaver.

I also have to give a shout-out to the helpful insights from the fan-posted comments on the Internet Movie Database for *The Creature from the Black*

Lagoon, *Dracula*, *Frankenstein*, and *The Wolf Man*. Your help greatly enhanced the fan's-eye view on these films, and also helped me look at these movies from much fresher perspectives.

Chapter Two: Kensington Gore

Sam Arkoff, *Flying Through Hollywood by the Seat of My Pants* (New York: Birch Lane Press, 1992).

Roy Ward Baker, *The Director's Cut: A Memoir of 60 Years in Film and Television*, (Richmond, UK: Reynolds and Hearn, 2000).

Joe Bob Briggs, *Profoundly Disturbing: Shocking Movies That Changed History* (New York: Universe, 2003).

Wheeler Winston Dixon, *The Films of Freddie Francis* (Lankam, Md.: Scarecrow/McFarland, 1991).

Flesh and Blood, directed by Ted Newsom, 1994.

Bruce G. Hallenbeck, "Hammer Heroines: Video Revival," *Femme Fatales*, July 1997.

Jack Hunter, editor, *House of Horror: The Complete Hammer Films Story* (London: Creation Books, 1973, 1994, 1996).

Christopher Lee, *Lord of Misrule: The Autobiography of Christopher Lee* (London: Orion Publishing, 2003).

Bruce Sachs and Russell Wall, *Greasepaint and Gore: The Hammer Monsters of Roy Ashton* (Sheffield, UK: Tomahawk Press, 1988).

Jimmy Sangster, *Inside Hammer* (Richmond, UK: Reynolds and Hearn Ltd., 2001).

David J. Skal, *Hollywood Gothic* (Boston: Faber and Faber, 1990, 2004).

Steve Swires, "Monster Moguls: Michael Carreras: Inside the House of Hammer," *Fangoria,* May 1987.

Al Taylor and Sue Roy, *Making a Monster* (New York: Crown 1980).

David Thompson and Ian Christie, *Scorsese on Scorsese* (London: Faber and Faber, 1989 and 1996).

Christopher Tilly, "Stop! Hammer Time," *Hot Dog,* December 2003.

Anthony Timpone, "Christopher Lee: The Last Horror Star," *Fangoria,* October 2003.

Uncredited, *Curse of Frankenstein* review, *Variety,* May 15, 1957.

Author interviews with Jay Cocks, Jimmy Sangster, and Ted Newsom.

Chapter Three: "The Signpost that Everyone Followed"

Gene Arkeel, "Passed Up Wages Alfred Hitchcock's Before-Taxes 'Psycho' Take of $5-Mil.," *Variety*, September 21, 1960.

Peter Bogandovich, *Who the Devil Made It?* (New York: Ballantine, 1997).

Sidney Gottlieb, editor, *Alfred Hitchcock: Interviews* (Jackson Miss.: University Press of Mississippi, 2003).

"Halloween": A Cut Above the Rest, Prometheus Entertainment/Compass International Pictures, 2003.

Aljean Harmetz, "Obituaries: Janet Leigh, 77, Shower Taker of 'Psycho,'" *The New York Times*, October 5, 2004.

Alfred Hitchcock, "A Lesson in PSYCHO-Logy," *Motion Picture Herald*, June 25, 1960.

Jim Hosney, "Screenwriter Joe Stefano Goes Psycho on Working with Hitchcock and Van Sant," E!Online Film School: Horror 101.

Janet Leigh with Christopher Nickens, *Psycho: Behind the Scenes of the Classic Thriller* (New York: Harmony Books, 1995).

Buzz McClain, "Music That Makes the Movies," *Playboy*, October 2005.

Patrick McGilligan, *Alfred Hitchcock: A Life in Darkness and Light* (New York: Regan Books/HarperCollins, 2003).

Alex Patterson, "Clockers," *Time Out London,* November 22, 1994.

Danny Peary, "Diabolique Henri-Georges Clouzot," The Criterion Collection.

Psycho Film Review, *Variety*, June 17, 1960.

Stephen Rebello, *Alfred Hitchcock and the Making of Psycho* (New York: St. Martin's Press, 1998).

Lowell E. Redelings, "The Hollywood Scene: The First Run Films in Review," *Hollywood Citizen-News,* August 11, 1960.

Philip K. Scheuer, "Psycho as Brilliant as It Is Disagreeable," *L.A. Times,* August 11, 1960.

Philip J. Skerry, *Psycho in the Shower* (New York: Continuum, 2009).

Steven C. Smith, *A Heart at Fire's Center* (Berkeley and Los Angeles: University of California Press, 1991).

Mark Summers, "From Sneer to Eternity," *Vanity Fair*, March 2006.

David Thomson, *Have You Seen . . . ?* (New York: Knopf, 2008).

David Thomson, "Scum of the Earth," *The Guardian*, July 26, 2003.

François Truffaut, *Hitchcock by Truffaut* (New York: Touchstone, Simon and Schuster, 1985).

Variety, June 17, 1960.

Variety, June 27, 1960.

Fiona Watson, "Great Directors: Henri-Georges Clouzot," *Senses of Cinema*.

Dick Williams, "See Hitchcock Film at Start or You'll Wait," *Mirror News View,* July 30, 1960.

Jim Windolf and Nathaniel Rich, "The 2008 Hollywood Portfolio Hollywood Classics," *Vanity Fair*, March 2008.

Charles Winecoff, *Split Image: The Life of Anthony Perkins* (New York: Dutton, 1996).

James Wolcott, "Death and the Master," *Vanity Fair,* April 1999.

Author interviews with Joseph McBride, John Carpenter, Alan Ormsby, Rita Riggs, Hilton Greene, Marshall Schlom, and Joseph Stefano.

Chapter Four: Building the Modern Zombie

Arkoff, *Flying Through Hollywood by the Seat of My Pants.*

Associated Press, " 'Blood Feast' B-Movie Producer David Friedman Dies," February 14, 2011.

Bob Bankard, "David F. Friedman and the Early Exploiteers," www .phillyburbs.com

Briggs, *Profoundly Disturbing.*

Ray Carney, *Cassavettes on Cassavettes* (London: Faber and Faber, 2001).

William Castle, *Step Right Up!: I'm Gonna Scare the Pants Off America* (New York: G. P. Putnam's Sons, 1976).

Paul Cronin, editor, *Roman Polanski: Interviews* (Jackson, Miss.: University Press of Mississippi, 2005).

Manohla Dargis, "Irredeemable 'Irreversible' Isn't Worth a Fainting Fit," *L.A. Times,* March 7, 2003.

Robert Evans, *The Kid Stays in the Picture* (New York: Hyperion, 1994).

Document of the Dead, directed by Roy Frumkes, 1985.

Karen Durbin, "A Devil of a Marriage, Scarier Than Ever," *The New York Times,* January 19, 2003.

Michael Etchinson, "Rosemary and the Devil," June 21, 1968. Clipping from Motion Picture Library file, publication unknown.

Mia Farrow, *What Falls Away* (New York: Nan A. Talese/Doubleday, 1997).

The Fearmakers Television Series, directed by Bret McCormick, written by John McCarty. Otherstream Entertainment Corporation, 1996.

Bob Fisher, "Dancing with the Devil," *MovieMaker,* Summer 2008.

David F. Friedman with Don Denevi, *A Youth In Babylon: Confessions of a Trash-Film King* (Amherst, N.Y.: Prometheus Books, 1990).

Paul R. Gagne, *The Zombies That Ate Pittsburgh* (New York: Dodd, Mead and Company, 1987).

Jeff Goldmsith, "Lost Scenes: Rosemary's Baby," *Creative Screenwriting* (July/August 2003).

James Greenberg, "A Life in Pictures," *DGA,* Winter 2009.

J. Hoberman and Jonathan Rosenbaum, *Midnight Movies* (New York: Harper & Row, 1983).

Ed Hulse, Jeremy T. Arnold, Kristin Lootens, and Emily Stone, "The Fifty Greatest Movie Posters of All Time," *Premiere,* August 2001.

Andrea Juno, Mark Pauline, *Re/Search: Incredibly Strange Films,* Re/Search Publications, 1986.

Michael Korda, "Movies" section, *Glamour,* September 1968.

Bill Landis and Michelle Clifford, *Sleazoid Express* (New York: Fireside Books, 2002).

Roy Loynd, "Par's Rosemary's Baby' Magic Pic—Magical BO," *The Hollywood Reporter,* May 29, 1968.

Chloe Malle, "There's Nothing to Be Scared About: Ira Levin's Park Pad Sells for $2.05 M.," *New York Observer,* January 5, 2010.

Harry Medved with Randy Dreyfuss and Michael Medved, *The Fifty Worst Films of All Time* (New York: Fawcett Crest, 1978).

Herschel Gordon Lewis, "The Incredibly Strange Film Show."

Mark Olsen, "King of Horror on Horror," *L.A. Times,* June 22, 2007.

Randy Palmer, *Herschel Gordon Lewis, Godfather of Gore* (Jefferson, N.C.: McFarland, 2000).

Pegasus Books Spring/Summer Catalogue 2010, Reissue of *Rosemary's Baby* entry.

Roman Polanski, *Roman* (New York: William Morrow, 1984).

Roman Polanski, Proust Questionnaire, *Vanity Fair,* March 2000.

Rosemary's Baby Press Notes.

Rosemary's Baby: A Retrospective, DVD making-of documentary.

John Russo, *The Complete Night of the Living Dead Filmbook* (New York: Harmony Books, 1985).

John Russo, *Making Movies* (New York: Dell, 1989).

John Russo, *Scare Tactics* (New York: Dell, 1992).

Dennis Schaefer and Larry Salvato, *Masters of Light* (Berkeley and Los Angeles: University of California Press, 1984).

Screenwriters on Film, Spencer Thornon and Lauri Berger, Encore/Starz/Showtime.

Gene Seymour, "All Roads to Horror Lead Back to 'Night' Creator," *L.A. Times,* January 10, 2003.

Eric Spitznagel, "George A. Romero: 'Who Says Zombies Eat Brains?'" vanityfair.com, May 27, 2010.

Sam O'Steen and Bobbie O'Steen, *Cut to the Chase*, Michael Wiese Productions, 2001.

"The Sunday Conversation: With George A. Romero," *L.A. Times,* May 30, 2010.

Tim Swanson, "Team Scream," Players Column, *Premiere,* November 2003.

David Thomson, *The New Biographical Dictionary of Film* (New York: Knopf, 2004).

John Thurber, L.A. Times obituary of Ira Levin, *L.A. Times,* November 14, 2007.

Uncredited, "Bill Castle's Low-Budgeter Ballyhoo Takes on $5-Mil Sophisticated Look," *Variety,* September 6, 1967.

Uncredited, "Even With Mia's $5,000 Haircut by Sassoon William Castle Is High on 'Rosemary's Baby,'" *The Film Daily,* August 21, 1967.

Variety, March 22, 1967.

Variety, September 6, 1967.

Variety, May 29, 1968.

Tom Weaver, *Interviews with B Science Fiction and Horror Movie Makers* (Jefferson, N.C.: McFarland, 1988).

Michael Weldon, *The Psychotronic Encyclopedia of Film* (New York: Ballantine, 1983).

Mason Wiley and Damien Bona, *Inside Oscar* (New York: Ballantine, 1996).

Susan Wloszczyna, "Back Among the Dead," *USA Today,* June 21, 2005.

Paul D. Zimmerman, "Devil Child," *Newsweek,* June 17, 1968.

Jason Zinoman, "Killer Instincts," *Vanity Fair,* March 2008.

Author interviews with Steve Frankfurt, William A. Fraker, Dave Friedman, Charles Glenn, Herschell Gordon Lewis, Andy Romanoff, George

Romero, John Russo, Joel Schiller, Jeffrey Schwartz, Russell Streiner, Anthea Sylbert, and Paul Sylbert.

Chapter Five: It's Only a Movie

A Decade Under the Influence, directed by Ted Demme and Richard La-Gravenese, Independent Film Channel, 2003.

Bill Baer, "The Exorcist: A Conversation with William Peter Blatty," *Creative Screenwriting,* vol. 10, no. 5 (September/October 2003).

Peter Biskind, *Easy Riders, Raging Bulls* (New York: Simon and Schuster, 1998).

Wiley and Bona, *Inside Oscar.*

Geoff Boucher, "William Friedkin: 'The Exorcist' Cast Was 'A Gift from God,'" *L.A. Times,* October 10, 2010.

John W. Bowen, "Of Unholy Light," *Rue Morgue,* no. 105, October 2010.

Peter Bracke, *Crystal Lake Memories* (Los Angeles: Sparkplug Press, 2005).

Briggs, *Profoundly Disturbing.*

Thomas D. Clagett, *William Friedkin: Films of Aberrration, Obsession and Reality* (Los Angeles: Silman-James Press, 2003).

"'The Exorcist' 25 Years Later: Director William Friedkin," October 11, 2000, online chat with *USA Today.*

Stephen Farber and Marc Green, *Outrageous Conduct: Art, Ego, and the Twilight Zone* (New York: Ballantine, 1988).

Anthony C. Ferrante, "Special Makeup FX: The State of the Art," *Fangoria,* no. 200, March 2001.

Jack Garner, "A Priest on Both Sides of the Camera," http://www.rochestergoesout.com, October 13, 1999.

David Grove, *Making Friday the 13th* (Surrey, UK: FAB Press, 2005).

Clive Hirschhorn, *The Warner Brothers Story* (New York: Crown, 1979).

Curt Holman, "Like a Man Possessed," Playboy.com.

Jim Hosney, "William Friedkin Takes the Podium and Makes Our Head Spin," E!Online Film School: Horror 101.

King, *Danse Macabre.*

Ernesto Lechner, "An 'Exorcist' for All Time," *L.A. Times,* October 15, 1998.

McDonagh, *Filmmaking on the Fringe.*

Don Kaye, "Living Their Death-Dream," *Fangoria,* no. 233, June 2004.

Susan King, "Wes Craven's Retirement Plan? 'My Goal Is Die in My 90s on the Set," *L.A. Times*, February 18, 2010.

Nick Owchar, "In His New Novel, 'The Exorcist' Author Balances Philosophy and Thrills," *L.A. Times*, April 1, 2010.

Julia Phillips, *You'll Never Eat Lunch in This Town Again* (New York: Random House, 1991).

Stephen Rebello, "Horror Loses Its Bite," *Playboy*, November 2003.

Jeffrey Ressner," "Devil's Playground," *DGA Quarterly,* Fall 2008.

Russo, *Scare Tactics*.

Nat Segaloff, *Hurricane Billy* (New York: William Morrow, 1990).

Fred Szebin, "Ellen Burstyn Remembers The Exorcist," *Filmfax,* no. 100, August/September 2003.

David A. Szulkin, "Last Housemates," *Fangoria*, no. 200, March 2001.

David A. Szulkin, *Wes Craven's Last House on the Left: The Making of a Cult Classic* (Surrey, UK: FAB Press, 1997).

Taylor and Roy, *Making a Monster*.

Calum Robert Waddell, "Crystal Lake Chronicles: An Interview with Director-Producer Sean S. Cunningham," *Shock Cinema*, no. 27, Winter 2005.

Calum Waddell, "Gem Cutting: An Interview with Editor-Producer Bud Smith," *Shock Cinema*, no. 32 (Spring 2007).

Weldon, *Psychotronic Encyclopedia*.

www.wescraven.com/bio_data.asp.

David E. Williams, "Demonic Convergence," *American Cinematographer,* August 1998.

Author interviews with Rick Baker, William Peter Blatty, Bob Clark, Wes Craven, Terrence Donnelly, Nessa Hyams, Marc Jaffee, Richard LaGravenese, Richard Lederer, Father William O'Malley, Alan Ormsby, Dick Smith, and Marcel and Carolyn Vercoutere.

Chapter Six: Just When You Thought It Was Safe

Ryan Adams, "Interviews: Paul Partain, Franklyn from The Texas Chain Saw Massacre," www.living-dead.com.

AP, "Jaws Author Peter Benchley Dead at Age 65," foxnews.com, February 12, 2006.

Steven Bach, *Final Cut* (New York: William Morrow, 1985).

Bill Baer, "Jaws: Bill Baer Speaks with Carl Gottlieb," *Creative Screenwriting,* May/June 2001.

John Baxter, *Steven Spielberg: The Unauthorized Biography* (New York: HarperCollins, 1996).

Biskind, *Easy Riders, Raging Bulls.*

Briggs, *Profoundly Disturbing.*

David Brown, *Let Me Entertain You* (New York: William Morrow, 1990).

John Charnay and Nicole Baker, "'Jaws' Gory Scenes Stir Unrest Over PG Rating," *Hollywood Reporter*, July 7, 1975.

Robert Allen, "Does Not Play Well With Others," ICG International Cinematographers Guild, October 2003.

Ellen Farley and William K. Knoedelseder, Jr., "The Real Texas Chain Saw Massacre," *L.A. Times*, September 5, 1982.

Bob Fisher, "Looking Back at Jaws," *MovieMaker* no. 59, vol. 12, Summer 2005.

Barbara Gips, "Shapping Up 'Jaws'—Hook, Line and Sinker," *L.A. Times*, September 12, 1975.

Peter Goldman and Martin Kasindorf, "Jawsmania: The Great Escape," *Newsweek*, July 28, 1975.

Earl C. Gottschalk, Jr., "In the Shark's Wake Watch For Piranhas, Gators, More Sharks," *The Wall Street Journal*, September 10, 1975.

Nancy Griffin, "In the Grip of Jaws," *Premiere,* October 1995.

Mark Harris, *Pictures at a Revolution* (New York: The Penguin Press, 2008).

Jim Harwood, *Variety,* June 2, 1975.

Dade Hayes and Jonathan Bing, *Open Wide: How Hollywood Box Office Became a National Obsession* (New York: Hyperion/Miramax Books, 2004).

Ellen Kanner, "Reality Bites, "The Paper Trail" column, *Pages,* January/February 2004.

Alex Lewin, "Adventures in the Scream Trade," *Premiere* (February 2001).

Patrick Jankiewicz, *Just When You Thought It Was Safe: A Jaws Companion*, (Duncan, Okla.: Bear Manor Media, 2009).

Stefan Jaworzyn, *The Texas Chain Saw Massacre Companion* (London: Titan Books, 2003).

L.A. Times, February 13, 2006.

Ray Loynd, "Around L.A.: In the Teeth of the Storm," *L.A. Herald-Examiner*, August 3, 1975.

Alison Macor, *Chainsaws, Slackers, and Spy Kids* (Austin: University of Texas Press, 2010).

Leonard Maltin, *Leonard Maltin's 2001 Movie and Video Guide* (New York: Signet, 2000).

The Making of Steven Spielberg's Jaws, produced by Laurent Bouzerau, 1995.

Masters of Horror, documentary, directed by Mike Mendez and Dave Parker, 2003.

Joseph McBride, *Steven Spielberg: A Biography* (New York: Simon and Schuster, 1997).

Legs McNeil, Jennifer Osborne, and Peter Pavia, *The Other Hollywood: The Uncensored Oral History of the Porn Film Industry* (New York: Regan Books, 2005).

Roy Morton, *Close Encounters of the Third Kind: The Making of Steven Spielberg's Classic Film* (New York: Applause, 2007).

A. D. Murphy, Jaws Film Review, *Variety*, June 18, 1975.

Mary Murphy, "Fields: VP from the Cutting Room Floor," *L.A. Times*, July 24, 1975.

Mary Murphy, "The Perils of a 'Chainsaw' Star," *L.A. Times*, November 20, 1974.

New England Out Way TV show, 1974, The Shark Is Still Working documentary.

Gerald Peary, *The Real Paper,* October 23, 1980.

John Podhoretz, "Shark Attack," *Weekly Standard*, June 21, 2010.

Quint, "Farewell and Adieu . . ." *Ain't It Cool News,* February 12, 2006.

Tom Shone, *Blockbuster: How Hollywood Learned to Stop Worrying and Love the Summer* (New York: Free Press, 2004).

Elizabeth Snead, "Recalling 'Jaws,' the First of the Summer Blockbusters," *USA Today,* July 9, 2000.

Mike Spring, "Jaws: An Interview with Carl Gottlieb," *DVD Angle*, July 11, 2001.

Talk Today "Jaws": Carl Gottlieb, http://www.usatoday.com/community/chat/.0710gottlieb.htm.

Charles Taylor, "DVD's," *The New York Times*, May 8, 2005.

Time, June 23, 1975.

Peter Travers, "Steven Spielberg," *Rolling Stone,* 40th Anniversary Issue, May 3–17, 2007. Issue 1025/1026.

Will Tusker, " 'Jaws' Cures Exhibitor Blues," *The Hollywood Reporter*, July 7, 1975.

"Twentieth-Century American Bestsllers," Graduate School of Library and Information Science, maintained by unsworth@uivc.edu.

Uncredited, "A Nation Jawed," *Time*, July 28, 1975.

The Universal Story, written and produced by Joan Kramer and David Heeley, directed by David Heeley. Universal, 1995.

Variety, May 22, 1974.

Edward Wyatt, "Peter Benchley, Author of 'Jaws' and Other Best-Selling Thrillers, Dies at 65," *The New York Times*, February 13, 2006.

Zinoman, "Killer Instincts."

Author interviews with Dan O'Bannon, Ron Bozman, Michael Chapman, Greydon Clark, Oscar Dystel, Al Ebner, Jim Fargo, George Fredrick, William S. Gilmore, Carl Gottlieb, Roger Kastel, Len Leone, Alison Macor, Joseph McBride, Thom Mount, Daniel Pearl, Dorothy Pearl, Fred Rappaport, Nikki Rocco, and Jim Troutman.

Chapter Seven: Giving the Devil His Due

A Decade Under the Influence.

Chas Balun, *Lucio Fulci: Beyond the Gates* (Key West, Fl.: Fantasma Books, 1997).

"Big Ballyho Gamble on 'Omen,' Fox Hopes Antichrist Is Saviour," *Variety*, June 30, 1976.

Peter Brunette, editor, *Martin Scorsese: Interviews* (Jackson, Miss.: University Press of Mississippi, 1999).

Building a Better Zombi, directed by William Helfire, interview by Mike Baronas and Kit Gavin, Shriek Show, 2004.

John Clark, "Filmographies: Nancy Allen," *Premiere*, July 1990.

Cameron Crowe, "Sissy Spacek Acts Her Age," *Rolling Stone*, October 18, 1979.

Manohla Dargis, "Mario Bava . . . Back from the Grave," *L.A. Weekly*, July 26, 1996.

Medved, with Dreyfuss, Medved, *Fifty Worst Films of All Time*.

Anthony Timpone, "Stephen King's Scariest Movie Moments," *Fangoria*, no. 238, November 2004.

Earl C. Gottschalk Jr., "Fox Is Counting on Rescue by 2 New Films, But Analysts Still Expect 'Down Year,' " *The Wall Street Journal*, July 12, 1976.

Earl C. Gottschalk, Jr., "It's Finally True: Movies Are Going Straight to the Devil," *The Wall Street Journal*, October 25, 1976.

Linda Gross, "A Clairvoyant Previews Her Death in 'The Psychic,'" *L.A. Times*, May 5, 1979.

Scott Holton, "Commentary: An In-Depth Interview on the Creative and Technical Aspects of Carrie," *Fantascene*, no. 3, 1977.

Troy Howarth, *The Haunted World of Mario Bava* (Surrey, UK: FAB Press, 2002).

Alan Jones, *Profondo Argento* (Surrey, UK: FAB Press, 2004).

Gregg Kilday, *L.A. Times*, August 31, 1977.

Laurence F. Knapp, editor, *Brian De Palma: Interviews* (Jackson, Miss.: University Press of Mississippi, 2003).

James K. Loutzenhiser, The Psychic Movie Review, *Box Office Review*, April 2, 1979.

Tim Lucas, *Black Sabbath (The Three Faces of Fear)*, DVD Liner Notes, Image, 2000.

Tim Lucas, *Black Sunday*, DVD Liner Notes, Image, 1999.

Tim Lucas, *Hatchet for the Honeymoon*, DVD Liner Notes, Image, 2000.

Tim Lucas, *I Vampiri*, DVD Liner Notes, Image, 2001.

Dave Kehr, "Critics Choice: The Mario Bava Collection, Volume 1," *The New York Times*, April 10, 2007.

King, *On Writing*.

Susan King, "Horrormeister Mario Bava Gets a Blood Thorough Retrospective," *L.A. Times*, March 13, 2008.

Jack Kroll, "Deviled Ham," *Newsweek*, July 12, 1976.

L.A. Times Film Clips, August 21, 1976.

L.A. Times, August 31, 1977.

Leslie Long, American Cinematheque Program Notes: The Haunted World of Mario Bava, October 8–10, 1993.

Clipp MacMillan, *Shock*, DVD Liner Notes, Anchor Bay, 2007.

Paul Malcolm, "The Haunted World of Mario Bava," *L.A. Weekly*, May 31, 2002.

Todd McCarthy, The Omen Movie Review, *The Hollywood Reporter*, June 8, 1976.

Morton, *Close Encounters*.

A. D. Murphy, The Omen Movie Review, *Variety*, June 6, 1976.

A. D. Murphy, Carrie Movie Review, *Variety*, November 3, 1976.

SOURCES 👁 551

Mary Murphy, "Movie Call Sheet," *L.A. Times*, April 12, 1976.
Noel Murray, "Brian De Palma," A.V. Club, November 15, 2007.
Gabriella Oldham, *First Cut: Conversations with Film Editors* (Berkeley and Los Angles: University of California Press, 1992).
The Omen Legacy, directed by Brent Zacky, Prometheus Entertainment, 2001.
Ron Rennington, Suspriria Movie Review, *The Hollywood Reporter*, August 23, 1977.
Rex Reed, The Omen Movie Review, *Vogue*, August 1976.
Bryan Reesman, "The Horror Within," *MovieMaker*, no. 76, vol. 15, Summer 2008.
Josh Rottenberg, "There's Something About Carrie," *Premiere* (August 2001).
Julie Salomon, *The Devil's Candy: The Bonfire of the Vanities Goes to Hollywood* (New York: Houghton Miffin, 1991).
Richard Schickel, "Bedeviled," *Time*, June 28, 1976.
Richard Schickel, *Clint Eastwood* (New York: Knopf, 1996).
Richard Schickel, "A Movable Feast," *Time*, November 8, 1976.
Michael Singer, *A Cut Above* (Los Angeles, CA: Lone Eagle, 1998).
666: The Omen Revealed, directed by J. M. Kenny, Twentieth Century-Fox, 2000.
Suspiria Press Notes.
Suspiria 25th Anniversary, directed by David Gregory and Gary Hertz, Blue Underground, 2001.
Christopher Tennant, "Back Talk: Everybody's All-American," *Talk*, December 2001/January 2002.
Kevin Thomas, "'The Omen' a Scare Package," *L.A. Times*, June 25, 1976.
Kevin Thomas, "Pity, Terror and Wit," *L.A. Times*, November 17, 1976.
Kevin Thomas, "Suspiria: Highly Stylized Horror," *L.A. Times*, August 26, 1977.
Anne Thompson, "The Big Bang," *Premiere*, May 1999.
Variety, July 16, 1980.
Will Turner, "Fox Big Promo Gamble on 'Omen' Goes to B.O. Test," *Variety*, June 24, 1976.
Chris Willman, "Paradise by the Dashboard Light," *L.A. Times*, May 28, 1995.
Stephanie Zacharek, "DVD's," *The New York Times*, May 8, 2005.

Author interviews with Howard S. Berger, Al Cliver, Jay Cocks, Joe Dante, Brian De Palma, David Forbes, Antonella Fulci, Jessica Harper, Donald Heitzer, Harriet B. Helberg, Daphna Krim, Alan Ladd, Jr., Alfredo Leone, George Litto, Tim Lucas, Barbara Magnolfi, Massimo Morante, Marcia Nasatir, David Seltzer, P. J. Soles, Lou Stroller, Mario Tosi, and Gareth Wigan. Lamberto Bava interview conducted for this book by Paolo Zelati.

Chapter Eight: The Night He Came Home

Robert Abele, "Knight of the Living Dead," *L.A. Times*, June 23, 2005.

Adrienne Barbeau, *There Are Worse Things I Could Do* (New York: Carroll and Graf Publishers, 2006).

Frank Barron, "'Halloween' Seen as Perennial Holiday Fare by Irwin Yablans," *The Hollywood Reporter*, November 10, 1978.

Erik Bauer, "Things That Go Bump in the Night," *Creative Screenwriting*, January/February 1999.

Gilles Boulenger, *John Carpenter: Prince of Darkness* (Silman-James Press, 2001).

Document of the Dead, directed by Roy Frumkes, 1985.

Terry L. Du Foe, "Back from the Dead with George Romero," *Filmfax*, no. 107, July/September 2005.

Halloween Unmasked, directed by Mark Cerulli, Anchor Bay, 1999.

Mark Cerulli, "Debra Hill: The First Lady of Fear," fangoria.com.

Mark Cerulli, "Moustapha Akkad: The Gentleman Producer," fangoria .com.

Gagne, *The Zombies That Ate Pittsburgh*.

George Romero Incredibly Strange Film Show.

Michael Gingold, "Halloween Producer Debra Hill Dies," Fangoria.com, March 7, 2005.

Anna Gorman, Elaine Dutka, and Ashraf Khalil, "For Arabs, a Man of Renown in Hollywood," *L.A. Times*, November 12, 2005.

Lee Grant, "'Halloween' in South Pasadena," *L.A. Times*, May 27, 1978.

Grove, *Making Friday the 13th*.

Martin A. Grove, "'Halloween Is Returning to Haunt Us," *L.A. Herald-Examiner*, October 6, 1980.

Halloween: A Cut Above the Rest, Prometheus Entertainment/Compass International Pictures, 2003.

Ed Harris, American Cinematheque Q and A, Egyptian Theater, Hollywood, Calif., January 9, 2010, notes provided by Raymond Lee Christian.

Hollywood Reporter, November 10, 1978.

Hollywood Reporter, December 28, 2006.

Jim Hosney, "Writer-Producer Debra Hill on Jamie Lee, Body Counts and Horror in Suburbia," E!Online Film School: Horror 101.

Mr. Beaks Interviews George Romero, *Ain't It Cool News,* May 25, 2010.

Myrna Oliver, "Debra Hill, 54; Pioneering Woman in Hollywood, Co-Produced 'Halloween,'" *L.A. Times,* March 8, 2005.

Patrick Jankiewicz, "Celebrating Halloween II," *Fangoria,* November 2009.

Jones, *Profondo Argento.*

Pauline Kael, *Halloween* Movie Review, *The New Yorker,* Februrary 19, 1979.

Bill Kelley, "Salem's Lot: Filming Horror for Television," *Cinefantastique,* no. 2, vol. 9, Winter 1979.

Sean Kennelly, "The Buzz" column, *Creative Screenwriting* (May/June 2005).

Stephen Lemons, "Scary Movie," *New Times,* October 12–18, 2000.

Jason Matloff, Debra Hill entry in "Women Who Broke the Mold," *Premiere,* Women in Hollywood, 1998 Edition.

Mark Olsen, "Toronto International Film Festival: The Spirit Moves John Carpenter Again," *L.A. Times,* September 14, 2010.

Danny Peary, *Cult Movies* (New York: Delta, 1981).

Mallory Potosky, "Halloween Too," *MovieMaker,* no. 70, vol. 14, Summer 2007.

Tony Rayns and Scott Meek, "Close Encounters with the Wunderkind . . . And an Ascendant Star . . . ," *Time Out,* March 10–16, 1978.

Paul Scanlon, "'The Fog': A Spook Ride on Film," *Rolling Stone,* June 28, 1979.

Spitznagel, "Who Says Zombies Eat Brains?"

Uncredited, "A Man Who Knows Where He's Going," 1978, article taken from www.theofficialjohncarpenter.com.

Uncredited, "John Carpenter's Halloween—Behind the Scenes," www .halloweenmovies.com/filmarchive/h1bts.htm.

Weaver, *Interviews with B Science Fiction and Horror Movie Makers.*

Zinoman, "Killer Instincts."

Author interviews with John Amplas, William Peter Blatty, Pat Buba, John Carpenter, Dean Cundey, Mick Garris, Kim Gottlieb-Walker, John Harrison, Debra Hill, Bob Rehme, George Romero, Tom Savini, Ray Stella, Austin Stoker, and Tommy Lee Wallace.

Chapter Nine: No One Can Hear You Scream

Alien Evolution, produced and directed by Russell Leven and Andrew Abbott, written and narrated by Mark Kermode.

Brad Abraham, "Grave Robber from Outer Space," *Rue Morgue,* March 2007.

Rachel Abramovitz, "Leave It to Weaver," *Premiere,* Women in Hollywood, 1998 Edition.

Brantly Bardin, "Idol Chatter: Sigourney Weaver," *Premiere,* March 2003.

John W. Bowen, "In the Shadow of the Tall Man," "The Complete Phantasmography," *Rue Morgue,* March 2007.

Vincent Canby, "Screen: 'Phantasm' a Horror Story," *The New York Times,* June 1, 1979.

Charles Champlin, "A Screamer in Phantasm."

Michael Coate, "Presentation Matters: The Original First Wave Engagements of Alien—A 25th Anniversary Trip Through Time (And Space)," in70mm.com, 2004.

David S. Cohen, "'Alien' Set Standard in Days Before Digital," *Variety,* July 28, 2003.

Fangoria Weekend of Horrors Phantasm Panel 2007.

Ferrante, "Horror Heroes Unite!"

Michael Fleming, "The Talented Mr. Ridley," *Playboy,* March 2001.

Paul R. Gagne, "Science Fiction Typographics," *Cinefantastique,* Spring 1981.

Earl C. Gottschalk, Jr., "Hit Picker: How Fox's Movie Boss Decides That a Script Is a Potential Winner," *The Wall Street Journal,* May 17, 1979.

Sam Kashner, "Producing the Producers," *Vanity Fair,* January 2004.

Glenn Kenny, "'Alien' Pops Again," DVD Dispatch, *Premiere,* July 1999.

Laurence F. Knapp and Andrea F. Kulas, editors, *Ridley Scott: Interviews* (Jackson Miss.: University Press of Mississippi, 2005).

Jack Kroll, "Scared Stiff in Outer Space," *Newsweek,* May 28, 1979.

Leonard Maltin, *The Whole Film Sourcebook* (New York: Plume/New American Library, 1983).

Harris, *Pictures At a Revolution.*

Hayes and Bing, *Open Wide.*

Dennis McLellan, "Dan O'Bannon 1946–2009: Sci-Fi Screenwriter Crafted Classic 'Alien,'" *L.A. Times,* December 19, 2009.

McDonagh, *Filmmaking on the Fringe.*

Gina McIntyre, "Happy Birthday, Tall Man! 'Phantasm' Turns 30," Hero Complex column, *L.A. Times,* October 16, 2009.

Danny Peary, *Omni's Screen Flights/Screen Fantasies* (New York: Dolphin, 1984)

Phantasm Review by "Berg," *Variety,* February 5, 1979.

Phantasm Press Notes.

Peter Rainer, "Phantasm: Coscarelli's One-Man Horror Show," *L.A. Herald-Examiner,* March 29, 1979.

Jeff Walker, "Alien: A Secret Too Good to Give Away," *Rolling Stone,* May 31, 1979.

Author interviews with Reggie Bannister, Roger Christian, Robert Del Valle, Steve Frankfurt, Alan Ladd Jr., Uncle Bob Martin, Dan O'Bannon, Bob Rehme, and Gareth Wigan.

Chapter Ten: Did You Check on the Children?

Jack Bond, "Terror Comes Calling," *Marquee* (September/October 1979).

Jones, *Profondo Argento.*

Bill Kelley, "Salem's Lot: Filming Horror for Television," *Cinefantastique,* vol. 9, no. 2, Winter 1979.

Janet Maslin, "A Killer Returns in When a Stranger Calls," *The New York Times,* October 12, 1979.

Robert Osborne on Location, *The Hollywood Reporter,* November 17, 1978.

Kevin Thomas, "It's a Scream for Three Unknowns," *L.A. Times,* October 29, 1979.

Uncredited, "Columbia Pickup on Simon Feature," *The Hollywood Reporter,* November 17, 1978.

Author interviews with Jules Brenner, Bob Clark, Mick Garris, Richard Kobritz, and Fred Walton.

Chapter Eleven: Be Afraid, Be Very Afraid

Barbeau, *There Are Worse Things I Could Do.*

Peter Biskind, "Any Which Way He Can," *Premiere* April 1993.

Peter Bogdanovich, "What They Say About Stanley Kubrick," *The New York Times Magazine*, July 4, 1999.

Boulenger, *Prince of Darkness.*

David Breskin, *Inner Views*, (New York: Da Capo Press, 1992).

Briggs, *Profoundly Disturbing.*

Garrett Brown, "The Steadicam and The Shining," *American Cinematographer,* August 1980.

Eric Caidin, "Lloyd Speaks!: An Interview with Actor Joseph Turkel," *Shock Cinema*, no. 20, Spring-Summer 2002.

Jonathan Dee, "David Cronenberg's Body Language," *The New York Times Magazine*, September 18, 2005.

Steve Dollar, "Barker Kept Head, Appeased Censors," *Atlanta Journal and Constitution*, December 23, 1988.

David Edelstein, "The Love Bug," *Rolling Stone,* October 9, 1986, no. 484.

Paul R. Gagne, "Stephen King," *Cinefantastique* (Spring 1981).

William Goldman, *Which Lie Did I Tell?* (New York: Pantheon, 2000).

Aljean Harmetz, "Shining and Empire Set Records," *The New York Times,* May 28, 1980.

Michael Herr, "Kubrick," *Vanity Fair*, August 1999.

Knapp, *Brian De Palma: Interviews.*

Vincent LoBrutto, *Stanley Kubrick: A Biography* (New York: Donald I. Fine Books, 1997).

Herb Lightman, "Photographing Stanley Kubrick's The Shining," *American Cinematographer*, August 1980.

Janet Maslin, "Screen: Nicholson and Shelley Duvall in Kubrick's 'The Shining,'" *The New York Times,* May 23, 1980.

Patrick McGilligan, *Jack's Life* (New York: W. W. Norton, 1994).

Mark Olsen, "King of Horror on Horror," *L.A. Times,* June 22, 2007.

Paul M. Sammon, "David Cronenberg," *Cinefantastique* (Spring 1981).

Scifi.com Chat with Andrew Niccol, June 11, 1998, www.scificom/transcripts/AndrewNiccol.html.

The Shining, Garrett Brown and John Baxter DVD commentary.

Thomson, *Have You Seen?*

Laurent Tirard, *Moviemakers' Master Class* (London: Faber and Faber, 2002).

Chris Todley, editor, *Cronenberg on Cronenberg* (London: Faber and Faber, 1992).

Joe Turkel, American Cinematheque Q & A, Egyptian Theater, Hollywood, Calif., September 18, 2009. Notes provided by Raymond Lee Christian.

John Carpenter: Fear Is Just the Beginning: The Man and His Movies, directed by Garry Grant, 2000.

Michel Ciment, *Kubrick* (London: Faber and Faber, 2001).

Uncredited, "Events and Revivals" Section, *L.A. Times*, February 24, 2005.

Uncredited, "WB Sees First-Week 'Shining' Tally of $1 Mil for 10 Screens," *The Hollywood Reporter*, May 28, 1980.

Variety review of *The Shining,* May 23, 1980.

Weldon, *Psychotronic Enclyopedia*.

Author interviews with Allan Arkush, John Board, Garrett Brown, John Carpenter, Dean Cundey, Pierre David, Mick Garris, Debra Hill, Cooper Layne, Bob Rehme, Tom Sherak, and Tommy Lee Wallace.

Chapter Twelve: Long Night at Camp Blood

Bracke, *Crystal Lake Memories*.

Dee, "David Cronenberg's Body Language."

David Grove, "Crystal Lake Memories," *Fangoria*, no. 212, May 2002.

Grove, *Making Friday the 13th.*

Jankiewicz, "Celebrating Halloween II."

Jankiewicz, *Just When You Thought It Was Safe*.

Lane Maloney, "Indie Filmmakers Has Major Luck with 'Friday the 13th,'" *Variety*, March 24, 1980.

The Making of Jaws 2, written, directed, and produced by Laurent Bouzereau, 2001.

Kim Masters, *Keys to the Kingdom* (New York: William Morrow, 2001).

McDonagh, *Filmmaking on the Fringe*.

Drew Struzan and David J. Schow, *The Art of Drew Struzan* (London: Titan Books, 2010).

Waddell, "Crystal Lake Memories."

Author interviews with Peter Bracke, John Carpenter, Harry Manfredini, Victor Miller, and Tommy Lee Wallace.

Chapter Thirteen: A Different Kind of Animal

An American Werewolf in London, Griffin Dunne and David Naughton DVD Commentary.

Barbeau, *There Are Worse Things I Could Do*.

Bauer, "Things That Go Bump in the Night."

Kevin Alexander Boon, "In Defense of John Carpenter's The Thing," *Creative Screenwriting*, January/February 1999.

Farber and Green, *Outrageous Conduct*.

Pablo F. Fenjues, Rocky Lang, *How I Broke Into Hollywood* (New York: It Books/HarperCollins, 2006).

Gagne, *The Zombies That Ate Pittsburgh*.

Beverly Gray, *Roger Corman: An Unauthorized Biography of the Godfather of Indie Filmmaking* (Los Angeles: Renaissance Books, 2000).

David J. Hogan, Michael Mayo, and Alan Jones, "The Making of The Thing and Rob Bottin's Eye-Popping, Razzle-Dazzle Make-up Effects," and "I Don't Know What It Is, But It's Weird and Pissed Off," *Cinefantastique*, November/December 1982.

Jason Lapeyre, Jovanka Vuckovic, and W. Brice McVicar, "The Bad Moon Rises Again," *Rue Morgue*, September 2009.

John Carpenter: Fear Is Just the Beginning.

Ron Magid, "Rob Bottin Part 1," *Make Up Artist*, August/September 2004.

Ron Magid, "Rob Bottin Part 2," *Make Up Artist*, October/November 2004.

Jason Matloff, "The Business of Insanity," *MovieMaker*, Summer 2007.

Ted Newsom, "There's No Thing Like an Old Thing," *Cinefantastique*, November/December 1982.

Russo, *Scare Tactics*.

Tom Savini, *Grand Illusions* (New York: Image, 1983).

Singer, *A Cut Above*.

Giulia D'Agnolo Vallan, *John Landis* (Milwaukee, Or.: M Press, 2008).

Author interviews with Rick Baker, John Carpenter, Joe Dante, David Foster, Mick Garris, John Harrison, John Landis, Uncle Bob Martin, Thom Mount, Tom Savini.

Chapter Fourteen: A Thunderstorm in a Bottle

Ryan Adams, "The Ladies of 'The Evil Dead,'" www.living-dead.com.

Peter Biskind, "The Crucible," Premiere Special Issue, *New York and the Movies,* 1994.

Bruce Campbell, *If Chins Could Kill: Confessions of a B Movie Actor* (New York: L.A. Weekly Books for Thomas Dunne Books/St. Martin's Press, 2001).

Roger Corman with Jim Jerome, *How I Made a Hundred Movies in Hollywood and Never Lost a Dime* (New York: Random House, 1990).

Frank DiGiancomo, "The Lost Tycoons," *Vanity Fair,* March 2009.

Robert Englund with Alan Goldsher, *Hollywood Monster: A Walk Down Elm Street with the Man of Your Dreams* (New York: Pocket Books, 2009).

Ferrante, "Horror Heroes Unite!"

Mikal Gilmore, "Fab Freddy," *Rolling Stone,* October 6, 1988.

Kris Gilpin, "Craftsmanship on a Lower Budget: An Interview with Sam Raimi," Reprinted on the Temple of Schlock Web site, May 28, 2009.

Lee Goldberg, "On the Set of Craven's 'Nightmare'—Where to Dream Is to Die," *UCLA Daily Bruin,* October 24, 1984.

Patrick Goldstein, "Pater Familias," *L.A. Times Magazine,* November 7, 1999.

Joshua Hammer, "A Cult-Film Cash Machine," *Newsweek,* September 12, 1988.

John Hodgman, "The Haunting," *The New York Times Magazine*, July 23, 2006.

Darrell Hope, "How to Make a Scary Movie . . . Sam Raimi on the Gift," *DGA Magazine,* March 2001.

Laurence Lerman, "Guest Shot," *Playboy,* March 2001.

Gina McIntyre, "Wes Craven on the Joys of 3-D and the Pain of 'Elm Street' Remakes," *L.A. Times,* October 7, 2010.

Ed Naha, *The Films of Roger Corman: Brilliance on a Budget* (New York: Arco Publishing, 1982).

Never Sleep Again: The Elm Street Legacy, directed by Daniel Farrands and Andrew Kasch, 1428 Films, 2010.

Nicanor Loreti, "Ted the Mighty: An Interview with Ted Raimi," *Shock Cinema,* no. 25, Summer 2004.

McDonough, *Filmmaking on the Fringe.*

Gina McIntyre, "Bruce Campbell on the Horror Franchise That Launched His Career," *L.A. Times,* September 1, 2010.

Sam Raimi Incredibly Strange Film Show.
John Russo, *Making Movies* (New York: Dell, 1989).
William Schoeel and James Spencer, *The Nightmare Never Ends* (New York: Citadel Press, 1984, 1992).
Szulkin, "Last Housemates."
Bill Warren, *The Evil Dead Companion* (New York: Griffin/St. Martin's Press, 2000).
Sharon Waxman, *Rebels on the Backlot* (New York: HarperCollins, 2005).
Author interviews with Josh Becker, Wes Craven, Kaye Davis, Sara Risher, Mark Shostrom, Scott Spiegel, and Rob Tapert.

Chapter Fifteen: To Stay Sane You Have to Laugh
Arkoff, *Flying Through Hollywood.*
Anne Billson, "Is the Future of Horror a Man Called Clive," *Sky*, August 13–26, 1987.
Martin Booe, "Deliciously Terrifying," *USA Weekend*, January 26–28, 1990.
Martin Burden, "Queasy Does It," *New York Post*, September 17, 1988.
www.clivebarker.info.
Murray Cox, "The Arts," *Omni*, October 1986.
Tom Crow, "Clive Wire," *Village View*, Ocotber 16–22, 1992.
Michael Flores, "It's Only a Movie," *Best of No 2—The Interviews*, 1989.
Gagne, *The Zombies That Ate Pittsburgh.*
Dwight Garner, "Disney Sees the Future," *The Times London*, October 6, 2002.
Mikal Gilmore, "Hell Raisers," *Rolling Stone*, February 11, 1988.
Hellraiser production notes.
Alan Jones, "Hellraiser," *Cinefantastique,* September 1987.
Alan Jones, "Hellbound: Hellraiser II," *Cinefantastique* (January 1989).
McDonagh, *Filmmaking on the Fringe.*
Bob Morrish, "A Literary Hellraiser," *Cinefantastique,* September 1987.
Reality Check TV Interview with Clive Barker.
Jeffrey Ressner, "Hellraiser," *The Hollywood Reporter*, August 6, 1987.
Don Swaim, CBS Radio, September 30, 1987.
Thompson and Christie, *Scorsese on Scorsese.*
Douglas E. Winter, "Raising Hell with Clive Barker," *Twilight Zone Magazine,* December 1987.
Jeff Zaleski, "The Relaunch of Clive Barker," *Publisher's Weekly.*
Author interviews with Stuart Gordon and John Harrison.

Chapter Sixteen: Having a Friend for Dinner

Andrew Kevin Walker, Fade-In Magazine Seminar, 1999.

Jim Emerson, "Man of Iron," *Premiere,* February 1991.

Joel Engel, *Screenwriters on Screenwriting* (New York: Hyperion, 1995).

Robert Englund IMDB Trivia Page.

Michael Fleming, "Playboy Interview: Kevin Spacey," *Playboy,* October 1999.

Michael Fleming, "Q & A with Social Network's Mike De Luca," *Deadline,* October 12, 2010.

Nigel Floyd, "Kiwi Fruit," *Time Out London*, May 12, 1993.

Stephen Galloway, "Punk. Prophet. Genius," *The Hollywood Reporter,* February 9, 2011.

Lawrence Grobel, *Above the Line* (New York: Da Capo, 2000).

Anthony Hopkins IMDb Trivia Page.

Robert E. Kapis, editor *Jonathan Demme: Interviews,* (Jackson, Miss. University Press of Mississippi, 2009).

Goldman, *Which Lie Did I Tell?*

Wiley and Bona, *Inside Oscar.*

Tom Matthews, "The Silence of the Lambs: Ted Tally—15 Years After the Lambs Stopped Screaming," *Creative Screenwriting,* January/February 2006.

Mike Medavoy and Josh Young, *You're Only As Good As Your Next One* (New York: Pocket Books, 2002).

Jeff Menell, Dead Alive Film Review, *The Hollywood Reporter,* January 21, 1993; *Time,* February 8, 1993.

Brian Mockenhaupt, "The Curious Case of David Fincher," *Esquire,* March 2007.

Dan Persons, "The Corman Connection," *Cinefantastique,* February 1992.

Dan Persons, "Jonathan Demme on Horror," *Cinefantastique,* February 1992.

Dan Persons, "Perfecting Performance," *Cinefantastique,* February 1992.

Dan Persons, "Production Design, Visualizing the Nightmare," *Cinefantastique,* February 1992.

Dan Persons, "Silence of the Lambs: The Making of Director Jonathan Demme's Instant Horror Classic, A Chiller for the '90s," *Cinefantastique,* February 1992.

Ian Pryor, *Peter Jackson: An Unauthorized Biography* (New York: St. Martin's Press/Thomas Dunne Books, 2004).

Claudia Puig, "Making 'Seven' Audience Snap to Attention," *L.A. Times,* November 3, 1995.

Claudia Puig and Richard Natale, "Violent Seven Outdraws Sexy Showgirls at Box Office," *L.A. Times,* October 20, 1995.

Stephen Rebello, "Telling It Like It Is," *The Santa Fean*, August 2001.

Mark Salisbury, "Sick, Seven, '8mm,'" *Fangoria,* no. 180, March 1999.

Mark Salisbury, Andrew Kevin Walker, *Seven, 8mm* (London: Faber and Faber, 1999).

Screen International, September 20, 1991.

Fred Schruers, "A Kind of Redemption," *Premiere* (March 1991).

Todd McCarthy, Se7en Movie Review, *Variety,* September 25, 1995.

Brian Sibley, *Peter Jackson: A Film-Maker's Journey* (New York: Harper-Collins Entertainment, 2006).

Dan Snierson, "Reiner's Reign," *Entertainment Weekly*, November 18, 2005, no. 850.

Terry Spaugh, "Silence of the Lambs," *Creative Screenwriting,* September/October 1998.

James Swallow, *Dark Eye: The Films of David Fincher* (London: Reynolds and Hearn, 2003).

Thom Taylor, *The Big Deal* (New York: Quill, 1999).

Kenneth Turan, "Seven Offers a Punishing Look at Some Deadly Sins," *L.A. Times*, September 22, 1995.

Uncredited, "Splatter King Looks Past Braindead," *Variety*, October 5, 1992.

Karen Valby, "Unbreakable," *Entertainment Weekly*, September 7, 2007.

Waxman, *Rebels.*

Author interviews with Mark Amin, Ron Bozman, Richard Francis-Bruce, Jay Cocks, Jesse Kornbluth, Daphna Krim, Michael Pellerin, Eric Pleskow, and Andrew Kevin Walker.

Chapter Seventeen: The Little Horror Films that Could

Ain't It Cool News, August 23, 2003.

Richard Alleva, "Spooky, Really Spooky," *Commonwealth*, September 24, 1999.

Michael D'Antonio, "I See Blockbusters," *Esquire*, August 2000.

Daniel Argent, "The Writing Sense," *Creative Screenwriting*, July/August 1999.

Ken Auletta, "Beauty and the Beast," *The New Yorker,* December 16, 2002.

James Bates, "Disney's Spreading of Financial Risk Made 'Sense' Then," *L.A. Times,* August 31, 1999.

James Bates, "Lionsgate to Buy Artisan Entertainment," *L.A. Times,* October 28, 2003.

Peter Biskind, *Down and Dirty Pictures* (New York: Simon and Schuster, 2004).

Chad Bixby, "Hollywood's Hottest Writer / Directors: Ed Sanchez and Dan Myrick," *Fade-In,* vol. V, no. 2, 1999.

Jess Cagle and Jeffrey Ressner, "Has Harvey Lost His Way?" *Time,* April 8, 2002.

Thane Christopher, "Hollywood's Hottest Writer/Director: M. Night Shyamalan," *Fade-In,* vol. V, no. 2, 1999.

John Colapinto, "The Big, Bad Wolves of Miramax," *Rolling Stone,* April 3, 1997.

Richard Corliss, "Scary and Smart," *Time,* August 2, 2004.

Ted Elrick, "Wes Craven DGA Magazine Interview," *DGA,* December 1997–January 1998.

Ben Fritz, "Sixth's Supernatural Lure," *Variety,* September 8, 1999.

Mark Harris, "Movies," *Entertainment Weekly,* August 6, 2004.

Zorianna Kit and Shari Roman, "The Unbearable Lightness of Being Kevin Williamson," *Fade-In,* vol. V, no. 2, 1999.

Paul Lieberman, "Keeping It Fresh with a Vengeance," *L.A. Times,* October 10, 1999.

Tod Lippy, "Directing Scream: A Talk with Wes Craven," *Scenario,* vol. 3, no. 1, Spring 1997.

Tod Lippy, "Writing Scream: A Talk with Kevin Williamson," *Scenario,* vol. 3, no. 1, Spring 1997.

Brian Lowry, "Film Review: The Village," *Variety,* July 29, 2004.

Kim Masters, "Harvey, Marty, and a Jar Full of Ears," *Esquire* (July 2002).

Todd McCarthy, Movie Review of The Sixth Sense, *Variety,* August 2, 1999.

Maitland McDonagh, "History of Horror, The '90s," *Fangoria,* no. 200, March 2001.

Gina McIntyre, "Wes Craven on the Joys of 3-D—and the Pain of 'Elm Street' Remakes," *L.A. Times,* October 10, 2010.

Ricahrd Natale, " 'Sense' Shows Its Powers," *L.A. Times*, August 9, 1999.

Timothy L. O'Brien, "The Curse of the Blair Witch," *Talk*, February 2002.

Jeff Otto, "Director Ed Sanchez and Dan Myrick Discuss 'Blair Witch' Influence," Bloody Disgusting.com, October 16, 2009.

Richard Schickel, *Time*, August 16, 1999.

Laura Schiff, "An Interview with Kevin Williamson," *Creative Screenwriting*, volume V, no. 1, 1999.

Sean Smith, "Curse of the Blair Witch," *Newsweek*, January 26, 2004.

James B. Stewart, *Disney War* (New York: Simon and Schuster, 2005).

Szulkin, "Last Housemates."

Bill Warren, "Reflections on Horror Part II: Joe Dante and John Landis," *Fangoria*, #200, March 2001.

Glenn Whipp, " 'The Blair Witch' at 10," *L.A. Times*, July 11, 2009.

Author interviews with Larry Cohen, Wes Craven, Michael Gingold, Robert Kerman, Barry Mendel, and Eduardo Sánchez.

Epilogue: "The Audience Is Always There for It"

Justin Chang, "Film Reviews: George A. Romero's Land of the Dead," *Variety*, June 20, 2005.

Corliss, "Scary and Smart."

Manohla Dargis, "Not Just Roaming, Zombies Rise Up," *The New York Times*, June 24, 2005.

Fangoria, no. 264, June 2007.

Nikki Finke, "Eli Roth Reacts Badly to Hostel II Failure; Says R-Rated Horror in Serious Jeopardy," *Deadline Hollywood Daily*, June 17, 2007.

Dana Harris, "Sequel Sees There's More to 'Saw,' " *Variety*, November 2, 2004.

Stephen Holden, "A Gore Fest, with Overtones of Iraq and TV," *The New York Times*, October 29, 2004.

L.A. Times, May 30, 2010.

Kim Masters, "The Next Blair Witch?" *The Daily Beast*, October 5, 2009.

Ian Mohr, "Lionsgate Stalks Horror Pic 'Saw,' " *Hollywood Reporter*, January 13, 2004.

Mark Olsen, "Toronto International Film Festival: The Spirit Moves John Carpenter," *L.A. Times*, September 12, 2010.

Robert W. Welkos, "From a Thriller to Legal Drama," *L.A. Times*, August 19, 2005.

Staci Layne Wilson, "Wes Craven on 'The Hills Have Eyes,'" horror.com, 3.11.06.

Author interviews with John Amplas, John Carpenter, Wes Craven, Stuart Gordon, Ehren Kruger, George Romero, and Tom Savini.

ACKNOWLEDGMENTS

Not every story a writer takes on is easy, and every book has its own particular obstacles and hurdles to overcome, but writing about horror films was great fun, and I'm very grateful for everyone's cooperation who spoke to me and helped me along the way, and they are, in alphabetical order: Forrest Ackerman, Scott Alexander, Mark Amin, John Amplas, Allan Arkush, Rick Baker, Reggie Bannister, Dan O'Bannon, Lamberto Bava, Josh Becker, William Peter Blatty, John Board, Ron Bozman, Howard S. Berger, Peter Bracke, Jules Brenner, Garrett Brown, Richard Francis-Bruce, Pat Buba, John Carpenter, Michael Chapman, Roger Christian, Bob Clark, Greydon Clark, Al Cliver, Jay Cocks, Larry Cohen, Wes Craven, Dean Cundey, Joe Dante, Pierre David, Kaye Davis, Brian De Palma, Terence Donnelly, Oscar Dystel, Jim Fargo, David Foster, William Fraker, Steve Frankfurt, Dave Friedman, Antonella Fulci, Mick Garris, William S. Gilmore, Michael Gingold, Charles Glenn, Basil Gogos, Stuart Gordon, Jessica Harper, John Harrison, Harriet B. Helberg, Donald Heitzer, Debra Hill, Jack Hill, Nessa Hyams, Marc Jaffee, George Clayton Johnson, Larry Karaszewski, Roger Kastel, Robert Kerman, Richard Kobritz, Jesse Kornbluth, Daphna Krim, Ehren Kruger, Alan Ladd Jr., Richard LaGravenese, John Landis, Cooper Layne, Richard Lederer, Alfredo Leone, Len Leone, Herschel Gordon Lewis, Geroge Litto, Tim Lucas, Alison Macor, Barbara Magnolfi, Father William

O'Malley, Harry Manfredini, Stanley Mann, Uncle Bob Martin, Richard Matheson, Joseph McBride, Barry Mendel, Victor Miller, Irene Miracle, Massimo Morante, Thom Mount, Marcia Nasatir, Ted Newsom, Alan Ormsby, Daniel Pearl, Dorothy Pearl, Michael Pellerin, Eric Pleskow, Fred Rappaport, Bob Rehme, Andy Romanoff, Sara Risher, Nikki Rocco, Rita Riggs, George Romero, John Russo, Eduardo Sánchez, Jimmy Sangster, Tom Savini, Joel Schiller, Marshall Schlom, Jeffrey Schwartz, David Seltzer, Carol Serling, Tom Sherak, Mark Shostrom, David J. Skal, Dick Smith, P. J. Soles, Scott Spiegel, Joseph Stefano, Ray Stella, Austin Stoker, Russell Streiner, Lou Stroller, Anthea Sylbert, Paul Sylbert, Rob Tapert, Mario Tosi, Jim Troutman, Robert Del Valle, Marcel and Carolyn Vercoutere, Andrew Kevin Walker, Kim Gottlieb-Walker, Tommy Lee Wallace, Fred Walton, Tom Weaver, and Gareth Wigan.

For finding this book a home, I'm eternally gratefully to my agent, Bob Diforio at D4EO Literary Agency, who has just been awesome from day one. I'm also very grateful that we landed with Rob Kirkpatrick at St. Martin's Press, who gave me great freedom to write this tome, and who also gave terrific suggestions and support from day one. (Thanks to Nicole Sohl, his assistant, as well.) And thank you to copy editor Sabrina Soares Roberts, and production editor John Morrone. Major thanks to Maryann Palumbo, for introducing me to Bob, and for all her help over the years. I couldn't have done it without you in a million years.

Thanks to Paolo Zelati for getting the Lamberto Bava interview for this book, and thanks to Raymond Lee Christian for research help as well, and for being a great friend. Thanks to Shawna Hogan for transcription help, and for being a great friend for many years, and thanks to my writing friends Paul Gaita, Chris Poggoli, Patrick Jankiewicz, Steve Ryfel, K. J. Doughton, David Rensin, Jay A. Fernandez, and Steve Rosen, for your help, encouragement, and support through several very trying years. A special shout-out to the memory of Jim Shaughnessy, a dear friend I miss every day, who lit the spark in me that launched my love of film. You are not forgotten, rest in peace.

Special thanks to Omid Rahmat, for hiring me at the greatest job I ever had; Rob Wright, my editor at Tom's Games, who was the best ally I ever had as a writer; and thanks to my editor at TGDaily, Aharon Etengoff. Also thanks to Adam Schragin at MadeLoud, and Neil Matsumoto at HDVideo Pro. It's hard to find editors that can help and enhance my work, and treat me like a human being, and I'm grateful you guys are among the good ones.

Also special thanks to my mother Sandra, father Steven, brother Drew, and grandmother Ginny, who were all very helpful and supportive. Thanks again to all. (And apologies to anyone I forgot.)

INDEX